DUTCH MUCK—AND MUCH MORE

Dutch Muck—and Much More:
Dutch Americans in Farming, Religion, Art, and Astronomy

Edited by Earl Wm. Kennedy
Donald A. Luidens
David Zwart

Copyright 2019 Van Raalte Press
All rights reserved

Van Raalte Press is a division of Hope College Publishing

A. C. Van Raalte Institute
Theil Research Center
9 East Tenth Street
PO Box 9000
Holland, MI 49422-9000

vanraalte@hope.edu
www.hope.edu/vri

Printed in the United States of America
978-0-9891469-8-2

Editor-in-Chief: Jacob E. Nyenhuis
Copy Editor: JoHannah Smith
Cover Art: *Het Kanaal* (2019), oil painting, by Chris Stoffel Overvoorde,
    in the collection of Robert P. and Diane Swierenga
Page Layout: Russell L. Gasero, Archivist, Reformed Church in America

Papers from the Twenty-First Biennial Conference of the Association for the Advancement of Dutch American Studies, Pella, Iowa, 2017.

Dedication

Richard H. Harms

*Scholarly preserver and interpreter
of Dutch American heritage*

and

Dutch American sons and daughters of the soil

Who transformed the wilderness and planted a legacy

Contents

Acknowledgments   ix

Introduction   xi

I. Dutch Americans and Farming

1. Time, Space, Worldviews, and Agricultural Landscapes
   Janel Curry   1

2. Dutch on the Muck: Celery Cropping in Michigan and Elsewhere
   Robert Swierenga   15

3. Onion Set Farming in South Holland, Illinois
   Ken Bult   65

4. Pea Pickers and POWs
   Mary Risseeuw   75

5. Dryland Strip Farming and the V-Blade: Dutch Canadian Innovations that Helped Stop Soil Drifting
   Don Sinnema   85

6. "This locality was settled by Hollanders": The Dutch in Wayne County, New York, since 1800
   Janet Sheeres   109

7. Impact of Farming on Dutch Settlement in Whiteside County
   Michael Swanson   125

II. Dutch American Rural Life

8. Rural Identity among Dutch Americans
   David Zwart   137

9. The "Many Children of God": The Role of the Religious Community in Dutch American Migration
 Justin Vos — 153

10. Dutch Immigrants and Nature: Environmental Observations in Letters from Dutch Pioneer Settlers in the United States, 1835-1860
 Henk Aay — 177

11. A Hunter's Experience: Henry Takken's Memoir and the Demise of the Passenger Pigeon (*Ectopistes migratorius*)
 Jan J. Boersema and Nella Kennedy — 207

III. Dutch American Leaders

12. His Name Was Klijn: Rev. Hendrik Georg Klijn, Reluctant Separatist
 Earl Wm. Kennedy — 221

13. The Michigan Years (1888-1893) of Geerhardus Vos
 George Harinck — 253

14. John Henry Vanderpoel—Who?
 Nella Kennedy — 275

15. A Mini Biography of Dutch American Astronomer G. P. Kuiper
 Huug van den Dool — 303

Index — 315

Van Raalte Press Publications from 2007 to 2019 in Chronological Order — 325

Acknowledgments

As dogs grow older, they proverbially learn fewer new tricks, but, as the Association for the Advancement of Dutch American Studies enters its third decade, it shows no signs of avoiding novelty. Thus, just as our fourteenth biennial conference met in June 2003 in the "Windy City" of Chicago to learn about the "Dutch in Urban America," our twenty-first gathering transpired in the rural city of Fulton, Illinois (population 3481 in 2010), due west of Chicago, to learn about, among other things, Dutch Americans as farmers and tillers of the soil. Perhaps our twenty-eighth biennial conference (note the precedent set by multiples of seven) may take us to outer space or to the subterranean world. In any case, we were happy in the present instance for the chance to get out into the country beside the Mississippi River, breathe the fresh air, and enjoy the hospitality of the denizens of Whiteside County.

The publication of the present volume—the product of the salubrious climate of Western Illinois and the assiduous labors of our fifteen contributors—has been brought to pass under the kind auspices of the Van Raalte Press and its editor-in-chief, Jack Nyenhuis, ably assisted by its copy-editor-in-chief, JoHannah Smith, as well as its layout editor-in-chief (and indexer) in faraway New Jersey, Russ Gasero, and his son, Matthew—all working under a tight deadline because of the prior commitment of the publisher to some other major publications. Our collective hats are doffed to these intrepid overtime workers and their long-suffering next of kin. We are also indebted to Bob Swierenga for allowing us to use his recently acquired, theme-supporting, painting on our front cover; it was created by the well-known artist, Dutch-born Chris Overvoorde. Last, we acknowledge with deep gratitude the support of the A. C. Van Raalte Institute, currently celebrating its silver anniversary.

Earl Wm. Kennedy
Donald A. Luidens
David Zwart

Introduction

Earl Wm. Kennedy

The invitation from the Fulton, Illinois, Historical Society, headed by Barbara Mask, to the Association for the Advancement of Dutch American Studies to hold its twenty-first biennial conference June 15-17, 2017, in that city provided AADAS with an opportunity to break new ground. The organization had customarily met at Reformed Christian colleges in towns at the center of large concentrations of North American Dutch, such as Holland and Grand Rapids, Michigan, and Pella and Orange City, Iowa.[1] Now, however, fresh from the novelty

---

[1] Since 1977, when the biennial conferences that soon (1979) became AADAS started, they have convened at Calvin College in Grand Rapids four times; Hope College in Holland six times; Central College in Pella thrice; Northwestern College in Orange City twice; and Trinity Christian College of Palos Heights, Illinois, Dordt College (Dordt University, as of May 2019) of Sioux Center, Iowa, and Redeemer University College of Ancaster, Ontario, all once. The two exceptions to this pattern are the Sheboygan, Wisconsin, meeting at Lakeland College (now University), affiliated with the United Church of Christ, and the Albany, New York, conference at the New Netherland Institute and the New York State Museum. The AADAS has not (yet) ventured west of Sioux County (in northwestern Iowa) for conference locations, although there are Dutch enclaves—with histories waiting to be explored—in California, Washington, Montana, Texas, and so forth, not to mention several provinces in Canada.

of meeting in 2015 in Albany, New York, AADAS decided to accept Fulton's request, thus marking another departure from its usual practice. The 2017 conference took place in the heartland, where Illinois borders Iowa. A further anomaly is that Fulton is not a college town and is the smallest municipality yet to host an AADAS gathering; its population is only about four thousand, being the fourth largest town in the predominantly agrarian Whiteside County. In keeping with this venue, a rural theme was selected for the conference: "Dutch Americans and Agriculture, Past and Present."

Named for the man commonly credited with inventing the steamboat (1807), the city of Fulton was founded in 1835 and boasts a significant number of people with Dutch surnames. Protestant immigrants, largely farmers from rural areas in the Netherlands, began to arrive there just after the Civil War, establishing Reformed and Christian Reformed churches. They were taking advantage of the cessation of hostilities, improved trans-Atlantic transportation, cheap government lands, and the coming of the railroad from Chicago to Western Illinois. Located on the Mississippi River, where it is crossed by the Lincoln Highway, Fulton can claim to be the birthplace of President Reagan's parents.

Conference participants from outside the area were treated to visits to the huge "De Immigrant" windmill (manufactured in the Netherlands and shipped piecemeal to Fulton) on the ("Dutch") dike at the edge of the Mississippi, as well as the nearby Windmill Cultural Center, with its exhibit of working miniature windmills. The windmill, unlike the dike (which protects from flooding by the river), is nonfunctioning. Further enlightenment on matters Dutch came by an evening presentation on Saint Nicholas (Sinterklaas) by Barbara Mask. We were introduced to some of the local Christian Reformed and Reformed churches and were taken out in the country to the Newton Zion Reformed Church (on Frog Pond Road), where we met a few members of its small but lively congregation. The conferees were more than well fed at a couple of the local churches as well as the Eagle Point Park Lodge, just across the river in Clinton, Iowa, overlooking the Mississippi.

We burned off these calories by mental exercise by hearing (and discussing) the presentations of seventeen speakers over the course of a day and a half, employing our "little grey cells" while sitting in the comfortable and electronically well-endowed conference center (auditorium) of the world headquarters of Fulton's premier business, Agri-King (appropriately named, considering the theme of the conference). Outside our "classroom," we learned even more from guided tours of the facilities of the firm, which specializes in tailor-making nutritious, "highly fortified" feed for the animals of large and small livestock producers "worldwide."

As with virtually all the AADAS conferences with a central theme, there were not (quite) enough proposed papers on agriculture and kindred topics to fill the schedule, so submissions were accepted on other Dutch American subjects as well. All but one of the sixteen papers read at Fulton were submitted for publication, and all of these have been accepted. Of the contributors, nearly half of the fifteen, namely seven, were born outside the United States (six in the Netherlands and one in Canada), and as far as can be ascertained, only two of the authors have no Dutch blood coursing through their veins—the keynote speaker and the lead editor.[2] Two of the contributors still live and work in the Netherlands. Eleven articles are about the land, farming, crops, and the environment, whereas the last four are about people relatively far removed from the soil.

Janel Curry, although not of Netherlandic extraction and new to AADAS, had a long association with Calvin College, noted for its Dutch roots, integration of faith and learning, and links with our organization. Her keynote address was intended to guide us in "reading" agricultural landscapes. This "reading" begins with discerning large-scale, global patterns of immigration, such as who came and whence and when they came. Next, national and regional factors are to be observed, like the availability of land (less of it as time passed), as well as ethnic and religious patterns; for instance, the mid-nineteenth-century second wave of Dutch Reformed immigrants became concentrated mostly in agricultural communities in the Midwest (Michigan and Iowa). Finally, on the local level, the openness of the Dutch immigrants to new technology and niche markets enabled them to utilize (seemingly) unpromising muckland, for example, for truck farming. In addition, the worldview of the Dutch Reformed may have been related to their frequently engaging in small, intense, diverse, farming, aided by "bonding" and "bridging" and openness to technological and other changes.

Robert Swierenga, the "dean" of Dutch American immigration historians, read a paper in 1977 at the very first of the biennial conferences that soon morphed into AADAS, and he appears to have

---

[2] Michael ("Mike") Swanson may have a Scandinavian surname, but his mother was a Huizenga (of the Groningen Huizengas).

attended and presented at all the ensuing gatherings, including of course the one at Fulton. His contribution on this occasion is a wide-ranging overview of Dutch involvement in the production of celery "on the muck." Most of Swierenga's article is focused on West Michigan, including Kalamazoo, Holland, Hamilton, Grand Haven, Muskegon, Montague, Fremont, Hudsonville, Allendale, Zeeland, Wyoming, Jenison, Byron Center, and Imlay City. Luce County in Michigan's Upper Peninsula is also studied. Elsewhere, the immigrant celery growers were active in the Chicago area; De Motte, Indiana; and Celeryville, Ohio; as well as Hollandale, Minnesota, and Wilhelmina Colony, Dunklin County, Missouri. Farther afield, Swierenga finds Dutch muck farmers in Holland Marsh, Ontario, Canada, and the Sacramento River delta in California. The immigrant muck farmer in the last-named place was also an aristocrat with an earned doctorate in law. Swierenga notes that the Dutch were inventive in developing celery varieties and managed to "dominate the market for celery, onions, and many other vegetables" in the late nineteenth and early twentieth centuries.

Speaking of onions, Ken Bult's article focuses on Dutch farmers growing "onion sets" around South Holland, near Chicago, and not far from his own hometown. South Holland was originally called Low Prairie (Lage Prairie) because of its elevation, which suggests the swampy nature of the area, with alluvial clay, a bit akin to the muckland discussed by Swierenga. Onion sets thrived in the sandy loam soil available in South Holland. The somewhat ambiguous term "onion sets" refers, according to the *Merriam-Webster* dictionary, to "a small onion bulb planted in the spring [instead of seed] to produce an early crop especially of green onions."[3] Bult divides his paper into two parts: the rise of South Holland as the "Onion Set Capital of the World," from about 1890 to 1939 (undergoing the Great Depression fairly well), and South Holland as leader in both producing and marketing of onion sets during the 1940s and 1950s. The success of the Dutch in this endeavor may be attributed to their thriftiness, clannishness, and (Calvinistic) work ethic. Chicago's (sub)urban sprawl in the latter part of the twentieth century ended the heyday of the South Holland onion producers.

---

[3] A further definition of onion sets: "Sets are grown from seed sown in the greenhouse earlier, and the little plants about 4 inches tall are "set" with planting machines in the spring. The harvest is a small onion, about an inch or smaller in size. These are packaged as a secondary seed onion, then planted in another season to grow a large bulb onion the second year." David Postma email to the editor, 7 Dec. 2017.

Another crop discussed at the Fulton conference was peas, that is, their processing, not their cultivation. Wisconsinite Mary Risseeuw tells the story of the pea-canning factories in her state in the early and middle decades of the twentieth century. Places like Cedar Grove and Oostburg in Sheboygan County and Waupun and Alto in Dodge County were centers of this industry. All went very well with the canneries until World War II, when young male workers were taken into the armed services. This meant that women and even German prisoners of war had to replace them in the canneries and also in the fields harvesting the crops. The POWs were often given hospitality in the homes of members of local Reformed churches, which later caused resentment among returning American servicemen who had been fighting the Germans overseas. The cannery experience of Risseeuw's brother adds personal color to this article.

Returning to the theme of the land, Donald Sinnema, who began life on a Dutch immigrant farm in Alberta, Canada, and is now immersed in the gigantic, esoteric work of editing the papers of the Synod of Dort for its quadricentennial, has taken time out here to return to his roots. He tells the story of two key inventions made by Dutch Canadians (one of whom was his shirttail relative) to help keep soil from drifting after plowing. The loss of topsoil was a major threat across the Canadian prairies and the American Great Plains during the 1910s, 1920s, and 1930s. To meet this problem, the two immigrant Koole brothers, of Monarch, Alberta, introduced strip farming in 1918, and twenty years later, their nephew, another Netherlander, George Williamson (originally Willemsen) of nearby Granum, Alberta, invented the Williamson single V-blade, which in plowing cut the roots of weeds but left a trash cover to prevent soil drifting. Another Albertan, Charles Noble, however, took over (seemingly somewhat deviously, by means of patent infringement litigation) and improved the latter invention, so that the Noble V-blade became widely popular in North America and other parts of the world in the 1950s and later.

In another contribution related to farming, this time within a small geographical area, Janet Sheeres employs her characteristic talent for sleuthing out neglected topics (like overlooked Dutch immigrant enclaves) by telling about nineteenth and early-twentieth-century Dutch immigrant farmers (and their descendants) in Wayne County, New York. She has divided her article into four parts: the place, the people, the produce, and the progress (like four peas in a pod; note Risseeuw's article). Regarding the "place," Wayne County has good soil (even some muck for potatoes and vegetables) and a temperate climate on Lake Ontario; it was linked to the outside world by the Erie Canal (1823) and railroad (1841). The "people" were the "new" Dutch immigration to the county, largely from the province of Zeeland, begun already in 1802 (long before 1847, when the better-known colonies of Holland and Pella were started), with Abraham Peper (1757-1845) and his family, and grew slowly from then until 1846. (Sheeres lists nineteen families or individuals who came during this period.) A larger influx came in 1845 from Zeelandic Flanders, led by Marinus Clicquennoi; it had many (other) people with French Huguenot surnames. Pultneyville and Pickleville (later East Williamson) were the immigrants' chief places of settlement. Jozias Bruijnooge of the latter place, writing in an 1849 Sheboygan newspaper, urged his fellow newcomers to speak Dutch and to obtain Dutch preachers; thus a Dutch Reformed congregation was organized there in 1851. As for the "produce," Sheeres details the occupations of men and women based on decennial federal censuses. The men (and their wives) were frequently farmers who either owned or leased their property, while fruit orchards, followed by potatoes and vegetables, were the major money makers. Fruit and vegetable canneries offered employment for many. German prisoners of war were brought in toward the end of World War II to help on the farms and in the factories. Under the rubric "progress," Sheeres offers reasons for the greater degree of assimilation (Americanization) of the Wayne County Dutch in comparison with other, larger, Dutch colonies; nevertheless, they remain proud of their heritage, still forming about 11 percent of the county's population

Continuing the study of Dutch immigrants in a single county is the contribution of Michael Swanson, who looks at his own locality, the mostly rural, Whiteside County, Illinois, as a place where Dutch immigrants put down roots. They began arriving in small increments just after the Civil War. Most of them were farmers who remained so in Whiteside County, where they were concentrated in Fulton and Garden Plain (its East Clinton area) Townships, usually near Reformed or Christian Reformed churches. Their chief crop was corn, but they also grew wheat, oats, and hay, as well as fruits and vegetables. Their livestock included horses (later replaced by tractors), cattle (for beef and milk), pigs, and chickens (for eggs and meat). Their farms, which—more often than not—they leased, were mostly small and diversified, prudently combining the aforementioned crops and animals, so as not to put all their eggs in one basket. The fruit of their labor was intended for both their own consumption and for sale (by means of truck farming, for instance). To support his narrative, Swanson provides several statistical charts covering the years from 1870 to 1925.

David Zwart, while relatively young, is rapidly becoming a veteran participant at AADAS conferences. His article examines the rural, farming sensibilities (self-image) of the midwestern Dutch in the twentieth century, as shown in the mini-histories composed for significant anniversaries (like centennials), as well as in Tulip Times, pageants, and other celebrations. He takes special note of the commemorative booklets about the founding and growth of nineteenth-century Reformed and Christian Reformed immigrant congregations. Highlighted in these (virtual) eulogies are the faith and sacrifices of the pioneers as they settled and tamed the wilderness and successively built ever-better sanctuaries. These stories were told with an eye to inspire the upcoming generation to emulate the piety and steadfastness of their forebears, in a time when rural congregations were facing unsettling change (world wars, depression, and modernity) and, frequently, decline. The sovereign, covenant-keeping God, who had given his people a mission, gave assurance for the future. Congregations in Holland, Michigan; Pella, Iowa; and Sheboygan County, Wisconsin, are among the many examples used. A wistful nostalgia for "the little white church" in the "heartland" pervades a significant number of these documents, as they idealize and romanticize the pioneers.

Justin Vos, a recent Dordt College graduate, is a doctoral student of Suzanne Sinke (former president of AADAS) in the History Department at Florida State University. His contribution aims to illustrate the decisive role religion played, even more than ethnicity (which he claims has been overemphasized in recent scholarship), in the case of a typical Dutch immigrant family. This perspective is also suggested but not argued in the articles of Curry and Zwart. Vos draws upon 185 family letters, written during a period of over thirty years, translated and published in the Netherlands in 1999, to show that religion was the foundation of at least some immigrants' communal experience. As he puts it, "the [De Jong] family's Calvinist faith provided a source of personal identity, fostered ethnic unification, and created an expansive ethnically inclusive community on shared religious values." Lieuwe and Tjitske de Jong and six of their children (including a married daughter and her husband) emigrated from Friesland to farm in New Holland, Douglas County, South Dakota, in 1893-94. Only their eldest, married daughter remained behind. Most of the letters are from Tjitske to her faraway daughter, telling the family news, while often (unsuccessfully) urging her and her family to join them. Vos examines the family's ties to the Netherlands, the role of church community and attendance (CRC), the motivation for Christian education, and the importance of church membership (one son, sadly, never joined). Vos also examines the efforts at familial reunification, as well as the use of religious language in the letters. The article concludes with a study of the implications of "Dutch Reformed geography" and the place of ethnicity within the Dutch Reformed community; although closely related, Reformed faith and Dutch ethnicity are not identical.

The next two articles are related in that they were both written by three (one article is coauthored) native Netherlanders and concerned with the natural environment as *observed* (flora and fauna) and as *disturbed* (fauna – passenger pigeons). The nineteenth-century Dutch immigrants, having known many fewer "wide open spaces" than they encountered in the New World, would, understandably, have been awestruck by the American "wilderness."

Henk Aay, like Janel Curry, is a geographer once associated with Calvin College, and like Justin Vos, relies principally on letters as the basis for his contribution. Aay's thorough study of the immigrants' (and visitors') environmental observations, knowledge, and behavior relies on their private letters and memoirs, as well as their published articles and letters in Dutch American newspapers and other publications. He focuses mainly on letters written between 1846 and 1860 by immigrants who had settled in the Midwest, particularly West Michigan, Wisconsin, Iowa (Pella), and Illinois (Cook County), in addition to letters composed in New York State while the newcomers were traveling to their future homes. In all, he draws upon 314 private letters and 38 public ones, totaling 351 documents, with 451 environmental observations. Public letters (intended for publication at the time of writing) had twice the percentage of comments on the environment (on its own terms) than private ones, much of it informational and promotional (something like "chamber of commerce" ads today). Private letters (unpublished at the time) to family and friends back home tended to view the environment more as it affected the settlers' daily lives and how it could be used, such as in farming. Aay provides statistical charts showing the relative frequency of the various kinds of observations. Almost a third of the environmental observations concern four categories: landscape, birds, plants (not crops), and animals (namely, new and different things the immigrants had seen in the United States), whereas the rest of the comments tell of the settlers' livelihood, their needs and wants, and the ways in which their lives are connected to the natural environment (the subcategories here are forestry, soil, climate, nature's impact on people, farming practices, and natural resources). Aay richly illustrates his findings with quotations from many personal letters, revealing the settlers' worldview regarding nature (believing that God's blessings or curses on the environment flow from human virtue or vice), weather and climate (hotter and colder than the Netherlands), landscape (amalgamating nature and culture), landscapes at the settlement (the settlers' reactions were both positive and negative), the natural world (wildlife of plants and animals), natural resources (soils), environmental practices (turning woodlands into farmlands), nature's good and bad impact upon the immigrants, and as observed on their journeys to their destinations in the United States. Finally, Aay periodically sprinkles in helpful comparisons between the Netherlands and the New World, as well as between the different areas of settlement in the Midwest.

Jan Boersema, aided by yet another Dutch-born scholar, Nella Kennedy,[4] has a much narrower focus than Aay. These coauthors tell the sad tale of the unforeseen, sudden extinction of the passenger pigeon in America during the latter part of the nineteenth century. The disappearance of not a few species of animals from the overpopulated Netherlands is a familiar story. And we have all heard about being "as dead as a dodo," a metaphor originating in the nineteenth century but referring to a bird which was last seen in Mauritius in the seventeenth century, when the Dutch ruled that island (named for Maurice, the stadtholder of the Netherlands). It is doubtless pure coincidence that Netherlanders were also (innocent?) bystanders at the extinction of the once-prolific passenger pigeon. However this may be, it is also one of the great mysteries of our time that so numerous a species should vanish so quickly, first from urban dinner tables and ultimately from the earth. Boersema, a biologist by vocation and an environmentalist by avocation, is well qualified to tell the story, while Kennedy, a historian of art and of the Dutch American scene, has led in transcribing and deciphering the obscure, difficult document used as the basis of this study. The manuscript's elusive author was Henry (originally Hendrik, nicknamed Henk) Takken (1839-1914), who had come in 1852 from the Netherlands with his parents to settle in the Western Michigan

---

[4] Her married surname may be Scots-Irish, but she was born a Breugem in Rotterdam, the Netherlands.

Dutch colony, where he remained for the rest of his days. He worked as a blacksmith (his father's vocation) and (mostly) as a wagon maker, but for recreation, Henry and his friends hunted what we might colloquially call "sitting ducks," but were then preeminently passenger pigeons, with some other birds and animals as well. In 1910, near the end of his life, Takken was asked to put down on paper the recollections of his early hobby as a small-game hunter. This he did, with pencil, in the mangled English and spelling of "the man on the street" operating in a foreign tongue. Since he did not sign the document, some sleuthing was required to identify him as the author. In the Netherlands, hunting with a gun had been a luxury, reserved for the upper classes, but in America, as is well known, anyone could use a firearm (of several types) for obtaining food, furs, and so forth; traps were also used to catch animals. Boersema lists on a chart thirteen different species, including passenger pigeons, hunted by Takken and his companions, together with their Latin names (doubtless unknown to Takken), such as deer, boar, mink, muskrat, otter, bear, fox, squirrel, duck, partridge, and others. About a third of Takken's brief narrative is taken up with shrewd observations about passenger pigeons and their ways. The article concludes with a lament over the tragic end of the unfortunate passenger pigeon, in addition to educated guesses as to its causes, chiefly over-hunting by men like Takken, as well as the genetic makeup of the birds.

The final four articles from the Fulton conference take us away from the muck, the farm, and the flora and fauna to the more "elevated" areas of theology and the arts and sciences. These concluding essays feature four Netherlands-born men, two erstwhile Christian Reformed leaders and two more "secular" figures but with roots in the old country's public church, the Hervormde Kerk (Reformed Church). The immediately preceding article on Henry Takken (and the carrier pigeons) already anticipates the concluding, biographical section of this volume. The quartet's individual histories are arranged in near-chronological order, with the two churchmen first, to be followed by an artist and a scientist.

Earl Wm. (Bill) Kennedy has given us the story of the erratic Rev. Hendrik Georg(e) Klijn (1793-1883), the sometime (1857) cofounder of the future Christian Reformed Church. The son of a Lutheran murderer, Klijn, who insisted on assuming his mother's surname, grew up in Utrecht to become a wallpaper dealer and a pioneer elder in the Utrecht Seceder Reformed congregation. Trained and ordained as a gospel minister by Rev. Hendrik Pieter Scholte (later founder of Pella,

Iowa), Klijn served two Seceder churches in the Netherlands before immigrating to western Michigan with some of his flock in 1849. He pastored, successively, three Reformed congregations (Graafschap, Michigan; Milwaukee, Wisconsin; and Grand Rapids, Michigan) until 1857, when he was badgered into seceding from the allegedly impure Reformed Church in the East. After only a few months' exile from the denomination, Klijn repented and returned to the fold, deeply sorry and apologetic for his unloving conduct toward his brethren in the Reformed Classis of Holland. His ministry then resumed in congregations in Kalamazoo and Chicago[5] until he took emeritus status in 1868, when he was seventy-five years old. But Klijn was not yet done, for in "retirement" he regularly supplied churches, successively, in Grand Haven, Michigan; Milwaukee; Chicago; and Pella, Iowa. In fact, even after this, he continued preaching on most Sundays for the last five years of his long life in Keokuk, Iowa, where he held forth in Dutch at home for a small group of hearers (there being no Reformed congregation in town) until one day after his ninetieth birthday. When he was unable to preach standing, he sat, and when he could no longer sit, he preached from what became his deathbed. From 1838 (his ordination) until 1883 (his death), he kept a logbook, recording every place and every sermon text he preached Sundays (often three times on the Lord's Day) and during the week (sometimes several times), especially in his preretirement years. This is a remarkable testimony to his perseverance in his calling. Klijn was almost always a peacemaker, except most notably when he temporarily broke with the classis in 1857, and even then, he made his exit with gracious words. He left this life far removed from the stigma of his father's horrific deed.

    George Harinck offers us insight into the early career and exodus of another onetime Christian Reformed leader, the biblical theologian Geerhardus Vos (1862-1949). Harinck has already published extensively on Vos, including an appreciative essay on his seven published volumes of Dutch poetry. Very much unlike Klijn, Vos was a "preacher's kid." Also, unlike Klijn, he was never ordained into the ministry, although he was theologically trained. His father, a Seceder Reformed pastor, had brought his wife and children to Grand Rapids in 1881. Harinck investigates why the brilliant, well-educated, young Geerhardus, with a newly minted doctorate from a European university, agreed to teach at the then subpar theological school of the Christian Reformed Church

---

[5] When Klijn was pastoring in Chicago, he organized the First Reformed Church of Fulton, Illinois, in 1866.

in Grand Rapids (it would become Calvin Theological Seminary), what he accomplished during his five years there (1888-93), and why he left Grand Rapids for an Old Testament professorship at the Princeton Theological Seminary of the Presbyterian Church in the United States (1893-1932). Vos accepted the Grand Rapids position primarily out of loyalty to his parents, his alma mater, and his denomination. He had to teach a very heavy load of courses, in many different subjects, to students who were often without any college education. He enriched the curriculum by introducing, among other courses, the history of philosophy. Vos's lectures on Reformed systematic theology were heavily influenced by Abraham Kuyper's neo-Calvinism, supralapsarianism, and doctrine of presumptive regeneration (see the article for definitions!); these were all minority positions in the Christian Reformed Church, not calculated to win him friends among his colleagues and constituency. He received considerable criticism for these views and kept a low profile preparing his lectures and teaching, largely refraining from publishing. In addition to helping to upgrade the school, Vos did some solid theological scholarship. The students were enthusiastic about him, not wishing him to go elsewhere. The "push" factors for his departure from the Grand Rapids school included his heavy workload, the sort of courses he had to teach (such as English for Dutch speakers), the inferior quality of the student body, the stifling theological sniping from non-Kuyperians, and last, but perhaps not least, his marriage in May 1893 to a "gentile," namely, a local American woman of non-Dutch, non-Christian Reformed heritage. *Cherchez la femme (fatale?)*. The "pull" factors drawing him to Princeton were a smaller teaching load focused more on his own central interests (like the exciting new field of biblical theology), teaching college graduates, and the larger world of the Presbyterian Church in the East. Vos's departure was a big loss for Grand Rapids and a major gain for Princeton, where he would serve until he retired almost four decades later. During Vos's time at Calvin, he had also almost accepted a position at Kuyper's Free University of Amsterdam. Something of an introvert, he remained a fish out of water during his entire career. Nevertheless, his books written at Princeton, such as those on Old and New Testament biblical theology and on the Pauline eschatology, became standard texts for conservative seminaries, remaining in print until now. And even his lectures on Reformed dogmatics, written while still in Grand Rapids, have just recently been published.

Speaking of the arts, such as Vos's poetry, we now segue, virtually seamlessly, to the visual arts with an essay by Nella Kennedy, herself an art historian in public and a creative artist in private, on the career of a once-prominent but now little-remembered instructor at the School of the Art Institute of Chicago, the Dutch American artist John Henry Vanderpoel (1857-1911). Five years older than Vos, Vanderpoel was baptized in the Dutch Reformed Church as Johannes van der Poel in a little municipality, now famous for being the location of the Schiphol Airport. He was the seventh of ten children, whose recently widowed innkeeper father took them suddenly in 1868 (under cover of darkness, to avoid his creditors) to begin life anew in Chicago. The elder Vanderpoel rose to importance as a chief clerk in the Cook County government. Following his lead, the family speedily Americanized, with John Henry marrying an American woman. He did, however, study abroad when he was young, mostly in Paris, in preparation for a career in art. Somewhat deformed and unusually short in stature, he showed artistic ability at an early age, especially excelling in drawing the undraped human form. He was beloved by his students at the School of the Art Institute for his kindly personality, effective teaching, and talent at draftsmanship. Vanderpoel's most lasting contribution, other than his influence on his students (one of whom was Georgia O'Keefe), is an illustrated textbook on the human figure that they urged him to publish. Originally appearing in 1907 and still in print today, it contains over three hundred drawings and marginal sketches. He was, moreover, in demand as a muralist and as a painter (in oils, pastels, and watercolors). Many of his and his students' works are on display at the John H. Vanderpoel Memorial Art Gallery, located in Chicago's Beverly (Hills) neighborhood and sponsored by the John H. Vanderpoel Art Association. A nearby public school and street also bear his name. Although almost his entire career as an art instructor was spent at the school in Chicago, his summers were spent teaching in various places in the United States and at an American artist's colony he initiated in Rijsoord in the Netherlands, near his father's family's farm. Vanderpoel left his Chicago employment for a position at the more prestigious St Louis People's University just a year before he died. A conservative in his field, he embodied the French beaux-arts traditionalism of the Art Institute of Chicago as over against modernism.

The last of the three Dutch-born contributors of biographical entries is Huug van den Dool, longtime AADAS participant, who might facetiously be called a "weatherman extraordinaire" but who properly is a professional meteorologist, a person engaged in the tricky "science" of short-term climate prediction, with a doctorate in physics and mathematics and many scientific publications to his name, including a book recently issued by the Oxford University Press. Van den Dool introduces us to the most recent of the Netherlanders featured in our volume, the world-renowned planetary scientist (one type of astronomer), Gerard Peter Kuiper (1905-1973). Incidentally, the fields of Van den Dool and Kuiper, climate and astronomy, are cousins, if not siblings. Kuiper is perhaps best known for the "discovery" of the eponymous Kuiper Belt—not to be found in haberdasheries but in the heavens; the term refers to trillions of primordial, icy bodies, including the dwarf planet Pluto, encircling our solar system beyond Neptune; Kuiper hypothesized the belt's existence, which has been confirmed since his death. This famous Dutch American astronomer, Gerard Peter Kuiper, began life as Gerrit Pieter Kuiper, in humble circumstances in a small community in the province of Noord-Holland, the son of a progressive Reformed tailor and his wife. G. P. had the talent and the determination to overcome his disadvantaged background and to jump through the hoops of the Dutch educational system and the prejudice against someone of his social class and West Frisian accent. He eventually gained entrance into the premier Dutch university, Leiden, during the golden age of astronomy in the Netherlands of the 1920s. The Netherlands had a surplus of astronomers, while the United States had a shortage of them, so during the 1930s, Kuiper became part of the Dutch supply that met the American demand. He quickly adapted to his adopted country, changing his name slightly, marrying an American, and largely shedding his Dutch identity. Kuiper became quite proficient in English but, strangely, seemed to have lost his facility in the Dutch language and was extremely reluctant to use it publicly during visits to the Netherlands. In any event, he had an illustrious career in the United States, hardworking, focused and driven, and aided by generous monetary grants and the use of gigantic telescopes; he was heavily involved in the anti-Soviet Cold War space race.

  Our contributors' topics thus run the gamut from muck to outer space. Enjoy!

I. Dutch Americans and Farming

CHAPTER 1

Time, Space, Worldviews, and Agricultural Landscapes

Janel Curry

I spent a semester in England as an undergraduate, and in my course on the history of Roman Britain, we spent one day each week working at a Roman archeological site. Finding Roman coins was interesting, but what I truly remember is the day that the archeologist walked us across a farmer's field. He talked about how each field carried a name passed down over the centuries—a clue to its history and potential artifacts dating back to Roman times and before. I think I became a geographer that day, and I began to see rural agricultural landscapes as open books that tell us stories about the past. We can "read" landscapes, and they can tell us about our past and perhaps our future. My goal today[1] is to help you learn to read agricultural landscapes. This increased literacy will help you interpret the layers of history behind farmlands, a unique visual expression of time, space, and worldviews.

I start with a model I have constructed to give you a framework to use in reading a landscape (below). Interpretation starts with looking at

---

[1] Because this was the keynote address for the conference, some of its lecture quality has been retained.

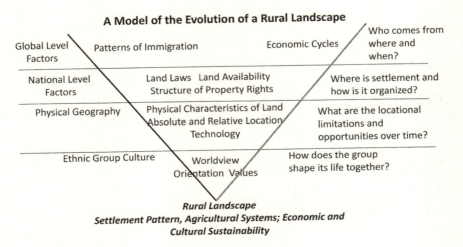

(*Janel Curry*)

larger-scale factors that shape cultural landscapes, then moving down to more regional and national-level scales, to actual physical characteristics of a particular place, to the worldviews of the ethnic groups that interact in that place—all forces that work to create the landscape we see. I will use Dutch American examples to illustrate the model, enabling me to identify potential research questions for scholars.

Global-level factors

The overarching perspective on immigration to North America must be a global one: Who came from where? and when? The broad pattern reveals the predominance of immigrants from Britain between 1500 and 1830, but smaller numbers of other groups also came during that time, such as the early Dutch settlers in the Hudson River Valley. The Americas also saw fifteen million Africans arrive through the institution of slavery.

Mass immigration ensued after 1830. Between the 1830s and 1880s, Northern Europeans dominated the immigrant ranks with the addition of Scandinavians, Germans, the second wave of Dutch immigrations, and the Irish. The Ellis Island era began in 1892, with 71 percent of the immigrants being from Eastern and Southern Europe. Post-World War II saw the third wave of Dutch immigration, along with others affected by the war. And, finally, the post-Vietnam War era was characterized by an increase in Asian immigrants, expanding to immigrants from all continents.

National-level factors

National factors that affected landscapes included the availability of land where settlement could take place and the process by which it was initially distributed. The actual availability of such land for settlement was shaped by federal relations with Native American populations and other, adjacent nations over time. Land laws, such as the Homestead Act (1862), shaped the distribution of available land. In this case, the law allowed for the granting of one hundred and sixty acres of land to individuals who would live on the land and cultivate it for five years. Federal land offices were established on the frontiers of European communities to facilitate the settlement of newly opened land. These national land laws also shaped settlement in terms of whether individuals or groups obtained land. Some ethnic groups worked harder than others in their attempt to re-create the work and residential patterns of their home countries, sometimes with great effort. The North American structure of land distribution emphasized individual land ownership on isolated plots, a model in stark contrast to the farm villages of continental Europe.

The settlement of North America by Europeans was thus primarily a process of east to west settlement that sorted groups by immigration era. For example, the earliest, pre-revolutionary wave of Dutch entry was to the East Coast, primarily the Hudson River Valley and New Jersey. The next wave of Dutch immigration, in the mid-nineteenth century, was to the Midwest. There are cases where the second generation moved even farther west for new land as well—the initial settlement of Pella, in southeast Iowa, spawned a next generation who moved to Sioux County in northwest Iowa and beyond. Finally, the post-World War II Dutch immigrants layered on top of previous settlement groups, settling in places like Ontario and British Columbia, Canada, and southern California. Therefore, "who went where" was largely dependent on when they came and what land was available.

Inasmuch as ethnicity is tied to faith tradition, we see the spatial pattern generated from this religious sorting mechanism. The diversity of the religious affiliation map tells us something of how opened or closed the immigrant group was, as well as the degree of consolidation of their settlement pattern. For instance, the Reformed community pattern shows very distinct and concentrated Dutch concentrations in Western Michigan and Northwestern Iowa.

The examples of the Norwegians and Ukrainians will serve to illustrate the impact of the timing of immigration on agricultural

Swan River rural church (*photo by Curry*)

ethnic rural settlements. Norwegians came in the latter part of the nineteenth century, while Ukrainians came after 1900. The Upper Midwest and Great Plains of the United States were open to settlement at the time of Norwegian immigration. The predominance of Lutherans in this region today is evidence of the concentration of this group in this region. Arriving later, Ukrainians who desired to farm bypassed the United States and settled in the Canadian Prairies. As a result, whereas one finds Lutheran churches in the rural upper US Midwest and Great Plains, rural Ukrainian Orthodox churches are found in Swan River, Manitoba, in west central Manitoba. In the United States, Ukrainians tended to become urban residents, a pattern that prevailed among many European immigrant groups.

The Dutch were an exception to this general pattern, where immigrants who arrived after initial settlement became urban residents. Late Dutch immigrants (those from the post-World War II wave) still chose agriculture, managing to layer their settlement on top of previous immigrant groups, often entering agriculture through intensive niche enterprises. We understand little about why the Dutch formed this exception. Questions rich for exploration include:

- What was their motivation?
- Were they more skilled at intensive agriculture?

- Was there a greater desire to maintain an ethnic agricultural landscape and community?
- Was there an anti-urban bias?

One of these areas of Dutch agricultural concentration that was tied to late immigration is the Niagara Peninsula in Ontario. This area, with its unique climate, is known for its vineyards and soft fruits, such as peaches. The region around St. Catherines is also home to more recent Dutch farmers. This type of intensive specialized agriculture often leads to the use of migrant farm labor. The relationship between Dutch farming and migrant labor offers another possible research opportunity. What is the state of labor relations in these communities? Is it different than in other agricultural communities?

Physical geography

Moving down the model to the local scale, the physical characteristics of a location play an additional role in community and agricultural development. The nature of the land may at first limit opportunities and cause an area to be bypassed by immigrants. The combination of technological advancement and market forces, however, may later provide a new opportunity for the formerly rejected site. Technology to overcome the limitations of the land and higher agricultural prices to pay for the new technology may combine to make the land an agricultural resource. It is possible that some ethnic groups, such as the Dutch, are more open than others to the adoption of new technology and to taking advantage of a potentially profitable niche market.

The Dutch settlement of Hollandale, Minnesota, illustrates the complexity of the unique opportunities offered by this site. Rice Lake Marsh, the future Hollandale, was consolidated into large land holdings because it was a swamp. The federal government gave swamplands, as well as land grants for the development of railroads, to state governments. The federal Swamp Land Act of 1850, together with railroad grants, facilitated the consolidation of land holdings within the Rice Lake Marsh area. The large landowners there attempted to either drain the land or find extensive uses for it, including hunting and fishing. And, in fact, swampland is usually not reclaimed for agriculture unless there are large landholdings or some centralized effort to assess the cost of the drainage. The cost of the technology and the needed coordinated effort requires this.

In the case of the Rice Lake Marsh, the right combination of factors came together in the late 1910s and early 1920s. High land prices, high agricultural product prices, and new technology led to an elaborate scheme to successfully drain the Rice Lake Marsh, part of an effort of the Albert Lea Farms company. The company specifically marketed the drained land to Dutch farmers who focused on intensive vegetable crop production. This has led to a correlation between the former natural boundaries of the Rice Lake Marsh and Dutch surnames.

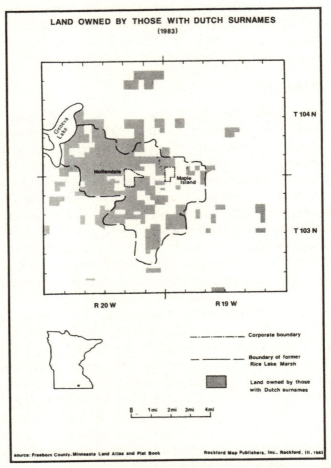

Land owned by those with Dutch surnames in Hollandale, Minnesota, 1983[2]

[2] Janel M. Curry-Roper and Carol Veldman Rudie, "Hollandale: The Evolution of a Dutch Farming Community," *Focus* 40, no. 3 (1990): 13-18, image p. 15.

Although Hollandale has its unique story, its case raises questions about the relationship between Dutch farm communities and the physical characteristics of land—muckland in particular. The Dutch seemed to be drawn to land with these physical characteristics (for instance, Celeryville, Wisconsin; Kalamazoo, Michigan; and Hollandale, Minnesota). Examples also exist of instances in which Dutch farmers took advantage of late development opportunities and congregated in the same area. One of the questions this raises is whether this was motivated by a desire to live in an ethnic/religious enclave. These opportunities are also often tied to niche markets, whether truck farms in New Jersey or dairy farms in California. More research needs to be done on whether this is a verifiable pattern and whether the Dutch might have a higher comfort level with the technological change associated with these niche markets. Are Dutch farmers more open to innovation?

Ethnic group culture

Finally, worldview factors affect the development of these agricultural landscapes. I want to draw on three interrelated worldview elements that I have found to be important. The first is the level of commitment to place and to rural life and this commitment's impact on agricultural patterns. The second is the communal orientation of a culture group. The third is a culture group's posture toward technology, change, and external resources. The differences in these worldview elements become evident through a comparison among groups in Iowa.

Average farm sizes and levels of product diversity in farms range widely among different ethnic groups. In a comparison of three neighboring communities, Dutch Reformed farm size was found to grow at a slower rate than in two other communities between 1960 and 1980.

Likewise, Dutch Reformed farms exhibited higher levels of diversity in their farm systems than most comparable groups.

Perhaps a reason for the smaller farms, in comparison to close neighboring communities, relates to the greater diversity in livestock. This pattern may be an indication of an effort by members of the community to stay in place and farm, in which case, these measures may reflect an overall commitment to a community with intensification through livestock as the means to this end. A comparison of communal orientations among differing communities does show the strength of the commitment of Dutch Reformed respondents to their community.

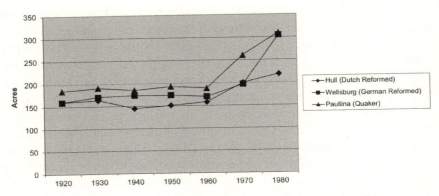

Trends in farm size among three Iowa communities[3]

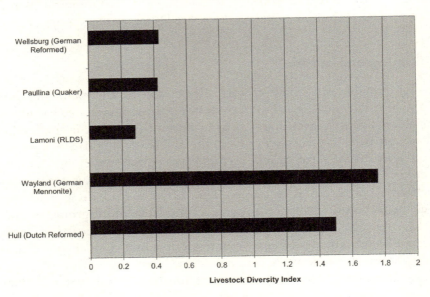

Farm diversity index among five Iowa communities[4]

Furthermore, this theorized commitment to place may be possible only because of a positive posture toward technology and change, along with an ability to tap external resources and expertise to take advantage of opportunities. Scholars talk about the importance of social networks

[3] Janel M. Curry, "Community Worldview and Rural Systems: A Study of Five Communities in Iowa," *Annals of the Association of American Geographers* 90, no. 4 (2000): 693-712, adapted from fig. 5, p. 707.
[4] Ibid., adapted from fig. 4, p. 706.

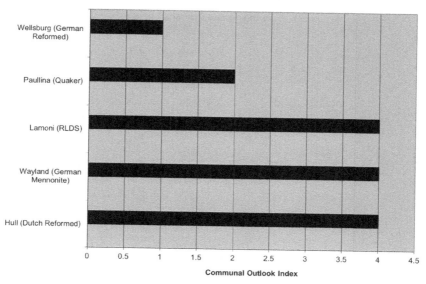

Communal worldview index among five Iowa communities[5]

in terms of a community being able to thrive and change in the face of new challenges. These networks of trust and reciprocity are referred to as social capital, of which, two aspects have been identified. The first is "bonding" or the inward-looking aspect of social capital that reinforces exclusive identities. The second is "bridging," which is outward looking and encompasses a diverse group of people. Bonding is good for developing specific reciprocity and building solidarity. Bridging networks are better for linkage to external assets and institutions, as well as for increased information flow. Both are needed for healthy communities. Bonding leads to the ability to undertake joint action, and bridging allows for the accessing of external resources and expertise. The Dutch Reformed are unique in having strong traits of both bonding and bridging. The data suggest that the Dutch may have a unique tendency to modernize (bridge) through accessing external information in order to intensify their agriculture and remain in a tight community (bond).

Summary

Global patterns of immigration affected who came from which places over time. These global patterns interacted with the national

[5] Ibid., adapted from fig. 2, p. 700.

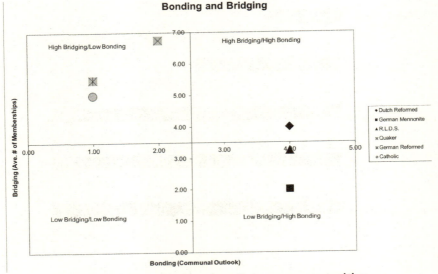

Social capital profiles for six Iowa communities

sequence and pattern of land openings, creating a general east-to-west migration model, with earlier immigrants settling in the East, nineteenth-century immigrants establishing farm communities in the Midwest and Great Plains, and later arrivals settling the Canadian Prairies. This pattern is greatly influenced by arrival times of immigrant groups and the availability of land.

In addition to land availability, the physical characteristics of land resources created limits on settlement. These constraints changed over time with technological development and market forces. Therefore, opportunities and limitations were not static. Finally, ethnic-group culture and worldview shaped the agricultural systems. Either an intentionality in maintaining an ethnic enclave or evidence of strong social bonding led to intensification of agriculture in place, differentiating this type of community from those that experience the extensification of agriculture, with expanding farm sizes and a generational shift out of agriculture.

Dutch Reformed agricultural communities exhibit some similarities to these general patterns and some differences, leading to interesting potential research questions:

- Dutch late arrivals chose agriculture—why?
- Do Dutch farmers have a higher level of comfort with technological change than other ethnic groups?

- Does the Dutch Reformed worldview lead farmers toward intensification and specialization, which in turn leads to smaller farms?
- How have Dutch Reformed farmers interacted with farm laborers?
- What is the long-term impact of the dual strength of bonding and bridging among Dutch Reformed farmers?

Given the interaction of global, national patterns, with the physical characteristics of our landed resources, increasingly impacted by climate change, how will these ethnic farm landscapes evolve?

Will the unique characteristics of Dutch Reformed agricultural communities lead to the expansion of their agricultural footprint in comparison to other ethnic groups?

Many rich questions for exploration are here for the taking.

Sources

Curry, Janel, Margaret McCallum, and Jorge Juan Rodriguez V. "Spiritual Care Education and Rural Systems in Swan River." *Journal of Pastoral Care & Counseling* 70 (March 2016): 53-62.

Curry, Janel. "Social Capital and Societal Vision: A Study of Six Farm Communities in Iowa," 139-52. In *Religion as Social Capital: Producing the Common Good*. Edited by Corwin Smidt. Waco, TX: Baylor University Press, 2003.

Curry, Janel, "Dutch Reformed Worldview and Agricultural Communities in the Midwest," 71-89. In *The Dutch-American Experience: Essays in Honor of Robert P. Swierenga*. Edited by Hans Krabbendam and Larry Wagenaar. Amsterdam: VU University Press, 2000.

Curry, Janel M. "Community Worldview and Rural Systems: A Study of Five Communities in Iowa." *Annals of the Association of American Geographers* 90, no. 4 (2000): 693-712.

Curry-Roper, Janel M. "Embeddedness in Place: Its Role in the Sustainability of a Rural Farm Community in Iowa." *Space and Culture*, no. 4/5 (2000): 204-22.

Curry-Roper, Janel M. "Worldview and Agriculture: A Study of Two Reformed Communities in Iowa," 17-32. In *Reformed Vitality, Continuity and Change in the Face of Modernity*. Edited by Donald A. Luidens, Corwin Smidt, and Hijme Stoffels. Lanham, MD: University Press of America, 1998

Curry-Roper, Janel M. "Community-Level Worldviews and the Sustainability of Agriculture," 101-15. In *Agricultural Restructuring and Sustainability: A Geographical Perspective*. Edited by Tim Rickard, Brian Ilbery, and Quentin Chiotti. Wallingford, UK: CAB Int., 1997.

Curry-Roper, Janel M. and John Bowles. "Local Factors in Land Tenure Change Patterns." *Geographical Review* 81, no. 4 (1991): 443-56.

Curry-Roper, Janel M. and Carol Veldman Rudie. "Hollandale: The Evolution of a Dutch Farming Community." *Focus* 40, no. 3 (1990): 13-18.

Curry, Janel M. "The Swamp Land Grant and the Root River Land District of Minnesota." University of MN: unpublished manuscript, September 1980. In partial fulfillment of a master's degree in geography.

CHAPTER 2

Dutch on the Muck: Celery Cropping in Michigan and Elsewhere

Robert P. Swierenga

The Dutch are masters of the muck,[1] and at the turn of the century, they knew something that other Americans did not: that wetlands, once drained, are ideal for growing vegetables. This type of intensive agriculture they knew first hand, and it supported their families. Their wooden shoes were ideal for working in wet soil, and even their horses were fitted with wooden shoes to keep them from sinking into the soft, wet soil as they pulled the plows.

Dutch muck farms are found in scores of townships across North America, each with its specialized cropping patterns, based on soil conditions, markets, and individual preferences. For example, Celeryville, Ohio, specializes in celery; Hudsonville, Michigan, in onions; and Holland Marsh, Ontario, in lettuce.

---

[1] In the terminology of North American agriculture, muck is a highly decomposed organic material found in drained wetlands. Such "black soil" vegetable cropping is an important part of agriculture in New York, Ohio, Michigan, Indiana, Illinois, Wisconsin, and Florida. American "muckers" often had roots in the Netherlands or eastern Europe, where their ancestors practiced a similar type of farming. The soils are deep, dark colored, and friable, often underlain by either marl or marl clay; https://en.wikipedia.org/wiki/Sapric.

Where wetlands were relatively small in acreage, the immigrants drained the land themselves, since it could be done with Dutch-style windmills and by ditching and tiling. But in regions like northern Indiana; Hollandale, Minnesota; and Holland Marsh, dewatering required massive drainage projects, undertaken by large companies with vast amounts of capital. In northern Indiana, Aaron Hart, wealthy Philadelphia land investor, cut Hart Ditch, which channeled Plum Creek from Dyer through Munster to the Little Calumet River. Cady Marsh Ditch drained lowlands from Griffith through Highland to the Little Calumet. Burns Ditch ran more than twenty miles from the Little Calumet River at Lake Station to Burns Harbor on Lake Michigan and drained thousands of acres.[2]

Albert Lea Enterprise of Minnesota used huge excavators that drained Rice and Geneva Lakes and created Big Marsh. The dredge "Swamp Angel" cut an eighteen-mile ditch, known as Big Ditch, twelve feet deep. The monster machine removed 1.7 million cubic yards of soil. When Big Marsh was drained, the company advertised for Dutch farmers to buy small plots and grow vegetables.[3]

Swamp Angel, Buckeye Ditching Machine (Hollandale the Wonderland *pamphlet*)

[2] http://www.encyclopedia.chicagohistory.org/pages/581.html; http://www.placekeeper.com/Indiana/Cady_Marsh_Ditch-449811.html; https://www.bing.com/search?q=burns+ditch+Indiana&form.

[3] Cheri Register, *The Big Marsh: The Story of a Lost Landscape* (St. Paul: Minnesota Historical Society Press, 2016), is a critical environmental portrayal of the draining of the Rice Lake "Big Marsh," pt. 3, "The Big Ditch."

Big Ditch cut out by Swamp Angel
(Hollandale the Wonderland *pamphlet*)

Holland Marsh was drained by a Toronto firm with a $137,000 contract, led by physics professor William Day. The canal runs over fifteen miles and is seven-and-a-half-feet deep. Dutch farmers were once again recruited.[4]

Breaking muck soil with ten-ton tractor with Caterpillar treads
(Hollandale the Wonderland *pamphlet*)

[4] Albert VanderMey, *And the Swamp Flourished: The Bittersweet Story of Holland Marsh* (Surrey, BC: Vanderheide Publishing Co., 1994).

Muckland is primarily composed of humus (peat) from drained swampland, which has been found up to forty-feet deep. Muck farming is controversial because the drainage of wetlands destroys wildlife habitat and results in a variety of environmental consequences. Peat is a natural resource. More such soils will not likely be created in the United States because of environmental regulations. Muck farms are prone to problems, such as the soil being very light, which often requires windbreaks to keep topsoil from blowing away when dry. Muck soils can catch fire and burn underground for months. When cropped, oxidation removes a portion of the soil each year, so muckland becomes progressively more shallow. Some muck farms have been reclaimed for wildlife preserves by state laws.[5]

West Michigan celery

West Michigan is the birthplace of celery production in the United States; Dutch muck growers first caught "celery fever" in Kalamazoo.[6] Before celery was domesticated and became a popular menu item, its bitter herb roots were used for seasoning and the hollow stalks as filler in soups. Celery stalks were also an ingredient in patent medicine, like, for example, Paine's Celery Compound Household Medicine. As a vegetable, celery had several advantages; it was a relatively high-value crop, with steady demand, seldom grown in home gardens, and very low in calories—eighty-two per stalk—which appealed to weight watchers.[7]

Michigan has approximately five million acres of muck soils, nearly one-seventh of the land area.[8] Dutch celery-growing areas were concentrated in West Michigan regions: Kalamazoo/Portage/Decatur, Holland/Hamilton, Zeeland/Hudsonville/Allendale, Wyoming/Byron Center, Grand Haven/Norton Shores/Muskegon, and Whitehall/Montague/Fremont, although production also spread to Imlay City

---

[5] https://en.wikipedia.org/wiki/Muck; accessed 17 April 2017. Healthy soils rely on water, oxygen, air, and a balanced supply of nutrients. Oxidation involves oxygen exchanges between water and inorganic materials that reduce nutrients.

[6] I am indebted to Larry Kieft and Robert "Bob" Poel, whose grandfathers were pioneer celery growers in Grand Haven, for sharing their first-hand knowledge of celery growing, and to Kieft for taking me on field trips in Grand Haven and Muskegon. William Braaksma of Kalamazoo shared an extensive file of celery newspaper stories and photos.

[7] John K. Trocke, "History of Michigan Celery Industry," in *The Michigan Celery-Carrot Industry* (Cooperative Extension Service, Michigan State University, n.d. [likely about 1965]).

[8] "Agricultural Regions in Michigan," http://geo.msu.edu/extra/geogmich/ag_regions.html.

Paine's Celery Compound Household Medicine, ca. 1900

and Decatur in the Thumb area and even to Newberry in the Upper Peninsula.

In 1885 the first fifteen celery farms in the state were in Kalamazoo, the nursery of celery production. Thirty years later, Kalamazoo had 248 farms, Portage 44, and Muskegon 22. By 1925 Hudsonville had 68 farms, Muskegon 33, Grand Haven 16, Tecumseh 11, and Decatur 9. The state total that year was 315 farms in seventeen counties, down from 322 farms in nineteen counties in 1915. By 1971 the Hudsonville-based Michigan Celery Promotion Cooperative had fifty-four active members. Over time, with tractors and mechanization, the size of farms increased to forty acres or more.[9]

Between 1958 and 1968, Michigan farms produced about one million standard, wire-bound crates of celery and two hundred thousand crates of celery hearts. In 2005 Michigan celery farmers were down to seventeen hundred acres, while California growers cultivated over twenty-five thousand acres, fifteen times as much. Michigan,

---

[9] "Michigan Celery Growers and Shippers," *Michigan State Gazetteer*, 1885-1931, a tabulation for twenty selected years, by county, compiled by Robert Poel. The 1971 numbers are from the 1971 membership list of the Michigan Celery Promotion Cooperative, compliments of Bruce Schreur.

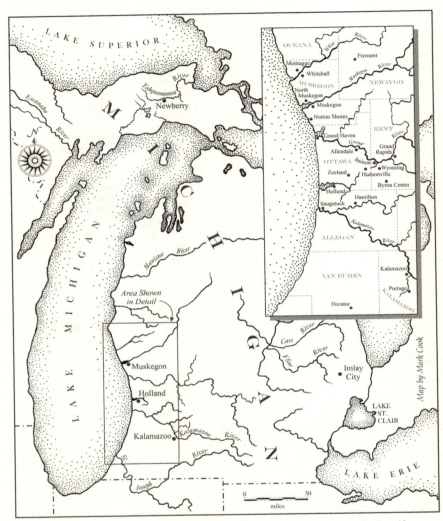

Celery cultivation areas in Michigan (*map by Mark Cook*)

however, was still in second place nationally in 2013, with 104 million pounds grown, valued at $20.4 million.[10]

Kalamazoo-Portage-Decatur

Scottish immigrant George Taylor first brought wild celery seeds to Kalamazoo from the marshes of southern England and served the

---

[10] Trocke, "History of Michigan Celery Industry."

strange vegetable at a Democratic Party banquet at the Burdick Hotel in late 1856. The positive reaction of the diners induced him to plant an acre the next year. Taylor's first greenhouse stood at what is now Henderson Park.[11]

Dutch immigrants fifteen years later developed celery and made it a treat on tables across America. Cornelius De Bruin, a barrel maker from the province of Zeeland, who immigrated in 1866, was the first Dutchman to grow celery. Tradition has it that he saw a strange plant while walking near the corner of Cedar Street and Westnedge Avenue. The celery stalks were hollow and tasteless, suitable only as a filler in soup. He asked for seed and raised a crop, which his children peddled from house to house. He also shipped bunches by train to a store in Three Rivers, twenty miles south, and then happily received more orders. In 1875 brothers Joseph and Peter Balkema began raising celery on the fertile Kalamazoo River bottomland. Lewis Ver Sluis began his multigeneration, celery-growing-and-shipping company in 1896.[12]

The popularity of this vegetable spread like wildfire, and demand greatly exceeded supply. Soon Dutch farmers were growing celery in two- and three-acre plots in the lowlands along Axtell Creek, a tributary of Portage River, in the southern part of the city. The season ran from mid-June to the first frost in October.[13]

By 1910 Zeelanders were clustered along Burdick Street, south of the city, and Groningers and Frisians were concentrated on Raven Creek lowlands north of the city around the intersection of Paterson and West Streets. Most farms drew on family labor for their intensive-style cropping. Celery fields soon stretched southward to Portage and eastward to Comstock. Names of Dutch celery growers in the 1910 Kalamazoo city directory fill six-and-a-half pages.

---

[11] John Kline, "The History of Kalamazoo Celery," in *Report of Michigan Muck Farmers' Association* (Feb. 1928), 27-29; "Scotsman in Kalamazoo Gave Nation 'Dutch Treat,'" *Kalamazoo Gazette*, 3 July 1966; Fred Peppel, "Stalking the Celery City," Feb. 2005, http://www.kpl.gov/local-history/business/celery.aspx, accessed 15 May 2017.

[12] Some sources credit Marinus De Bruin as the first Dutch grower, but Cornelius is correct. "History of Celery in Kalamazoo," http://www.migenweb.org/kalamazoo/celery.htm, accessed 26 May 2017; Peppel, "Stalking"; Dave LeMieux, "By 1951, Muskegon was Michigan's 'Celery City,'" *Muskegon Chronicle*, 18 Sept. 2012, quoting a 16 Sept. 1907 article in the same paper; Byron E. Carpenter, "US Celery first Grew in Kalamazoo," Michigan Celery Promotion Cooperative, n.d.

[13] Herbert Brinks, "Celery," *Origins* 16, no. 1 (1998): 31-35; Peppel, "Stalking"; John A. Jakle and James O. Wheeler, "The Changing Residential Structure of the Dutch Population in Kalamazoo, Michigan," *Annals: Association of American Geographers* 59, no. 3 (Sept. 1969), 441-60, esp. 446-60.

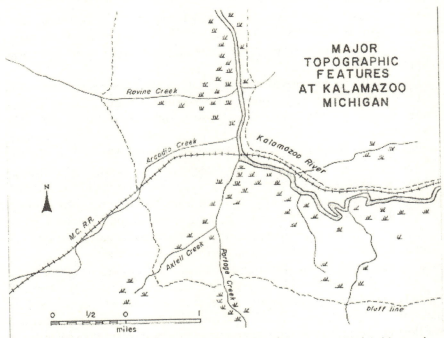

Major topographical features in the Kalamazoo area (*Jakle and Wheeler* [see footnote 13], *fig. 1, p. 446*)

Gerrit Vander Kolk cuddles a huge bundle of celery grown on his father's farm in Kalamazoo, 1911 postcard. The site today is near the Crosstown Parkway (*courtesy Robert Poel*)

Dutch on the Muck: Celery Cropping in Michigan and Elsewhere

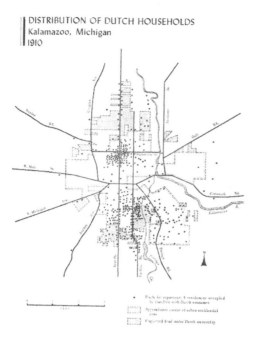

Distribution of Dutch households, Kalamazoo, Michigan, 1910. Unplatted land under Dutch ownership (shaded areas on map) are celery farms (*Jakle and Wheeler, "The Changing Residential Structure," map p. 450*)

Harvesting blanched celery, Kalamazoo, 1920 (*courtesy Robert Poel*)

Growing celery requires keeping the soil drained, while providing the plants with plenty of fresh water—celery is a thirsty vegetable. Having large families was a boon for the hard labor of grubbing in the dirt for long hours. Growers also needed efficient ways to market their vegetables. Fortunately, Kalamazoo stood astride the direct New York-Chicago rail line. Trucks later supplanted trains.

Kalamazoo Dutch developed yellow (blanched) celery, prized for its sweet taste. Blanching required the back-breaking work two weeks before harvest of placing 2' x 16' boards astride each row to shelter plants from direct sunlight. This process blanched the stalks. Large iron brackets held the sixteen-foot boards in place. Some growers covered growing plants with soil to block sunlight completely. The blanched variety brought premium prices at the market. In the 1930s, "Kalamazoo celery," a variety known as Golden Self Bleaching, was featured on the menu of Chicago's fashionable Palmer House hotel. In the late 1940s, blanched celery gave way to the pascal (or green-stalk) variety that dominates the market today because it is less labor intensive.[14]

Henry Schippers, one of the most prominent growers, recalled that to raise celery, he "worked from early morning till late at night, digging and raking, cultivating, sprinkling, and planting," often on hands and knees. Henry Nanninga Sr. was the celery-growing champion in 1913, with—if the news report can be believed—a twelve-foot stalk, weighing forty-six pounds, which he cut from his field at what is now Lovers Lane and Centre Streets in Portage.[15]

John Gernaat Jr.'s immigrant parents began growing celery on a five-acre plot in 1917. Gernaat, in his memoirs, describes the primitive methods they used.[16] Seeds were germinated in a large enamel dishpan in moist soil and placed in the kitchen over a heat register. The sprouts were broadcast over a bed of soil in a greenhouse heated with coal stoves, until they reached about two inches and were then transplanted in one-inch squares into seedbeds. When the danger of frost was over, the celery was planted by hand in forty-rod rows, kept straight by a fishing line stretched from both ends. Weeding was done in the same way. Clothes caked with muck had to be left at the door. If the temperature

---

[14] "Kalamazoo Won Fame as 'Celery City' in '30s," *Kalamazoo Gazette*, 28 Aug. 1961; Robert P. Swierenga, *Holland, Michigan: From Dutch Colony to Dynamic City*, 3 vols. (Holland, MI: Van Raalte Press; Grand Rapids: Eerdmans, 2014), 2:1102.

[15] "Celery Man Tells Kazoo Rotary Club about Philosophy of Hard Work, Success, and Contentment," *Kalamazoo Gazette*, 18 Oct. 1925; Crunchmobile," *Kalamazoo Gazette*, 6 Oct. 1985.

[16] Brinks, "Celery," quotes Gernaat's memoirs at length.

Arend DeYoung (*left*) and hired hands (*l-r*): Reinder Vanden Berg and Lester and Henry Ryskamp stand ready to cut (yellow) celery blanched by boards, 1920 (*courtesy Raymond Vander Roest*)

dropped to thirty-five degrees, the young plants were sprinkled from hoses fitted with nozzles every thirty inches, fed by pumps from a well. Plants were fertilized with whatever manure was at hand—from cows, pigs, and chickens, as well as from the outhouse.

When celery reached about twenty inches and was two weeks from harvest, blanching boards were set up. At maturity, each plant had to be cut off at the root with a large knife, within days of ripening. This had to be done in the wee hours of the morning to prevent "wilting." Trimmings were spread on the ground for fertilizer. Stalks in field crates were loaded on horse-drawn wagons and taken to wash houses, where women worked on packing lines to trim, wash, and package the stalks in crates 16" x 16" x 26" in size, known as "highballs." Celery hearts were packed in smaller, square-sized crates, known as "little squares." After putting in from two- to six-dozen stalks, depending on size, men nailed the top on the wooden crates. Growers later turned to wire-bound crates, which eliminated the time-consuming step of nailing "slats" on the top. The plants ready for shipping were marketed through a broker.[17]

In the late 1920s, mechanized planters were invented by Holland Transplanter Co., which allowed two men to plant thousands of

---

[17] Clarence Poel, "Celery Farms Were Big in Area [Grand Haven] in Early 1900s," *Muskegon Tribune*, 8 Oct. 1999.

26 DUTCH MUCK—AND MUCH MORE

Holland Transplanter machine, late 1920s, manufactured by Holland Transplanter Co. of Holland, Michigan. The men faced backward to set the celery seedlings (*courtesy Howard Poll*)

Annual Kalamazoo Celery Growers/Shippers, by year, 1883-1959. Source: *Michigan Gazetteers* (*courtesy Robert Poel*)

seedlings per day while sitting on the machine. Lightweight Grand Haven-made tractors with mechanical cultivators were invented in the 1930s. John Gernaat Sr. and two brothers, over time, expanded their acreage sufficiently to support four families.[18] By 1950 Kalamazoo city had twenty-four growers, including Gernaat and brothers Arthur and Lewis Ver Sluis. The Ver Sluis brothers were Kalamazoo's last celery-shipping company, handling two thousand crates a week.[19]

In the 1960s, celery production moved to large corporate farms in California and Florida. The Ver Sluis brothers, in an interview in 1966, attributed the celery collapse around Kalamazoo to urbanization, the unwillingness of young people to work that hard ("When the old folks quit, there was no one left to take over"), and the failure to adapt early enough from rail to trucks to bring crops to market. They failed to see the impact of Sunbelt competition, where growers operated on a huge scale.[20]

In the mid-1960s, the few celery growers left were Kenneth Dusseljee, Clarence and Melvin Klooster, Art Meints, Jacob W. Slager and Sons, Jon Slager, Chris Wenke, and the growers/shippers Posthumus Brothers (Claus and George). In 2000 Kalamazoo had only one grower left, with three hundred acres. Celery by then had given way to plants and shrubs.[21]

Along Rural Route 3, in Decatur (Van Buren County), in southwest Michigan, a cluster of Dutch celery growers included the families of John De Feyter, Wybren Hoekstra, Houtman Brothers (Adolph and Jerry), Henry Penning, Martin Schreuder, and Mike Schuur. Henry Schuur farmed in nearby Dowagiac.[22]

Portage celery center

In 1989 Portage city fathers decided to memorialize the celery crop that put Kalamazoo on the map as the world's leader in celery

---

[18] Summarized from John Gernaat's recollections, printed in Brinks, "Celery."
[19] Swierenga, *Holland, Michigan*, 2:1103-4; "Kalamazoo Won Fame"; Mic Adams, comp., "Celery Growers 1920s-1950s, Kalamazoo City," http://www.migenweb.org/kalamazoo/celery.htm.
[20] "Scotsman in Kalamazoo." Descendants of Rudophus Balkema, a 1911 immigrant, in the 1950s owned a trucking company that hauled celery to Chicago (Joe Brinks, AZO Services, Management, Kalamazoo, to author, 19 Oct. 2017).
[21] "Celery," Pure Michigan Agriculture, www.michigan.gov/mdard; "Michigan Celery" http://michigancelery.com/; Trocke, "History of Michigan Celery Industry."
[22] Trocke, "History of Michigan Celery Industry"; "26 Companies in Celery Farming," http://www.amfibi.directory/us/14029-celery_farm; "Celery Farms in Michigan," http://www.manta.com/mb_45_C00A10BB_23/celery_farm/michigan.

production. They erected an outdoor center with historic and working displays and artifacts, such as celery beds, a washer, railroad carts, plowing equipment, and old photos and newspaper accounts. Kalamazoo-based Upjohn Co. and the Battle Creek-based Kellogg Foundation each donated $100,000 toward the $235,000 cost of the celery center.[23]

Holland-Hamilton

Dutch farmers in other Michigan communities also caught "celery fever." Holland's most innovative nurseryman, George H. Souter, promoted the cultivation of celery in the early 1880s.[24] Since celery had become a successful cash crop in Kalamazoo, Souter in 1885 planted twenty-five thousand celery seedlings on drained wetlands at Hudsonville. The *Holland City News* jumped on Souter's bandwagon. There were five hundred acres of muckland in the immediate vicinity of Holland—ideal for celery, the editor asserted—and four hundred men could be put to work raising the tasty plant. John Huizenga, J. Regnerus, and the De Bruyn family, among others, answered the call and marketed excellent celery.

South of Holland, along Allegan Road (M-40), toward Hamilton, was a small section of prime muckland. In 1926 John Nevenzel bought seventeen acres of "worthless" marshland and transformed it into a prime celery field. Nevenzel's Fillmore Township farm was one of an eventual five-hundred-acre tract devoted to celery.[25]

In the 1930s, Henry Eding started with sixteen acres, and today his descendants operate a 185-acre celery farm, combined from fourteen different farms. Henry's son, Alvin, took over and, in turn, passed it to his grandsons, Ron and Dale. The Edings improved their growing practices over the years by using crop covers, better pest management, and crop rotation with onions. They planted oil seed, radish, and sorghum-Sudan grass for cover crops. Their celery is now sold to Meijer and other chain stores. Eding Brothers' Celery Farm received the 2010 Master Farmer Award from the Michigan Vegetable Council. Eding Bros. and other growers formed the Hamilton Celery Growers Association

---

[23] "Celery Center to Open in Portage Next April," Associated Press, undated clipping, summer 1988. This venue continues as the Celery Flats Interpretive and Historical Center.
[24] Swierenga, *Holland, Michigan*, 2:1101-2.
[25] *Holland City News*, 25 Oct. 1884, 27 June 1885, 3 Aug. 1889, "Forty Years Ago Today," 5 Jan. 1939; *De Grondwet*, 27 Jan. 1889.

to market a sweet, crisp variety— Hamilton Golden Brittle. Dale Eding died in 2015, and Ron has carried on with his nephews Jeff and Mike. Edward Miskotten owned a celery field in Hamilton in 1940, and in the post-1945 period, Paul Veldhoff also raised celery in Hamilton.[26]

In the end, however, there was not enough muckland around Holland for commercial celery production. Production moved eastward to Vriesland and Hudsonville and southward into Fillmore Township in Allegan County (see below).

Grand Haven, Hancock and Kieft

Grand Haven celery soils lay on the northeast side along the mouth of the Grand River, where a half-dozen bayous host wetlands, lowlands, and sandy and organic black soils, nourished by thick native grasses. According to Larry Kieft, there were more than thirty Dutch growers in Grand Haven from the 1890s to the 1950s.[27]

The first celery grower was a Yankee, George Hancock, who in 1887 began on a half-acre plot at the corner of Washington and Wallace (now South Beacon Blvd., or US-31). He started with carnations and soon added celery *seedlings* (not stalks) and tomatoes, all under glass. Eventually he had fourteen greenhouses covering seven acres (25,000 square feet), an entire city block. The buildings were located between Columbus and Washington Streets and Eighth and DeSpelder Streets. Hancock & Sons annually grew over three hundred thousand carnation plants for cut flowers sold to the Chicago market. The firm at its apex in 1905 also shipped eight hundred thousand celery seedlings a year to other parts of Michigan, New York, and Ohio and processed eighty-five thousand cans of tomatoes per year. About 1908 Hancock sold out to James Frank, a relative by marriage. Dutch celery growers bought Hancock's greenhouses and moved them to their small parcels to raise their own seedlings.

One of the first Dutch celery growers was Martin Kieft, son of Jan (John) Kieft, an 1853 immigrant from Groningen. In 1856 Jan Kieft erected a house at 327 Fulton Avenue that still stands in the oldest part of the city. The family joined the nearby First Reformed Church on the corner of Washington Avenue and Third Street.

---

[26] "Celery Crop a Cut above the Rest," *Holland Sentinel*, 27 Dec. 2010; "Celery," in Bob Lucas, *Muck Industry*, 1968.
[27] For this and following paragraphs, I relied on Larry L. Kieft, *The Kieft (Kijft) Family, 1600-ca.2000, Netherlands to America: A People of the Soil, A Family of Farmers* (privately printed, 2017).

Team and wagon hauling celery crates to market
(*courtesy Larry Kieft*)

About 1890 Martin Kieft, born in the Grand Haven house in 1856, planted celery on five acres at 1015 Fulton Street at Ferry Street. His farm eventually grew to twenty-five acres, including greenhouses on Ferry Street, and several islands—one covering seventy acres—in the Grand River watershed. The soil in northeast Grand Haven was organic black muck over a subsurface of sphagnum peat. A drainage ditch emptying into the Grand River provided plenty of water for the thirsty vegetables.

By the late 1890s, there were six hundred persons working in celery operations in the Grand Haven area, and by 1912, they exported 110,000 crates of celery annually. This included Peter and Henry Roossien, who immigrated in the 1860s. Marriage conjoined the Peter Roossien and Kieft farms. Harm Roossien had a windmill atop his wash shed on Beechtree Street, south of Waverly.[28]

In the 1920s, Martin Kieft's sons, Martin (Ted) Jr. and Peter, took over. During harvest time in the 1930s, they employed up to forty school children, earning from ten to twenty cents per hour. The family farm planted two crops of celery seedlings in their greenhouses, raising nine hundred thousand seedlings in the first crop and six hundred thousand

---

[28] Larry Kieft interview.

Boys crating celery, 1950 (*courtesy Larry Kieft*)

in the second. After meeting their own needs, most seedlings were then sold to other Michigan celery farmers.

In the 1960s, Martin (Ted) Kieft's son, Larry, took over for a brief time. By the 1970s, "upfront money" to raise a celery crop—heat and light for greenhouses, seeds, fertilizer, and so forth—had climbed to $5,000 an acre. Besides celery seedlings, the Kiefts also raised greenhouse tomatoes, lettuce, and other leafy vegetables. The ideal system was to grow under glass year-round, starting with celery and flowering plants

Field crew poses after harvesting yellow celery with sideboards in foreground, late 1920s (*courtesy Larry Kieft*)

in the spring, then moving to tomatoes and celery in the summer, and ending with lettuce and flowers in the fall and winter. Their greenhouse tomatoes, celery, and leafy vegetables were marketed through the Grand Valley Cooperative. To further expedite marketing, Larry Kieft owned and operated a national horticulture-floriculture brokerage firm.

Other early celery growers included C. J. Bos, at Beacon Street and Jackson Avenue, who erected a typical Dutch windmill for pumping water to his field. Bos sold acreage on Taylor Street to four Welling brothers. Cousins John and Jake Welling lived on the 400 and 500 blocks of Grant Street and farmed ten acres south of Taylor Street, next to the railroad tracks. Jake and son John Welling moved from a Coopersville dairy farm to Grand Haven to grow celery. They eventually accumulated ten acres on Fulton Street from J. Deursma, Harm Roossien, and Abe Kooiman. The Fulton Street Wellings were distant relatives of the Grant Street Wellings.

Adrian Poel farmed ten acres north of Fulton Avenue, and the Tysman, Duerwarder, Peterson, and Arie Klop families worked the muck along Robbins Road east of South Ferry Street. Other celery growers were Daane, De Ryke, Geldersma, Van Arkel, Ver Berkmoes, and other Kiefts—Fred, John, Paul, and Tom. Most of these had sons and grandsons who inherited the family farm, making some growers three- and four-generation operations. By 1970 there were only three growers left, and Adrian Poel ultimately was the last celery farmer in Grand Haven.[29]

Marketing

In the early decades of celery farming in West Michigan, growers along the lakeshore shipped their crates on lake steamers overnight to reach Chicago and Milwaukee markets at dawn. Later, trucking firms, such as Holland Motor and Heidema Bros. of Zeeland, delivered the crates to Chicago's South Water Market. Each grower put his own stamp or stencil on every crate, so should any problem arise, the product could be traced to a particular grower.

In the 1930s, two commission brokers, Marty and Nate Roth of Chicago, began brokering Michigan celery, buying it from growers and selling it to retailers, mainly Jewish-owned restaurants and grocers. John Mulder of Zeeland was the West Michigan field representative of Roth Bros. Competing brokers were Bosgraaf in Hudsonville and De

---

[29] Poel, "Celery Farms Were Big in Area."

Henry Roossien's farmhouse, water tank, and windmill, built about 1890, ca. 1895. The windmill was a major tourist attraction. Dake Engine Co. of Grand Haven made the gears from Roossien's hand-carved wooden models (*courtesy Larry Kieft*)

Peter Roossien greenhouses erected in the 1890s, ca. 1920s (*courtesy Larry Kieft*)

Heidema Bros. tractor trailer delivering celery from Kieft Farms in Grand Haven to M. Roth & Sons, South Water Street Market, Chicago, ca. 1955 (*courtesy Larry Kieft*)

Bruyn and Talsma in Zeeland. Most Dutch growers preferred to deal with outsiders like Roth Bros., who kept business dealings confidential. The Roth firm continued until the end of the golden era in 1970.

Michigan Celery Production Cooperative

Celery farmers in West Michigan formed the Celery Growers Association in 1916 to equalize prices by grading celery into three classes, giving both growers and consumers a fair deal. A related trade group was the Michigan Muck Farmers Association, founded in 1919.[30]

In June 1951, Dutch growers formed the Michigan Celery Production Cooperative in Muskegon as a price-setting board. The first meeting was held in the home of Martin Kieft Jr., at 1015 Fulton St., in Grand Haven. The cooperative is now based on Chicago Drive at Fortieth Avenue in Hudsonville. Every celery grower joined to obtain economies of scale in purchasing and marketing. They were increasingly forced to compete with large corporate farms in Southern California and Florida that benefitted from long growing seasons.

Until the 1950s, California growers, based on a gentleman's agreement, shipped only in the winter and allowed Midwest growers to sell in the summer. In the 1960s, the Lyndon B. Johnson Administration, to supply cheap food for social welfare programs, created "corporate

---

[30] *Holland Sentinel*, 13 Nov. 1916; Michigan Muck Farmers Association, "Michigan's Mucklands, Early History," 3-6, Muck Farmers Week, 1968–50th Annual Meeting, Michigan State University.

farms," ranging in size up to twenty thousand acres in the Salinas Valley of Southern California. California growers then began shipping celery in refrigerated rail cars, and by the 1960s, they were able to send Fruit Growers Express "produce trains," loaded with celery and other leafy vegetables, to Chicago, New York, and other large cities. This broke the back of Michigan celery growers. Duda Farms, Florida's largest grower, today contracts up to four hundred acres of celery in Michigan for grower-direct summer sales. Large markets like Meijer, with its over 240 stores, have bypassed the middlemen and buy directly from growers, like the Eding family in Hamilton.

As celery farming yielded to large growers, old farms were variously distributed. Larry Kieft, Martin's son, donated the last thirty acres of the family's seventy-acre island in the Grand River to the Audubon Society as a wildlife refuge. It adjoins a Grand Haven city park. Harm Roossien's farm on South Beechtree Street is now the site of Woodland Commons condominiums. The original windmill and home can still be seen on the two-acre site.[31]

Muskegon-North Muskegon-Norton Shores

The Salmon family is credited with being the first in 1882 to "cut muck" along Ryerson Creek in the Muskegon area to grow celery. Again, Dutch immigrants caught celery fever. By 1907 thirty-three Dutch farmers were raising celery in Muskegon County—seventeen farmers in the Ryerson Creek Valley, eight in the Muskegon River Valley, two in Bear Swamp, and six in Peck's Bayou. Their farms ranged from one to five acres. In 1942 there were more than one hundred growers with four hundred acres in production, enough to fill ten refrigerated boxcars per day in season. By 1951 seven hundred acres were devoted to celery, making Muskegon "Celery City," instead of Kalamazoo.[32]

Simon Workman family of Norton Shores

The major grower was Simon Werkman (anglicized to Workman), the progenitor of Silver Buckle Celery Brand & Farms. He emigrated in 1883 as a twenty-five-year-old day laborer from the province of Groningen. In 1899 Workman bought from William Moorman forty

---

[31] Swierenga tour of Grand Haven celery and tomato farms with Larry Kieft and Hank De Young, 10 Oct. 2016.
[32] LeMieux, "By 1951, Muskegon was Michigan's 'Celery City.'" LeMieux lists each farmer and his acreage in the various celery fields in Muskegon County.

36 DUTCH MUCK—AND MUCH MORE

Simon Workman, turning sod for second field, on Cleveland "CLTRAC" tractor, 1910s (*courtesy David Workman*)

acres in the 108-acre Norton Shores marsh and began raising celery. Big Black Creek flowed through his field and provided plenty of fresh water.[33] Herbert Klug, Jacob Wagenmaker, and Ed Cepilina each worked ten acres adjacent to Workman, who later bought the three out, increasing his field to seventy acres, a huge operation. On the south side of the creek, Nelson Scott, Casey Fisher, and Jacob Wagenmaker each farmed ten acres in celery.

For many years, Workman grew the tender celery "hearts," harvested as young plants, as well as the highly desired blanched variety, both delicacies for which customers were willing to pay a premium. Like every grower, he tried to "beat the market" in June by selling the first local crop, which could pad profits for the entire season.

Workman built a washing plant and cold storage that held twenty thousand crates of packed celery. This allowed him to sell as market prices dictated until about Thanksgiving Day, the limit for cold storage. All the families erected homes on higher ground along Getty Street on the northern border of the marsh; the southern border was Norton Road. The marsh, totaling some 108 acres, today lies within sight of the US-31 and I-96 intersection. In 1947 the US Army Corps of Engineers straightened Big Black Creek and erected dykes to contain the water.

---

[33] Frank T. Halpin, "Muskegon's Oldest Celery Grower," *Muskegon Chronicle*, 25 July 1947.

Simon Workman Sr., Muskegon's oldest active grower, at his packing table in 1947, Getty Street, Norton Shores, Michigan (*courtesy David Workman*)

Workman was blessed with six sons, all of whom joined the business. In full production, Workman & Sons shipped fifteen hundred crates per day and from twenty-five to thirty-five thousand crates per season. Each trailer truck load held from five to six hundred crates.

By the 1930s, Workman & Sons distributed 40 percent of their crop to the Milwaukee-based supermarket chain, E. D. Godfrey & Sons. At first, Workman hired Heidema Trucking to haul their celery to the cooler in Hudsonville. In the 1930s, Workman & Sons purchased their own semitrailer, which allowed them to ship directly to Godfrey's Milwaukee warehouse. The remaining 60 percent of their crop was divided almost evenly between Marty Roth in Chicago, the renowned vegetable broker, and the Michigan Celery Cooperative.

After many years of successive celery cropping to the very edges of the field, the topsoil thinned, and more important, the plants developed a soil fungus of the genus *Fusarium*, which virtually wiped out the Michigan celery industry in the 1940s. *Fusarium* yellows caused plants to wither in midseason, turn yellow, and die. An insecticide was developed in the 1950s to treat the fungus, but the ideal treatment was to plant onions every second or third year, since onions somehow counteracted *Fusarium*. In the late 1970s, a new strain of *Fusarium* yellows

Workman & Sons' Silver Buckle Celery truck, late 1930s (*l-r*): John, Simon Sr. (father), Bill, Tom, Simon Jr., and Jim (*courtesy David Workman*)

Aerial view of S. Workman & Sons' celery fields, ca. 1985, about two hundred acres in all (*looking east*), Getty Street on bottom, Norton Road on left, and Big Black Creek on right, US-31 northbound lane on upper left, Workman greenhouses on lower right. On upper right are Scott and Fisher farms (*courtesy David Workman*)

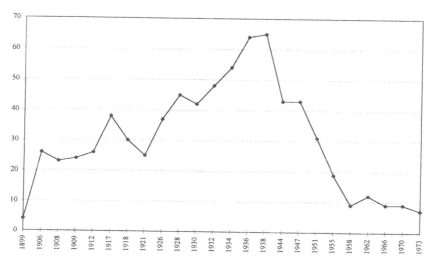

Muskegon Area Celery Growers/Shippers, by year, 1899-1973.
Source: *Michigan Gazetteers* (courtesy Robert Poel)

(called Race 2), appeared in Michigan, and celery growers around the state have had to treat it with insecticide.[34]

Workman & Sons, unfortunately, did not have enough land to set aside a third for onions. The Godfrey grocery chain called for more—not less—Workman celery, but they were not able to keep up with the demand. David Workman and his cousin, Bill Workman, were the last celery growers in Muskegon County in the 1990s.

Workman & Sons had only a few options: shift to onions or some other crop, rent their land to other celery growers, or sell the rights in perpetuity to Michigan Land Conservancy. The Gorman-Anderson Act of the Michigan legislature in 1980 mandated that, after not cropping for five years, the right to crop is forever forfeited. Workman & Sons decided to accept an offer from the Department of Natural Resources to buy a lease in perpetuity on their farm and allow the land to return to its natural marshlands. An added feature was that the site is part of the major West Michigan waterfowl flyway. The marsh now has water up to

---

[34] MSU Extension, "Celery: Commercial Vegetable Recommendations (E130)," Dec. 1986.

eight feet in depth at the low end and a countless number of migratory waterfowl. It has become a birders' paradise.[35]

Smaller Muskegon growers included Fisher Brothers (Joe, Bernard, and Casey), Albert Hekkema, Herbert Klug, and Jacob Wagenmaker & Son (Alvin). North Muskegon, until the 1970s, had a large concentration of Dutch celery growers, including the Bosma Brothers (Donald and Richard), Marinus Van Eck, and Albert Hekkema of White Lake farms.

Montague—Whitehall—Fremont

Weesies family of Montague

Edward Weesies, as a fresh immigrant, worked in celery fields in Montague, until buying fifty acres of muck soils in 1910, complete with a barn. He and his wife, Elizabeth, had ten children by then, plus three more soon thereafter, which was more than enough to work fifty acres. The family planted vegetables, mainly celery and lettuce, and peddled the produce by horse and wagon in Montague and Whitehall and at Lake Michigan resorts. They also raised cows, chickens, and pigs. In 1917 Edward bought his first truck and erected a greenhouse to raise seedlings.

The 1920s were as prosperous as the 1930s were desperate. In the late 1920s, Edward's three oldest boys—Claude, Harry, and John—joined a partnership with him, named E. Weesies & Sons. The firm added acreage in the 1930s, when land was dirt cheap. The best years were during the Second World War, when Weesies & Sons bought four hundred undeveloped acres along the White River and built dikes to drain the land for celery production, much of it sold to the military. The Weesies firm also bought four used greenhouses and moved them to the farm. German POWs provided much-needed labor during the war, and Mexican migrants were hired in the 1950s. At midcentury, disease wiped out the prized yellow variety of celery, and Weesies turned to the hardier Pascal green celery.

In 1959, after older brother Claude's death, the remaining four brothers reincorporated as Weesies Brothers Farms, with one hundred acres of celery in production. In the 1960s, seven Weesies families were in the business, clustered along Walsh Road in Montague, along

---

[35] Notes on Swierenga and Larry Kieft interview, 27 Oct. 2016, with David Workman, at his home.

with Casey Timmerman, a close relative. Weesies Farms was one of the largest celery operations in Michigan. In 1976 the third generation came in, and more greenhouses were built for what was becoming mainly a potted-flower operation. Celery production declined due to disease, competition, low prices, and high labor costs. Since 1997 Weesies Farms, as the firm was renamed, has operated garden centers in Montague, Spring Lake, Hart, and Manistee. It is one of the largest flower growers in Michigan, with three hundred acres devoted to potted flowers.[36]

Hekkema & Sons continue to grow celery on Silver Creek Road in Whitehall, while Peter Van Singel and Bruce Willbrandt crop celery in Grant. Bolthouse Farm raised celery at nearby Cedar Springs in the 1960s.[37]

Wagenmaker Farms of Fremont

In Fremont (Newaygo Co.), Alvin and Gordon Wagenmaker, sons of Jacob, in 1964, opened a 160-acre celery farm on North Maple Island Road. Gordon soon bought out Alvin, and his sons joined the company. The secret of success for Wagenmaker Farms is a marketing agreement with Campbell Soup Company. The Wagenmakers own sufficient land to alternate crops of celery and onions. They have also developed improved celery strains and more efficient cropping and harvesting practices. The firm generates $1 million in annual revenue from vegetables, melons, and flowers.

Hudsonville-Allendale-Zeeland

Hudsonville muckland was an ancient river bottom that stretched fifteen miles from Grandville through the future Hudsonville (Georgetown Township), Vriesland, and Zeeland. Government surveyors in the 1830s found two streams in the old channel, with a perceptible divide between their headwaters—Rush Creek flowed east to the Grand River, and Black River (now Macatawa River) flowed southwest into Black Lake (now Lake Macatawa). This south channel from the Y in the river at Grandville eventually became the "long swamp" that stretched from the Tamarack Swamp west of Hudsonville through Vriesland to

---

[36] Greg Means, "Weesies 100 Years later," *White Lake Beacon*, 26 July 2010; "Wally Weesies: A Lifetime Sowing Community Commitment," *White Lake Beacon*, 23 Aug. 2004. Lemieux, "By 1951, Muskegon was Michigan's 'Celery City.'"

[37] "Celery," Bob Lucas, *Muck Industry*, 1968.

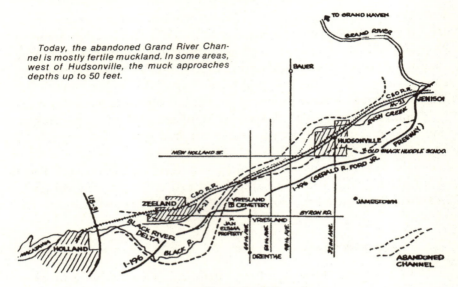

Today, the abandoned Grand River Channel is mostly fertile muckland. In some areas, west of Hudsonville, the muck approaches depths up to 50 feet.

Hudsonville - Zeeland Channel

This former water channel is now some of the richest muck land in the area.

Abandoned Hudsonville-Zeeland Grand River channel (*courtesy Gary Byker Memorial Library, Hudsonville, Michigan*)

the Cedar Swamp in Zeeland Township. The Tamarack Swamp proved to be the most valuable, with deposits of peat up to fifty-feet deep.[38]

In the early 1870s, after a rail line from Grand Rapids was laid along the south ridge of the swamp (M-121 now parallels those tracks), Dutch farmers recognized the value of the "worthless" marsh and began ditching it by hand with back-breaking shovels to drain off standing water. Farmers then cleared the heavy underbrush and felled trees with two-man saws, and horses hauled the logs to saw mills. Stumps were removed by mounting special tripods with a screw borer that horses pulled around and around in a circle. Ultimately, the fields were tiled to keep water off. Horses on the muck had to wear "muck shoes" made of metal plates, burlap bags, and sometimes wooden shoes fit for hooves, so they could gain traction and not sink into the muck. Caterpillars later solved this problem.[39]

[38] Dan Hager, "Treasure from Rattlesnake Swamp," *Grand Rapids Press*, 13 Oct. 1974. Tamarack is a native conifer that grows in swampy or boggy soil and loses its needles in the fall. I thank director Melissa Huisman and her staff at the Gary Byker Memorial Library, Hudsonville, for opening their rich archives and scanning many photos.

[39] Hager, "Rattlesnake Swamp"; "Hudsonville's Agricultural Beginning," in Hudsonville Chamber of Commerce booklet, *Hudsonville, MI* (1984), 10-14.

Dutch on the Muck: Celery Cropping in Michigan and Elsewhere

Google map of Hudsonville muck soils, showing former Macatawa (originally Black) River bed that deposited up to fifty feet of muck soils

Lambert Yonkers and son Albert began cultivating onions and celery in Vriesland in 1875, and about 1879, they moved to the Hudsonville muck. This family was probably the first to grow celery in Hudsonville. Gerrit Gelder began growing the stalks in the 1890s on his farm at Chicago Drive and Sixty-Fourth Avenue. Gerrit Schreur, progenitor of Schreur Farms, married one of Gelder's daughters.[40] By 1897 the swamp was still largely undeveloped, with nonresident speculators offering land at twenty dollars per acre. This relatively cheap price attracted Dutch farmers from the Holland/Zeeland area, who bought and developed several thousand acres in the next decades.[41]

[40] I am grateful to Bruce Schreur for sharing his extensive knowledge of celery production in West Michigan and for providing documentation and photographs.
[41] Evelyn Sawyer and Shirley Krombeen, compilers, *Pictorial Glimpses of the Hudsonville Area*, 66.

By 1914 *De Grondwet* of Holland reported that celery production in the Hudsonville area surpassed that of Kalamazoo, although the two regions ran neck and neck for several decades. Kalamazoo celery, however, had the cachet of premium quality, and Ottawa County growers wisely marketed their celery in Chicago, under the famed Kalamazoo brand. Land prices in Hudsonville skyrocketed; in 1919 Jacob Dyke sold his forty acres of muckland for $1,000 per acre, and this was considered cheap, although it set a record for this region. (By the 1980s, the same land was selling for $10,000 per acre.)[42]

In 1922 celery fields were thick between Zeeland and Hudsonville, ranking Ottawa County third in the state, behind Kalamazoo and Muskegon Counties. In 1923 an astounding 410,000 cases of celery were shipped out of Holland harbor. Every year in the 1920s, $1 million in celery and other vegetables from Ottawa and Allegan County muck farms was shipped to Chicago's South Water Market. In the 1930s, trucking overtook rail shipments to save time and provide door-to-door service. The early celery growers were William Steenwyk, John Smit, Cornelius Spoelman, Gerrit Bolhuis, Albert Holthof, Tom Bosgraaf with son-in-law Albert Blauwkamp, Albert Bytwerk, and Martin Ver Hage.[43]

To the west, Arie and Gerrit Schreur, Andrew Gelder, and the Palmbos family farmed the muck at Beaverdam. They were known as

Dredging Rush Creek, 1910s
(*courtesy Gary Byker Memorial Library, Hudsonville, Michigan*).

[42] *De Grondwet* (Holland, MI), 6 Jan. 1914; *Holland City News*, 16 Nov. 1905, 2 July 1914, 16 Oct. 1919; *Grand Rapids Press*, 24 Jan. 1991.

[43] *Holland City News*, 24 Aug. 1922, 1 Feb., 26 July, 12 Dec. 1923, 28 Oct., 23 Dec. 1926; "Michigan's Mucklands, Early History," 3-6; Gloria J. Byle, "A Story of the Hudsonville Lowlands," Jan. 1998, in Gary Byker Memorial Library; Trocke, "History of Michigan Celery Industry."

Cornelius Spoelman (in suit holding aloft a celery stalk) in his field on Van Buren Street, c. 1910. The field hands were recent immigrants from the Netherlands, all sponsored by Spoelman (*courtesy Gary Byker Memorial Library, Hudsonville, Michigan*)

the "Vriesland Growers," because the Pere Marquette rail siding at Sixty-Fourth Avenue carried that misnomer.[44]

The Ottawa County drain commissioner maintained the ditches, and average farm sizes increased from ten acres in the 1920s, to fifty acres in the 1970s, and up to several hundred acres currently. Major

Albert Schut Sr. (*right*), son George (*center*), and son Albert Jr. (*left*) cultivate weeds on the family farm on New Holland Street, c. 1910. Brother Lambert Schut's farm bordered on the east (*courtesy Gary Byker Memorial Library, Hudsonville, Michigan*)

[44] Bruce Schreur interview, 26 Nov. 2017.

vegetables grown on the Hudsonville muck today are onions and celery, with lesser patches of pumpkins, radishes, and squash. Growers in 1951 joined the Michigan Promotion Celery Cooperative, housed in a small office in Zeeland, with its processing facility in Muskegon. In 1981 the cooperative consolidated its offices and processing plant in Hudsonville, the new celery center.[45]

From the 1940s through the 1970s, dozens of Dutch farmers clustered along New Holland and Van Buren Streets, north of M-121: John and William Arens; Tom Bosgraaf (Superior Brand Produce); John, Ralph, and Al Blauwkamp; Chester Brower and son Harvey; Willard Brower; Earl De Good; Fred De Witt; Norman De Weerd; Albert, Dick, and Clarence Dykema; Bernard Dyke; John and Stanley Emelander; Henry Gemmen; Case, Simon, and Stanley Grasman; Wally Hamburg; Gerrit Kiekover; Chester and Stuart Krikke; Andrew Machiele; Gordon Martinie; Art Nykamp; William Roeters; Andrew Schreur and son Richard (Rick); Herman Schreur and son Bruce; Harold Schut; Henry and John Smit; John Teune; and Ver Hage Farms (Martin's sons Ernest and Terry). These families made Hudsonville the "Celery Center" of Michigan. In recent years, most of these farmers have grown celery under contract with Duda Farms of Florida, which leases some four hundred acres in Hudsonville.[46]

Superior Brand Produce, founded by Tom (Tiete) Bosgraaf on seven-and-a-half acres on Van Buren Street, in 1918, expanded in 1932. Tom's business partner, Albert Blauwkamp, who married Tom's daughter Sadie, kept the books. Tom's son, Ben, worked the farm, and son Ralph handled greenhouses and maintenance work. In the early 1940s, the firm began shipping to Chicago and other Midwest markets. After an injury in 1943, Ben built a cold storage warehouse on Fortieth Avenue for his onion patch, with sons Ted and Jack. By the time Tom retired in 1957, his son Ralph's son Jerry was managing field hands, and Albert Blauwkamp's son Terry was the sales manager. Celery crops then covered twenty-six acres, rising to fifty acres by 1972. The firm packed over one thousand crates a day, in season, and the dry storage building, built in 1958, held up to twenty thousand crates. More recently, five

---

[45] Hager, "Rattlesnake Swamp."
[46] Trocke, "History of Michigan Celery Industry"; "The Good Earth" [Chester Brower Farm], *Grand Rapids Press*, 7 Oct. 1984. Interviews with Harvey Gemmen, Bruce Schreur, and Roger Lutke of Hudsonville, 28 Sept. 2017. Lutke manages the Michigan Celery Cooperative; *Hudsonville: A History of Growth*, booklet (July 1996), 8 (quote).

Mart Hart and Gerald Blauwkamp (with military hat), home on furlough from World War II, on mechanical celery planter at Simon's Forty-Eighth Avenue farm in Blendon Township (*courtesy Gary Byker Memorial Library, Hudsonville, Michigan*)

families have owned the company—Albert Blauwkamp and son Terry, Ralph Bosgraaf and son Jerry, and Elmer Haaksma.[47]

Schreur Farms (Bruce and son Eric) is the largest producer in Hudsonville today, with more than two hundred acres. Bruce Schreur's grandfather, Gerrit, of Zeeland, began raising celery before 1910, followed by his father, Herman. Now Eric's son Mitchell works the farm. Some 70 percent of their crops end up in regional supermarkets, and the remainder is shipped to food processors, such as Campbell's, for soup and V-8 juice. Because few American seed companies are working on new celery varieties, Schreur Farms is doing cultivar selections and crossings.[48]

William Talsma and son Gene have marketed their Crispheart celery brand since 1940—almost eighty years. Brothers Gerald and Ron Miedema, sons of Ted, a Dutch immigrant, of Jenison, in 1971 started Miedema Produce, which specializes in radishes, along with onions, cucumbers, lettuce, and other vegetables. In 1998 the firm expanded production to Phoenix, Arizona.[49]

[47] Paul Courter, "A Farm Business Built from the Ground (7½ acres) Up," *Michigan Farmer*, 20 May 1972; Bosgraaf Sales Company, Gary Byker Memorial Library, Hudsonville, MI.
[48] Brice Schreur interview, 26 Nov. 2107.
[49] "Celery Producer Crispheart Produce Celebrates 75th Anniversary," Miedema Produce, Hudsonvile, MI; "Radishes: Our Humble Beginning," http://www.miedemaproduce.com.

Hall's Express truck hauling Bosgraaf Produce vegetables
to Fruit Growers Rail Express rail siding
in Grand Rapids for timely marketing, 1960s
(*courtesy Gary Byker Memorial Library, Hudsonville, Michigan*)

Andrew Schreur bought a twenty-acre farm on Van Buren Street in the 1940s and with his son Rich began growing celery. An ounce of seeds nurtured in their greenhouses produces one hundred and fifty thousand plants, which yield from thirty- to thirty-five thousand plants per acre. Fortunately, most years were not like 1980, when a crate of celery cost from $5.50 to $6.00 to produce, and the market price was in the same range. There was no profit for a long season of work.[50]

Planting celery on Gerrit Schreur's farm, c. 1934. While Gerrit (*standing*) looks on, son Herman (*right*) and hired hand (*left*) ride Holland Transplanter (*courtesy Bruce Schreur*)

[50] Maureen Nolan, "Hudsonville Celery Farmers Stalk Muck Farms," *Grand Valley Advance*, 28 Apr. 1891.

Dutch on the Muck: Celery Cropping in Michigan and Elsewhere

Schreur Farms sign, surrounded by Bruce and Sheryl Schreur (*left*), son Eric and wife Heather (*right*), and grandchildren Gerrit, Ellie, Grace, and Mitchell (*seated*)—the fifth generation to work the land (*courtesy Bruce Schreur*)

The area of Allendale around Sixty-Eighth Avenue and Lake Michigan Drive (M-45) also hosts muck soils. Albert Sall and son Russell farmed a mile north, and Dale Buist and son Robert, Howard Kraker, and Fred Le Febre farmed a mile west. John Van Timmeren and son Cal raised celery four miles to the northwest until 2012, when the Michigan Department of Natural Resources purchased the farm and returned it to natural wetlands. Near the Van Timmerens was Agle Farms on Northwood Highway.

The major celery area in Zeeland Township was around the intersection of Chicago Drive and Ninety-Sixth Avenue, down the hill from the city of Zeeland, owned by the Kroll family. By the 1940s, the Krolls were raising perennials. In 1942 the Widow Kroll and her daughters, Dena and Harriet, hired Dennis Walters to work the family farm and help raise perennials. Dennis later married Harriet, and the business became Kroll and Walters Perennials. This business was so successful that Dennis was able to bring his four brothers into the growing operation. When Dena retired, the company was rebranded as Walters Gardens, which continues to the present day.[51]

---

[51] https://www.waltersgardens.com/history.php.

Celery growers in Zeeland and surrounding areas marketed their crops through De Bruyn Produce Co., a brokerage run by Donald, Robert Sr. and Robert Jr. De Bruyn; John Smallegan; and John Workman out of a warehouse on Washington Street in Zeeland. The firm aggregated celery crates until it had full truckloads for to the Chicago market. The family from 1915 has also operated a general store, De Bruyn Seed Co., at the same location, which continues today.[52]

Wyoming—Jenison—Byron Center

In the Wyoming area, celery farms were concentrated in a two-square-mile area from Twenty-Eighth Street to Forty-Fourth Street and from Ivanrest Avenue to Kenowa Avenue. Part of that area had muck up to eleven feet deep. From the 1920s to the 1970s, the farms of John Tamminga, the four sons of Peter Kelder (John, William, Thomas, and Peter), John Berends, and John Bont stood along Byron Center Avenue south of Twenty-Eighth Street, while those of Lou Roossien, Charlie Van Dyken, and Peter Yonker dotted Twenty-Eighth Street between Byron Center Avenue and Burlingame Avenue. Peter Huizenga had a large wholesale greenhouse on Twenty-Eighth Street at about Sharon Avenue. When the celery farms gave way to subdivisions, the muck soils were bagged and sold at garden stores.[53]

Andrew Buist, Gerrit Kiekover, George Sall, Clarence Talsma, Casey Visser, Lucas and Ted Vredeveld, and the Westrate Brothers (Marinus and Matthew) raised celery in Jenison and Harold Roelofs in Grandville.

Byron Center was blessed with thousands of acres of muck soils, and the village even boasts a street named Celery Avenue. Bruce Van Solkema Farms (later Byrle and Wesley) grew celery there for four decades, along with C. Steenwyk & Sons on Ninety-Second Street, and K & V Celery Farms, both on Eighty-Eighth Avenue. Growers as late as the 1970s included Simon C. Grasman, Henry J. Holstege & Sons (Harvey and Jay) and Gerrit and Leonard Holstege, Melvin Kapteyn, Vernon Kramer, John Lubbers & Son (Gerald), Clarence Mast, and Steenwyk Brothers (Clarence and Ray). As Grand Rapids spread into the suburbs, farms gave way to housing developments, which have proven to be a more profitable use of the land.

---

[52] www.debruynseed.com.
[53] I am indebted to Jacob E. Nyenhuis for this information. He grew up in the vicinity and knew these families in the 1940s and 1950s. He worked for John Taminga for three years and for Peter Huizenga for a year. Nyenhuis lived on acreage purchased by his father from Peter Yonker.

Imlay City

Imlay City in the Thumb region had a large muck soil area to the east and north that attracted Dutch farmers from Kalamazoo, Zeeland, and Hudsonville. In 1922 John De Haan, a young man from Hudsonville, cleared some muckland and began growing celery. His success prompted Harry E. Palmer of Imlay City to raise celery on ten acres of his muckland as a test crop. Following the successful test, Palmer and two local partners, in 1923, established Bella River Celery Company and recruited Peter Laarman of Hudsonville, a native of Amsterdam, to manage celery and onion production for the company. Laarman and his new wife Cora were lured by cheap land prices—from $10 to $50 per acre, compared to $800-$1,000 in West Michigan—and the prospect of selling directly to Detroit markets rather than being at the mercy of brokers. Laarman's brother Andrew, and Arthur Vander Ploeg and family, arrived within days of Laarman in February, and the trio planted fifty-five acres that spring.[54]

News reports of opportunities in Imlay City in the next five years brought Dutch farmers from Kalamazoo, Zeeland, Byron Center, and other West Michigan muck farms. These included Frank Yonkman, Heine Ettema, John Stryker, Marinus Vandenberg, John Vlieg, and Almon Brandt. They ditched and tiled their land for vegetables, beginning with celery and onions, and expanded to carrots, spinach, beets, parsnips, and peppermint, among others. The Imlay City Celery Co. was formed in 1928, and the chamber of commerce in 1930 began hosting Muck Farmer Days. Celery was king; it brought growers $1,000 per acre in 1935, according to one newspaper report.[55] Growers John and Henry Vlieg, Fred Hoeksema, and Heine Ettema, in 1937, were officers in the Imlay City Onion and Produce Growers Cooperative.[56]

Bella River Celery Company in 1925 recruited home missionary Rev. John R. Brink to establish the Imlay City Christian Reformed Church, and later the members founded Imlay City Christian School; both institutions anchored the Dutch community. Muck farms continue in the hands of second- and third-generation Hollanders, such as Ettema Brothers (Alvin, Bernard, and William), Warner Hoeksema,

---

[54] Maria Mulder Brown, "The Dutch at Imlay City, Michigan" *Origins* 25, no. 2 (2007): 31-35; J. Dee Ellis, "Pioneer Families and History of Lapeer County, Michigan" (Lapeer MI: Lapeer County Genealogical Society, 1979), 116.

[55] E. M. Foster, "Imlay City celery brings growers $1,000 on an acre," *Lapeer County Press*, 13 Mar. 1935, cited in Brown, "Imlay City."

[56] Brown, "Imlay City," 33.

Arthur Groenewoud breaking his forty acres of muckland, ca. 1935-36 (*courtesy Maria Mulder Brown*)

Jake and Lewis Jager, Sidney Lousma, and Ralph Vlieg. But celery gave way to other vegetables already in the 1960s, due to competition from corporate farms in Southern California and Florida. Van Dyke Farms is a leading producer of head and leaf lettuce.[57] Many growers gave up farming, bagged their rich humus, and sold it by the hundreds of truckloads a day. Hoeksema Brothers (John and William, sons of Fred) and their descendants farmed the last muckland in the mid-1990s.

Newberry—Upper Peninsula

A federal land grant to a railroad in 1879 of 1.4 million acres in Luce County in the central Upper Peninsula included swamplands. In 1883 a railroad commissioner formed the Newberry Celery and Improvement Co., which drained a few acres and raised thirty-eight thousand celery plants. But no one knew how to grow celery. So farm manager, Harry Harris, ran an advertisement in a Kalamazoo newspaper, and he managed to recruit John G. Van Tuyl, a celery field worker, who came in 1898 and took charge. Van Tuyl drained more acres and made a going business. After a few years, he bought land next to the Harris farm and started the OK Celery Garden. Van Tuyl shipped his Golden Plume blanched variety by rail to urban markets and built a very successful business. He was killed in 1925, when his car was struck by a train. His married daughter, Bertha Van Tuyl Lone, took over the farm and continued to grow celery until 1995.[58]

---

[57] Ibid., 33-34.
[58] Robert Poel, "Newberry: Michigan's Upper Peninsula Celery Farming Pioneers," unpublished ms., 2017.

Chicago area

In the 1840s and 1850s market gardeners on the far south side of Chicago drained marshlands along the Little Calumet River and its tributaries, in order to farm the rich soils. At the turn of the century, Dutchmen raised celery on small patches of muckland after it was drained by the major public works projects noted in the opening paragraphs. Most truck farmers in northern Indiana along Ridge Road—the prehistoric shoreline of Lake Michigan, farmed clay or sandy loam soils, on which they raised onion sets and a variety of vegetables for Chicago wholesale markets. Muck soils did not predominate in this region.[59]

De Motte, Indiana

De Motte in Jasper County, Indiana, was a Dutch colony of the Ton (Richard and Jon) Realty Company of Roseland, who in the 1890s

---

[59] Richard A, Cook, *South Holland Illinois: A History, 1846-1966* (South Holland, IL, 1966); David L. Zandstra, "The Dutch of Highland, Indiana," paper presented at Ninth Biennial Conference, Association for Advancement of Dutch American Studies, Calvin College, 9 Oct. 1993; Robert P. Swierenga, *Dutch Chicago: A History of Hollanders in the Windy City* (Grand Rapids: Eerdmans, 2002), 551-64.

purchased a large parcel of swampland some forty miles to the southeast. By 1893 some thirty-five families took possession of the recently drained marshlands, and they made work of founding a Reformed church. The two largest muck farms by the late twentieth century were the Kingma and Broertjes farms, which were recently merged into Kal-Bro Farms of De Motte. Kal-Bro Farms raises vegetables for the Chicago and Indianapolis markets and operates a farmers market and garden center in De Motte.[60]

Willard and Celeryville, Ohio

In 1895 Henry Johnson, an entrepreneur in Willard, Ohio, about fifty miles south of Sandusky on Lake Erie, realized that an extensive marsh near the town could produce good celery if it was drained. He knew that Dutch immigrants could do the job, so he recruited several families with experience in celery cultivation from Kalamazoo. They came and built a canal system to drain the swamp. The muck soil grew celery and other vegetables faster than other areas and even allowed for some double crops in a single growing season. Ohio State University maintains an agricultural extension at Willard.[61]

The Hollanders formed the Willard Christian Reformed Church in 1896 and later Celeryville Christian School, which anchor the unique agricultural community of Celeryville. Muck farming continues to be prosperous, although celery is now one of about three dozen vegetables their descendants market through Kroger, Meijer, Walmart, and other retailers. Migrant workers come yearly to tend and harvest the crops. Willard Christian Reformed Church presently has sixty families (140 souls), and the school serves some seventy students.[62]

Three families came to monopolize celery production in Celeryville—Buurma, Holthouse, and Wiers. Buurma Farms was founded in 1896 by Frans (Frank) Buurma, a Dutch immigrant who first worked in the Kalamazoo celery fields. When Buurma learned of the cheap swamp land, he and other countrymen, including Wiers, Cramer, Moll, Holthouse, Van Zoest, Shaarda, Kok, and Postema, decided to move to Willard. The men built dikes, windmills, and canals to drain

---

[60] https://www.facebook.com/pg/KalBroFarms.
[61] Miriam Jordan, "One Ohio Town's Immigration Clash, Down in the Actual Muck," *New York Times*, 18 June 2017.
[62] Henry S. Lucas, *Netherlanders in America: Dutch Immigration to the United States and Canada, 1789-1950* (Ann Arbor: University of Michigan Press, 1955; rep. Eerdmans, 1989), 321.

the swamps to get to the fertile muck below. They divvied up the land and began growing celery, hence the name "Celeryville." Over time, they added other vegetables. Frank Buurma's farm initially consisted of only four acres, which he worked with his four sons—John, Gerry, Hank, and Anco—who took over operations after his death. Children in the family worked the soil until the 1940s, after which, growers came to rely on Hispanic migrants.

The Buurma operation eventually grew to eight hundred acres, and in 1976 the company ventured into Michigan by buying some twelve hundred acres of muckland near Gregory (Livingston County). The firm marketed twenty different crops under "Buurma" and "Holland Brand" labels. Currently, Buurma Bros., incorporated in 1982 as Buurma Farms, consists of twenty-five hundred acres that support thirty different crops, including radishes, beets, lettuce, parsley, southern greens, sweet corn, green onions, and celery. In recent years, celery is no longer grown in Celeryville due to the "yellowing" disease. But the Michigan farm continues to grow celery.

There are now twelve Buurma descendants that own the company and another six, mainly the young, are full-time employees. The company employs upward of five hundred workers during the busy

Frans (Frank) Buurma, progenitor of Buurma Farms, proudly shows off his late 1930s International "semi." The printing on the door reads: "F. Buurma & Sons, Garden Produce, Willard, Ohio, Phone 5735." The twenty-eight-foot Fruehauf trailer was used for storage until a year ago (*courtesy Loren Buurma*)

Crew in the packing house running celery hearts for Ohio grocery stores, 1940s (*l-r*): Jack Buurma, Jack Van Laar, Harriet Meyers, Frank Buurma

Aerial view of Buurma Farms in the early 1960s
(*courtesy Loren Buurma*)

summers and ships two million packages annually, mostly to urban consumers east of the Mississippi River.[63]

Holthouse Farms has produced high-quality produce for over one hundred years, beginning in 1870, with Dutch-born Jan Holthuis, another migrant from Kalamazoo celery fields. He and sons, Rudy and Jacob, established what would become Holthouse Farms in 1903.

Rudy and Jacob managed the business when their father retired, followed by Rudy's sons, Jordon, Stanton, and Mark, and Jacob's son, Wayne, who worked together for several years. When Rudy and Jacob retired, Wayne started his own farm, while Rudy's sons continued Holthouse Farms. The farm is run today by Jordon's sons, Ken and Steve, and Stanton's sons, Kirk and Kevin, who continue to grow the business by distributing produce both locally and to major cities east of the Mississippi River. To help accommodate the expanding business, Holthouse Farms purchased Doug Walcher Farms in 2003, an operation that specializes in green bell peppers, cucumbers, summer and winter squash, eggplant, and fall ornamentals. With the addition of Walcher Farms, Holthouse Farms was able to offer wet produce (lettuce, green

Jan Holthuis (*standing on left*) with his children: standing *l-r:* Harm, Rudy, Jacob; seated *l-r:* Alice, Grace, John, Dena

[63] www.buurmafarms.com/about/history.

Holthouse Farms sign (*courtesy Holthouse Farms*)

onions, parsley, radishes, etc.), making them a "one-stop shop" for their customers.

As Christians who believe in good stewardship of the land, the Holthouse family is dedicated to the principle of sustainability, which they have made an intrinsic part of the business from the beginning. As Ken Holthouse said, "We've been caretakers of the land for over a 100 years. We've always known that we have to take care of the land if we expect it to take care of us."[64]

Henry Wiers, an 1881 immigrant to Kalamazoo, in 1896 traveled with his family and other Dutch immigrants to purchase five acres in the mucklands of Celeryville. At that time, the muck was poorly drained, but Wiers, along with others, employed draining techniques from the Netherlands to make the land arable. Wiers and his compatriots supplied local markets by horse and wagon and urban markets by rail. By 1934 there were thirty-seven families and twenty-seven farms in the Celeryville area, cultivating a combined 210 acres of celery.

Henry Wiers in 1906 helped finance and build the Celeryville Christian Reformed Church. The second generation took over the farm in 1922 when Wiers passed his ten acres to his sons, Edd and Garrett. In 1940 the third generation, the five sons of Edd Wiers—Henry, Frank, Corwin, Norman, and Eddy—took over the operation. In 1965 the state built a seventy-five-acre reservoir to collect rainwater, which allows Celeryville farmers to irrigate their crops even in severe droughts.

[64] https://www.holthousefarms.com/about.

Edd Wiers, late 1950s (*courtesy Wiers Farms*)

In 1970 the fourth generation of Jim, Ed, John, Tom, Ben, and Jerry Wiers began entering the business, and they realized the importance of on-time delivery and flexibility. In 1975 Wiers, under the name "Dutch Maid Produce," purchased eight tractor trucks and ten trailers to gain control of delivering their produce.

Radish Gang— Corwin Wiers, *far left*, Edwin Wiers is the youngest, third generation, 1940s (*courtesy Wiers Farms*)

Intergenerational Wiers partners on Celeryville farm
(*courtesy Wiers Farms*)

Hollandale, Freeborn County, Minnesota

Albert Lea Farms Company of Omaha, headed by George H. Payne, by 1919, had acquired from various owners the fifteen-thousand-acre Rice Lake marsh located north of Albert Lea in Freeborn County, Minnesota. These acres had been drained a decade earlier by capitalists Bryant Barber and P. D. McMillan. Turtle Creek was the major drainage artery through Rice Lake. Albert Lea Farms paid $337,500 ($22.50 per acre) for the tract and brought in a seventy-six-ton Buckeye Ditching and Road Building machine (the Swamp Angel) that further opened Turtle Creek to twelve feet wide and seven feet deep, with large clay tiles laid on the bottom for drainage. The company borrowed $650,000 for the land, for ditching fifty-seven miles, and for laying out nineteen miles of roads. By 1919 six thousand acres were ready for farming.[65]

The Payne Investment Co. advertised exclusively for Dutch farmers skilled in muck soils in Dutch-language newspapers, such as *De Volksvriend* in Orange City, Iowa, and *De Grondwet* in Holland, Michigan, and in Netherlands papers. Payne invited a committee from Dutch Reformed churches in Sioux County, Iowa, to come, the carrot being the promise of five acres for a church and parsonage. The name "Hollandale" was chosen for the community, which was platted in 1922. The Peter Louters family were the first settlers in early 1922 and helped build the Hollandale church and school. The town grew so fast that the original church could accommodate only one-third of the worshipers.[66]

[65] Register, *The Big Marsh*, 189-201.
[66] Janel M. Curry-Roper and Carol Veldman Rudie, "Hollandale: The Evolution of a Dutch Farming Community," *Focus* (Fall 1990): 13-18; "Hollandale, Minnesota," [Hollandale Colony brochure, 1924] *Origins* 18, no. 1 (2000), 39-43; Lucas, *Netherlanders in America*, 175-76.

Hollandale celery field and homes of Henry Voss and Henry Posthumus (Hollandale the Wonderland *pamphlet*)

The land was touted to be twice as valuable as Iowa farmland and offered for $32.50 per acre. The soil was especially good for sugar beets, potatoes, onions, cabbage, carrots, and Golden Heart celery that Kalamazoo Dutch growers had already made a delicacy. Hollandale celery would bring higher prices than Kalamazoo celery, the promoters declared. Hollandale celery farms averaged twenty acres each, ten times larger than typical Michigan celery farms. In 1922 one Dutchman produced celery that brought $700 per acre. Cabbage, onions, and potatoes also brought good prices.

Henry Posthumus and Henry Voss came from the Kalamazoo celery fields in 1924 and soon Posthumus was the celery king of Hollandale. By 1926 Hollandale was a model Dutch American community, and Albert Lea Farms boasted of forty farms with fourteen hundred acres under tillage.

Excessive flooding from heavy rains from 1926 to 1928 wiped out all celery production, and Albert Lea Farms went bankrupt in the Great Depression. Dutch farmers who stuck it out survived by raising mainly potatoes and onions and more recently corn and soybeans, along with potatoes. The light muck soil had long given way to heavy clay loam.

Vorden Polder, California

In 1879 P. J. van Löben Sels, a lawyer from Zutphen, province of Gelderland, who had recently immigrated to California, was hired to drain an 8,800-acre polder, fifteen miles north of Sacramento, California, in the Sacramento River delta, which he named Vorden. Van Löben Sels was appointed director of the Vorden polder, which he successfully drained by building levees to hold back annual flooding and then rented to farmers for the rich soil. He later purchased for himself and drained another 5,100 acres nearby. The polder could have become an immense Dutch settlement like Holland Marsh, but only a few Dutch immigrants came, notably the Pijlman brothers in 1890. So Japanese gardeners came to dominate the polder. The farms produced immense quantities of asparagus and sugar beets. Today Vorden is known for its flower farms.[67]

Wilhelmina Colony, Dunklin County, Missouri

Wilhelmina was a Dutch Catholic settlement founded in 1909-10 by Father Julius E. De Vos of Chicago, a member of the Norbertine Order, with the help of Fathers Vincent Tesselaar and F. F. Peeters of Noord Brabant. The colony, named after Netherlands Queen Wilhelmina, was planted on fertile swamplands with muck thirty feet deep along the St. Francis River. A venture of the Catholic Colonization Society, Wilhelmina did not flourish, despite the soil being choice to raise garden vegetables or cash crops of corn, potatoes, and cotton. Most Catholic immigrants preferred larger cities.[68]

Holland Marsh, Ontario

Albert VanderMey's 1994 book, *And the Swamp Flourished*, has the subtitle, *The Bittersweet Story of Holland Marsh*. Vander Mey tells the story of the "Salad Bowl of Ontario," the twenty-two thousand-acre Holland Marsh that Canadian professor William Henry Day and associates, in the 1920s, drained into Lake Simcoe. The canal and adjoining dike road were completed by 1930. Realizing the agricultural value of the black gold, John Snor, a Dutch agent of the Netherlands Emigration Foundation, saw the marsh as ideal for Dutch farmers. John Sytsma was the first to come, in 1931, and he and friends bought 125 acres for $35-40 an acre. It was a steal. They subdivided the land into five-acre plots and fifteen Dutch immigrant families, mainly from Groningen and Friesland, came in 1934 to start farming the muck. Each house stood cheek by jowl along the dike road.

[67] Lucas, *Netherlanders in America*, 393. Pieter Justus van Löven Sels (1851-1927), from an old aristocratic family, earned his law doctorate at Utrecht University in 1878 with a dissertation on the American Civil War. In California, he married the daughter of the Dutch consul in San Francisco and pursued a career in law. He became the United States ambassador to Paraguay and received an honorary knighthood from King William III of the Netherlands. https://www.findagrave.com/memorial/78868682/pieter-justus-van_loben_sels. I am indebted to Earl Wm. Kennedy for this biographical information.

[68] Lucas, *Netherlanders in America*, 455-56l; Van Hinte, *Netherlanders in America*, 734.

The village of Ansnorveldt[69] was platted that year as a homogeneous Dutch colony. In 1935 the settlers erected a small Dutch Reformed Church, which in 1938 became the Holland Marsh Christian Reformed Church.[70]

Holland Marsh expanded rapidly in the next decade, especially during the Second World War. Most growers reduced risk by raising a little of everything—celery, onions, carrots, lettuce, beets, radishes, spinach, and so forth. All the farming was done by hand, but gradually, specialized machines were invented to work the wet, loose soils. Caterpillar-type tractors were required when tractors became bogged down in the muck.[71]

As in West Michigan, in 1946 five hundred Holland Marsh growers formed the Bradford Co-operative Storage facility to provide cold storage for their vegetables, so they could be sold over the winter months at higher prices. Larger farmers erected their own packing sheds to keep vegetables "harvest fresh" by packaging them in ice and shipping by truck and rail across Canada and to Detroit, New York City, and other urban centers. In 1948-49 the Canadian National Railway alone transported 1,036 carloads valued at nearly $7 million.

Over time, the percentage of Dutch declined from 100 percent in 1935 to 40 percent in 1961 and 25 percent in 1994, and it is still dropping. The heyday of Dutch muck farming in California was in the 1940s and 1950s. By the sixties, heavily capitalized corporate farms were buying the small family plots and consolidating them into large-scale mechanized operations. The soil, worth $15,000 an acre in 1994, is as fertile as ever, but the Hollanders are largely gone.[72]

Conclusion

Dutch immigrants were not the first to farm the muck, but they developed celery varieties that made this common vegetable a "Dutch treat" on American tables. They had the knowledge, work ethic, fortitude, *and proper shoes*, to ditch and tile their fields, grow under glass,

---

[69] http://www.king.ca/Visitors/HistoryandHeritage/History/Ansnorveldt/Pages/default.aspx; www.wiewaswie,nl; www.ancestry.com. Ansnorveldt was a corruption of the Dutch *aan Snors veld*, meaning "on [or at] Snor's field," *not*, as is sometimes claimed, "Ann Snor's field," for the wife of John (Jan Jacob) Snor, since her name was Cornelia.

[70] VanderMey, *And the Swamp Flourished*; Harry Vander Kooij, "Holland Marsh" *Origins* 24, no. 2 (2006), 16-21.

[71] VanderMey, *Swamp Flourished*, 19-28, 131-35.

[72] Ibid., 135-37.

make genetic improvements, and develop labor-saving techniques and machines to plant, weed, and harvest, all of which enabled them to dominate the market for celery, onions, and many other vegetables. In recent times, competition from California mega-farms prompted many celery growers to shift to horticulture—either flowers and shrubbery or various cash crops. But pockets of celery growers continue to fend off California competitors, notably in Hudsonville, Michigan, and Celeryville, Ohio.

CHAPTER 3

Onion Set Farming in South Holland, Illinois

Ken Bult

South Holland is a village in Cook County, Illinois, located about twenty miles south of downtown Chicago. Immigrants from the Netherlands first settled the area in 1846. The town, originally called De Laage Prairie (Low Prairie), was built on the Calumet River. A few miles to the north, along the Thornton-Chicago Road, was another Dutch settlement named De Hooge Prairie (High Prairie). Settled in 1849, it is now the Roseland neighborhood of Chicago. By the end of the nineteenth century, these regions became world renowned for their success in raising onion sets.

The history of commercial onion-set production and marketing for South Holland and environs can be divided into two periods: (1) from 1890 to 1939, when South Holland began to compete as a real player in the onion set industry; and (2) from 1940 to the 1950s, when South Holland became the leader in both the production and marketing of onion sets.[1]

---

1 Arvin William Hahn, *The South Holland Onion Set Industry* (South Holland, IL: South Holland Trust and Savings Bank, 1952), 31.

The early years, 1890 - 1939

Soon after local farmers began raising onion sets in 1892, South Holland became known as the "Onion Set Capital of the World."[2] By the 1920s, South Holland had become "the onion town *par excellence.*" So prominent had onion sets become that their husbandry had replaced grain and cattle farming, which had been the two primary agricultural endeavors in the region until that time.[3]

Onion sets are small, dry, partly grown onion bulbs, raised from seeds the previous year. They are similar in appearance to very small scallions. Onion seeds are densely planted at about fifty pounds per acre. This thick planting stunts the growth of the onion and produces the "sets." The harvested sets themselves are very easy to nurture into fully developed onions. Replanted with just their tops showing, the onion sets soon start growing, eventually becoming marketable onions. They must be planted with space (at about six pounds per acre, like other farm produce) to mature and fill out. The amount of space required depends on the type of onion intended for harvest.

One advantage of planting onion sets is that they can be planted as soon as the soil can be worked, and a frost will not hurt them. As a result, onion sets provide the earliest crop from a vegetable garden. In addition, onion sets can also be harvested all summer long if they are planted at different times throughout the spring.

When depositors of the South Holland Trust and Savings received their bank statements in 1932, they found an image of onion sets and the words, "The Home of the Onion Set." For years the economic life of the South Holland region centered on this cash crop, which made the community financially sound.[4]

The later years, 1940 – 1950s

By 1940 about twenty-five hundred acres were devoted to farming onion sets, and the area was producing more than 1.5 billion sets annually. This trend continued until well after World War II, when the proximity to Chicago and the arrival of the subdividers changed

---

[2] http://www.encyclopedia.chicagohistory.org/pages/1173.html.
[3] Jacob Van Hinte, *Netherlanders in America: A Study of Emigration and Settlement in the Nineteenth and Twentieth Centuries of the United States of America.*, ed. Robert P. Swierenga, trans. Adriaan de Wit (Grand Rapids MI: Baker Book House, 1985), 792-93.
[4] Dodson, L. S., *Social Relationships and Institutions in an Established Urban Community, South Holland, Illinois* (Social Research Report no. 16, Washington DC, Feb. 1939), 47.

The Dutch Valley Growers was a group of South Holland onion set farmers that formed a cooperative in 1933. Walter De Graff, Ted De Graff, William Gouwens, Howard Pals, and Arnold Dalenberg were among the organizers

the rural nature of the region.[5] In 1920 South Holland dealers were marketing 85 percent of the total commercial crop of onion sets, and by 1950, they were selling more than 90 percent.[6]

Other than Thornton Township (which includes South Holland) and Bloom Township (to its south), the other twenty-two townships in Cook County had fewer than one thousand acres in onion set production. The Calumet region, with its light sandy soils, is well suited to produce garden crops, especially onions. The soil, for the most part, is the remains of an old glacial lake bottom.[7] In South Holland, the change to onion sets led to farmer co-ops that kept agriculture a major

---

[5]   Cook, Richard A., *A History of South Holland, Illinois [1846-1966]* (South Holland, IL: South Holland Trust and Savings Bank, 1966), 86.
[6]   Hahn, *The South Holland Onion Set Industry*, 41.
[7]   Walker, J. C. (John Charles), 1893-; Edmundson, W. C. (Wilbur Clifford), 1888- & Jones, H. A. (Henry Albert), 1889-. Onion-set production book, May 1944; Washington, DC. (digital.library.unt.edu/ark:/67531/metadc6157/: accessed 2 June 2017), University of North Texas Libraries, Digital Library, digital.library. unt.edu; crediting UNT Libraries Government Documents Department, 2.

A portable onion mill from 1912. Although most milling was done in the warehouse, this portable mill was also used in the fields

factor in South Holland until well after the end of World War II. In order to avoid the dangers of a one-crop dependence, often onion set farmers raised other garden crops for the local markets as well.

Why the Dutch?

An interesting question arises from the foregoing discussion. Why were the Dutch so engaged in onion set farming? Was there anything unique about their culture and community that fostered this occupation?

The majority of Dutch farmers who raised sets in the first thirty years were either immigrants or first-generation Americans. Although there is no independent verification, Dutch familiarity with other bulb crops so prominent in the Netherlands may have been a factor in their success with onion sets. Holland, Michigan, and Momence, Illinois— both areas dominated by the Dutch— have bulb-growing industries. The well-known tulips of Holland and gladioli in Momence are perfect examples of similar bulb plants.[8]

---

[8] Ibid., 36.

According to Arvin Hahn in *The South Holland Onion Set Industry*, "Of the five hundred farm operators in the two townships in which the South Holland Area is situated (Thornton and Bloom), more than forty per cent raise onion sets and more than ninety per cent of the set growers are of Dutch origin." Farm sizes and acreage remained relatively stable from 1921 to 1950.[9] Three character traits of the region's Dutch culture that may have been contributing factors to their prominence in onion set growing were: (1) a tendency toward thriftiness, (2) a particularly clannish nature, and (3) a deeply imbedded work ethic.[10]

Historians of the Christian Reformed Church suggest that the Dutch propensity toward "thrift and stability" were reasons that Dutch immigrants were more readily welcomed to America than some other immigrant groups.[11] Thriftiness meant that Dutch farmers lived frugally, generating savings that could be put back into more land and improved machinery as it developed. In this way, they built up considerable land holdings.

Moreover, these new and improved methods remained in the Dutch ghetto because, according to Dodson, who did a social study of the region in the 1930s, one of the first impressions to be had of South Hollanders was their unfriendliness toward strangers. Villagers as well as outsiders realized that such coldness existed and freely admitted it.[12]

Dodson tells the story of a Dutch minister from a nearby village who remarked that the Dutch in other towns considered South Holland such a tightly closed enclave that even *they* were not fully accepted.[13] Arvin Hahn noted, as late as 1952, a reluctance of the regional onion set growers to discuss their methods.[14]

This tight-knit community arrangement extended even to the financing of onion set farms. A special system of financial assistance was developed among the onion set growers and bankers of South Holland. Onion sets require fifty pounds of seed per acre, compared with from six to eight pounds per acre for other crops (and for mature onions). At $1 a pound, onion seed would cost $500 for ten acres, compared with from $60 to $80 for other crops. Due to the trust that existed in

---

[9] Hahn, *The South Holland Onion Set Industry*, 7.
[10] Ibid., 37.
[11] Jacob T. Hoogstra, ed., *One Hundred Years in the New World 1857-1957. The Christian Reformed Church Centennial* (Grand Rapids, MI: CRC, 1957), 25.
[12] Dodson, *Social Relationships*, 17.
[13] Ibid., 18.
[14] Hahn, *The South Holland Onion Set Industry*, 37.

such a close-knit community, interest-free loans were made by bankers at the beginning of the planting season and were either repaid over time or taken out of production payments at the end of the season.[15] Most farmers settled up at the end of the year. There is no evidence that any such system was in place in any other onion set production regions.

Other local businesses made accommodations for this once-a-year payday as well. According to retired village doctor Carl Walvoord, South Holland farmers carried their banking pattern over to his practice; they paid their doctor's bills in cash once a year. But they added a unique wrinkle: although they settled up at the end of the year, they always left a dollar on the books. It was considered bad luck to pay the doctor in full—if you paid up, you would get sick for sure.[16] This unusual business model seemed to work well; the South Holland Trust and Savings was one of the few banks that remained open for business throughout the depression of the 1930s. Most Dutch depositors simply would not withdraw their hard-earned money.

Last, it has been suggested that it was a strong Calvinistic work ethic that promoted Dutch thriftiness.[17] A good work ethic was not unique to the region or to the Dutch, but it was a contributing factor to the overall success of the Dutch onion set growers. The very process of farming onion sets demands a strong work ethic, its hours are long and year-round. On the one hand, onion set farming requires short, concentrated periods of attention.[18] At the same time, it requires year-round attention, which deterred many farmers outside the region from growing onion sets. The rigorous annual schedule reflects the changing seasons:

1. Soil preparation—late fall and early spring
2. Cultivation and weeding—late spring and early summer
3. Harvesting and curing—late summer and early fall
4. Storing and processing—late fall through early spring

All things being equal, soil preparation and weeding remain the same as with most crops; harvesting, however, and curing are a different story. These unique tasks, initially carried out by hand, exact tremendous

---

[15] Ibid., 38.
[16] http://articles.chicagotribune.com/1986-10-29/news/8603220369_1_lake-michigan-onion-farming.
[17] Ronald Findlay and Kevin H. O'Rourke, "Commodity Market Integration, 1500–2000," National Bureau of Economic Research-Globalization in Historical Perspective (Jan. 2003), 29.
[18] Ibid., 12.

commitment and diligence. A strong work ethic was imperative to carry them out successfully.

In the early days, the sets would be loosened by a cultivator and then picked up by hand and placed in a shaker screen

After being cleaned by the sifter, the onion sets are placed by hand into crates to cure. The crates are of a special design that allows air to circulate

The crates are then stacked in the fields from thirty to forty days

The First Christian Reformed Church of South Holland, Illinois, can be seen in the background

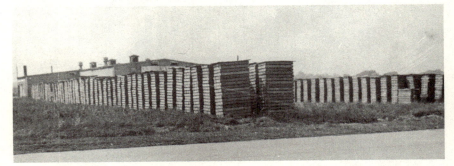

Most of the time, onion sets would be stacked in the fields to dry, but sometimes they would be stacked to dry near the warehouse so the fields could be made ready for next year

These girls are sitting on a pile of chaff that the onion mill would blow out during the milling process. The girls worked picking mud and sprouts out as the sets passed on a belt

Sometime around the end of July and the beginning of August, the tops of the sets would start to turn yellow, which indicated that it was ready to harvest. A cultivator would loosen the sets from the soil, and they would be picked up by hand and placed in a shaker screen to remove the loose dirt. After being cleaned in this manner, they would be placed by hand into crates to cure. The crates were designed for air circulation and remained stacked in the field for thirty or forty days. Sometime in late September or early October, the crates would be brought to the warehouse where they would be restacked to be processed as orders were received.

Before distribution, the sets would be run through a fanning mill, which removed the remaining dirt, dust, loose scales, and withered sets. Finally, they were separated by size and packed for shipment. Most distribution took place between December and April.

Last, the importance of nurturing marketing relationships for thirty years or more cannot be underestimated as a reason for the success of Dutch onion set growers. Along with the large production numbers, which meant any order could be filled regardless of size, the sets were of a consistently high quality. To facilitate marketing, several associations were developed among the farmers, further insulating them from outsiders as well as assuring fiscal solvency among themselves. One such association was Dutch Valley Growers, a group of South Holland onion set farmers that formed a cooperative in 1933. Walter De Graff, Ted De Graff, William Gouwens, Howard Pals, and Arnold Dalenberg were among the organizers. The Dutch Valley Growers continues today with James Paarlberg and his sons.[19] They operate a multiwarehouse facility in La Crosse, Indiana. Their motto remains, "Dutch pride in every bag."

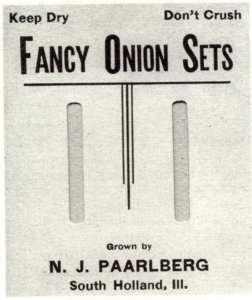

Conclusion

Onion set farming came early to the rich soil south of Chicago. By the late nineteenth century, South Holland and environs were recognized as a central producer of onion sets, earning the sobriquet, "Onion set capital of the world," at the height of its success. The unique culture which the Dutch immigrants brought with them and that they enmeshed in their communities facilitated their remarkable accomplishments. Among other traits, their thriftiness, clannish unity, and hard work enabled them to prosper well into the twentieth century, when urban expansion finally redirected the local economy.

[19] James Paarlberg is a descendent of Antje Paarlberg née Waagmeester (1808-1885) more commonly known as the Widow Paarlberg. Antje settled in South Holland in 1847. She was the inspiration (although misrepresented) for Selina Peake DeJong, the main character in Edna Ferber's 1924 Pulitzer Prize-winning novel, *So Big*.

CHAPTER 4

Pea Pickers and POWs

Mary Risseeuw

As with many rural Dutch towns at the turn of the twentieth century, the villages of Cedar Grove and Oostburg in Sheboygan County and Waupun and Alto, in Dodge County, Wisconsin, were quite self-sufficient. There was a general store, a bank, a mill, and many of the types of businesses that supplied the daily needs of the villagers and local farmers. The soil was fertile, and the price of acreage was within the grasp of a small farmer starting out.

The land along Lake Michigan in Sheboygan County was blessed with a microclimate especially suited to growing peas. Warm days and cool nights provided the perfect growing conditions. Because the sugar in peas turns to starch if it is too hot, peas were always harvested before the Fourth of July. This was a great cash crop for farmers, because the canneries would sow, spray, and harvest. Because of the fragile nature of the crop, planting was staggered, so that only a prescribed number of acres were ready each day.

Pea pickers of 1914 (*courtesy Sheboygan County Historical Research Center*)

Early canneries of peas and other produce

The Dutch Canning and Pickling Company in Cedar Grove was incorporated in 1908. The only product packed in the early years was peas. The very first year, the wooden floor, which was set on posts, collapsed under the weight of the canned peas, mixing them up and causing considerable damage and a huge loss. It was a one-line plant, with a capacity of about thirty thousand cases for the first two years; each case contained ninety cans. In these early years of canning factories in Wisconsin, there was a great deal of competition and rivalry. The above-named packing operations in Cedar Grove, then owned by the Huenink family, were initially under the supervision of a Fred Dusold, who had experience running other plants in Wisconsin and Illinois. In a letter to the Wisconsin Canners Association, Ben and John Huenink, sons of founder J. B. Huenink, wrote: "Fred Dusold [upon departing the company] would not tell us how he made the brine, or how long the peas should be blanched or processed, nor were we able to secure this information from other factories."[1] The brothers, however, were

---

[1] Frederick A Stare, *Story of Wisconsin's Great Canning Industry* (Madison: Wisconsin Canners Association, 1949), 388.

Oostburg Canning Company (*courtesy Jackie TeRonde Swart*)

not to be outwitted by Dusold but were ultimately able to secure this vital information and build a very successful business. They served as managers from 1908 until 1940. Equipment for corn was added in 1910 and a second line for peas in 1916. By 1920 they dropped the reference to pickling and became the Dutch Canning Company.

About the same time, Henry Verhulst, operator of a Sheboygan cheese firm, and his friend, John E. De Master, a garage owner, decided that a pea-canning business might be an interesting new venture. They purchased a sadly neglected factory near Kaukauna, Wisconsin, a village largely of Dutch Catholic immigrants. This location would not compete with the Cedar Grove plant, and they incorporated as the Calumet Packing Company. They eventually merged with the Cedar Grove plant to become Calumet Dutch Canning Company. Although the crops being processed at all the plants were light in the early years, the quality of the grades far exceeded that being produced in other states.

Peas were not the only farm produce then being processed in Wisconsin. The Oostburg Canning Company was established in 1902 for the purpose of canning corn, tomatoes, and apples. Within a year, they were unable to secure adequate acreage of tomatoes and apples, and both were dropped. Ed Faas served as manager and president from 1905 to 1940, joined by his son J. B. Faas and Peter Daane, Henry Woordes, and Sam Huibregtse. There were also smaller factories in Waldo and Sheboygan Falls. All of the original officers in the Oostburg and Cedar Grove plants owned and operated a number of canning factories in Sheboygan, Ozaukee, and Manitowoc Counties.

Although all these canneries battled the challenge of weather close to Lake Michigan, the presence of local farmers supplying them with produce provided them with stability. The truckers were usually the farmers themselves and trucking fewer than ten miles from field to factory ensured the freshest canned goods. In 1927, sixty percent of the canned peas in the United States were canned in Wisconsin. That equaled from ten to thirteen million cases, and Wisconsin peas were considered the highest quality in the country.[2]

The canneries and German prisoners of war

The onset of World War II created an agricultural labor crisis throughout the United States. Many of the workers in the canneries were women and younger men. Many of the latter went to war, while some of the women who had been laboring in the fields replaced the men in the war-related factories. There were therefore very few workers left to pick fruit in the orchards and tend to the fields. At the same time, the United States found itself with hundreds of thousands of German soldiers held as prisoners of war. To imprison them overseas would have required thousands of troops and supply ships, and all basic necessities would have had to be transported to Europe. The military, therefore, decided to transport the POWs on returning empty ships and house them at existing stateside military bases. This reduced the logistical nightmare of supplying and guarding them overseas. The utilization of POW labor developed later.

There were approximately 430,000 POWs brought to the United States. They included German, Italian, and Japanese, but 380,000 were German.[3] The United States established 156 base camps throughout the country, and only four states did not house POWs at any time during the war. Wisconsin housed about 10 percent of the POWs. Camp McCoy in Monroe County, Wisconsin, was one of the first base camps established in 1942, and POWs were housed in the state until June of 1946. There were fourteen branch camps in Wisconsin, and this study will concentrate on the two camps in Sheboygan County and the one in Waupun in Dodge County. In Sheboygan County, the POWs were housed at the county fairgrounds in Plymouth and at the former Sheboygan County Asylum on Sheboygan's west side. In Waupun, they were housed at the Dodge County fairgrounds.

[2] Stare, *Story*, 37.
[3] Ron Robin, *The Barbed-Wire College: Re-educating German POWs in the US during World War II* (Princeton, NJ: Princeton University Press, 1995), 6.

POWs working at the pea vinery
(*courtesy of Sheboygan County Historical Research Center*)

In 2002 *Stalag Wisconsin* was published, providing a wealth of information previously unknown (or forgotten) on this subject. Author Betty Cowley was a retired history teacher who had discovered many skeptics about POW camps in Wisconsin and very little available historical information. The National Archives informed her that all the information on branch camps had been destroyed in the 1950s. In further investigation, she discovered that many government reports remained classified. The declassified information that was available at the Wisconsin Historical Society was very general in nature. Mrs. Cowley's research turned to community and oral histories, particularly personal encounters with the men of the camps. Newspaper coverage regarding the camps was heavily censored during the war, but Sheboygan County newspapers ignored that directive and provided a great deal of general information about the camps.

The POWs were contracted to the canning companies in Wisconsin to help harvest and process crops that would have gone to waste. They also helped to bale hemp and to work in nurseries, tanneries, and dairies. Even as the war was coming to an end, the farmers and factories begged

Sheboygan County Asylum (*courtesy of Sheboygan County Historical Research Center*)

the government to keep the prisoners for the entire 1945 harvest. In Wisconsin it was estimated that the POWs realized $3.3 million for the government.

Farmers and food processors paid the government the going civilian rate for the labor of prisoners, supposedly to avoid unfair competition with those businesses that used American civilian labor. In many worker markets, the presence of a POW labor pool kept civilian wages low. The prisoners received eighty cents a day for their work and ten cents a day as a gratuity for their personal needs. It was paid in camp scrip, instead of cash, and could be used only at the camp canteen. They were also allowed to establish a personal savings account, so many men went home with cash in their pockets.[4]

The asylum barracks in Sheboygan housed 450 prisoners. Because it was from ten to twelve miles to the factories in Cedar Grove and Oostburg, civilian drivers or canning company workers transported the POWs to the fields and factories in the morning and picked them up again at night. Some were supervised; many were not. Initially the military provided meals, and the employer supplied water, but there were many exceptions to this rule. Prisoners who worked the sugar beet fields for the Wassink family were treated to their meals at the kitchen table with the other farm workers. Marilyn Wassink Hanson, a young girl at the time, remembers clearly her mother inviting the men inside and telling her that they should be treated like the other hired help.[5]

Prisoners assigned to the Oostburg Canning factory tired of the lunch provided by the base and started to frequent the Knotty Pine Restaurant in Oostburg, operated by the Te Ronde family. Family

[4] W. Pfister, "US Army Doing Fine Job Running POW Camp," *Sheboygan Press* (24 July 1944) 10.
[5] Marilyn Wassink Hanson, personal communication to the author, 19 March 2017.

German POWs at the Sheboygan County Asylum Camp (*courtesy of Sheboygan County Historical Research Center*)

members recounted stories of locals coming into the restaurant for lunch and finding most of the seats occupied by prisoners.[6]

Herbert Prange, a year-round employee of the Oostburg factory, worked alongside many of the prisoners year after year. Many of the immigrants in this area were from the Achterhoek in Gelderland, and in the 1940s, there were still some descendants who spoke Dutch and the local dialects. Their ability to communicate with the German POWs made operations in the factories and fields more productive and friendlier. Herbert Prange's wife and young daughter, Sharon, often came to the factory to pick him up at the end of his shift. One of the POWs who worked alongside Mr. Prange for some time took a liking to Sharon, and in his spare time at the camp he fashioned a toy for her as a Christmas gift.[7]

From Camp Waupun in Dodge County, 150 Germans were employed at the Waupun Canning Co., and another 100 worked for the Stokely Foods plant in Brandon, Wisconsin. Many of the men at the camps throughout Wisconsin functioned in the same way as migrant workers. They were moved from camp to camp and state to state to follow the harvest. In Dodge County, as in Sheboygan, many of the men remained after the pea harvest until the corn pack was finished in October.

[6] Jackie TeRonde Swart and John Swart, personal communication to the author, 12 May 2017.
[7] Sharon Prange Claerbout, personal communication to author, 2003.

Camp Waupun viewed from the roof of the canning company (*courtesy of the Wisconsin Historical Society*)

The labor shortage also affected the Waupun and Alto area, lacking American men between the ages of eighteen and thirty-five to take these jobs. Alto was quite small and rural. The Klosterboer farm near Alto utilized the POWs when the owner left for the service. The Glewen family responded by cooking meals and taking them across the road to the men in the fields and, at other times, by inviting the men into the house. Strongly criticized for this, Mrs. Glewen said she felt it was the Christian thing to do.[8] That sentiment was also expressed by the Alto Reformed Church, who reserved the front pews for the POWs during the canning season of 1945.[9]

Designed more to establish a boundary than to prevent escape, the camp was surrounded by a snow fence. Civilians were ordered to stay away from the camp but at the same time to extend some hospitality. The biggest problem was with the young women who hung around the fence and exchanged notes with the prisoners. There were only about twenty-eight hundred attempts at escape at all the camps in the United States. In reality, the POWs were well fed and well housed. In Sheboygan, with a large German immigrant population, there were prisoners who had family members living in the area who had emigrated before the war. Prisoners were given a relative amount of freedom to visit their local families.

---

[8] Kenneth Glewen, personal communication to author, 24 April 2017.
[9] Betty Cowley, *Stalag Wisconsin* (Oregon, WI: Badger Books, 2002), 260.

A number of Sheboygan County Dutch men who had served in Germany during the war, and some who had been held as POWs there, were incensed to return home and hear the stories of how well many of German POWs had been treated. When they discovered that the Germans had also been invited into American homes, they were very upset. An editorial in the *Sheboygan Press* expressed it bluntly: "Here is the Nazi attitude toward our boys. Not even the wounded are to be allowed a kindly word or gesture. And yet we waste sympathy upon the healthy, well-treated, well-fed Nazis housed comfortably at the fairgrounds."[10] One of the reasons the military claimed that records about the camps had been destroyed was an attempt to keep POWs from being targets for those who had lost sons in the war. Even now there is great reluctance to discuss the disparity in treatment.

Before and after the war, East Central Wisconsin also employed a great many Mexican migrant workers. Because of the fair treatment they had received, by the early 1950s, many of them chose to stay permanently. Although it is rarely discussed openly, many of the German POWs felt the same way and after the war came back to Sheboygan County to establish a permanent home, a few even marrying local women.

Personal postscript

My oldest brother, David Risseeuw, worked in the Cedar Grove factory in the early 1960s for fifty cents an hour. His hours averaged

Warehoused peas at Calumet Dutch Canning Company
(*courtesy of Sheboygan County Historical Research Center*)

[10] W. Pfister, "How About Our Boys?" *Sheboygan Press* (24 July 1944), 6.

from 100 to 120 hours per week. No canning was done on Sunday in either Cedar Grove or Oostburg, but if the crops came in on Saturday, they canned until the midnight cutoff. This was my first consumer education lesson as a child. The question our mother asked every day when my brother got up to go back to work was, "Who did you can for yesterday?" Peas were graded by hand and then canned. On the same day, canning could be done for A & P and for the Le Sueur brand—which sold fancy baby peas, grown on the same field but with a big price difference. Not all of the canned goods were shipped immediately. They were warehoused by grade, and labeling was done on a year-round basis as orders came in.

One of the ways my brother and the other college guys alleviated some of the boredom of this work was that every day at 3:49 p.m., one tennis ball was canned in a #10 can. My brother said they were always curious what the reaction was when someone opened that can of peas and found a tennis ball.[11]

---

[11] David Risseeuw, personal communication to author, 2 April 2017.

CHAPTER 5

Dryland Strip Farming and the V-Blade: Dutch Canadian Innovation that Helped Stop Soil Drifting

Donald Sinnema

"Canada is the land of agricultural miracles." So wrote the author of a classic 1943 volume about Montana in a chapter on soil drifting.[1] If it were not for four of these "miracles"—summer fallow, Marquis wheat, strip farming, and the V-blade—much of the western Canadian prairies and the northern plains of the United States might well be a barren wilderness, rather than part of the "wheat basket of the world." Of these four Canadian innovations, the latter two were made by Dutch Canadians.

---

[1] Joseph K. Howard, *Montana: High, Wide, and Handsome* (New Haven, CT: Yale University Press, 1943), 275. In a similar vein, Herbert Chester, from the Dominion Experimental Station at Lethbridge, Alberta, wrote in 1953: "It is generally conceded that soil drifting control as now practised on the Canadian prairies and, to a considerable extent, in the United States was pioneered in Southern Alberta." Herbert Chester, "The Development of Soil Drifting Control in Southern Alberta," (Dominion Experimental Station, Lethbridge, seminar, 5 March 1953), 1; Lethbridge Research Center, xx, D18. Cf. *Lethbridge Herald* (hereafter *LH*), 19 July 1935; James Gray, *Men Against the Desert* (Saskatoon: Western Producer Prairie Books, 1978), 242.

In 1886 Angus MacKay of Indian Head, Saskatchewan, invented summer fallow to contend with drought. In 1904 Charles Saunders of Ottawa developed early ripening Marquis wheat to avoid frost.[2] In 1918 the Koole brothers of Monarch, Alberta, introduced strip farming to combat soil drifting, and in 1938, George Williamson of neighboring Granum, Alberta, invented the V-blade, also to counter soil drifting.[3]

The menace of soil drifting

A combination of years of drought, winds, and poor farming methods had created the problem of soil drifting across the Canadian prairies and the American Great Plains beginning in the 1910s, 1920s, and especially in the Dust Bowl years of the 1930s. In southern Alberta, soil drifting became a major problem already by 1914,[4] only a decade after the land was first tilled. The disappearance of virgin soil fibers was the main factor leading to soil erosion after a decade of tillage. Soil erosion was especially intense from the Pacific through the Crowsnest Pass of the Rockies, due to prevailing Chinook winds that blew across the prairies from the southwest. One of the worst areas was the Chinook belt around Lethbridge, especially in the winter and spring months. In 1917 the newspaper reported that "drifting became so severe that entire fields were denuded; fences, trees, and buildings were covered; and roads blocked with dunes of drift soil."[5] Serious drifting threatened to make a desert out of the Monarch district in the dry years from 1918 to 1922.[6] Fields lost up to three inches of top soil in a year. One observer noted, "On June 9, 1920, farmers around Monarch had to light their lamps at four o'clock in the afternoon to see through the red murk that pervaded their houses."[7] From 1931 to 1937, a severe drought afflicted the prairies. By 1934, soil erosion had driven a third of the farmers out of southern Alberta.[8]

[2] The story of the discovery of summer fallow and of Marquis wheat is told by Paul de Kruif, *Hunger Fighters* (NY: Harcourt, 1928), ch. 2.
[3] Although Charles Noble of Nobleford must be credited with developing the straight blade earlier in 1935, and it was his later manufacturing of the Noble V-blade on a large scale that had the greatest impact on preventing soil drifting, he did not invent the V-blade.
[4] Asael Palmer, *When the Winds Came: How the Battle Against Soil Drifting was Won on the Canadian Prairies* [Lethbridge: 1968], 11.
[5] Palmer, *When the Winds Came*, 12.
[6] *LH*, 1 Aug. 1931.
[7] P. M. Abel, "Strip Farming," *Country Guide* (2 Dec. 1929).
[8] Ted Byfield, ed., *Alberta in the 20th Century* (Edmonton: United Western Communications, 1998), 7:217.

Since much of the Canadian prairies and western Great Plains is semi-arid (avg. 10-20 inches of annual rainfall),[9] the land did not have enough moisture to sustain good crops year after year. MacKay's development of the method of summer fallowing—leaving crop land fallow every other year so that it would have time to build up moisture and nutrients for the next year's crops—was critical. Fallow land, however, needs to be cultivated a few times to kill weeds, which rob the soil of moisture. The usual methods of cultivating summer fallow were by plow or disc, which not only killed weeds but also turned over the soil, leaving it bare and black on top. Early in the century, the theory of "dust mulch" summer fallow prevailed, the idea being that a finely tilled black field of pulverized soil would help conserve moisture.[10] The field (or duckfoot) cultivator came into broad use in the 1920s, but this implement tended to clog up in heavy stubble, leading to the common practice of stubble burning. These methods of summer fallowing and cultivating made the land especially susceptible to soil drifting.

Strip farming

Various methods were tried to combat soil drifting. These included creating lumpy ridges by listing, seeding cover crops, seeding winter rye or grasses, and planting trees as a windbreak. Strip farming turned out initially to be the most successful. Strip farming was a method of alternating planted crops and fallow land in narrow strips, perpendicular to prevailing winds, in order to prevent soil drifting. Strip farming was distinct from the age-old practice of "strip cropping," which alternated strips of different crops.

The Koole brothers of Monarch, in southern Alberta, are widely credited with starting strip farming as a way to prevent soil drifting.[11] In 1890 Leendert (Leonard) (1881-1948) and Arie (1882-1963) Koole had emigrated to Northwest Iowa with their parents from Pernis in the

---

[9] From 1902 to 1936, average annual precipitation at Lethbridge was 15.7 inches; *LH*, 24 Dec. 1936.
[10] Palmer, *When the Winds Came*, 10-11.
[11] E.g., *LH*, 1 Aug. 1931, 3 July 1935, 11 Dec. 1947, 23 Feb. 1952; Chester, "Development," 2; Palmer, *When the Winds Came*, 12-13; Gray, *Men Against the Desert*, 73; Grant MacEwan, *Charles Noble, Guardian of the Soil* (Saskatoon: Western Producer Prairie Books, 1983), 155; Ian Frazier, *Great Plains* (NY: Farrar, Straus and Giroux, 1989), 5; David Granatstein, *Dryland Farming in the Northwestern United States* (Pullman: Washington State University Cooperative Extension, 1992), 9; David Jones, *Empire of Dust* (Calgary: University of Calgary Press, 2002), 149.

Monarch, Nobleford, Granum, Barons area in southern Alberta

Dutch province of Zuid-Holland. They grew up on a farm near Sheldon, and then moved to southern Alberta, where they took up homesteads a couple of miles northwest (14-10-24 W4) of Monarch in 1904.[12] There they were part of the flourishing Dutch settlement that had begun in the Granum-Monarch-Nobleford district of southern Alberta in 1903.[13]

In 1915 Lorenzo Tuff of nearby Coalhurst first proposed the idea of what was later called strip farming, but there is no evidence that he had implemented it.[14] The Koole brothers at Monarch apparently independently came up with this innovation and first put it into practice in 1918.[15]

Accounts differ somewhat about the precise origin of the practice of strip farming and whether it was first done in 1917 or 1918. The

[12] *Sons of Wind and Soil*, 254-57.
[13] Donald Sinnema, *The First Dutch Settlement in Alberta: Letters from the Pioneer Years 1903-1914* (Calgary: University of Calgary Press, 2005).
[14] Lorenzo P. Tuff presented his idea to the *Lethbridge Herald* (7 Aug. 1915), but he was not able to test the idea on his farm; instead, in this article, he asks the experts to give their opinions, which did not happen. Tuff arrived at Lethbridge in the 1890s and claimed a homestead in 1908, just north of Coalhurst, about ten miles southeast of the Kooles. His wife died in 1914, leaving him with seven children. He remarried and gave up farming in 1918; then he moved to Washington, where he died in the 1919 influenza epidemic. *LH*, 16 April 1914, 21 Sept. 1918, 17 Feb. 1919, 7 March 1987; *Sons of Wind and Soil* (Nobleford: Nobleford-Monarch History Book Club, 1976), 374.
[15] "Monarch Home of Strip Farming," *LH*, 11 Dec. 1947; Gerrit Koole, "History of Strip Farming in Southern Alberta," *Fort Macleod—our Colourful Past* (Fort Macleod: Fort Macleod History Book Committee, 1977), 114-15.

Leendert Koole
(*courtesy Brenda Rogers*)

Arie Koole
(*courtesy Debbie Carrell*)

earliest version is an article in the *Country Guide* from 1929, based on an interview with the Koole brothers:

> Back in 1917, the year of the first serious drifting, one of the Koole brothers had a 40-acre field, a half-mile strip, 40 rods wide, lying north and south athwart the prevailing wind. The western edge of it was protected by a rank stand of stubble. They noticed that the western edge of this field did not suffer, but the two-thirds farthest from protection was badly blown.... But if stubble would protect a strip thirteen-and-a-third rods wide, why not put all the crop in strips of that width with stubble in between? And,

if summer-fallowing every other year is the best safeguard against failure from drought, why not crop alternate strips one year and fallow them the next?[16]

In his 1943 volume, Howard gave a rather similar account of this discovery:

> In 1917 the first of four great drouth years, . . . they watched as the wind snatched the topsoil from their fallow fields. They talked it over with their neighbors, other Dutchmen in the little colony. Someone (the Kooles did not claim the credit) remarked that the westernmost edges of the fields broadside to the wind had not drifted; the blow did not start until the wind had swept some distance into the fields. . . . They had the answer. Why not narrow the fallow field? Why not alternate strips of crop and strips of fallow? Why not place the strips at right angles to the wind, . . . with a shelter belt of crop or stubble to protect the fallow strip?
> The Kooles tried it in 1918, on 240 acres. It worked, and so came strip farming, salvation of the northern plains.[17]

Asael Palmer of the Lethbridge Experimental Station later reported that Arie Koole told him that he had come upon the idea of strips of grain and fallow during a visit the previous winter to his family at Sheldon, Iowa, where he had seen alternate strips of corn and grain (strip cropping).[18]

To summarize, the details of these accounts may all be factors in the origin of strip farming. It seems apparent that the initial idea of strip farming first occurred to the Koole brothers in 1917, when they observed that a fallow field did not drift for some distance east of a crop field. But it was in 1918 that they first initiated the practice of strip

---

[16] Abel, "Strip Farming."

[17] Howard, *Montana* (1943), 279. Some sources state that the Kooles introduced strip farming in 1917 (first stated in the 1950s), while other sources say 1918. The details Howard offers lend credibility to his account. The earliest sources indicate 1918, e.g., the *Weekly Newsletter of the Lethbridge Experimental Station* (*LH*, 5 May 1934): "The use of strip farming in Alberta was tried by a few farmers in the Monarch-Nobleford district back in 1918 as a means of checking the soil drifting, which had then become so serious that many farms were being abandoned. Today most of the farms in that locality are stripped, and it is one of the most successfully farmed dry land areas in Western Canada." Cf. *LH*, 17 Dec. 1963.

[18] Palmer, *When the Winds Came* (1968), 12-13; cf. *Sons of Wind and Soil*, 254. Visits by Arie and Leendert Koole to Sheldon, Iowa, during the winter of 1917-18 were reported by *De Volksvriend*, 8 Nov. 1917 and 10 Jan. 1918. This also confirms 1918 as the date when the Kooles started strip farming.

Strip farming near Monarch, Alberta (*courtesy Glenbow Archives*)

farming on part of their land at Monarch, after Arie had seen alternate crop strips in Iowa.

For a few years, the Koole brothers experimented with various methods of strip farming. Eventually, they divided their farms entirely into strips, running north and south, more or less at right angles to the prevailing Chinook winds.[19] The newspaper reported, "One of the brothers [Leendert] said he started with a 40-rod strip, and then found that width was too great. His strips were now 20 rods, while his brother [Arie] used 13-rod strips."[20] Soon it was found that strips from ten to twenty rods wide were most successful in preventing drifting.[21]

Initially, a few neighbors followed their example, including Leendert's brothers-in-law Chris and Neil Withage. It was not until after the Big Blow of 1920, when soil drifting was widespread, that the practice became more widely adopted. By 1924 the Monarch-Nobleford district was almost completely strip farmed.[22] Good crops in the years

[19] Abel, "Strip Farming."
[20] "Farmers in Nobleford-Claresholm-Monarch Triangle Launch Movement to Grapple with Soil Drifting Problem in Community Way," *LH*, 24 Feb. 1927.
[21] *LH*, 5 May 1934.
[22] Chester, "Development," 2. Cf. *LH*, 18 Sept. 1926. Jacob Dekker, "Strip Farming as a Way to Stop Wind Erosion," *The Furrow* (Canadian ed. published by John Deere), Sept.-Oct. 1936, described how best to do strip farming. Dekker was another Dutch farmer at Monarch.

from 1923 to 1929 slowed the progress of strip farming, although a conference held at Nobleford in 1927 urged strip farming as the most effective means to check soil drifting.[23] With dry years in the 1930s, strip farming soon became practiced widely throughout southern Alberta. In these years, the practice was strongly advocated by the Dominion Experimental Station at Lethbridge, the Canadian Department of Agriculture,[24] and by the *Lethbridge Herald*.

In 1932 the newspaper reported, "The strip farming method borrowed from the good Dutch farmers of the Monarch district has spread steadily, until it is now well established at Nobleford and Barons, and it is rapidly being adopted throughout the Carmangay and Champion areas, and even some districts further [sic] north are trying it out."[25] In 1933, during one severe wind of up to sixty-nine miles per hour at Monarch, damage was practically nil.[26] In 1934 strip farming was starting to be practiced in southeastern Alberta, and in the same year, due to the failure of cover crops, strip farming began to spread north from Macleod to High River.[27] By 1939 about 80 percent of the crop land in the Chinook belt from Pincher Creek to Medicine Hat was being strip farmed.[28]

Devastating drought and winds consumed the year 1935. The Legislative Assembly of Alberta adopted an act that year which required farmers to control soil drifting and prescribed strip farming (no wider than 20 rods) as one effective means.[29] The owner of a drifting field was held responsible for damage to adjacent land. This was a real impetus to the spread of strip farming in Alberta.

Farmers in other localities in Saskatchewan and Montana heard of the success at Monarch and came to investigate.[30] Thus, in 1931, there was strong interest in Saskatchewan to begin strip farming.[31] In September a group of farmers from Rosetown visited Monarch and then started the practice.[32] Within a few years, strip farming spread to

---

[23] *LH*, 24 Sept. 1927.
[24] E. Hopkins, S. Barnes, A. Palmer and W. Chepil, *Soil Drifting Control in the Prairie Provinces* (Ottawa: Dominion of Canada Department of Agriculture, 1935; also 1937, 1938, 1946 eds.), 10-13.
[25] *LH*, 10 Sept. 1932.
[26] *LH*, 28 Feb. 1933.
[27] Ibid., 17 Sept. 1934, 27 July 1934.
[28] William Dickson, "Soil Drifting Control in the Prairie Provinces," [1939]. Glenblow Archives, Calgary, A. E. Palmer fonds (hereafter GA, Palmer), M-6880-37.
[29] *The Control of Soil Drifting Act*, Statutes of Alberta 1935, c. 40. The Act passed 23 April 1935 and came into force 1 March 1936. Cf. *LH*, 13 April, 3 May 1935.
[30] *LH*, 19 July 1935, 18 May 1940; Palmer, *When the Winds Came*, 13.
[31] Ibid., 18 July, 1 Aug. 1931.

the Bushville, Springwater, Gull Lake, and Swift Current areas.[33] By 1938 a survey found that 63 percent of cultivated land was under strip farming in eleven townships in southwestern Saskatchewan.[34]

Again, Hobart D. Myrick, regarded as the father of strip farming in Montana, first brought the practice to Square Butte in central Montana in about 1927.[35] In 1932 he hosted the first strip farming tour for many Montana farmers.[36] During a visit to Alberta, W. H. Reed of Turner noticed strip farming, and he introduced the practice to northeastern Montana in 1931. From there, the idea spread to the Shaunavon district of southwestern Saskatchewan, after about one hundred farmers visited the Reed farm in 1934.[37] At Shaunavon, the first of many local strip farming associations was formed.[38]

Furthermore, by 1934 strip farming had spread to western North Dakota,[39] and by 1937, the adoption of strip farming had increased tremendously in many counties of Montana.[40] Soon strip farming became widely practiced throughout the Canadian Prairies and the northern Great Plains of America—in Montana and western North and South Dakota.

Although strip farming was very helpful in combatting soil drifting, it did not completely eliminate the hazard, especially in the dry years of the thirties. Where soil was light, some drifting continued on summer fallow with bare soil on the surface, leaving ridges of drift soil along the western edge of stubble strips. Weeds tended to grow along these margins. Also, narrow strips were somewhat inefficient to farm. The most serious drawback to strip farming was an increased infestation of sawflies, caused by the added number of borders, since sawflies concentrated around the edges of wheat fields.[41]

Because of its limitations, strip farming was only a partial solution to soil drifting. Already in the 1920s, it was realized that,

---

[32] Ibid., 28 Sept. 1931, 2 Jan. 1934.
[33] Ibid., 24 Aug. 1934, 2 April, 17 July 1935, 3 Sept. 1937.
[34] Asael Palmer, "Cultural Practice for the Control of Wind Erosion of Soils in Western Canada," *Empire Journal of Experimental Agriculture* 13 (July 1945), 127.
[35] *Havre Daily News*, 27 June 1932; Howard, *Montana*, 279-80.
[36] *Helena Daily Independent*, 5 July 1932; *LH*, 2 July 1932.
[37] *LH*, 7 July 1934; *Winnipeg Free Press*, 18 Sept. 1934.
[38] Ibid., 16 July 1934.
[39] Leroy Moomaw, "Summer-Fallow," North Dakota Agricultural Experiment Station, Circular 54 (May 1934), 3-4; *LH*, 15 Nov. 1935.
[40] *LH*, 25 Oct. 1935, 2 April 1937.
[41] [Asael Palmer], "Success, Failure and Development of Strip Farming and Ploughless Tillage Throughout the Prairie Provinces," [1938], GA, Palmer, M-6880-7; Hopkins, *Soil Drifting Control*, 13; *LH*, 6 Aug. 1934, 18 Sept. 1936, 2 July 1938, 30 Aug. 1943.

besides strip farming, a method of plowless cultivating was needed that left a "trash cover" of stubble and dead weeds on the surface of summer fallow instead of black soil, in order to preserve moisture and prevent soil drifting.

At many gatherings throughout the 1920s and 1930s, Asael Palmer, assistant superintendent of the Lethbridge Experimental Station, strongly advocated the need for summer-fallowing with a trash cover.[42] In 1916, J. H. Bohannan, of Sibbald in east central Alberta, first introduced the idea of "plowless fallowing" when he put aside his moldboard plow and started doing his summer fallowing with a field cultivator, leaving a partial trash cover.[43] Neil Withage, from the Dutch community at Nobleford, was the first to introduce plowless fallowing to the Monarch-Nobleford district in 1930 when he did his summer fallow with a stiff-tooth cultivator and found that his yields were just as good as his neighbors who plowed.[44]

But there was resistance to eliminating the plow, especially among those who had adopted strip farming. At a meeting of about 170 farmers at Nobleford, in March 1932, organized by Charles Noble, Asael Palmer spoke of the merits of plowless tillage. He later reported:

> Then, Leonard Koole, one of the originators of strip farming, and a very successful farmer, spoke, "I cannot understand this idea that good farming can be done without moldboard plowing. My father told me in Holland good plowing was the basis of good farming, and I have always noted good farmers are good plowmen. Please do not ask me to stop plowing. If I cannot plow, I cannot farm."
>
> His brother-in-law Neil Withage interjected: "Leonard, you are a better farmer than I am. I haven't plowed for two years but have received yields as good as yours and had no soil drifting on my fallow strips, while you've had some on yours."
>
> The discussion continued, some favoring and some opposing plowless tillage. Before the meeting closed, however, all who were still plowing said they would try at least half a 20 rod strip as plowless fallow the next summer.
>
> Within two years, Leonard Koole was an enthusiastic advocate of plowless, trash-cover farming. The Nobleford, Monarch, Barons district became the first in western Canada and

---

[42] *LH*, 21 July 1934, 2 Nov. 1953.
[43] Ibid., 4 Feb. 1955, 2 April 1955; Gray, *Men*, 74.
[44] Chester, "Development," 3.

perhaps in the world to abandon the plow and adopt plowless, trash-cover fallowing completely. The result was that during the "dirty thirties," there was practically no drifting in those areas.[45]

Despite its limitations, strip farming, along with plowless tillage, prevented southern Alberta from being ravaged in the mid-1930s like the Dust Bowl states of Kansas and Oklahoma. The *Bulletin* of the University of Alberta's College of Agriculture went so far as to say that strip farming "saved a region apparently doomed for destruction."[46]

The V-blade

As the practice of plowless tillage of summer fallow gradually became accepted, the challenge was to find an implement that would leave a trash cover on the surface. The one-way disc was widely used as a substitute for the plow, but it still turned over the soil and buried the plant residue. The duckfoot cultivator and the rod weeder came into common use in the 1920s, but these implements did not work in hard ground or heavy stubble. The duckfoot cultivator left a partial trash cover, but in heavy stubble, it tended to clog.[47]

A better implement, which killed weeds on summer fallow and left a good trash cover to prevent soil drifting, was needed. This was most effectively accomplished with the introduction of the blade cultivator in the latter 1930s.

Charles S. Noble, a large-scale farmer at Nobleford, Alberta, and an avid promoter of new farming methods, has deservedly received credit for his enormous contributions to dryland farm technology. His invention and production of the Noble blade was a crucial means to combat soil drifting by leaving a trash cover on fields of summer fallow.[48] But Noble was not the only contributor to significant developments in farm machinery that killed weeds in summer fallow and prevented soil drifting.

The first effort was in 1935, when John Turner and Otto Wobick, farmers from the neighboring town of Barons, invented what they

---

[45] Palmer, *When the Winds Came*, 30; *LH*, 18 March 1932.
[46] Quoted by Howard, *Montana*, 279.
[47] Asael Palmer, "Dry Land Tillage and Equipment: Recent Developments and Practical Application" (early 1940s), GA, Palmer, M-6880-7; Asael Palmer, "The Development of Soil Drifting Control in the Chinook Belt of Alberta" (c. 1954), GA, Palmer, M-6880-8; Donald Wetherell with Elise Corbet, *Breaking New Ground: A Century of Farm Equipment Manufacturing on the Canadian Prairies* (Saskatoon: Fifth House, 1993), 114-38.
[48] MacEwan, *Charles Noble*, chs. 17-18.

called the Paul Bunyan cultivator. This was constructed from an old multibottom, sod-breaking plow by removing every second plow bottom and the moldboards from the remaining ones, then welding a sixteen-inch plowshare onto the left side of the remaining shares to make thirty-two-inch duckfeet. The result was an implement with three or four duckfeet—essentially, oversized cultivator shovels. This implement successfully cut the roots of weeds below the surface of the soil and left a trash cover. But not many of these cultivators were produced because of limited availability of large gang plows. Also, the Paul Bunyan frame was too low to clear in heavy stubble when Russian thistles were present.[49]

In the winter of 1935-36, Charles Noble, while on vacation in California, invented the straight blade.[50] This farm implement pulled a nine-foot-long tilted blade about five inches beneath the surface of the soil to cut the roots of weeds, while leaving the weeds and stubble on the surface. The limitation of this implement was that it was heavy to pull, and the straight blade could be damaged if it hit a large rock.

Then, in 1938, George Williamson, of nearby Granum, invented a variation of this implement—the single V-blade. It had two tilted blades in the shape of a large V that cut the roots of weeds and left a trash cover in a manner similar to Noble's straight blade, but it sliced through the ground at an angle. This innovation was to become a standard design of the blade, since the V-blade pulled easier than the straight blade and was much less liable to damage when the blade struck a large rock.

George Williamson (anglicized from Willemsen) was part of the same Dutch community in Southern Alberta where Leendert Koole farmed. In fact, Koole was George's uncle. George's grandparents had immigrated from the cotton-factory town of Nijverdal in the Dutch province of Overijssel to the silk factories of Paterson, New Jersey, in 1892. Then, a decade later, they moved to Manhattan, Montana, to take up farming. Finally, in 1905, they crossed the border into Alberta to claim a free homestead at Granum.[51]

Born 7 June 1916, George grew up on his father's farm (NW 26-10-25 W4), nine miles east of Granum, in the Rocky Coulee district, and

---

[49] Chester, "Development," 5; Asael E. Palmer, "History of Dry Farming on the Canadian Prairies and Especially in Southern Alberta" (paper presented to the Lethbridge Historical Society, 24 Oct. 1961), GA, Palmer, M-6880-9; Palmer, *When the Winds Came*, 16. Turner and Wobick did not file for a patent on their machine.

[50] *Sons of Wind and Soil*, 304, and MacEwan, *Charles Noble*, 166-67, tell the story of Noble's invention of the straight blade.

[51] Family information collected by the author.

George Williamson
(*courtesy Alice Williamson*)

it was there in his father's blacksmith shop that twenty-two-year-old George invented the V-blade in the fall of 1938.

His original V-blade was bolted to a wooden frame, but when he tried it in the field, the wooden implement fell apart. So George immediately improved the machine by mounting the ten-foot V-blade on a metal frame. The blade was rather light, and there was difficulty keeping it in the ground, so George piled some rocks on the machine to make it heavier. That fall he successfully worked the stubble on his father's farm section after the harvest. The crop in 1939 was better than it had ever been, and he used the V-blade again that fall after harvest.[52]

The machine consisted of two tilted blades bolted to a support, in the shape of a single large V, about ten feet wide. The angle of the V was about 110 degrees. George used three plow beams as curved standards to connect the blade support to the frame of the implement, one in the middle and one close to each end. The standards were curved so that weeds and stubble would slide upwards and off the beam rather than clog up the machine. In 1939 George added eight rods with curved ends behind the blade in order to lift weeds to the surface of the soil. The

---

[52] "A Farmer's Invention Helps," *Family Herald and Weekly Star*, 16 Feb. 1949; "Cultivator Improved by Red Deer Inventor," *The Albertan*, 27 March 1948.

Williamson V-blade on his father's farm (*courtesy Alice Williamson*)

machine was supported by two car wheels that could be adjusted for height by a central rotating crank, so that the blade could be raised or lowered into the ground.

The implement proved to be a successful means of killing weeds, while leaving a trash cover on the surface. Soon neighbors expressed interest in such a machine, so George made a few similar V-blades for them.[53]

Young George, however, lacked the capital to manufacture his V-blade on any significant scale. He asked Peter Kooy (1894-1954), another blacksmithing farmer in the Dutch community, to help him make several V-blades, and Kooy offered George the opportunity to join him in manufacturing the blade on his farm (SE 14-10-23 W4), four miles east of Monarch and south of Nobleford. Peter Kooy's parents had emigrated from the Netherlands to Chicago in 1906, but soon moved to Vesper, Wisconsin, and then in 1910, they settled at Monarch.[54] So in 1939 George linked up with Kooy to begin manufacturing the machine on Kooy's farm. George lived for some time with the Kooy family, also helping Kooy do his farm work.[55]

Initially, Williamson and Kooy worked together to make some improvements to George's original design. They made the frame of the blade heavier. Instead of the original car wheels, they used steel wheels, purchased from a local John Deere dealer. And they replaced

[53] *The Albertan*, 27 March 1948.
[54] *Sons of Wind and Soil*, 259-60.
[55] Information from Bertha Hofman, a daughter of Peter Kooy.

Williamson-Kooy blade (*courtesy Delbert Kooy*)

the center rotating crank with two levers, one at each wheel. At some point in this early period, Charles Noble visited the Kooy farm to see how the Williamson V-blade worked.[56] Already in 1939, the Williamson blade (later also called the Kooy blade) was being sold commercially to neighbors in their district. One was made for George's uncle, Chris Withage (another Dutch farmer in the community), who managed the Lethbridge Experimental Station substation on his farm at Nobleford.[57]

At a field day at Pincher Creek, on July 19, 1939, Asael Palmer, assistant superintendent of the Dominion Experimental Station at Lethbridge, gave an address on "Soil and Moisture Conservation," in which he recommended use of either the Noble blade or the Williamson blade to prevent soil drifting.

> Mr. Palmer gave a comprehensive review of soil drifting preventatives, stressing as the most important means strip farming, [sub]surface cultivation, cover crops, and emergency methods, some of which are straw scattering, listing, and contour stripping. In order to lay a trash cover after surface cultivation, he advocated the use of a rod weeder, Noble blade, or Williamson blade.[58]

In April 1940, a report from the Experimental Station on "Blade Cultivators for Ploughless Tillage" (probably written by Palmer), described the three blade-type cultivators then in use:

[56] As recalled by Johanna Konynenbelt, a daughter of Peter Kooy.
[57] "A Farmer's Invention Helps."
[58] "Farmers Gather on Cyr Place at Pincher Creek for Field Day," *LH*, 22 July 1939.

Three general types of heavy blade implements are now being used, especially in Southern Alberta, that promise to meet the requirements for the ploughless tillage of dryland wheat farms. These are a straight blade, a single-wide duckfoot shaped [single V] blade, and a gang of three or four large heavy duckfeet, each [from] three- to three-and-one-half feet wide. These machines have two principles in common, namely, they are heavily built for penetrating hard, unploughed land, and the blades are large and tilted, so that they will lift the soil and disturb it sufficiently to kill small weeds, at the same time leaving the stubble and other trash almost undisturbed on the surface to serve as protection against wind action.

The straight blade in use was developed by Mr. C. S. Noble of Nobleford, Alberta, and consists of a straight heavy blade usually about ten feet long, mounted on a heavy frame and supported by two wheels. Mr. Noble has tried a number of different shaped blades and finally has developed a convex blade that seems to give good penetration, shears through the soil with little difficulty, and disturbs the surface sufficiently to give a good weed kill where conditions are satisfactory. Over one hundred of this type of blade cultivator are now in successful use in Alberta and seem to have definitely found a place.

A large duckfoot blade has been developed by Mr. Williams[on] of Monarch, Alberta, and is being used successfully by a few farmers. It has not been tried as extensively as the straight blade, so its merits are not so well determined.[59]

The heavy 3 or 4 gang duckfoot [Paul Bunyan] cultivator first came to the writer's attention on the farms of Messrs. Turner and Wobick of Barons, Alberta, and is now being used on a number of farms in this territory.

All three of these machines have been in use for three or four years. Those who are using them feel that they embody the principles that are required for ploughless fallowing land that has a cover of stubble or weed growth that will serve as a trash protection for wind proofing the soil through a summer fallow year.[60]

[59] Nine months later, the weekly letter of the Lethbridge Experimental Station reported: "There is no reason why any type of wide blade machine such as the Williamson "V" blade weeder would not be as successful to use as the Noble blade." *LH*, 24 Jan. 1941.

[60] Typescript dated 22 April 1940, Lethbridge Research Center, 13, B1; published in *LH*, 10 May 1940; cf. *LH*, 10 Jan. 1941, 12 July 1941.

On July 11, 1940, the Lethbridge Experimental Station sponsored a field day at its Nobleford substation on the Chris Withage farm. The featured event was a field demonstration of the three blade implements: the Paul Bunyan cultivator, the Noble straight blade and the Williamson V-blade. All three machines worked well to kill weeds in summer fallow, but in a pull-on-the-drawbar test, the Williamson blade required much less draft power than the Noble blade.

> Here it was found that all three blades on demonstration would go through weeds and trash so extensive that under ordinary farming conditions this amount of trash would never be found.
>
> After this, the pull on the draw-bar test was staged, and with each machine put down at the same depth, that is, about five inches, it was found that the Paul Bunyan cultivator exerted a pressure of 2075 pounds on the draw-bar.
>
> The Williamson blade then tried, and this machine had a draw-bar pressure of 2150 pounds. The Noble blade had 3150 pounds.
>
> It must be pointed out here that both the Paul Bunyan and the Noble blade cut a width of eleven feet, while the Williamson blade cuts ten feet.[61]

According to one report, on seeing the performance of the Williamson blade, Charles Noble exclaimed, "By golly, them boys have got something there!"[62]

In mid-August 1940, Peter Kooy went to the *Lethbridge Herald* to seek some free promotion for the Williamson blade. The *Herald* then reported on the development of the Williamson blade and included Kooy's own story of the blade and its merits:

> The other day Peter Kooy who farms 4½ miles south and 1 mile east of Nobleford came into the office with the accompanying pictures. Mr. Kooy was a youngster when he moved into the district with his father in 1910. He went through the first soil drifting in the district, and when he later acquired land for himself, he did what he could to combat the menace. . . . But he is proudest of the fact that he has helped young George Williamson to develop the Williamson blader, now being built on the Kooy farm. Mr. Kooy

---

[61] *LH*, 19 July 1940; see also 13 July 1940.
[62] As reported by Joe Konynenbelt, who was present at the demonstration.

says any blader is good because it does the cultivating job the right way, but he likes the Williamson machine best for various reasons.

The article continues in the words of Peter Kooy himself:

We all know the story. There ensued a battle against drouth, soil drifting, grasshoppers, weeds, and worms. Man used as weapons tools of tillage that had been standbys for decades, but they proved of no avail in the combat. The struggle became a defeat. Many gave up in despair, abandoned their life's dreams and trekked away.

But some stayed.... These same men believed, too, that soil drifting could be stopped, and the grasshoppers, worms and the weeds beaten....

Through years of ceaseless toil they found the answer. Sub-surface cultivation! It stopped soil drifting. It keeps the snow and rain where it falls and holds it there for a crop to nourish itself. It attacks the weeds at their most vital point, the roots, and destroys grasshopper eggs....

The most ingenious and practical implement ever devised for sub-soil cultivation is the Williamson blade cultivator. It handles every phase of below-surface cultivation so that it is the only implement needed for the manifold requirements of this new method of tillage. It performs the functions of a plow, disk, one-way, duck-foot cultivator, harrow and a rod weeder. Once the land has been broken up, it is the only tillage implement required on a prairie farm.

The Williamson blade cultivator is a product of inventive mechanical ingenuity and stern, hard-fisted experience. It was first made for the personal use of the inventor to combat the very thing that was defeating life in what had become to be known as the "dry belt"—drought, soil drifting, grasshoppers, worms and weeds. So successfully did the first machine perform, and so striking were the results of its cultivation that soon neighbors clamored for like machines of their own. And so today many of those who were ready to give up their struggle against the vicissitudes of the dry belt remained on their farms and are prospering.

The needs of the neighbors were first supplied from the home workshop. Eventually a manufacturing plant had to be consulted to meet the demand.⁶³ But the founders remained at the helm. The machine is still built by its originators whose interests and experience have been rooted in the soil since their babyhood. Into its construction have not gone the notions of theorists pushing pencils behind office desks, but the ideas and innovations of men moved by stark necessity and a lifetime of field experience.

The V-type blade travels below the surface of the area being cultivated. It lifts the soil up, loosens it and breaks it to admit air and moisture, but it leaves the stubble erect and the trash on top, anchored to the broken bits of earth to shade it from the blistering sun, to stop soil drifting, and to collect all the snow and rain into the upright covering. The loosened earth absorbs the moisture like a sponge, and the trash on top keeps the soil cool and checks evaporation. The same operation cuts the weeds at their roots and the special shaped rods behind the blade lift them to perish on the surface.

The V-type blade has been scientifically designed for both strength and light draft. The V-type design imparts a pushing and sliding to the edge of the blade. This combination of motions makes for easiest possible cutting. . . . This design for light draft and most efficient cutting possible will mean gallons and gallons of fuel saved every year in the operation of the machine.

Because, too, of the V-type construction of the blade, the machine handles any kind of soil, whether it be a heavy gumbo or clay, light sand, or earth studded with rocks—wet or dry, it handles them under all conditions. The slicing action of the edge of the V-blade makes short work of the most stubborn weeds, such as rose bush, sweet clover, Canada thistle, and others with thick roots that slide past ordinary cultivators.

The Williamson blade cultivator has received its stamp of approval from the results it has produced for practical farmers consistently over a period of years, from the heads of experimental farms and other agricultural authorities. In offering it to the public, the makers do so with every confidence that it is the best machine ever produced for sub-surface cultivation.⁶⁴

---

[63] Probably the Matthews Manufacturing Co. of Calgary.
[64] "Inventiveness of Nobleford-Monarch Farmers Beats Soil-Drifting Menace: Peter Kooy Tells Story Behind Development of Williamson Blader," *LH*, 16 Aug. 1940.

Williamson-Kooy blade (*courtesy Delbert Kooy*)

On December 16, 1940, Williamson and Kooy filed for a Canadian patent on their improved design of the V-blade; this patent was issued in December 1944.[65] There it was called a "V-blade cultivator and rod weeder." Williamson is listed as the inventor and Kooy as having a half interest in the invention. The focus of the patent was on the single V-blade design and the curved standards. Charles Noble had originally filed for a patent on his straight blade in 1937; but it was not issued until 1948.[66]

To make their production of the blade more efficient, Williamson and Kooy asked August Matthews of Calgary, in 1940, to install one of his newly invented gas torches on the Kooy farm. Matthews had invented the Matthews fluid-gas torch in 1938 as a cheaper alternative to the acetylene cutting and welding torch.[67]

Williamson worked with Kooy for about five years producing small numbers of the Williamson blade, until about 1944. Since most parts were made by hand with a forge and a cutting/welding torch, and since farm work also needed to be done, it took some time to make

[65] Canadian Intellectual Property Office, patent no. 424,584; *The Canadian Patent Office Record* (19 Dec. 1944), 3334.
[66] Patent no. 448,326. Noble applied in 1940 for another patent on his modified machine, with the straight blade behind the wheels; it was issued in 1946; patent no. 435,907.
[67] "Cultivator Improved by Red Deer Inventor," *The Albertan*, 27 March 1948; "Red Deer's New Industry," *Red Deer Advocate*, 2 April 1947.

a single blade. Because of the small numbers, they did not need to advertise. The blades they produced sold by word of mouth in the local market.

In 1944 George's mother sold him the southeast quarter section of the Williamson farm (SE 26-10-25 W4), which was in her name. There George lived in a trailer and built a blacksmith shop where he made some of the blades.[68] He farmed this quarter until he moved north to Red Deer in 1948.

After George no longer worked with him, Peter Kooy continued to make the V-blades on his farm. In early 1946, when Kooy's eldest son Ralph returned home from World War II military service, where he gained welding experience, he helped manufacture the Williamson-Kooy blade on the Kooy farm. After Peter Kooy retired from farming and moved to Abbotsford, British Columbia, in 1949, Ralph Kooy took over the Kooy farm and continued making small numbers of the blade. He produced the V-blade in various widths (8, 9½, 11 and later 12½ feet), and with optional steel wheels or rubber tires, and in 1951, he added the option of an hydraulic pump instead of levers to raise and lower the machine.[69] In the mid-1950s, Ralph began to regularly advertise new and used V-blades in the classified pages of the *Lethbridge Herald*.[70] This continued until about a year before Ralph quit farming and moved to Quincy, Washington, in late 1961.[71]

Claiming patent infringement, in late 1955, Noble asked Ralph Kooy to pay a royalty of 2½ percent on each blade he manufactured. After initially denying that there was any infringement, Kooy signed a licensing agreement in 1956 to pay such royalties, and at the end of that year, he paid the royalty for two V-blades that he sold during the year, each for $445.[72]

In all, production of small numbers of the Williamson-Kooy blade continued for about twenty years as either a one- or two-man operation.

---

[68] Interview with Klaas Poelman, 25 Aug. 2017.
[69] V-blade papers of the Ralph Kooy family, Quincy WA, including price lists for 1950-53, 1957 and 1960.
[70] The ads appeared regularly from 7 July 1955 until 31 May 1960. The latest new price was $480 for an eleven-foot blade.
[71] On the Kooy family, see *LH*, 16 Jan. 1946, 28 Jan. 1949, 21 Oct., 7 Dec. 1961.
[72] Glenbow Archives, Charles S. Noble fonds (hereafter: GA, Noble), Series 5, M-7697-5. After Noble was issued his original patent in 1948, his company raised issues of patent infringement against several other small companies that manufactured the Victory blade, Johnson blade, Renn blade, and Gareau blade, all of which started manufacturing after Noble and Williamson. Like Kooy, Victory and Gareau entered into licensing agreements with Noble and paid royalties on blades they produced. GA, Noble, Series 5, M-7697-1, M-7697-2, M-7697-6, M-7697-7.

Meanwhile, a few Williamson blades were also manufactured by the Matthews Manufacturing Company of Red Deer, north of Calgary. August Matthews had started this company to manufacture his gas torch. But he remained interested in the Williamson blade, and in about 1947, he invented an improvement of the blade—a mechanism with vacuumatic controls, operating off the tractor's intake manifold, enabling the operator, by means of fingertip controls, to raise and lower the blade at will, instead of moving cumbersome levers. Matthews purchased from Williamson and Kooy the right to manufacture the blade, and by early 1948, he began production in his Red Deer shop, making the first two blades with this improvement.[73] He modified Williamson's original design by using three smaller V-blades instead of the single V.

George Williamson married Alice Mason of Granum in December 1947, and the following year, he farmed the three quarters of his father's Granum farm, along with his own quarter. In the fall of 1948, George went to Red Deer to work for Matthews just for the winter, but he and his wife liked living in Red Deer, so they stayed and settled there.[74] George continued to work for Matthews, but he mostly worked on producing gas torches. Since the Matthews' shop was small, the two men rented a larger facility in early 1949 as a small factory in which they hoped to begin production of the Williamson V-blade.[75]

George worked in partnership with Matthews Manufacturing to produce a few of the Williamson blades until 1951, when the Noble corporation forced them out of business over the issue of patent infringement. Noble first raised this issue in March 1949. On the one hand, Noble could legitimately claim that its 1948 patent for the straight blade covered the blade assembly—the blade and blade support that cut weeds beneath the surface of the soil, leaving a trash cover. On the other hand, Williamson's 1944 patent covered the concept of a V-shaped blade. Williamson claimed that his patent exonerated him from the charge of infringement. Noble's high-powered, patent-attorney firm, Fetherstonhaugh and Company, of Winnipeg, however, contended that Williamson had an exceedingly narrow patent that was not prepared by an experienced patent attorney. With threat of litigation, Fetherstonhaugh and Company claimed that Noble's 1948 patent covered the blade and carrier combination, regardless of whether

---

[73] "Cultivator Improved by Red Deer Inventor," *The Albertan*, 27 March 1948.
[74] Interview with Alice Williamson, 19 Nov. 2016.
[75] "A Farmer's Invention Helps;" letter of Noble to Fetherstonhaugh, 24 May 1949; GA, Noble, Series 5, M-7697-8.

Williamson employed a V-shaped blade and carrier or a straight one.[76] The infringement issue lingered for two years while Williamson and Matthews continued to make a few of the V-blades. Finally, when Noble decided to take legal action, Williamson and Matthews, succumbing to the pressure, decided not to legally defend their case, and before July 1951, they ceased operations.[77] A year earlier George had taken up farming near Red Deer.[78]

Williamson did, however, hold a valid legal patent focusing on the V-blade concept, and it was Charles Noble who actually took over from Williamson the idea of the single V-blade. He modified it to develop models of the Noble V-blade that became extremely popular.

Noble's first blade cultivator of 1935-36 had a straight blade in front of the wheels. In late 1937, Noble placed the straight blade behind the wheels.[79] His first blades were made in the machine shop of his Nobleford farm, but with increasing demand, he built a manufacturing plant in Nobleford in 1941, later expanding his operations in a large new plant in 1951.[80]

It was first in 1941 that Noble produced a model of his straight blade that had an interchangeable attachment consisting of two "shovels" or V-blades, connected to the two standards that otherwise held the straight blade.[81] Then in 1948, Noble adopted the single V-blade concept in his popular model M Noble blade.[82] This was a single

[76] Letter of Fetherstonhaugh & Co. to George Williamson, 13 June 1949; GA, Noble, Series 5, M-7697-8.
[77] Correspondence in GA, Noble, Series 5, M-7697-8. Letter of George Willamson to Noble Cultivators, 31 July 1951. On the issue of patent infringement, I have benefitted from the legal advice of Glen Poelman, a federal justice of the Court of Queen's Bench, Alberta.
[78] Always an inventor, Williamson continued to design a number of inventions, most notably a fifteen-bale manual stooker in 1964 and then an automatic six-bale stooker in 1970, both of which he manufactured. He died in 1985.
[79] Charles Noble letter to S. Visser; GA, Noble, M-7198-42.
[80] On the invention and development of the Noble blade, see MacEwan, *Charles Noble*, ch. 18; S. F. Noble, "Noble Blade Meets West's Farm Needs," *LH*, 23 Feb. 1952.
[81] "Dry Farming Adventures," *Family Herald and Weekly Star* (15 Oct. 1941), 6; brochure, "Noble Cultivator and Attachments for Cover-Cultivation," advertises the "new '42 blade, shovel and weeder combination;" GA, Noble, Series 5, M-7198-71 (incorrectly dated 1939). Charles' son Shirley later wrote, "It was not for some 4 or 5 years after we started with the straight blade that we included the Vs in our line." Shirley Noble letter to O. S. Longman, 14 June 1956; GA, Noble, Series 5, M-2427-2.
[82] Noble's Canadian Price List (May 26, 1947) contains models A, B, C, and D, all consisting of varying sizes of the straight blade, with weeder blade and two-shovel attachments, not yet the single V-blade; GA, Noble, Series 5, M-7697-10. Cf. Noble ad in *LH*, 11 Dec. 1947.

V-blade that was narrower and heavier than the Williamson blade. The blade was attached to the sturdy frame by a single standard in the center (rather than the three on Williamson's blade), and the angle of the V was sharper. It was also fitted with an hydraulic pump to raise and lower the machine.[83] In the mid-1950s, Noble's very popular model K was made, again employing a single V-blade. Noble's modified design of the single V-blade was superior to the Williamson V-blade, and Noble had the resources to manufacture the blade in large numbers in his manufacturing plant in Nobleford.

The Noble V-blade, especially models M and K, soon became a standard farm implement for summer fallowing throughout the Canadian Prairies and American Great Plains, as far south as Texas, and it was also exported abroad to Australia, Russia, Argentina, South Africa, India, and other countries.[84] Though it was Noble who captured the market for the V-blade, which proved to be the most effective means of combatting soil drifting by leaving a trash cover, it needs to be recognized that his version was a modified form of the single V-blade, originally invented by George Williamson.

Together, strip farming and the V-blade were effective means of preventing soil drifting for a half century. Summer fallowing was phased out in the 1990s with the advent of no-till farming, chemical weed killers, and fertilizers.[85] At any rate, credit for the two innovations that had such a profound impact on preventing soil drifting goes to the creative ingenuity of Dutch Canadian farmers in Southern Alberta.

---

[83] Brochure, "Noble Model 'M' Cultivator," GA, Noble, Series 5, M-2429.
[84] By 1979 Noble had sold more than 10,000 blades.
[85] W. Carlyle, "The Decline of Summer Fallow on the Canadian Prairies," *The Canadian Geographer* 41 (1997), 267-80.

CHAPTER 6

"This locality was settled by Hollanders": The Dutch in Wayne County, New York, since 1800

Janet Sjaarda Sheeres

"This locality was settled by Hollanders." With this short sentence, W. H. McIntosh, author of *The History of Wayne County, NY,* dismissed the Dutch who had settled in Wayne County.[1] But there is much more to the story. This chapter will cover the place, people, products, and progress of Wayne County, New York.

The place

Wayne County is located on the southern shores of Lake Ontario in the Finger Lakes district of New York State. It was part of the Holland Land Company—land purchased by a Dutch consortium in 1792 and 1793.[2] The ground is exceptionally fertile with the soil having

---

[1] W. H. McIntosh, *The History of Wayne County, NY* (Pultneyville, NY: Yankee Peddler, Bookshop, 1975), 189. This 9x12, 298-page, densely written, 6-pt.-font book has 75 biographical entries of outstanding men in Wayne County, NY, without one Dutch-born person mentioned.

[2] The Holland Land Company was an unincorporated syndicate of thirteen Dutch investors from Amsterdam, who in 1792 and 1793 purchased land in central and western New York State, and western Pennsylvania. The syndicate hoped to sell

been formed over thousands of years after the last Ice Age. A layer of clay under the peat keeps the water in, but with proper drainage, the land can be highly productive. The large areas of muck are conducive to growing potatoes and a variety of other vegetables. Great stretches of profitable agricultural land were cleared by cutting down forests.

As far as the climate is concerned, temperatures of extreme heat and cold are modified by the influence of Lake Ontario. The lake provides a longer, cooler spring, so blossoms are protected, and a longer warmth in the fall for the fruit to ripen and be harvested. The cool nights and warm days in the summer help develop the starch in the fruit into sugar.

In 1823 the Erie Canal came through the county. Running from Albany to Rochester, it provided a valuable link to markets. In 1841 the Rochester and Syracuse Railroad brought about another opening for commerce. This meant that early in the century, Wayne County provided a splendid delivery system for goods coming in and products going out. It was an ideal place for settlement—villages along the canal benefited from the barge traffic, and property values remained high.

The people

Although Pultneyville in Wayne County was one of the earliest settlements of Dutch-born immigrants in the United States in the nineteenth century, it now ranks near the bottom of being recognized as such. In fact, few historians, except for Jacob Van Hinte and Henry Lucas, have spent any time describing it.[3] This is curious because Pultneyville was settled by at least a few Dutch-born families some years before Van Raalte arrived in the United States and founded Holland, Michigan.

Even though the Cayuga and Seneca Indian tribes consider this part of New York State their ancestral home, Wayne County did

---

the land rapidly at great profit. Instead, for many years, they were forced to make further investments in their purchase; surveying it, building roads, and digging canals to make it more attractive to settlers. They sold the last of their land interests in 1840, when the syndicate was dissolved.

3   Jacob Van Hinte, *Netherlanders in America: A Study of Emigration and Settlement in the 19th and 20th Centuries in the United States of America*, ed. Robert P. Swierenga, trans. Adriaan de Wit (Grand Rapids: Baker Book House, 1985), 804-6; Henry S. Lucas, *Netherlanders in America: Dutch Immigration to the United States and Canada, 1789-1950* (Grand Rapids: Eerdmans, 1989), 38, 39. Hans Krabbendam mentions Pultneyville, NY, only in passing in *Freedom on the Horizon: Dutch Immigration to America, 1840-1940* (Grand Rapids, Eerdmans, 2009), 43, 70, 81, 201.

not have large settlements of these indigenous people. The only early peoples were small Indian tribes and white fur traders passing through. The first pioneers, mostly from the New England states, arrived in the 1780s. These settlers were given land grants as a reward for their efforts in fighting against the British in the War for Independence. Some of their family names were Van Dusen, Vander Veer, Van Camp, Vanderbilt, Van Tassel, Van Valkenburg, Voorhis, and so forth. These old New York Dutch pioneers should not be confused with the later Dutch-born settlers who arrived early in the nineteenth century and are the subject of this chapter.

The earliest nineteenth-century, Dutch-born settlers in Wayne County came from the province of Zeeland in the Netherlands. They likely followed the first settler, Abraham Peper, who hailed from that area and drew others from the same region.

War often unsettles and displaces people. Such was also the case with Abraham Peper, a farmer living in Oost-Souburg, near Vlissingen, on the Dutch island of Walcheren, in the province of Zeeland. In 1795 the French invaded the Netherlands, and in 1801, Peper, according to the family's written account, had an altercation with one of the French soldiers billeted in his home.[4] When one of them insulted his family, Peper became angry and attacked the soldier with a farm implement. He was brought to trial but was acquitted on the basis of defending his own home. Nevertheless, his friends advised him that he should seriously consider leaving the country before the French confiscated his property. Accepting their advice, Peper held an estate sale in March 1802, the proceeds of which, including those of the real estate, amounted to approximately five thousand gold guilders.[5] Later that month, he and his family boarded the SS *Factor* in Den Helder and sailed to America. Although Antwerp would have been more convenient, Peper assumed it would also have been more perilous, since the port was in French hands, so instead, he traveled north, first to Amsterdam and then to Den Helder, from which the family departed.[6]

---

[4] A. P. van Langevelde, "De Peper-familie uit Holland," in *In Den Vreemde, Een blad voor geinteresseerden in Emigratie en Immigratie* (4 June 1993), 57-58.

[5] Lilian Dominicus, *Zeeuwen in Amerika: verhalen van emigranten door de eeuwen heen* (Kats: De Buitenspelers, 2011), 50.

[6] Lucas, *Netherlanders in America*, 28. Peper may have wanted to stop over in Amsterdam to purchase land from the Holland Land Company agent so that he did not have to travel with a chest full of gold guilders. Lucas names Peper as one of several Hollanders settling on Holland Land Company.

Peper was born on November 2, 1757, and in 1784, as a widower, he married the five-years-younger Willemina Blommert. Of their eight children, seven emigrated with them. In the Netherlands, Peper was a well-respected person, addressed as *Burger* (citizen), which, during the French occupation, would have been *Citoyen*. He was a lodge member in the Netherlands and later a founder of the Masonic Lodge in Pultneyville.[7] He also came with a glowing testimony from his church in Oost-Souburg, signed on March 2, 1802, by his pastor, Rudolph Englebert.[8] That he was a faithful church goer is evidenced by the fact that in America he was called "Deacon Peper."

In the 1810 United States Federal Census, Peper is listed as living in Cazenovia, Madison County, New York. Cazenovia was named after Theophilus Cazenove, one of the Holland Land Company agents. This verifies Lucas's statement that "Several Hollanders indeed settled on [Holland Land Company] lands, but they failed—among them, J. Butin, Abraham Peper, and Simon Didama."[9] By 1814 Peper was living in Pultneyville, in Wayne County, where he purchased acreage and began farming.[10] Beginning in 1808, the land around Williamson had become available for settlement, and the first roads were laid in 1810. In 1814 Abraham Peper Sr.'s and Abraham Peper Jr.'s names appeared on the road-tax rolls. Shortly after his arrival in Wayne County, Abraham Peper Sr. planted an orchard between the cemetery and his house on Lake Ontario.[11] He died May 9, 1845, at age eighty-eight and is buried in the Lakeview Cemetery in Pultneyville. Peper Jr. also lived the remainder of his life in Pultneyville, where he kept sheep.[12]

---

[7] Pultneyville Lodge #159 is a Regular and Recognized Masonic Lodge, having a charter through the Grand Lodge of NY, F&AM, recognized by the United Grand Lodge of England.

[8] *In den Vreemde* 4, no. 2 (June 1993).

[9] Lucas, *Netherlanders in America*, 28. Van Hinte, *Netherlanders in America*, 115, states that in 1801 Buffalo, NY, was laid out by the Holland Land Company as the city of New Amsterdam, but the name did not catch on.

[10] The family records put an Abraham Peper in Wayne County by 1810, while there is still an A. Peper listed in the 1810 United States Federal Census (hereafter USFC) in Cazenovia, so either he came right after that, or it may have been Abraham Peper Jr. still living in Cazenovia.

[11] America's oldest apple tree is believed to be the one planted by Peter Stuyvesant in 1647. He was the governor of "New Amsterdam" at the time he planted the tree in his Manhattan orchard. It was still bearing fruit 219 years later in 1866 when it was run over by a derailed train.

[12] The 1820 USFC of Wayne County list the following Dutch born: John De Kruyf, Abraham Pepper (Peffer), Abram Pepper (probably Abraham Jr.), and John Pepper.

Even though the elder Peper corresponded with friends in the Netherlands, at first, few took him up on his invitation to emigrate. As time passed, however, more people joined him. Research on the people who arrived, and whence they came, demonstrates a classic example of "cluster and chain" immigration. The following Dutch, all from the same area in the province of Zeeland, joined Peper during the first half of the 1800s.[13]

1802: John De Kruif (De Kruijft) (1773-1853), who married Maatje Peper in April 1803, in Deerfield, New York.

1811: The Albright family (Jan Albregts and Pieternella Louwerse), from Oost-Souburg, Vlissingen.

1830: William Wilhuis.

1832: Hubertus Luitwieler from Vlissingen, with wife and seven children.

1836: Jan Cappon from Walcheren, settled near Pultneyville and wrote letters home.[14]

1837: Jacob Hijnolf/Hinolf (Hinold), with wife and two children, from Vlissingen.

1839: Arnold Jobse, farmer (48), with wife, Pieternella Zachariase, and eight children, from Zoutelande, near Vlissingen; Willem Stoutenburg.

1840: Pieter Vander Driest (23), farmer, from Westkapelle.

1841: Jannis Cappon from Cadzand, with wife and four children; D. De Lelys (de Lelijs).

1842: The Daane family from Westkapelle; Jan Bruzijn/Brusijn from Zuidzand; Pieter Vander Driest's mother, Aplonia Willeboordse (56), widow of Jan Vander Driest.

1843: Jacobus and Jacob Pieter Eernisse families from Cadzand, who later settled in Rochester.

---

[13] A. Vergouw, *Emigranten naar Amerika uit West Zeeuws-Vlaanderen 1840-1970* (Kapelle: Werkgroep Emigratie van de afdeling Zeeland van de Nederlandse Genealogische Vereniging, 1993); Dominicus, *Zeeuwen naar Amerika*; USFC, Wayne County Genealogical information at http://wayne.nygenweb.net.

[14] Donna Martha Dean, *The Dutch Immigration into Wayne County*, Hoffman Essay 57-01, Wayne County Historian's Office.

1843: Elizabeth Callieux (18 and single) and Elizabeth Callieux (63), from Retranchement; Maarten den Hollander from Oostkapelle.

1844: Jacob Puijenbroek, from Aardenberg (born 12-16-1785), saw the possibilities of agriculture in the area and wrote enthusiastic letters home. Isaac du Bois, with wife and seven children; Pieter Jacob and Abraham Eernisse families, who later settled in Rochester.

1844: Jacob Bril, 76, wife and two children from Cadzand; Jan Bakelaar; Adriaan Bakelaar from Retranchement.

1844: Pieter Caillieux, farmer, wife Elizabeth Butijn/Butin, and four children from Retranchement.

1844: Pieter Bouwens, blacksmith, married to Adriana Clicquennoi, sister of Marinus; Joosse family.

1845: Leendert Faas family from Oostburg and Jan De Die (64) and wife from Biervliet; De Ruijscher family from Oostburg.

1845: Marinus Clicquennoi and party of 156 people.

1846: Peter Bom from Kapelle; Johannes De Visser (lay pastor) from Vlissingen. Isaac Pleijte (Plyte).

In 1846 and 1847, two large groups, including many from the province of Zeeland, emigrated with the Revs. Van der Meulen and Van Raalte to Zeeland and Holland, Michigan, but the large numbers make it difficult to track the individual immigrant to his or her final settlement.

Marinus Clicquennoi from Cadzand was the leader of what is regarded as the first and only, large organized group of West Zeeuws Flemish immigrants. The group arrived in New York on the *Henry Shelter* on June 7, 1845, and settled in East Williamson, about five miles southwest of Pultneyville.[15] The group of mostly poor laborers consisted of 156 people—from seventy to eighty adults and the remainder children. Clicquennoi was the widower of Sara de Bruijne, who died in 1836 in the Netherlands. His in-laws (Sara's parents)—the de Bruijne and Pleijte families—were in the group. In Wayne County, he married Jenny (last name unknown at present).

---

[15] Dominicus, *Zeeuwen in Amerika*, 70.

The adult men tried to find work in the Rochester flour mills and factories, but because they were uneducated and did not speak English, they found it difficult to obtain employment. In order to find work and housing, two of them, Johannes and Levinus Buurman, moved to Williamson, where they found work in the saw mills. Marinus Clicquennoi and Johannes Platschaert followed the Buurmans to Williamson and found employment as blacksmiths. Soon, others of the Clicquennoi group joined them, so these families were already living in the area when Van Raalte came through in 1846. He stopped in Rochester and found many wealthy and hospitable families of Dutch descent who may have told him about the colonies in Williamson, Sodus, and Pultneyville.[16]

Many of the 1845 immigrants to Wayne County originated in Zeeuws Flanders and were descendants of the French Huguenots. Their names betray their origin: Caillieux, Platschaert, Clicquennoi, DuBois, Du Mez, De Bert, Lefebre, Neufeglise, and so forth. The Zeeuws people had suffered as much, if not more, as other Dutch people from the French during the French (Napoleonic) occupation. Indeed, their persecution stretched further back to the Dutch Eighty Years' War with Spain. When the Dutch and Spanish finally signed the peace accord on June 5, 1648, which had to be ratified by the various provinces of the republic, the province of Zeeland refused to sign. Officially, therefore, the province was still at war with Spain when these emigrants set sail.[17] This streak of independence among Zeelanders would characterize their Americanization process. They soon anglicized their names. Caillieux (the Dutch Callieuy and Calijouw, Kaljouw) to Callicutt; Bruijnooge to Bruno; Albrecht/Albregtse/Albregts/Albrecht to Albright; Bakelaar to Buckley; Koets to Coats; de Bruijne to De Brine; Platschaert to Prescott; Van Huizen to Fenhouse, and so forth.

Jozias Bruijnooge, of Pickleville (later East Williamson), tried to preserve the Dutch language among his fellow settlers. In the November 17, 1849, issue of *De Sheboygan Nieuwsbode*, he begged his "fellow Dutch brethren" to subscribe to this Dutch-language newspaper, because "This could serve as a useful purpose for your children to maintain and cultivate your so dear mother tongue." He lamented the fact that in many areas there were no Dutch school teachers and that Dutch

---

[16] Adrian Van Koevering, *Legends of the Dutch* (Zeeland, MI: Zeeland Record Co., 1960), 141.

[17] Geert Mak, *De levens van Jan Six, een familie geschiedenis* (Amsterdam: Atlas/Contact, 2017), 58.

was not preached in worship services.[18] He garnered some results. The January 8, 1850, issue of the *Nieuwsbode* acknowledged the receipt of six dollars and printed the names of at least six subscribers in Wayne County.[19] By November 1850, Jozias had become the newspaper's agent for Wayne County.[20] Because many of their fellow Zeelanders had settled in Sheboygan, Wisconsin, the newspaper, no doubt, was read not only to keep up the Dutch language but also to keep up with the news of Sheboygan and, for Sheboygan readers, the Wayne County Dutch folks.

Jozias's complaint about the lack of preaching in Dutch came because there were already several established churches preaching in English. Already in 1812, the Methodists had established a congregation in Ontario, and in 1816, the Presbyterians established a congregation in Williamson. In 1824 the Reformed Protestant Dutch Church (now the Reformed Church in America) formed a mission station in Pultneyville. According to Vergouwe, Rev. Johannes Visser, an immigrant from Zeeland, was already preaching there.[21] There were enough Reformed-minded people to form congregations in 1851 in East Williamson, in 1860 in Marion, and in 1883 in Newark. The East Williamson Reformed Church began in 1847 as the Presbyterian Church of Pickleville (later East Williamson).[22] Not until 1907 did the Christian Reformed Church succeed in establishing a congregation in East Palmyra.[23]

The produce

After clearing the land, the first settlers in Wayne County farmed for home consumption only. Besides farming, they engaged in work in

---

[18] *De Sheboygan Nieuwsbode*, J. Quintus, ed. (17 Nov. 1849). Bruijnooge is referring to the fact that some of the churches in the area had been founded by earlier, English-speaking settlers.

[19] Ibid. 8 Jan. 1850.

[20] Ibid. 24 Oct. 1850.

[21] Johannes (de) Visser, with his wife, emigrated in 1846 from Vlissingen, Zeeland; www.Zeeuwengezocht.nl.

[22] George W. Cowles, *Landmarks of Wayne County, New York* (Syracuse, NY: D. Mason & Co., 1895), 192-93.

[23] Russell L. Gasero, *Historical Directory of the Reformed Church in America* (Grand Rapids, MI: Eerdmans, 2001), 620. In 1824 the Reformed Church began a mission station in Pultneyville Station, NY, with missionary Jonathan F. Morris. It lasted one year. According to McIntosh in the *History of Wayne County*, 125, the Reformed Church of Marion was organized in 1860. The church was first legally organized by Rev. J. W. Warnshuis, in 1870, with fifty-six members. The wooden edifice, 40' x 72', was built in Marion in 1872 and seated five hundred people. It was dedicated during that same fall. The valuation of that church property was $8,000. In 1871, J. W. Warnshuis was installed as pastor and continued serving until October 1876; after that, it was served by many pastors but finally disbanded in 1998; Gasero, *Historical Directory*, 581-82.

sawmills, carpentry, and blacksmithing, as well as potash and charcoal production. By midcentury, with improved avenues of transportation opening markets, fruit, grain, and dairy farming gained in importance.

In a lengthy article in the February 1, 1853, issue of *De Sheboygan Nieuwsbode*, Jacobus A. Buerman (Buurman) described the conditions in Williamson (including Pultneyville and Pickleville), Wayne County, as follows:

> [T]he southern area is hilly, but the northern area is flat and made up of clay and pebbly soil that produces excellent crops. Three-fourths of the land is arable, with the remainder forest filled with outstanding trees for lumber such as ash, maple, beech, hemlock, etc., all fetching high prices. In the summer, it is pleasant to walk the straight roads through the beautiful farms and orchards and see the countless varieties of fruit trees heavily laden with fruit. The land here sells for $25 to $50 per acre, and yields 25 bushels of wheat per acre, which we sell for $1.00 per bushel.... I advise Dutch immigrants who want to purchase land to settle their families in Rochester first, then come here and look around, and then go to Sheboygan, Wisconsin. When the immigrant has seen both areas, he will say, "In Pickleville and Pultneyville are the most thriving Dutch areas; the farmers' barns are filled with cattle, and the fields are teeming with crops." The laborer who had nothing in the Netherlands can become a landowner here. We live here with some 800 Hollanders and have plentiful food, because everyone who wants to work can and is able to earn more than he needs to live on, because the wages here are very high. Last summer one could not find enough people willing to work for $1.00 to $1.25 a day. We have about forty farms in our settlement, many that may be compared to the ones in Zeeland [the Netherlands]. We have two Dutch stores, a smithy, a steam sawmill, two shoemakers, a mason, a carpenter, a Dutch school, and two Dutch churches. A Presbyterian church built of wood, 24 by 40 feet and 12 feet high, and a Dutch Reformed church built of stone, 34 by 50 feet and 20 feet high. And, while eight years ago there was no Dutch spoken here, now you hear almost nothing else.[24]

According to Buerman, the Dutch-born immigrants in Wayne County were comfortable with their work environments, including the

---

[24] *De Sheboygan Nieuwsbode* (1 Feb. 1853). I have translated only the salient parts.

fruit industry. Already in the Middle Ages, fruit was cultivated back home in the Kapelle area and was, in fact, a sizable industry in Zeeland. The Zeelanders also knew how to grow potatoes and vegetables on clay by draining it.[25] Thus, their involvement in fruit and vegetable husbandry in Wayne County came naturally.

These industries provided high employment for the Dutch immigrants, including married women and school children, who helped harvest and pack the fruits and vegetables. The people worked first for other landowners before they could rent and then finally purchase their own land. According to Isaac Faro, many new immigrants also turned to share cropping as a beginning enterprise.[26]

Still, the acquisition of land was a slow process. Thirty years after Buerman's article in the *Nieuwsbode*, the 1880 federal census reported that of the 893 Dutch-born males, 237 were listed as farmers and 161 as farm laborers. The remaining occupations included blacksmiths, carpenters, masons, merchants, and so forth. In the 1891-92 list of the 328 property owners in Williamson, only sixty had Dutch names, and some of these may have been second generation.[27]

The 1880 federal census also listed 854 Dutch-born women.[28] Unfortunately, the census takers did not record the occupations of the married women, even though they were mandated to do so. All the married women in Wayne County were listed as "keeping house." We know that there must have been a number of seamstresses, milliners, laundresses, midwives, and others. Four of these Dutch-born immigrant women who worked as midwives were: Susan Tack Brill Ameele (1848-1929) and Katherina Plattenberg Langeraad (1820-1915) in the early years and Suzanne E. Wisse Den Hartogh (1865-1963) and Margaret Wisse Tack (1870-1955) in later years.

The same census recorded all the fifty-five young single women in Wayne County working as domestic servants, three of whom were just thirteen years old.[29] Domestic service seems to have been the only option open to these newcomer single women. In an 1849 letter to a friend in the Netherlands, Magdalena Elias wrote from Pultneyville,

---

[25] http://www.fruitteeltmuseum.nl/vaste-expositie.html.
[26] Isaac Faro, *Dutch Immigrant* (n.p., 1984), 40.
[27] *The Wayne County Directory for 1891-92* (Newburgh, NY: L. P. Waite & Co., 1892).
[28] Age ranges were: born between 1810 and 1830 (276); 1830 and 1850 (310); and 1850 and 1870 (268).
[29] They were Jenny Bridge (Brugge), Carry Gilsy (Gillis), and Susan Mayow (Mahieu).

I was twenty-two weeks at one place and received 22 dollars, one dollar a week, which is really 55 Netherlands guilders. . . . The name of the place is Palmyra. I live here with eleven Holland girls. If Holland girls are available, people won't hire others. They have high regard for the Holland people because they're good workers and can be trusted.[30]

Magdalena was born in 1823, in IJzendijke, Zeeland, and arrived in Wayne County in June 1848, a year before writing her letter. At twenty-six, she was one of the oldest domestics. Most young women had married by that age. The youngest Dutch-born domestic servant recorded in Wayne County was twelve-year-old Magdalena Eernisse who worked for Dr. Alvin W. Marsh and his wife in the town of Arcadia in 1850. She would remain a domestic all her life, later moving to Rochester, where she died at the age of forty-nine, still single.

The 1900 federal census for Wayne County lists 1,220 Dutch-born males. Not counting the males too young and too old to work, the following occupations were listed: 518 farmers, 403 farm and day laborers, 7 teamsters, 9 masons, 4 carpenters, 4 clerks, 2 teachers, 2 blacksmiths, 2 salesmen, 2 merchants, and 1 pastor. If we count the small business workers with the farm laborers, the ratio of laborers to farmers is almost equal.

There were also 1,107 Dutch-born females recorded in the 1900 federal census, with 816 of those listed as married and 109 widowed. Of the remaining 181 single women, 53 were domestic servants, and the balance were girls too young to work. The usual female occupations of the era were dressmaker, milliner, teacher, and nurse. These roles were all reserved for women born in the United States. The fact that none of these occupations was filled by Dutch-born women reflects the fact that the immigrant female still had an uphill climb to achieve an occupation besides that of domestic servant, even at the turn of the century. For those immigrants engaged in growing fruits and vegetables, it may be safely assumed that the married women worked side by side with their husbands.

As the twentieth century progressed, so did the production of fruits and vegetables in Wayne County. Fruit trees included apple, pear, peach, cherry, and plum, and according to the 1920 census, the number

---

[30] Magdalena Elias to Adriaan de Priester and wife, letter dated 1849, col. 78, box 22, ACC.

of fruit trees of fruit-bearing age in Wayne County was 1,487,242, broken down as follows: 906,938 apple, 195,628 peach, 216,982 pear, 145,453 cherry, and 22,242 plum.[31] Today Wayne County ranks third in the state of New York for the number of fruit trees, first in the number of apple trees, and second in the production of orchard fruit.[32] The most intensively farmed fruit areas are in the towns of Sodus, Williamson, Ontario, Huron, Walcott, Rose, Marion, and Walworth, with the first two the most extensive. Since Sodus, Williamson, and Ontario are where the most Dutch are concentrated, it may be assumed that most of them are engaged in this work, either as farm owners or laborers or in ancillary and support services.

Also lucrative to the area's income was the processing of fruits and vegetables. Canning factories had developed by 1910, providing paid work for women as well as men. Drying fruit became another way to add to the area's economy. So important was the apple crop to the military that, during WWII, Wayne County was granted the benefit of German prisoners of war to help harvest and process the fruit. The *Sodus Record* reported that 115 German prisoners of war arrived from Florida on September 7, 1944, and were placed at various farms and factories. Fifty-five of the prisoners went to work immediately. The others stayed in the camp to help fix up their quarters.[33] Later, freezing and related processing of produce would continue the development of the local agricultural economy.

Vegetables raised in Wayne County included potatoes, celery, onions, spinach, and kidney beans. Peppermint was also a highly profitable crop.[34] Peppermint processing began in the early 1820s and at one time was the chief agricultural product of the state, dictating the market. Peppermint is a bush-like plant that grows in wetlands to a height of about three feet. Farmers cut the plant with scythes and piled it in rows to dry. Oil from the peppermint plants was processed in laboratories and bottled in bottling rooms. Early bottles were cobalt blue and made at the Ely Glass Works located in Clyde, New York.

Thanks to the pluck and hard work of generations of residents, Wayne County has become one of America's foremost orchard areas, with

[31] All Wayne County statistics from the United States Census Bureau at: https://www.census.gov/quickfacts/fact/table/waynecountynewyork/PST045216.
[32] All Wayne County fruit growing statistics from the United States Dept. of Agriculture at https://www.agcensus.usda.gov/Publications/2012.
[33] http://www.historicsoduspoint.com.
[34] See: http://www.lifeinthefingerlakes.com/minty-history-lyons.

Dutch immigrants and their descendants undoubtedly contributing to its success. Unfortunately, the federal censuses described the orchard keepers simply as farmers, so it is difficult in the end to tell exactly who and how many of the Dutch engaged in fruit growing. In any case, Wayne County prospered not only because of the presence of the Erie Canal but also because of its fruit and vegetable production.

The progress

A third-generation Dutch American who grew up in Wayne County remarked, "I never got the feeling that it was a 'Dutch' community."[35] Several factors may have contributed to this lack of a sense of Dutch identity:

1. Despite his five thousand gold guilders, Peper was not a colonizer; he had no great aspiration to establish a "Dutch" colony like Van Raalte had done in Holland, Michigan.
2. The Dutch immigrants who came to Wayne County did not emigrate because of religious persecution, and there was no leading Dutch clergyman to form a Dutch "nucleus" and encourage cohesiveness. Rather, they came for economic or political reasons and wanted to merge quickly into their new communities.
3. The first Dutch-born settlers were too poor to purchase farms. They worked primarily for other farmers or in trades, such as blacksmiths and carpenters. As a result, leadership from well-to-do, Dutch-born landowners or professional people was lacking. The early township and county supervisor positions do not list any Dutch-born names. In other words, there was no early Dutch-born leadership. Even a century after Peper's arrival in Wayne County, the only professional person of the 278 Dutch immigrants listed in the 1910 federal census of the township of Arcadia (situated just south of the township of Sodus), was the pastor. The others were: 115 farmers, 49 farm laborers, 42 day-laborers, 26 in skilled trades, and 45 in various other non-skilled jobs.[36]

---

[35] Interview with Rev. Kenneth Havert in Grand Rapids, MI, Dec. 2016. His grandfather had immigrated in 1906 from Breskens, Zeeland.
[36] R. Hoeltzel, *Hometown History, Village of Newark, Village of Arcadia* (Newark, NY: Gene McLellan for Arcadia Historical Society, 2000), 102.

4. With few other Dutch-born immigrants available as potential spouses, eligible Dutch men and women intermarried with non-Dutch neighbors, accelerating the Americanization process.
5. With the towns and roads already named and laid out, the Dutch-born were not able to put their own stamp on their surroundings; rather, they just "fitted in" to existing, non-Dutch communities.
6. According to Van Hinte, these Zeeuws-Flanders immigrants did not have the strong ties to the Netherlands that the more inland Dutch had. They were never really Dutch to begin with, he maintained. Van Hinte put it this way:

> Real leaders, men of some education, were not found among them. For this reason, and also due to the gradual growth of the area, we have heard and still hear so little of this settlement. This lack of leaders also explains why these Hollanders, who at times settle amid the descendants of their 17th-century fellow Dutch, nevertheless kept so little of their Dutch characteristics but have become Americanized largely due to the New England elements that arrived and soon outnumbered the Old Dutch.[37]

7. By 1850 there were 237 Dutch-born residents in Wayne County.[38] At the same time, there were a total of 902 Dutch-born immigrants in Ottawa and Allegan Counties in Michigan.[39] The latter had a much larger core of Dutch-born to begin with and were able to maintain their ethnic identity as a result.
8. Many Dutch immigrants who arrived in Wayne County stayed only long enough to earn funds to travel on to more "Dutch" communities, like Sheboygan, Wisconsin. Therefore, a critical mass of Dutch people never took hold.

This may also explain why there is no Dutch Tulip Time in the county to celebrate its Dutch roots and identity. Of the sixty festivals or festivities held annually in Wayne County, there are no specific Dutch events. The Williamson-Pultneyville Historical Society gets together

---

[37] Van Hinte, *Netherlanders in America*, 804.
[38] In the neighboring counties of Monroe (including Rochester), there were 236 Dutch-born and 258 Dutch-born living Erie County (including Buffalo).
[39] In Michigan, the numbers per county were 1,892 Dutch-born living in Ottawa County, 546 Dutch-born living in Allegan County, and 356 Dutch-born living in Kent County. In the same year, there were 1,619 Dutch-born living in Wisconsin and 406 Dutch-born living in New Jersey.

once a year in the spring for a Dutch dinner in the Pultneyville Reformed Church. Bob Hoeltzel, Arcadia town historian, states,

> Although Dutch *huisvrouws* were noted as good cooks, only such Dutch dishes as *sla* (a mixture of boiled potatoes cut in small cubes, small cubes of fried pork, shredded lettuce and boiled eggs) and *saucijzenbroodjes* (pigs in the blanket) have caught on with the non-Dutch population. I don't recall a single Newark restaurant ever featuring Dutch food.[40]

This is not to say that the Dutch in Wayne County are not proud of their heritage. Peper's descendants are scattered throughout the United States, and all those with the surname of "Peper" are descendants of Abraham, including the founders of two of America's largest newspapers, the *Chicago Tribune* and the *New York Times*.[41] Members of the current generation with Dutch roots living in Wayne County know exactly where Zeeland, the Netherlands, is on the world map, and they can pronounce names like "Nieuwvliet" and "Schoondijke" without hesitation. While many names have been Americanized, there are still many that have retained the original spelling—De Kraker, Leenhouts, Van Hanegem, Van Houte.

According to the American Community Survey, the ethnic demographic makeup in Wayne County in 2005 was as follows: 18.0 percent German, 12.8 percent Italian, 12.6 percent English, 11.6 percent Dutch, 11.4 percent Irish, and 8.9 percent American ancestry. According to the 2000 federal census, 95.7 percent spoke English as their first language, 2.2 percent spoke Spanish, 1.8 percent spoke French, and 0.2 percent spoke another language.[42] Realizing that in the overall ancestry groups in the United States, the Dutch rank at only 2.5 percent compared to the Germans at 23.3 percent, the Irish at 15.6 percent, and the English at 13.17, the representation of the Dutch in Wayne County is above average.[43] And they should be recognized and celebrated in the annals of Dutch American history.

---

[40] Hoeltzel, *Hometown History*, 99.
[41] Dominicus, *Zeeuwen naar America*, 54.
[42] The *American Community Survey* (ACS) is an ongoing statistical survey by the US Census Bureau. https://en.wikipedia.org/wiki/American_Community_Survey.
[43] Loretto Dennis Szucs and Sandra Hargreaves Luebking, eds., *The Source, A Guidebook of American Genealogy* (Salt Lake City, UT: Ancestry. 1997), 447.

CHAPTER 7

Impact of Farming on Dutch Settlement in Whiteside County

Michael L. Swanson

The Dutch presence in Whiteside County, Illinois, primarily in and around the city of Fulton, had modest beginnings. The first Dutch-born person to settle there was Thomas Smith[1] in 1856. Individuals and families who had already settled elsewhere in the United States arrived in the Fulton area over the next five years, and the first inhabitants who came straight from the Netherlands began to arrive after the Civil War. Growth of the colony was always of a gradual nature. Many of the Dutch who came to Whiteside County were from the largely rural areas in the northern part of Groningen province. In 1891 the *Fulton Journal* documented the growth of the colony by reporting that in 1872, there were 50 families; in 1883, there were 120 families; and in 1891, there were 200 families.[2]

Emigration from the Netherlands during the latter half of the nineteenth century was spurred primarily by economic considerations.

---

[1] He was born 5 June 1821 as Thomas Pieters Smit in Leeuwarden, Friesland. Thomas emigrated as a seceder in 1846 and probably lived in New York and then around Zeeland, MI, before coming to Fulton. www.genlias.nl.

[2] "The Reformed Church in America at Fulton Ill.-Its Origin and Development." *Fulton Journal*, 15 Dec. 1891.

Day laborers and other common workers saw emigration as a way to improve conditions for themselves and their families more quickly and easily than if they remained in the Old Country. Emigration itself was not the solution, but through sacrifice and hard work, it could improve their condition. In the Fulton area, railroads and sawmills provided jobs to some Dutch immigrants, while other immigrants became merchants or other laborers. Even greater opportunities, however, were at hand for those who desired to work the land.

Illinois is in the heart of the corn belt in the Midwest. "Corn belt," however, is a bit of a misnomer; it belies the other farm activities taking place in this region. Like many other counties in Illinois, Whiteside County is mostly rural and contains rich farmland amenable to growing cash crops. To analyze farming practices in more detail, the various agricultural censuses, produced by the US Department of Agriculture since 1840, provide an array of state and county information.[3] Census data from 1870 through 1925 were selected for this study because: (1) this period reflects the growth of Dutch settlement in Whiteside County resulting from direct immigration, and (2) it covers the years when this immigrant generation transitioned to adult, first-generation, Dutch Americans. This period, moreover, reflects much of the era when farming was reliant upon people and animals rather than machinery to perform farm operations.

The typical farm of this era would have incorporated a combination of farming practices to protect against economic disaster in any given sector. Potential disasters could be widespread crop failure or infectious disease among livestock. As a result, a typical farm operation would have grown crops for feed and market, had dairy cattle for milk and related products, raised beef cattle and hogs for butchering, kept chickens for eggs and meat, and maintained gardens and orchards for vegetables and fruits.

Table 1 provides statistics for Whiteside County regarding numbers and sizes of farms, plus livestock that were typically found on these farms. Although the data do not separate out Dutch-owned farms from others, they can be assumed to reflect the fortunes of both Dutch and non-Dutch enterprises. According to data from the Bureau of Land Management, much of the land in Whiteside County was transferred

---

[3] Historical Census of Agriculture data have been digitized and are available at https://www.agcensus.usda.gov/index.php. Censuses were every ten years through 1920, though only statewide data is available for that census year. From 1920 through 1950, censuses were taken every five years. In some cases, census data were reported for agricultural activities from the previous calendar year.

Census Year	No. of Farms	Ave. Size (acres)	Horses	Cattle (% dairy)	Swine
1870	2485	140	14,944	35,264 (37%)	37,765
1880	2903	136	15,477	52,746 (35%)	82,313
1890	2717	150	20,846	68,806 (34%)	96,880
1900	2886	150	20,132	70,312 (32%)	125,000
1910	2898	144	20,004	57,683 (41%)	84,509
1925	2671	152	15,213	43,372 (39%)	91,926

Table 1: Whiteside County statistics for numbers of farms, average sizes, and numbers of animals

from the federal government to individuals (i.e., land patents) in the 1840s and 1850s.[4] There was an increase in the number of farms in Whiteside County from 1870 (2,485) to 1880 (2,903), suggesting that these years represent the end of the pioneer stage of farm units.[5] After this, the number of farm units showed little variation (less than 10 percent) through 1925. The average size of farms in acres remained relatively constant throughout the time period analyzed, ranging from 136 acres to 152 acres. These numbers reflect total farm size, including buildings, pastures, and wooded areas, rather than tilled acreage alone. The average size of Whiteside County farms was slightly smaller than the standard quarter section (160 acres) made available on the Great Plains and elsewhere—mainly west of the Mississippi River—by the Homestead Act of 1862.

For farm animals, statistics from 1870 to 1880 show that on average there were from five to six horses on each farm. This number increased to seven or eight horses per farm over the next three censuses and then decreased somewhat by 1925. Horses were relied upon not only for field work but also for transportation. The base numbers for 1870 and 1880 could reflect the start-up phase in terms of acquiring horses for farm work. They are also an indicator of the improved breeding in the latter part of the 1800s to produce horses suitable for the demands of farm work.[6] The gradual decrease by 1925 is likely due

---

[4] Searchable information on land patents for public land states is available on the Bureau of Land Management website, https://glorecords.blm.gov/default.aspx.
[5] Allan G. Bogue, *From Prairie to Corn Belt: Farming on the Illinois and Iowa Prairies in the Nineteenth Century* (NY: Ivan R. Dee Press, 2011), 8-10.
[6] Bogue, *From Prairie to Corn Belt*, 119-22.

Census Year	Corn (Bu x 10⁶)	Wheat (Bu x 10³)	Oats (Bu x 10⁶)	Hay (Tons x 10³)	Potatoes (Bu x 10³)
1870	2.16	458	0.88	54.83	219
1880	5.22	196	1.11	71.75	177
1890	3.83	45	1.70	113.96	316
1900	5.66	25	3.15	65.24	288
1910	5.23	110	2.10	78.39	385
1925	3.65	661	2.82	48.70	144

Table 2: Whiteside County Statistics for Yields
of Crops, Hay, and Potatoes
(Bu x 10⁶ = million bushels; Bu x 10³ = thousand bushels)

to the advent of tractors and cars to replace horses. The decision by farmers to change from horse power to tractors was not as simple as one might think. Additional outlays in capital for equipment to pull behind tractors, such as planters and balers, were required to utilize tractors to their full potential.[7]

For cattle and swine, there were increases in the total numbers, reaching the highest values from around 1890 to 1900. Per farm, the numbers were fairly modest in relation to modern farming practices. At the peak in 1900, there were an average of twenty-five cows and forty-four pigs per farm. Again, advances in breeding were crucial to the successful incorporation of cattle and swine on Whiteside County farms[8]. The proportion of dairy cows to beef cows remained relatively constant throughout the period. In addition to these animals, chickens were commonplace on Whiteside County farms, but sheep and goats were not found in great numbers.

Table 2 shows the production of crops and other plants on Whiteside County farms. Not surprisingly, corn was the dominant crop, with yields of just over two million bushels in 1870 to more than five million bushels in 1880, 1900, and 1910. Throughout the selected period, about 25-35 percent of all acreage in the county was devoted to growing corn.[9] The decrease in corn production by 1925 was likely

---

[7] Allan G. Bogue, "Changes in Mechanical and Plant Technology: The Corn Belt, 1910-1940," *The Journal of Economic History* 43, no. 1 (March 1983): 1-25.
[8] Bogue, *From Prairie to Corn Belt*, 86-113.
[9] See n. 3.

caused by the depletion of soil nutrients.[10] In 1870 wheat production approached half-a-million bushels in Whiteside County. This was overwhelmingly spring wheat, less hardy than winter wheat, sown in the fall and harvested the following year.[11] As a result, wheat production decreased significantly in Whiteside County from 1870 through 1900. Because of a rising demand for flour domestically and internationally, coupled with the adoption of winter wheat, cultivation increased again in the county between 1900 and 1925.[12] Farmers could get more than $2.00 per bushel of wheat compared to about $1.50 per bushel of corn after World War I, but these prices quickly dropped as markets once again stabilized.

Oats were another common crop, with yields of from one to three million bushels in Whiteside County. Oats were used for animal feed and also sold for cereal production. Hay is a generic term for various dried cut grasses, grown for animal feed during the colder months when fresh grass was not available on pasturelands. These grasses were also important for crop rotation because they added nutrients to the soil depleted by other crops. Potatoes are included in table 2 to show that this human food staple was a common item grown on farms in the county.

With this information in mind, where were the areas commonly farmed by the Dutch in Whiteside County? The Whiteside County township map above includes shaded areas that indicate the location of the prominent cities and towns. As noted earlier, the center of Dutch settlement was in and around Fulton, and the spread of the Dutch throughout Whiteside County could be generally determined by the location of Dutch churches.

The initial Dutch churches, First Reformed and First Christian Reformed, organized in 1866 and 1886, respectively, were both located in Fulton. The next church, Ebenezer Reformed, which began at a schoolhouse in Union Grove Township, was organized in 1896 and erected its edifice nearby in the county seat of Morrison. And in 1909, two rural churches were organized: Spring Valley Reformed in Ustick Township and Newton Zion Reformed in Newton Township.

To quantify the pattern of Dutch farming, federal census data for six townships were used to determine the total number of farming

---

[10] James O. Bray and Patricia Watkins, "Technical Change in Corn Production in the United States, 1870-1960," *Journal of Farm Economics* 46, no. 4 (Nov. 1964): 751-65.
[11] See n. 3.
[12] George Montgomery, Wheat Price Policy in the United States. http://ageconsearch.umn.edu (accessed 12 Oct. 2017).

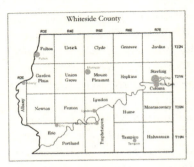

Township map of Whiteside County including cities and towns (size of shaded dots indicates relative population

households in relation to those operated by Dutch farmers.[13] The criteria for identifying Dutch farming households were: (1) whether the head of household was enumerated as a farmer in the census, and (2) if the head of household was born in the Netherlands or was a first-generation Dutch American (one or both parents born in the Netherlands). Typically, if the head of household was female, she would have no occupation attributed to her. In these cases, the household would qualify as a farming household if the oldest son had been recorded as a farmer in the census. If the census showed that the head of household or oldest son was a farm laborer, rather than a farmer, the household was not included in the count, because the individual would have been employed by a different farm household.

Table 3 shows the number of Dutch farming households compared to the total households in selected townships of western Whiteside County. Because there were few Dutch families in the county by 1870, the first census used for analysis was 1880, when there were about eighty such families. As expected, the highest concentrations of Dutch farming households were in Fulton and Garden Plain townships (42 out of 50 households in the townships studied). Many Dutch settled in the northwest part of Garden Plain Township, in an area called East Clinton (see plat map below). In the later 1800s, this area was informally known as "Holland Town" because of the number of Dutch families who lived there. In an article about the East Clinton School in 1892,[14] it is mentioned that there were fifty-six children in the school, all with Dutch parentage.

In 1900 there were about 350 Dutch families in Whiteside County. By this time, direct immigration was starting to wane, so the numbers

---

[13] Federal census records have been indexed and are searchable online at http://www.ancestry.com.

[14] "East Clinton School," *Fulton Journal*, 16 Dec. 1892.

Impact of Farming on Dutch Settlement in Whiteside County 131

Census Year	Fenton	Fulton	Garden Plain	Newton	Union Grove	Ustick	Totals
1880	0/116	19/71	23/163	0/136	4/156	4/162	50/804
1900	1/105	24/48	71/164	7/142	25/139	30/157	158/755
1910	20/106	40/69	74/147	31/130	50/144	50/151	265/747
1920	14/104	38/58	86/149	25/142	58/154	49/153	270/760

Table 3: Number of Dutch farm households compared to all farm households for selected Whiteside County Townships (number of Dutch households in Whiteside County from a search of the population schedules were: 83 in 1880; 361 in 1900; 569 in 1910; and 773 in 1920)

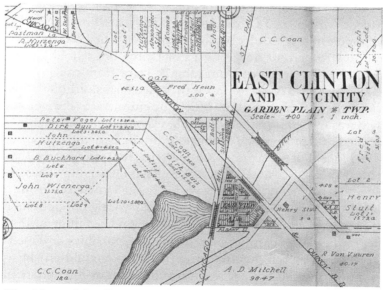

Plat Map of the East Clinton area of Garden Plain Township, 1912. Note that some of the Dutch names have been misspelled (Standard Atlas of Whiteside County Illinois [*Chicago: Geo. A. Ogle & Co., 1912*])

also reflect newly created families as children of Dutch immigrants were beginning to marry and have children of their own. In this census, about 160 Dutch farming households were found in the six townships analyzed, with nearly two-thirds of these in Fulton and Garden Plain townships. The greater the distance from Fulton, the fewer Dutch farming households were found (e.g., compare numbers for Fenton and Newton to Ustick and Union Grove). Dutch farming households were 50 percent of the total in Fulton Township by 1900 and reached this same level in Garden Plain Township by 1910. Over the entire period analyzed, the total number of Dutch farm households increased from 50 to 270. Expressed as a percentage of all farm households, Dutch farm households were only 6 percent of the total in 1880 but reached 35 percent in these six townships by 1910.

Further analysis of Dutch farm households in Whiteside County was conducted to assess the ratio of tenant farmers to farm owners. From the various censuses of agriculture, tenant farmers steadily increased in numbers from 1880 to 1920 (see table 4). Farms were rented either for cash or for shares of products. Although this level of detail is available on the agricultural censuses at the county level, it is not provided for individuals on the population schedules.

Identifying owned farms versus rented farms, however, is possible on the population schedules beginning in 1900. For 1900 and 1910, 72 percent and 75 percent, respectively, of Dutch-household farms were leased in the six townships from table 3. Data from the 1920 census shows a similar ratio of rented farms to owned farms, although there are more instances in this census in which the enumerator did not know if the farm was owned or rented. These levels of tenancy are significantly higher than the county-wide numbers from the agricultural censuses.

The usual land acquisition pattern for midwestern farmers progressed through a series of stages to farm ownership. These stages are general in nature, rather than specific to the Dutch as a group. If an immigrant or first-generation American was young enough, he likely would have worked as a farm laborer, either on the family farm or for another farmer. After earning sufficient funds, possibly combined with changes in his personal circumstances (marriage or children), he would then support himself by renting a farm for cash or for a share of the yield. If he became more financially secure, and the right opportunity presented itself, he could then purchase a farm. Finally, when the rigors of farm work became too much due to age, the farmer would usually retire and move "to town." Decisions would need to be made at that time whether to have a son or other family member take over the farm operations or to rent or sell the farm outright. The fact that Dutch farmers remained tenants over the decades suggests that they did not follow the usual pattern of tenancy to renter to owner. It is not self-evident why leasing farms was more prevalent among the Dutch

Table 4: Proportion of farms operated by tenant farmers in Whiteside County as reported on the agricultural censuses

Census Year	% Tenant Farms
1880	29
1890	37
1900	47
1910	52
1920	56

in Whiteside County. Perhaps they were more comfortable with being tenant farmers for the longer term, rather than actively using tenancy as a stepping stone to farm ownership.

Some insights can be gained from specific examples of Dutch farming activities around the Fulton area. Clearly, these examples do not address all aspects of farm operations in Whiteside County, but they do provide detail about some of the efforts of local Dutch farmers. These three examples of tenant farming discuss corn growing, dairy farming, and the rental of a larger farm:

> F. Sterenberg[15] who lives on W. C. Fellows' farm, has 40 acres of corn up large enough to plow. He is very fortunate in securing a good stand and has 40 acres more just coming through the ground.[16]
>
> Mr. Akker[17] is a tenant on one of Harry Smith's farms and is engaged extensively in the dairy business. He is now milking twenty-seven cows, and during the month of January the milk from the herd brought him $280.[18]
>
> John J. Damhoff,[19] who had been a tenant on the Fellows farm east of town for the past five years, Thursday moved to the Burnett farm in Gardenplain [sic], which he has leased for a term of years. It is a well improved farm and consists of 240 acres.[20]

The purchase of farms was also reported in the local paper and four examples provide details about those transactions:

---

[15] Fred Sterenberg was from Usquert in Groningen province and came to Fulton in the early 1860s after living in Muskegon, MI.
[16] Untitled, *Fulton Journal*, 1 June 1883.
[17] Harry Akker was born in IL to Dutch immigrants.
[18] Untitled, *Fulton Journal*, 15 Feb. 1910.
[19] John J. Damhoff was born in IL to Dutch immigrants.
[20] Untitled, *Fulton Journal*, 1 Feb. 1910.

Among the large sales of real estate made this week is the transfer made by B. Robinson of this city. He has sold his fine farm in Garden Plain, five miles from Fulton, for the sum of $10,500, to John Damhoff.[21] This is at the rate of $65.625 per acre, and it is evidence that real estate in Whiteside County is not depreciating on account of Dakota emigration, or from any cause.[22]

Today S. Akker[23] purchased of E. Lockhart a farm of 160 acres two miles north of Garden Plain for $6,750, of which $1,000 was cash. Six years ago, Mr. Akker was in debt which he has paid by farming on a rented farm.[24]

J. B. Kearns sold his farm in Garden Plain to Louis Jaarsma[25] last week. The farm consists of 120 acres, and the consideration was about $60 an acre.[26]

Cornelius Vogel,[27] who for several years has been a tenant on the farm owned by Mrs. Mary E. Kain, southeast of town, Wednesday, by J. M. Eaton as agent, purchased the farm, which comprises 120 acres. It has good buildings and is convenient to town, being one and one-fourth miles southeast of the Mississippi Valley Stove factory. The consideration was $12,000, or $100 per acre.[28]

In addition to traditional farming practices, some truck farming of locally grown produce took place among the Dutch of Whiteside County. Two of the early Dutch settlers, John Munneke and Al Van Dellen,[29] were occasionally mentioned in the *Fulton Journal* regarding the fruits and vegetables that they sold in local markets. As Dutch settlement increased, a few others were involved in truck-farming ventures. In the early 1900s, greenhouses were built and operated in Fulton by some Dutch individuals for the growth and sale of fresh fruits and vegetables.

---

[21] This John Damhoff (father of John J. above) was from 't Zandt in Groningen province and came to Fulton in the 1860s.
[22] Untitled, *Fulton Journal*, 8 Sept. 1882.
[23] Sjabbe Akker (van Akkeren) was from Den Andel in Groningen province and came to Fulton in the 1860s with other family members.
[24] Untitled, *Fulton Journal*, 9 March 1883.
[25] Louis Jaarsma emigrated from Warffum in 1881.
[26] Untitled, *Fulton Journal*, 27 Dec. 1898.
[27] Cornelius Vogel emigrated from Warffum in 1881.
[28] "Fulton Farm Sold for $100 an Acre." *Fulton Journal*, 23 Sept. 1910.
[29] John (Jan) Munneke and Al (Alje) Van Dellen were both from Groningen province and lived in Muskegon, MI, before coming to Fulton in the early 1860s.

Apart from the Dutch, the Germans in Whiteside County were renowned for their agricultural practices. In a 1908 history of Whiteside County,[30] Germans and "Hollanders" were compared. Both groups were characterized quite favorably, particularly for their piety, work ethic, and thriftiness. The Germans were most numerous in the townships of Jordan, Hopkins, and Genesee in the eastern half of the county. Farming was in their blood according to this history. "The German takes to the soil as a duck to water. He is a natural farmer.... They believe in large barns, spacious corn cribs, warm shelters for stock."

Conclusion

The rich, abundant farmland in Whiteside County was like the call of the siren for many of the Dutch immigrants seeking a better life on the Illinois prairie. These Dutch adapted quickly to the various and changing agricultural activities practiced on Whiteside County farms. "Green Hollanders" likely learned from experienced farmers about local farming practices, though advances in animal breeding, plant varieties, fertilization, crop optimization, and machinery meant that even seasoned farmers would have to be open to new ideas to get the most out of their efforts.

In the period analyzed, most Dutch farm households were in the townships of Fulton and Garden Plain. Over time, Dutch farms spread generally to the east and south. The impact of agriculture on Dutch settlement in Whiteside County was quite significant during the immigration phase of the latter 1800s. About 60 percent of all Dutch households in the county were farm households in 1880. As more Dutch arrived, many of them also took to farming, as evidenced by the tripling of the number of farm households from 1880 to 1900 in the townships analyzed. At this point, Dutch farming households still represented about 44 percent of all Dutch households in the county. The number of farm households may be somewhat greater, since the Dutch also began farming in townships not included in this study.

In the early 1900s, more of the Dutch in Whiteside County followed the general trends brought about by the industrial revolution by living in towns and villages rather than on farms. The number of Dutch farm households in the six townships had stabilized by 1910, although the total number of Dutch families in the county continued

---

[30] William W. Davis, *History of Whiteside County, Illinois: From Its Earliest Settlement to 1908* (Chicago: Pioneer Publishing, 1908), 229-30.

to grow. It is also noteworthy that the Dutch favored tenant farming to a greater degree in comparison to the county-wide farm owning patterns. Reasons are not apparent for their leasing arrangements, so any explanation of this difference would be speculative. Articles in the *Fulton Journal* make clear that some Dutch did not have an issue with being tenant farmers for a period of several years or longer.

Agriculture continues to be a significant economic driver for Whiteside County, although this now includes a diverse array of agricultural-related businesses, in addition to farming practices. The propensity of Dutch settlers in the Fulton area to choose to farm was an important factor in the success of the colony. Farming instilled a sense of community among the rural Dutch at local churches and other gatherings. Without the significant agricultural opportunities available to the early Dutch, one wonders if the Dutch settlement in Whiteside County would have prospered as it has for more than 130 years.

II. Dutch American Rural Life

CHAPTER 8

Rural Identity among Dutch Americans

David Zwart

Pioneering settlers to America's rural landscape played a starring role in the collective memory of Dutch Americans in the twentieth century. Stories about and images of these pioneers clearing forests and cutting prairie sod laid the foundation for the identity of Dutch Americans in the twentieth century. This emphasis on rural settlement, while diminishing urban life, reflected important cultural assumptions that fit broader cultural trends in the United States. Yet, Dutch Americans added a twist to how they thought about their life together and how they constructed their institutions within the United States.

Dutch immigrants and their descendants in the twentieth century emphasized the rural aspects of their history in both community and institutional commemorations. This reflected the social reality of the rural background of many of the Dutch immigrants, as well as cultural forces within and outside of the group. Nostalgia for rural pastoralism and theological ideas combined to create a collective identity around a story of settling the land and building institutions. This rural perspective shaped how Dutch Americans positioned themselves within the broader context of American identity. Twentieth-century Americans embraced a popular image of rural America as the "heartland" of the country. As David Danbom articulated, "Rural America ... exercised an influence on the American mind and public policy far out of proportion to the numbers of farmers in the population."[1] The importance of rural themes in commemorating the past and fitting into the United States were similarly important for Dutch Americans.

Commemorative histories, written by and for Dutch Americans in the twentieth century, reflect and highlight several rural themes. Stretching across the twentieth century, these examples come from a variety of geographic locations. A variety of forces, both internal and external to the ethnic group, shaped these rural sentiments. An understanding of context and brief comparisons to other ethnic groups of the same era show the emphasis of the Dutch American rural sentiments that explain how they constructed an ethnic identity within the United States, while maintaining many separate institutions.

Interest in identity formation and—more broadly—collective memory, has over the past thirty years had historians asking new questions about Dutch Americans. Michael Douma's *How Dutch Americans Stayed Dutch* is a prime example of examining this ethnic identity.[2] Terence G. Schoone-Jongen's focus on Tulip Time festivals shows how celebrations functioned in Dutch America.[3] These books have highlighted various aspects of the identity-formation process of Dutch Americans. Rob Kroes' examination of Amsterdam, Montana, incorporated a geographic aspect to how Dutch Americans viewed themselves.[4] Hans Krabbendam added another geographic dimension by examining the impact of the Great Plains on Dutch Americans.[5] By examining the way rural sentiments contributed to a Dutch American identity, I will add another aspect to the matrix of what people living in the twentieth century meant when they called themselves Dutch American.

Endnotes
[1] David B. Danbom, *Born in the Country: A History of Rural America* (Baltimore: The Johns Hopkins University Press, 1995), x.
[2] Michael Douma, *How Dutch Americans Stayed Dutch: An Historical Perspective on Ethnic Identities* (Amsterdam: Amsterdam University Press, 2014).
[3] Terence G. Schoone-Jongen, *The Dutch American Identity: Staging Memory and Ethnicity in Community Celebrations* (Amherst, NY: Cambria Pres, 2008).
[4] Rob Kroes, *The Persistence of Ethnicity: Dutch Calvinist Pioneers in Amsterdam, Montana* (Urbana: University of Illinois Press, 1992).
[5] Hans Krabbendam, "The Return of Regionalism: The importance of Immigration to the Plains for the History of Dutch in America," in *Dutch Immigrants on the Plains*, ed. Paul Fessler, Hubert R. Krygsman, and Robert P. Swierenga (AADAS 2006), 1-21.

Rural sentiments in commemorative histories

The Dutch Americans who commemorated a rural past looked to the experiences of many Dutch migrants in the nineteenth and early twentieth centuries. The reality of rural immigration is an important aspect to explain the rural narrative. Most of the migrants from the Netherlands to the United States from 1835 to 1880 came from rural areas. These rural immigrants were a mix of craftsmen and day laborers. Even after 1900, more Dutch migrants to the United States left rural areas than urban areas.[6] These rural migrants, like other European immigrants, sought land in rural Midwest. As Jon Gjerde noted, "The vast tracts of open land in the West enchanted Euro-Americans who saw it as a heaven for both the oppressed and the entrepreneur."[7] These European immigrants benefited from US policies that encouraged their settlement.[8]

The first Dutch settlements of the nineteenth century set the dominate pattern for Dutch Americans. The founding of Holland, Michigan, and Pella, Iowa, as well as Sheboygan County, Wisconsin, in rural landscapes, played a key role in setting the theme for later collective memories. These settlements were the archetype for Dutch American communities. Centered around churches and expanding outward, these communities came to be a dominant factor in the identity of many Dutch Americans. Although many immigrants did settle in Chicago and Grand Rapids, rural communities influenced how people imagined Dutch America. Rural communities were the oldest in the Midwest and the base for future enclaves both near and far.[9]

Celebrations throughout the twentieth century highlighted the rural aspects of Dutch immigrants. Beginning with the semicentennial celebration in Holland, Michigan, on August 25, 1897, the story of settling the rural landscape dominated the framework of remembering the past. The 1897 celebration included addresses collected into a book of reminiscences. These addresses, by prominent men in the

---

[6] Robert P. Swierenga, *Faith and Family: Dutch Immigration and Settlement in the United States, 1820-1920* (NY: Holmes and Meier, 2000), 57, 68.

[7] Jon Gjerde, *The Minds of the West: Ethnocultural Evolution in the Rural Middle West, 1830-1917* (Chapel Hill: University of North Carolina Press, 2002), 27.

[8] David B. Danbom, *Born in the Country: A History of Rural America* (Baltimore: Johns Hopkins University Press, 1995), 132-49.

[9] The settlements of Dutch Americans have been well documented. For a recent overview, see Hans Krabbendam *Freedom on the Horizon: Dutch Immigration to America, 1840-1940* (Grand Rapids, MI: Eerdmans, 2009).

community, help interpret the first fifty years of Holland. For instance, Hope College's president Gerrit J. Kollen began his address by noting the "rich material resources" the Dutch immigrants found. He continued, "dense forests have made room for laughing harvests—the dark swamps have been converted into rich gardens . . . by able efforts, wise plans and fruitful labor of the Fathers." Gerrit Diekema echoed the same sentiments in his address, "Forests and swamps have given way to fields and gardens, to flowers of summer and waving golden harvests of autumn."[10] These rural images of farming and harvests framed how other celebrations would remember the Dutch immigrant experience.

The same settlement and cultivation themes were evident in other public celebrations in the early twentieth century. A pageant performed by Hope College students in 1936 in celebration of the ninetieth anniversary of Holland's founding recalled how the 1847 settlers felled trees to clear the land and build cabins. The pageant's flowery language celebrated how "The smell of upturned soil, the birds singing, the sunlight through the trees . . . filled [the colonists'] hearts to overflowing with the joy of living."[11] These rural images framed how the pageant presented the story of Holland and of Dutch Americans: as valiant pioneers who had cleared and conquered the land, which in turn produced rich bounty.

Rural and pastoral images dominate the way Holland, Pella, and Orange City, Iowa, presented themselves in their annual Tulip Time festivals that began in the late 1920s and early 1930s. Early promotional brochures in Holland include images of rural scenes of tulips and of children in "traditional" costumes. Pella's brochures include more rural images, such as "The Old Holland Milk Cart" in 1936. Both Pella and Orange City publicity include many depictions of windmills. The choice of these images says much about what the organizers viewed as legitimate Dutch symbols that they understood and their reflections of broader American cultural perceptions of the Netherlands as a pastoral, rural place.[12]

---

[10] "Semi-Centennial Reminiscences," Semicentennial Celebration, box 1, Programs 1897, Holland Historical Trust (HHT).

[11] "The Pageant of 1936," 7-8, Anniversaries of Hope College, JAH.

[12] See Douma, *How Dutch Americans Stayed Dutch*, 121-36; Suzanne Sinke, "Tulips are Blooming in Holland, Michigan: Analysis of a Dutch American Festival" in *Immigration and Ethnicity: American Society – "Melting Pot" or "Salad Bowl,"* ed. Michael D'Innocenzo and Josef P. Sirefman (Westport, CT: Greenwood Press, 1992), 3-14; and Annette Stott, *Holland Mania: The Unknown Dutch Period in American Culture and Art* (Woodstock, NY: Overlook Press, 1998).

By the 1947 centennial of the founding of Pella and Holland, themes of clearing and cultivating the land were accepted notions of how these places presented themselves and their place in the American cultural landscape. Pella's celebration included a program of character sketches of early pioneers, as well as the pageant *City of Refuge*.[13] The pageant highlighted the success of the community based on farming the "fine" land and ended with a farming metaphor of the community as whole: a seed planted and growing into a sturdy stalk.

The Holland centennial was an even bigger event, which used the resources of the larger settlement to tell the story of the past in many venues. Henry Lucas's *Ebenezer: Memorial Souvenir of the Centennial Commemoration* provides a lasting popular artifact of the overall narrative of Dutch American settlement. The book highlights how Dutch Americans had created "splendid farms."[14] The pageant in Holland told a familiar story of conquering the land through hard work and suffering.[15] And a booklet of pioneer stories told by Ruth Keppel also valorized the way the founders had settled the land.[16]

Cedar Grove in Sheboygan County, Wisconsin, also celebrated the centennial of its founding by Dutch immigrants in 1947. Its simple pageant highlighted the way mail was brought to the rural area. The pageant also depicted the building of churches and schools by the founders of the community.[17]

Although community celebrations, other than Tulip Time festivals, decreased in the 1960s and 1970s, the thematic pattern for the remaining festivities had been set: to emphasize the settling and cultivating of the rural landscape. The Dutch immigrants had worked hard to develop the land and construct buildings for their institutions, such as churches and schools. The emphasis on the hard work and struggle of the founders often overlooks the benefits and encouragement they received from state and federal policies that encouraged European immigration and that built railroads when Native Americans were being pushed off the land.

---

[13] *The City of Refuge*, 15-17 May 1947, produced by John B. Rogers Production Co. in Pella, Iowa, Pella Anniversary 100th, folder 1947, Pella Historical Society Archives.

[14] Henry S. Lucas, *Ebenezer: Memorial Souvenir of the Centennial Commemoration of Dutch Immigration to the United States held in Holland, Michigan, 13-16 August 1947* (Netherlands Information Bureau, 1947), 14.

[15] "A Historical Pageant Spectacle," 13-15 Aug. 1947, produced by John B. Rogers Production Co. in Holland, MI. Willard Wichers Papers, box 4, HHT.

[16] Ruth Keppel, *Trees to Tulips: Authentic Tales of the Pioneers of Holland, Michigan*, Centennial of Holland, MI, 1947, box 1, *Trees to Tulips* 1947, JAH.

[17] *Cedar Grove Centennial Homecoming Souvenir Program*, 1947. Church files, Cedar Grove First Reformed, JAH.

A nostalgia for pioneering rural life was at the center of American identity in the second half of the twentieth century, particularly in the Midwest. John Bodnar noted that images of patriots and pioneers dominated state commemorations after World War II.[18] This reflected a longing for a nice story to help them make sense of the present as they experienced economic and cultural changes. Particularly in the years after World War II and into the 1960s, many rural people struggled with changes to their lives. Farmers sought out labor-saving chemical and mechanical technology because of reduced labor availability. Farm size grew as farmers could cultivate more land and raise more livestock. The choices farmers made, with the support of farm policy, altered the social and physical rural landscape.[19] This resulted in higher production but lower prices, so farm income dropped compared to income in the United States in general.[20] At the same time, rural people's expectations changed as radio and television brought mass culture to the farms and villages. Automobiles connected them more quickly to larger population centers. Patterns of daily life changed slowly but noticeably. People moved out of rural areas, changing the demographics permanently.[21] The Dutch were not immune to these cross currents in an evolving rural world.

Rural nostalgia in congregations

Settling in rural areas did require significant sacrifice on the part of the founding pioneers. They broke the ground, cleared the forests, built the first structures, and organized their communities. The frontier, with the coming of institutions like churches, made American democracy, so the story went. Churches played a central role in the story of what made America exceptional via the Turnerian frontier.[22] In their relative

[18] John Bodnar, *Remaking America: Public Memory, Commemoration, and Patriotism in the Twentieth Century* (Princeton, NJ: Princeton University Press, 1992), esp. ch. 6, "Memory and the Midwest after World War II."

[19] J. L. Anderson, *Industrializing the Corn Belt: Agriculture, Technology, and Environment, 1945-1972* (De Kalb: Northern Illinois University Press, 2009), 8. The migration from rural to urban areas resulted in a smaller percentage of the population living on farms. For specific numbers, see David Danbom, *Born in the Country*, 244-48. For a good general overview of conditions in the Midwest after World War II, see J. L. Anderson, ed., *The Rural Midwest Since World War II* (De Kalb: Northern Illinois University Press, 2014).

[20] Dorothy Schweider, "Cooperative Extension and Rural Iowa: Agricultural Adjustment in the 1950s," *Annals of Iowa* 51, no. 6 (Fall 1992): 604-5.

[21] Robert Wuthnow, *Remaking the Heartland: Middle America Since the 1950s* (Princeton, NJ: Princeton University Press, 2011).

[22] Frederick Jackson Turner, "The Significance of the Frontier in American History," in *Proceedings of the State Historical Society of Wisconsin*, 1883.

isolation, churches served as the center of these rural settlements. Across the rural Midwest, ethnic churches and communities covered the landscape to create a "heavily churched landscape." Robert Ostergren points out that the church "played a major role in the organization and development of community on nineteenth-century American frontiers, especially in the Middle West."[23]

The same was true for Dutch Americans. Robert Schoone-Jongen has pointed out the importance of churches to the success of settlements in Minnesota.[24] The church was more than just a religious meeting place. Robert Swierenga called it a "cultural nest, integrating families, social classes, and nationality groups. It gave members a cultural identity and status and socialized them into the community."[25] The successes and strains on these iconic rural churches played a significant role in how Dutch Americans constructed their shared story about their community formation.

Rural people in congregations, particularly in the Midwest, imagined themselves as the heart of America. Across a variety of denominations, these rural congregations commemorated their past by emphasizing the importance of the church in building America. The commonalities across denominations show the important place of the church in the rural landscape even as the position of the church might diminish.

Some events of the twentieth century, however, pulled at rural congregations: from broad-scale migration of rural sons and daughters to more promising occupations in urban centers, to anti-immigrant sentiments during World War I, to the Great Depression, to service members being shipped throughout the country and world during World War II, to the cultural shifts of the 1960s. Despite these cultural changes, rural churches have continued to serve as a symbol of a stable force in society.

Dutch American congregations had much of the same kind of nostalgia for pioneer farming as did other congregations in the Midwest. The theme of taming the land and making it productive often set the background for building a church. For instance, the Gibbsville,

---

[23] Robert C. Ostergren, "The Immigrant Church as a Symbol of Community and Place in the Upper Midwest," *Great Plains Quarterly* 1, no. 4 (Fall 1081): 225.
[24] Robert Schoone-Jongen, "A Time to Gather, A Time to Scatter: Dutch American Settlement in Minnesota, 1885-1920" (PhD dissertation, University of Delaware, 2007).
[25] Robert P. Swierenga, "The Little White Church: Religion in Rural America," *Agricultural History* 71, no. 4 (Autumn 1997): 416.

Wisconsin, Reformed Church in its 1956 centennial booklet, noted how their pioneer ancestors "saw nature change from forests to fertile acres. . . . These sturdy pioneers endured extreme hardships while they blazed the trail to civilization."[26] The First Reformed Church of Hull, Iowa, noted in its 1960 booklet that pioneers "were sons and daughters of the soil. They wrestled with the sod that had laid untouched through the centuries of time. They did not have modern power machinery to plow the ground and break the sod. A team of horses or a yoke of oxen provided the power by which the sod was broken, and the seed sown."[27]

Into the 1960s and 1970s, rural themes of dominating the land could be found in the way congregations framed their congregational histories. The writers of the congregational history for the First Reformed Church in Fremont, Michigan, wrote, "Life was hard in those days as roads had to be cut through the forests and land had to be cleared for crops and homes."[28] The authors of the Peoria, Iowa, Christian Reformed Church booklet explained how the pioneers had moved "over the river" east of the Skunk River because "land was becoming more difficult to obtain" closer to Pella.[29] This emphasis on obtaining land for farming framed many congregational stories.

Another way rural congregations demonstrated that they were at the center of the American story was by emphasizing the progress their churches had made. Often framed with the details of building projects, congregations reflected a belief that the church's success showed the overall success of the immigrants and their descendants and America's progress in general. These congregational commemorations usually include pictures of meeting places starting in homes or other temporary quarters and moving to more permanent—albeit simple—structures. The stories usually include how the congregation met in ad hoc buildings before building more substantial framed buildings. Often a third (or fourth) building project was required to deal with either natural disasters (lightning strikes and fires were surprisingly common) or growing congregations. Of course, the most successful congregations could boast of even more impressive brick buildings.

---

[26] Gibbsville Reformed Church, "Our First Century for Christ, 1856-1956," 3. Church Files, Gibbsville Reformed Church, JAH.

[27] First Reformed Church, "75th Anniversary, 1885-1960." Church Files, Hull, IA, First Reformed, JAH.

[28] First Reformed Church, "Centennial Anniversary, 1869-1969," Fremont, MI. Church Files, Fremont First Reformed Church, JAH.

[29] Peoria CRC, "Seventy-Fifth Anniversary, 1894-1969." Peoria, IA, ACC.

Even if progress was hard for many rural congregations, the memory of past progress was an important history to tell to encourage themselves.

Dutch American congregations followed this same self-congratulatory pattern, often emphasizing the building projects they had completed. Sometimes they listed in their official histories the details of each building. Often the successive buildings would be used to break up periods of the congregation's history. This could take the form of photos of each of the church buildings and careful descriptions of the unique features of each succeeding sanctuary. The covers of commemorative booklets often graphically depicted this progression of buildings. The cover of the Hingham, Wisconsin, Reformed Church booklet in 1965 shows this memorable progression.[30] Another clear example is the 1966 cover of the Overisel, Michigan, Reformed Church.[31] As in nonrural sections of the denomination, these images showed that success in the rural congregation meant being able to build bigger and more impressive edifices.

This progress narrative gave a gloss to what might actually have been happening in rural congregations, as noted by some history books. For instance, as late as the 1970s, some congregations told the story of a strong rural life even in the face of rural decline.[32] The Calvary Evangelical Lutheran Church of Swede Home, near Stromsburg, Nebraska, celebrated its centennial in 1973. The writers of their history emphasized their Swedish beginnings and that they were "staunch" Lutherans. But they also worried about the "problems of the rural church," while reminding readers that "what counts is its quality of spiritual growth, witness, and service."[33] Congregations might have concern about filling the pews of their building, but they reveled in the faithfulness of those who came before them and built their structures.

The reality of decline was felt with fewer people in the pews and with merging or closing congregations. Children and beloved neighbors moved away as mechanization required less labor. Struggling with economic realities brought others to move off the farm. These changes caused some to feel as though the ground were shaking under their feet. Old patterns of church life, which had seemed so steady, now changed.

---

[30] Hingham Reformed Church, "75th Anniversary, 1890-1965," Hingham, WI, church files, JAH.
[31] Overisel Reformed Church, "Centennial," Holland, MI, church files, JAH.
[32] Wuthnow, *Remaking the Heartland*.
[33] Calvary Evangelical Lutheran Church of Swede Home, "One Hundredth Anniversary, 1873-1973," Stromsburg, Nebraska. Swenson Swedish Immigration Research Center, Augustana College, Rock Island, IL.

But the image of the little white church remained important for how people thought about rural life. In a time of sudden and continual change, people seemed to pine for a simpler time, when churches truly served as the center of a pastoral, agricultural community. In the collective memory of Dutch Americans, the little white church continued to be important. Commemorations provided a time to remind members of the importance of the church.

Although building projects showed success and a narrative of progress, emphasizing the faithfulness of founders reminded rural congregations of what made them the heart of America. The nostalgia of the rural past can be seen in the religious commitment of early settlers who acquired the land, usually without mentioning how they had acquired the land. For instance, the Big Canoe Lutheran Church near Decorah, Iowa, commemorated its centennial in 1953. The history written emphasizes the hard work of the pioneers to settle the land. At the same time, these settlers were portrayed as "faithful" and "devout."[34] The St. John's Evangelical Lutheran Congregation (a Missouri Synod Lutheran congregation) of Germantown, Iowa, in 1963 even went so far as to wonder aloud, "In all our present day moving, do we always think of the church [like the founders did]?"[35] Being faithful, like the founders, is emphasized over and over in congregational histories.

Nostalgia for rural churches among Dutch Americans, but also across the spectrum of denominations, reflects the values of people who longed for a "simpler" time, with the church at the center of life in the face of unsettling changes. This nostalgia reflected, at least partly, the values of rural people, even if contemporaries could no longer live them out. They longed for an imagined time of simplicity and faithful church members. The iconic "little white church" played a large role in the heart of the story of America. A lone structure on the prairie or in the woods, surrounded by a cemetery filled with saints who had passed on, maybe with a parsonage on the same property. These buildings and their congregations within covered the landscape of the nineteenth century, and they continued to play a role in the twentieth century, in both actuality and memory.

General themes and patterns in rural congregations across denominations reflected larger cultural patterns, but the theology of

---

[34] Big Canoe Lutheran Church, "One Hundredth Anniversary: 1853-1953" (Big Canoe, IA; Luther College Archives, Decorah, IA).

[35] St. John Evangelical Lutheran Church, "Anniversary Booklet: 1878-1963" (Germantown, IA; Concordia Historical Institute, St. Louis, MO).

Dutch American Calvinists also shaped how these rural congregations constructed their story. A strong sense of a sovereign God and of covenant theology mattered in how Dutch Americans thought about themselves and their churches. Congregations were not just places where individuals came together but where a sovereign God had called his chosen people. The cause of the success—whether in the lives of individual parishioners or of the congregation more generally—was quickly laid at the feet of God. Staying in the church mattered because God had chosen them and their children. Worrying about the next generation seemed to matter even more for Dutch American Calvinists than for other denominations.

When telling their history, the structure of the history written in commemorative books emphasized Calvinistic theology. The framework of this history stressed that God had done great things among his chosen people. Sully, Iowa, Christian Reformed Church celebrated fifty years in 1946. The story told in this church history is one of continued growth because of faithfulness. The congregation started a Christian school to train "covenant children."[36] Often pastors set the tone with their introductory remarks for these books. For instance, Rev. J. B. Hulst wrote in the 1958 Ireton Christian Reformed Church book that "all these blessings flow through Jesus Christ. . . . It is through His covenant of grace that you are kept. It is through His irresistible grace that you have been brought in the Church."[37] The Newkirk, Iowa, Reformed Church in 1957 titled its book "75 years of growth" and told the congregation to "dedicate this occasion to the glory of God." It included a poem with the first line "God Bless our little country church."[38] Of course, this theology also affected urban believers, but the use of it by those in rural areas, in their relative isolation, makes it all the more important for keeping small pockets of Dutch Americans loyal to their own congregations even as they dealt with significant changes all around them.

As suggested, the Dutch American congregations emphasized how they needed to keep the next generation faithful. This emphasis on the next generation's faithfulness meant that the congregation often dedicated the commemorative booklet to them, or at least the pastor's message of introduction to the booklet would clearly point out the goal

---

[36] Sully CRC, "Fiftieth Anniversary, 1896-1946" (Sully, IA. ACC).
[37] First CRC, "50th Anniversary: 1908-1959" (Ireton, Iowa, ACC).
[38] Newkirk Reformed Church, "Seventy-five Years of Growth: 1882-1957," Hospers, Iowa, Church Files, JAH.

of the covenant youth staying faithful. Concern about keeping youth in the church might seem to be a more urban concern than a rural one, yet many rural congregations framed their commemorations around encouraging the next generation.

Encouraging faithfulness among sons and daughters was portrayed in later years as a fundamental focus of the founding fathers and mothers. Stories of pioneers' struggle and perseverance because of their faith drove the narrative of most of the commemorative booklet histories. These booklets characterized the founders as remaining faithful despite all their hardships. As they built a life for themselves and their descendants, so the story went, they created a way of life that should be emulated.

Conclusion

The story of clearing and settling rural land is a familiar one to most Americans. This story frames much of how Dutch Americans, among many others, conceived their own legacy and placed themselves in the larger "America" story during the twentieth century in community celebrations, public narratives, and congregational histories. The little white church played a role not only in the settling of America but also in how Americans perceived the heart of America. Rural congregations, including Dutch American congregations, used this iconic image to frame their twentieth-century story. To this country-wide model, Dutch American congregations added affirmations of God's sovereignty and the importance of keeping the next generation faithful to him.

The focus on stories of the rural aspects of Dutch American identity, as well as collective memory, may identify another aspect of the construction of a Dutch American identity. I propose that rural sentiments have shaped the general Dutch American collective memory. This framework allowed Dutch Americans to present themselves as part of the mainstream American culture, even as they maintained separate institutions. Rural settlements and churches dominate many stories of the past among Dutch Americans, and although the story of settlement and expansion is largely driven by a search for land, collective memory has recast this search as a providential mission, affirmed in its many signs of success.

Emphasis on the rural aspects of settlement, however, may have masked certain historical realities of the number of Dutch Americans settling in cities like Chicago and Grand Rapids. The rural paradigm as central to the Dutch American identity might over emphasize rural isolation instead of neighborliness and interaction with other city dwellers. In other words, the collective identity of Dutch Americans may have been too centered on a rural story of conquering the land, developing independent land owners, and idealizing an isolated rural way of life, while overlooking the urban experience of rubbing shoulders with other Americans.

For much of the twentieth century, Dutch Americans had exhibited a kind of rural mindset based on their historical experience and wistful nostalgia. America was a land they helped to create, and the rural way of life lay at its heart. Recent books examining rural American politics emphasize how rural folks have a "rural consciousness" and see themselves as "strangers in their own land" who have been "left behind."[39] Many Dutch Americans seem to exhibit this aspect of the rural mindset, even those who do not reside in rural areas. The historical development of this rural mindset among Dutch Americans reveals much about their twentieth-century identity.

---

[39] Katherine Jean Cramer, *The Politics of Resentment: Rural Consciousness in Wisconsin and the Rise of Scott Walker* (Chicago: University of Chicago Press, 2016), Arlie Russell Hochschild, *Strangers in their Own Land: Anger and Mourning on the American Right* (NY: New Press, 2018), and Robert Wuthnow, *The Left Behind: Decline and Rage in Rural America* (Princeton, NJ: Princeton University Press, 2018).

CHAPTER 9

The "Many Children of God": The Role of the Religious Community in Dutch American Migration

Justin Vos

> *"May praying be our comfort also at great distance, and God willing, may we see one another again on earth or may the Lord be with you and us and may the Lord bless us here."*[1]

After arriving on the vast plains of South Dakota in 1894, Tjitske Lijkeles Memerda De Jong wrote the words above to her eldest daughter, Baaye, who remained in the Netherlands. Just as Tjitske's faith provided comfort and connection to family left behind, it also joined her and her family to a new community in the United States. The religious

---

[1] Ulbe Bakker, ed. and trans., *Sister, Please Come Over: Experiences of an immigrant family from Friesland, the Netherlands. Letters from America in the period 1894-1933* (In Dutch: *Zuster, kom toch over: Belevenissen van een emigrantenfamilie uit Friesland. Brieven uit Amerika in de periode 1894-1933* [Kollum, NL: Trion G.A.C., 1999]) 2nd ed. (Winsom: Ulbe Bakker, 2000), Tjitske De Jong to Baaye and Gerrit Bakker, New Holland, SD (26 April 1894), 45. Due to the majority of citations coming from this collection, unless otherwise cited, all further citations from *Sister, Please Come Over* will provide the letter details, followed by the letter number and the English translation page number. Therefore, anyone desiring the original Dutch, rather than the English translation, may refer to the letter number.

commitment demonstrated within the letters of the De Jong family offers a perspective on the Dutch Protestant community as a primarily *religious*, rather than a primarily *ethnic* community maintaining religious ties. Recognizing religion, rather than ethnicity, as the foundation for the immigrants' communal experience allows us to gain a deeper understanding of the relationship between faith and ethnicity.

Tjitske and her husband, Lieuwe De Jong, boarded the SS *Westerdam* in Antwerp, Belgium, on March 10, 1894, after having traveled to Antwerp from their former home in Friesland, a northwest province of the Netherlands.[2] The couple left Antwerp with their sons Pete, Teake, Nick, and Jessie, and their daughter Renske and her husband Albert. They arrived on March 27 in South Dakota to reunite with their children, Nellie and George, who had emigrated ahead of their parents in August of 1893 to find housing.[3] Altogether, by 1894, nine members of the De Jong family had immigrated to New Holland, South Dakota, but Baaye, the eldest daughter, and her husband Gerrit had decided to stay in Friesland.

This separation of parents from their daughter, and siblings from their sister, created a chain of correspondence that stretched over thirty years. The "American De Jongs" wrote many letters to the "Netherlands De Jongs," Baaye and Gerrit, describing their lives in America and urging them to follow in their footsteps. In total the collection includes 185 letters. These letters, mostly from the American De Jongs to the Netherlands De Jongs, and only a handful of late letters from America, provide a detailed account of the migration process.

The goal of this chapter is to analyze the role of religion in the life of the De Jong family. What role did personal piety play within their daily life, and how did their Calvinist beliefs and involvement in a broader Reformed community impact their migration experience? Through examination of the De Jongs' letters, I argue that the family's Calvinist faith had provided a source of personal identity, fostered

---

[2] Renske and Albert Hiemstra to Baaye and Gerrit Bakker, Antwerp, 10 March 1894, letter 1:39. I have titled the letters according to whom the writer identified in the greeting and salutation. For example, many of the letters titled "Renske and Albert Hiemstra to Baaye and Gerrit Bakker" were written by Renske to Baaye. I, however, have added the additional names to demonstrate the original intention of the sender and to note who would have read the letter.

[3] Lieuwe De Jong to Baaye and Gerrit Bakker, New Holland, SD, 4 April 1894, letter 2:43. Note: despite the earlier use of "Nelly" by her parents and siblings, during Nellie's adult life, she spelled her name "Nellie," and so I have chosen to use this spelling consistently throughout this chapter.

ethnic unification, and created an expansive, ethnically inclusive community based on shared religious values.[4] Thus, the De Jongs' story suggests fuller ways of understanding religion and ethnicity within the migration process.

This study focuses on Dutch American Protestants, even though Catholics, Jews, and nonreligious migrants made up a significant portion of the Dutch American population.[5] As others have noted, the international nature of Catholicism created a different experience for Dutch American Catholics.[6]

Studying the De Jongs within a specifically Dutch Reformed (Calvinist) framework allows for a greater focus upon the theological particularities of the Reformed tradition and its impact upon the family's experience in America. I begin with the De Jong family's ties to the Netherlands, followed by an exploration of the role of the church community and church attendance, the motivation for Christian education, the importance of church membership, efforts towards familial reunification, and the use of religious language. Finally, the paper concludes with a study of the implications of "Dutch Reformed geography" and the place of ethnicity within the Dutch Reformed community.

Ties to the Netherlands

By moving to New Holland, South Dakota, in 1894, the De Jongs became a link in the expanding westward chain of Dutch immigration. West of the Mississippi River, Dutch immigrants had originally moved to the town of Pella, in south-central Iowa, and had spread to northwest Iowa, before venturing into Minnesota and then South Dakota.[7] As the Dutch kept moving westward, they continued to form churches similar

---

[4] The De Jongs' experience parallels the thesis of Jon Gjerde that the Midwest created a paradox in which European immigrants maintained a unique ethnic identity while simultaneously adopting American patriotism. See Jon Gjerde, *The Minds of the West: Ethnocultural Evolution in the Rural Middle West, 1830-1917* (Chapel Hill: University of North Carolina Press, 1997), 4.

[5] For Dutch American Catholics, see Yda Saueressig-Schreuder, *Dutch Catholic Immigrant Settlement in Wisconsin, 1850-1905* (NY: Garland Pub, 1989). For Dutch American Jews, see Robert P. Swierenga, *Faith and Family: Dutch Immigration and Settlement in the United States, 1820-1920* (NY: Holmes & Meier, 2000), 193-212.

[6] Yda Saueressig-Schreuder, "Urbanization and Assimilation Among the Dutch Catholic Immigrants in the Fox River Valley, Wisconsin, 1850-1905," in *The Dutch American Experience: Essays in Honor of Robert P. Swierenga*, ed. Hans Krabbendam and Larry J. Wagenaar (Amsterdam: VU Uitgeverij, 2000), 143-54.

[7] Swierenga, *Faith and Family*, 76-79.

to those they had left in the Netherlands.⁸ The religious community the De Jongs joined in New Holland was no exception. In the Netherlands, Lieuwe helped begin the Christian Reformed Church (CRC) in Hijlaard, Friesland. The Christelijke Gereformeerde Kerk in Nederland (CRC in the Netherlands) separated from the Hervormde Kerk (the Dutch State Church) in 1834, due to worries about the state church's loyalty to traditional Reformed doctrine, the rewriting of the Church Order, and the development of a new theology that stressed a personal relationship with Jesus instead of established Calvinist principles. The state church majority labeled CRC members as Seceders, considering them unpatriotic schismatics. By leaving the Hervormde Kerk, Lieuwe had made a religious statement, proclaiming a commitment to the stricter Calvinism of the Christelijke Gereformeerde Kerk (CRC).⁹

In New Holland, South Dakota, the De Jong family became a part of the Christian Reformed Church in North America (CRCNA), a separate denomination from their former church home, the CRC in the Netherlands.¹⁰ Soon after their arrival, Lieuwe and Tjitske took part in communion.¹¹ Participation in the sacrament required church membership; one can therefore assume that the De Jongs' church memberships in Hijlaard transferred to their new church in New Holland.¹² A personal level of fellowship existed between the two denominations, due to their closely related theological understandings.¹³

---

8   Swierenga describes religion as a bridge between the Old World and the New World, creating ethnic community and aiding the assimilation process; *Faith and Family*, 154-55.
9   Footnote for Lieuwe De Jong to Baaye and Gerrit Bakker, New Holland, SD, 4 April 1894, letter 2:421. For greater detail on the separation, see Karel Blei, *The Netherlands Reformed Church*, trans. Allan J. Janssen (Grand Rapids, MI: Eerdmans, 2006), 61-66. See also, Gerrit J. tenZythoff, *Sources of Secession: The Netherlands Hervormde Kerk on the Eve of the Dutch Immigration to the Midwest* (Grand Rapids, MI: Eerdmans, 1987).
10 The CRCNA was not named as such until later, but I use the term for clarity's sake and to mark a clear difference between it and the similarly named denomination in the Netherlands.
11 Pete De Jong to Baaye and Gerrit Bakker, Joubert, SD, 1894, letter 7:53.
12 At the time, church membership involved an official process of membership papers, which transferred from one church to another. Richard H. Harms describes the early desire of the CRCNA to gain affiliation with the Seceders in the Netherlands and the growth of the denomination due to continuing migration. See Richard H. Harms "Forging a Religious Identity: The Christian Reformed Church in the Nineteenth-Century Dutch Immigrant Community," in Krabbendam and Wagenaar, *The Dutch American Experience*.
13 Swierenga and Bruins describe the 1882 Masonic controversy, which created a new wave of secession from the RCA to the CRC and shifted the allegiance of the CRC in the Netherlands from the former to the latter. See Robert P. Swierenga and Elton

Church magazines provided another link between the De Jongs' "Netherlands church" and their new "American church." In January of 1903, Nellie wrote, "I read in our church magazine that you have a new minister.... I hope that you will enjoy being led by him."[14] *De Wachter*, the magazine of the Christian Reformed Church in North America, carried news of ministerial changes within the Christelijke Gereformeerde Kerk in Nederland, a sign that the two denominations maintained regular communication. Again in 1911, Baaye sent Nellie a church magazine from the Netherlands.[15] The De Jongs in America desired to maintain knowledge of continuing developments within their old church home.[16] Church news linked the De Jongs to the Netherlands. The two sisters freely shared news of new congregations, ministerial changes, and theological debates within the churches of both countries. Church news in general flowed from the United States to the Netherlands; for example, in 1909, Tjitske sent cutouts from *De Wachter* to her daughter Baaye.[17]

The De Jongs' understood the two denominations, the Christian Reformed Church in both the Netherlands and America, to be part of an international Dutch Reformed circle.[18] In 1903 Renske described their new minister as similar to their former minister in the Netherlands. Additionally, she wrote, "You (Baaye) wrote about Ulbe de Vlas, Albert says he should come over here, he can become a minister here much more easily and at much less cost, that is in Grand Rapids."[19] The

---

J. Bruins, *Family Quarrels in the Dutch Reformed Churches of the 19th Century* (Grand Rapids, MI: Eerdmans, 1999), 130-31.

[14] Renske and Albert Hiemstra to Baaye and Gerrit Bakker, New Holland, SD, 17 Jan. 1903, letter 116:267.

[15] Nellie De Jong to Baaye and Gerrit Bakker, Zuni, NM, 18 Oct. 1911, letter 147:323.

[16] In describing the Christianity of Korean Americans during the first half of the 19th century, David K. Yoo stressed the transnational connections that Korean American Protestants maintained with churches in Korea. Similarly, Dutch Calvinism became a transnational religious tradition. See David K. Yoo, *Contentious Spirits: Religion in Korean American History, 1903-1945*, (Stanford, CA: Stanford University Press, 2010), 17-33.

[17] Pete and Dina De Jong to Baaye and Gerrit Bakker, New Holland, SD, 4 July 1909, letter 130:295.

[18] Hans Krabbendam argues that Dutch Americans exhibited few characteristics of transnationalism, but he also points out that religion may be the one transnational outlier, providing "a framework of meaning that tied immigrants together." Hans Krabbendam, "They Came to Stay: The Weak Transnational Relations of the Dutch in America," in *Sharing Pasts: Dutch Americans Through Four Centuries*, ed. Henk Aay, Janny Venema, and Dennis Voskuil (Holland, MI: Van Raalte Press, 2017), 22.

[19] Renske and Albert Hiemstra to Baaye and Gerrit Bakker, New Holland, SD, 17 Jan. 1903, letter 116:269.

seminary of the CRC in North America, Grand Rapids, Michigan, trained many ministers in the denomination. Albert and Renske saw little difference between training for the ministry in the Netherlands and undertaking ministerial studies in Michigan. Migration did not radically alter the De Jongs' religious observance; instead the CRC in North America provided an institution that reinforced their Calvinist faith in their new home.[20]

The church community and church attendance

The De Jongs' Dutch Reformed Calvinism connected them to their former denomination in the Netherlands; it also, however, tied them to their new community in New Holland, South Dakota, an established Dutch community with a Christian Reformed church. The family attended church their very first Sunday in New Holland. Lieuwe De Jong wrote, "We went to church here Sunday morning, someone was reading a sermon; the minister was away, he had received a call, the people here are churchgoers."[21] The De Jongs had moved to a place with similar people: Dutch Reformed Church members.

Church attendance defined life in New Holland. On Sunday mornings, the faithful converged on the church. "There are two large horse stables near the church," reported Lieuwe. "Each one has room for 40 horses, every farmer can have two horses stabled and has his own numbered place in the stable. They come from everywhere with two horses pulling the carriage."[22] Renske expressed joy when her son described the message of a sermon to her. She wrote to Baaye saying,

> When I was so very ill, Hieltje came home from church and said that the minister had preached about the cross of Christ. He said that the minister had said that we must not set our hearts upon worldly things . . . but only glory in the cross of Christ . . . I told

---

[20] The connection to the Netherlands is evident in the literature read by the De Jongs. When ill in 1908, Renske described reading books written by Abraham Kuyper, the former prime minister of the Netherlands and a leader of the neo-Calvinist movement away from the Dutch state church. Renske and Albert Hiemstra to Baaye and Gerrit Bakker, Harrison, SD, 8 April 1908, letter 120:277. The translation of *Zuster, kom toch over* (*Sister, Please Come Over*) is books *lent* by Kuyper; a more accurate translation, however, is books *written* by Kuyper.

[21] Tjitske De Jong to Baaye and Gerrit Bakker, New Holland, SD, 26 April 1894, letter 3:45.

[22] Ibid.

it all later to the minister, and he got tears in his eyes and was touched with joy that a child should listen with such care.[23]

Church attendance provided both community and a source of personal comfort and joy. Shortly after the family's arrival in South Dakota, Renske wrote that they had a one-hour wagon ride to church.[24] Two years later, Tjitske, tired of the long Sabbath commute, wished that she lived closer to church. Four year later, in the fall of 1900, Tjitske got her wish as she and Lieuwe moved to a farm nearer to the church.[25] Church attendance defined Lieuwe and Tjitske's sense of space. Specifically, the De Jongs defined this space by proximity to a Christian Reformed church.

Pete went to Capron, Illinois, in March of 1896, to be a farmhand for a man who had moved there from New Holland. The De Jongs had bought nineteen cows and two horses from this man, so Pete worked there to pay off the rest of their debt from the livestock and to earn money to buy more cattle in the future.[26] Without a Dutch community and Reformed church, Capron disappointed Pete. He wrote:

> I am still in good health and satisfied with my service. The only thing that bothers me is that I cannot visit a Dutch church, for there are no Dutch here, and I have not heard a word of Dutch in 15 months, but can speak American well . . . and now I can go to the English church, but I think it a great joy to go to church with one's own people."[27]

Despite the financial benefits, Pete's move had two major negatives: no Dutch community and no Christian Reformed Church. For Pete, an "English church" did not offer the same experience as a Dutch congregation.

The provision of both community and personal worship is further demonstrated in Nellie's experience in New Mexico. Nellie served as a

---

[23] Renske and Albert Hiemstra to Baaye and Gerrit Bakker, Harrison, SD, 11 Jan. 1909, letter 127:289.

[24] Renske and Albert Hiemstra to Baaye and Gerrit Bakker, New Holland, SD, 5 Aug. 1894, letter 9:61; and Nellie De Jong to Baaye and Gerrit Bakker, Charles Mix County, SD, 31 Oct. 1896, letter 46:143.

[25] Nellie De Jong to Baaye and Gerrit Bakker, New Holland, SD, 28 Sept. 1900, letter 84:213.

[26] Renske and Albert Hiemstra to Baaye and Gerrit Bakker, New Holland, SD, 17 Nov. 1895, letter 28:103.

[27] Pete De Jong to Baaye and Gerrit Bakker, Capron, IL, 2 May 1897, letter 54:157.

schoolteacher in Zuni, New Mexico, as part of the CRC's missionary efforts.[28] She ministered among the Zuni in an area with few churches and therefore had little opportunity to attend a regular service, which proved to be a challenge. Nellie wrote:

> We do sometimes feel quite lonely here, especially on Sundays. Only once I have heard a sermon since I arrived here and that in 6 months. We celebrated then the Lord's Supper and we had to travel 100 miles on the wagon, that is the only means of transport that we have and it is an open one at that.[29]

Like Pete, Nellie believed in the importance of church attendance, enduring many miles to participate in a formal worship service.

Christian Reformed worship emphasized the importance of the sermon, for it "imparted theological knowledge to the laity."[30] Renske expressed joy when her son described the message of a sermon to her. She wrote to Baaye:

> When I was so very ill, Hieltje came home from church and said that the minister had preached about the cross of Christ. He said that the minister had said that we must not set our hearts upon worldly things . . . but only glory in the cross of Christ. . . . I told it all later to the minister and he got tears in his eyes and was touched with joy that a child should listen with such care.[31]

Church attendance provided both community and a source of personal comfort and joy.

Even when the weather did not allow for church attendance, the De Jongs carefully observed Sabbath worship. On Sunday, February 17, 1895, before Pete left for Illinois, he wrote:

> We were supposed to go to church today, but there is a strong wind blowing, and there is so much dust in the air that we cannot drive. It is an hour's drive, and when it is so cold, driving is no good. Father reads a sermon on Sundays.[32]

---

[28] Nellie De Jong to Baaye and Gerrit Bakker, Zuni, NM, 17 Oct. 1908, letter 124:283.
[29] Renske and Albert Hiemstra to Baaye and Gerrit Bakker, Harrison, SD, 11 Jan. 1909, letter 127:291.
[30] Ibid.
[31] Ibid., 289.
[32] Pete De Jong to Baaye and Gerrit Bakker, Charles Mix, SD, 17 Feb. 1895, letter 18:83.

During ministerial absences, congregational elders routinely read prepared sermons. In 1892 the CRC Synod (the governmental body of the denomination) decided to distribute these sermons through bookstores, giving the laity the opportunity to purchase them for their own private use. Eventually, Synod created a committee with the sole responsibility of organizing these written sermons.[33] Therefore, sunshine or blizzard, minister or no minister, the De Jongs had the opportunity to hear the exposition of Reformed theology.

Christian education

Similar to the importance of doctrinal preaching, the De Jongs strove to impart theological knowledge to their children through religious education. Lieuwe explained the process of church education when he wrote:

> Nick and Jessie are going to catechism classes and so will the others, but they will have to go to New Holland, since we go to church there and shall continue doing so for some time, I think. It is a bit over five miles from our place, but the minister gives catechism classes in a school three or four miles away from here.[34] He gives catechism classes in three or four different schools and in church every week."[35]

The minister traveled to the various country schoolhouses, teaching multiple lessons every week. The Heidelberg Catechism served as the foundation of doctrinal understanding and provided the primary benchmark for church membership.[36] The many years of study and memorization created a lasting impression on those who completed

---

[33] CRCNA, *Index of Synodical Decisions of the Christian Reformed Church in North America* (Grand Rapids, MI: CRCNA, 2001), 507. Synod disbanded the Sermons for Reading Services Committee only in 2015, after the internet made sermons more readily available.

[34] By 1914 Platte, New Holland, Harrison, Corsica, and Armour each had their own CRC congregation. Harrison, SD, is 4 miles east of New Holland, and Corsica is 6 miles east of Harrison. Armour is 20 miles southeast of New Holland, while Platte is 15 miles west of New Holland. *Yearbook of the Christian Reformed Church in America* (Grand Rapids, MI: Eerdmans-Sevensma Co., 1914): 124-26.

[35] Lieuwe and Tjitske De Jong to Baaye and Gerrit Bakker, Charles Mix, SD, 27 Oct. 1894, letter 12:69.

[36] Henry Beets, *The Christian Reformed Church in North America; Its History, Schools, Missions, Creed and Liturgy, Distinctive Principles and Practices and Its Church Government* (Grand Rapids, MI: Eastern Avenue Book Store, 1923), 216-19.

catechism classes. On hearing the news of the death of her cousins, Nellie wrote, "What a great blessing is the enormous comfort in both life and death, to know that we are the property of our faithful Savior Jesus Christ."[37] Nellie directly alluded to the first question and answer in the Catechism.[38]

Similar to the importance of catechetical education, the De Jongs believed in the importance of Christian day schools. In a letter to Baaye and Gerrit in 1899, Nellie included a two-dollar gift for their old Christian school in Hijlaard.[39] A year earlier, Tjitske reported to Baaye, "We have not yet any special denominational schools, but there is freedom. The Bible is used in most schools and prayers and grace are said."[40] By 1916, however, the New Holland CRC established a denominational school. Teake described this development to Baaye and Gerrit:

> We also have the privilege of being able to send our children to a Christian school, even though it is quite a sacrifice: the public school is only half a mile from here and the Christian school is at two and a half miles' distance. When the weather is cold or turbulent they often have to be taken to and from school. . . . The school has existed for about three years; apparently the Lord wanted to bless it. This work started in the vestry of the church, but now there is a sizable school with a stove, meeting all the current requirements, without any debts. Christian education is rapidly increasing in America, but here in Dakota, New Holland is the first one, although a second one is to be founded soon.[41]

The De Jongs experienced inconvenience and hardship in choosing Christian education for their children, after already sending them to the public school for a number of years. Lieuwe and Tjitske's

---

[37] Nellie De Jong to Baaye and Gerrit Bakker, Zuni, NM, 15 Dec. 1908, letter 126:287.
[38] Q and A 1 of the Heidelberg Catechism: "What is your only comfort in life and death? Answer: That I, with body and soul, both in life and death, am not my own, but belong unto my faithful Savior Jesus Christ." The connection to the catechism is clear with Nellie's use of "comfort in both life and death" and "property of our faithful Savior Jesus Christ." Catechism quoted from the CRC, *Psalter Hymnal: Centennial Edition* (Grand Rapids, MI: Publication Committee of the CRC: 1959), 24.
[39] Nellie De Jong to Baaye and Gerrit Bakker, Armour, SD, 24 Sept. 1899, letter 74:199.
[40] Tjitske De Jong to Baaye and Gerrit Bakker, New Holland, SD, 1 March 1898, letter 63:173.
[41] Teake and Maggie De Jong to Baaye and Gerrit Bakker, Harrison, SD, 26 Dec. 1916, letter 158:339.

dedication to the church community and their commitment to a Christian upbringing for their children led them to make this decision.

The De Jongs' decision to send their children to a Christian school developed out of a broader history within the Dutch American community. Janet Sjaarda Sheeres argues that the right to freely educate their children is what motivated the original Dutch Seceder settlement, led by Albertus C. Van Raalte to western Michigan in 1847. Sheeres describes the unwillingness of the Dutch government to grant the Seceders the right to start their own schools; the Seceders therefore saw the United States as a place where they could educate their children as they saw fit.[42]

The development of neo-Calvinism, through the political and theological philosophy of Abraham Kuyper, provided another possible influence on the De Jongs' choice of Christian education.[43] Kuyper, prime minister of the Netherlands and a neo-Calvinist theologian, led a second group of dissenters, the Doleantie, out of the Hervormde Kerk in 1886.[44] As prime minister, Kuyper developed the concept of *verzuiling* (pillarization), which divided society into three groups: Reformed, Catholic, and "neutral" (liberal/socialist). Robert Swierenga describes the concept as

> place[ing] the three faith communities on an equal basis at law and allow[ing] for tax-supported separate schools and universities, newspapers, trade unions, media outlets, health and welfare agencies, and sports associations.[45]

---

[42] Janet Sjaarda Sheeres, "The Struggle for the Souls of the Children: The Effect of the Dutch Education Law of 1806 on the Emigration of 1847," in *The Dutch in Urban America*, ed. Robert P. Swierenga, Donald Sinnema, and Hans Krabbendam (Holland, MI: JAH, 2004), 34-47.

[43] Jon Gjerde, in *Minds of the West*, argues that the religious thought of nineteenth-century European immigrants should not be considered traditional or less modern. Neo-Calvinist thought among Dutch immigrants provides an example of European immigrants transplanting contemporary religious and political thought to America. The De Jongs did not simply cling to an old tradition but engaged a contemporary Dutch debate about religion's role in society. See Jon Gjerde, *The Minds of the West: Ethnocultural Evolution in the Rural Middle West 1830 - 1917* (Chapel Hill: University of North Carolina Press, 1997), 17.

[44] For details concerning the religious developments in the Netherlands, see TenZythoff, *Sources of Secession: The Netherlands Hervormde Kerk on the Eve of the Dutch Immigration to the Midwest* (Grand Rapids, MI: Eerdmans, 1987).

[45] Robert Swierenga, *Dutch Chicago* (Grand Rapids, MI: Eerdmans, 2002), 51. Swierenga provides greater detail on the distinction between the Seceders and the Doleantie, along with the response of Chicago Dutch Calvinists in the second chapter of *Dutch Chicago*.

In accordance with this philosophy, Kuyper proposed dividing the upper chamber of the Dutch legislature by spheres, giving seats to business, labor, education, agriculture, and industry. Kuyper's proposal, however, never came to fruition.[46] Consequently, members of the Doleantie, along with the earlier Seceders who supported Kuyper's neo-Calvinist theology, encouraged the creation of Christian day schools. The importance of Christian schooling demonstrates the embedded nature of the De Jongs' worldview in a specific Dutch Reformed milieu.

Church membership

Because the Calvinist faith played such a large role in De Jong family life, church membership served as a mark of belonging. As described above, catechetical instruction provided the gateway to full church membership. Once the De Jong children completed religious education, the church expected them to become members. When George did not fulfill this expectation, questions arose. In January of 1903, Nellie expressed her concerns to Baaye: "George has not yet joined the church and does not seem to take it seriously, at least as far as we can see, but we do often judge wrongly and hope that to be the case as far as this is concerned."[47] By April 1908, concerns had transformed into blatant criticism when Renske described George as "weak and worldly and irreligious."[48] In October of the same year, Nellie described the tragedy that befell George and his wife Rika through the death of their twin children:

> [George and Rika's twins] were sick before I left, this is really sad; they were growing so well. God is not bound to admit only the [covenant children],[49] but what grounds for hope do we have for our children if we have withdrawn ourselves from the Lord. Hopefully this will be a stimulation to bring the parents back to the Lord."[50]

Nellie hoped for the salvation of the children, despite her worry concerning the spiritual state of George and Rika.

---

[46] James D. Bratt, *Abraham Kuyper: Modern Calvinist, Christian Democrat* (Grand Rapids, MI: Eerdmans, 2013), 139.
[47] Nellie De Jong to Baaye and Gerrit Bakker, New Holland, SD, 6 Jan. 1903, letter 115:267.
[48] Renske and Albert Hiemstra to Baaye and Gerrit Bakker, Harrison, SD, 8 April 1908, letter 120:277.
[49] "Covenant children" is my translation of the Dutch *verbondskindren*, rather than the given translation "children of the alliance."
[50] Nellie De Jong to Baaye and Gerrit Bakker, Zuni, NM, 17 Oct. 1908, letter 124:285.

Ultimately, George and Rika did not achieve the spiritual transformation for which Nellie had hoped. In 1910 she wrote that George still had no interest in spiritual advancement.[51] Finally, in 1927, she wrote:

> We see and hear little of George and his family. We have very little contact with him. Why this is, I have no idea. It seems that he wants to have nothing to do with us. That they live completely outside the church may have something to do with it.[52]

George's rejection of the church, in comparison to the rest of the family's strong religious convictions, caused a rift between them. George's religious indifference created a major stumbling block for the family. Calvinistic religion set the De Jongs apart from the world around them. Nellie described George as "worldly," marking him as outside of the community.[53] George chose to adopt a different identity, one not formed by religious belief.[54] A common religious belief and heritage held together the Dutch Reformed community and network.[55] With a rejection of the religion came a separation from the community.

---

[51] Nellie De Jong to Baaye and Gerrit Bakker, Zuni, NM, 23 Sept. 1910, letter 135:303.

[52] Nellie De Jong to Baaye Bakker, Eagle Butte, SD, 24 Sept. 1927, letter 163:355. By 1927 Gerrit had passed away.

[53] Renske and Albert Hiemstra to Baaye and Gerrit Bakker, Harrison, SD, 8 April 1908, letter 120:277.

[54] George's rejection of the CRC community represents one form of identity formation. Besides George, the rest of the De Jong family represents a very devoted strand of Dutch Calvinism, as seen in their joining the Seceders in the Netherlands. Other forms of Dutch American identity are seen in the De Jongs' experience. After marrying John De Haan, Jessie left the CRC to join the RCA. Various correspondents clearly noted this denominational difference. For example, Sy Bakker wrote, "We went to the *Reformed Church* [emphasis mine] to meet uncle John De Haan, he belongs to that church." The Dutch immigrant community could recognize the religious differences among themselves. A range of religiosity existed among Dutch Americans from strict Calvinists to members of the more Americanized RCA to the nonreligious. For Bakker's comment see Sy Bakker to Baaye and Gerrit Bakker, Harrison, SD, 22 Dec. 1927, letter 169:369.

[55] In his study of Manhattan, MT, Rob Kroes in *The Persistence of Ethnicity* (Urbana: University of Illinois Press, 1992), highlights the importance of the Reformed faith for maintaining the Dutch community. Kroes describes the separation that occurred between the CRC and the Protestant Reformed Church, a splinter group that left the CRCNA in 1924. Kroes argues that despite religious disagreements that tore the community apart, the division was part of a common Reformed heritage. The religious division solidified the community's uniqueness and common background, which set them apart from the broader American culture. This sense of being set apart is visible within the divide that occurs within the De Jong family.

Reuniting the family

Despite strained family relations with George, the De Jong family continuously tried to persuade Baaye and Gerrit to emigrate to the United States, motivated by the immigrants' desire to see their daughter and sibling (and her husband). Religious orthodoxy and church community lowered the barriers for resettlement. Lieuwe and Tjitske stressed to Baaye and Gerrit the religious faithfulness of their Dutch American community. In 1898 Tjitske explained to her daughter, "In religious matters we are just as well served. . . . And as far as teachers and young men's and young women's fellowship is concerned, it is so good here that I think there are not many such where you are."[56] On December 17, 1910, Lieuwe wrote,

> Well, Gerrit and Baaye, what about it, are you prepared to come over, or haven't you made up your minds yet? . . . And, dear children, you do not have to remain in the Netherlands for the religion either. There is a congregation here of one hundred families and a large church, a presbytery. The [minister] has a stipend of 900 dollars, and on Sunday afternoons the place is so full of people and carriages that there is nearly no way of getting through. . . . And Lieuwe does not have to stay at your place for his study. We have good [ministers] here too, and it is not expensive, but I do not want to force you.[57]

Lieuwe hoped that the presence of a CRC community would convince Baaye and Gerrit that coming to America would not require a spiritual sacrifice.

In 1911 Renske wrote to Baaye and Gerrit describing the stories of multiple families who had successfully moved to the United States. Furthermore, she reminded them that "it is however the same God,

---

To borrow from Kroes, when George De Jong left the church, he left the game of Frisian fives; Kroes, *The Persistence of Ethnicity*, 120. Friesian fives is a ball game that consists of two teams of three participants each whom are playing against each other on a fives court, similar to handball.

[56] Tjitske De Jong to Baaye and Gerrit Bakker, New Holland, SD, 1 March 1898, letter 63:173. Fellowships for young men and women were Bible studies and social groups sponsored by the church for the teenagers within the congregation.

[57] Tjitske and Lieuwe De Jong to Baaye and Gerrit Bakker, Harrison, SD, 17 Dec. 1910, letter 138:309. The word "minister" in parentheses notes my translation of the word *dominie* from the original Dutch instead of "vicar," which was provided in the original translation. The word "presbytery" should really have been translagted as "classis."

who reigns; that is comforting. It is the same Gospel that is preached here for which you can go to the house of worship."⁵⁸ The family described their church life to Baaye and Gerrit in order to stress that the orthodox Reformed faith did not exist only in the Netherlands. The Dutch American community held the same values. By the spring of 1914, however, Lieuwe and Tjitske's hope of reuniting their family began to slip away, as Lieuwe wrote:

> And if crops are high over there, then you should sell everything except your clothes. . . . We, your parents and grandparents, await you, if you do not come shortly you probably will not come at all, since we are growing old and God does not really request you to.⁵⁹

Lieuwe and Tjitske desperately desired to see their children and grandchildren and have their whole family united; after twenty-four years of separation, however, they realized that their dream would not become a reality.

Letter writing and religious language

Suzanne Sinke's study of Dutch immigrant women provides valuable insight into the use of religious language within letters, especially during times of hardship. Sinke argued that Dutch immigrants expressed their difficulties through biblical language and religious terminology.⁶⁰ The De Jong family conforms to this pattern of using biblical language during times of sorrow and loss. On the first anniversary of their emigration from Friesland, Tjitske wrote:

> Let us pray that the Lord will see to it that it was not our last meeting, let us continually ask the Lord about his intentions with regard to us and let us pray that He may remain our source of comfort, we are so unfaithful to the Lord, although He favors us with many blessings.⁶¹

In reflecting on this momentous life change, Tjitske relied upon religious terminology; she could express the emotional pain

---

⁵⁸ Renske and Albert Hiemstra to Baaye and Gerrit Bakker, Harrison, SD, 1 Aug. 1911, letter 144:319.
⁵⁹ Lieuwe and Tjitske De Jong to Bouwe and Tjitske Strikwerda [grandchildren], Harrison, SD, 26 May 1915, letter 156:337.
⁶⁰ Suzanne M. Sinke, *Dutch Immigrant Women in the United States, 1880-1920* (Urbana: University of Illinois Press, 2002), 193.
⁶¹ Tjitske De Jong to Baaye and Gerrit Bakker, Charles Mix County, SD, 5 March 1895, letter 19:85.

of separation from her daughter only through divine appeals. With the birth of her second child, Renske described the Lord's generosity and mercy, quoting from the book of Psalms.[62] Less than a year later, however, the child died. Renske tried to cope with this loss by gaining consolation from her belief in the child's presence in heaven, but that did not end her sorrow. She wrote to Baaye that the loss "rips a wound that will bleed till our grave, and it appears that all joy of life has disappeared just like that."[63]

Religious expression of grief did not always translate into unqualified belief. For Renske, self-doubts emerged in the sorrow of her loss. She confided to Baaye:

> I sometimes had to collapse from my work by the cradle and beg the Lord for salvation and mercy for this little one, for then I felt the sin and guilt press my heart so.... Oh to see that lamb suffer so for our sins, that breaks my heart, but he has accomplished it, as did his Saviour, whose days we now also commemorate.[64]

The pain of her experience caused Renske to blame the weight of her own sin for the death of her child. Although not an orthodox Reformed belief, Renske's emotional expression tied the biblical concepts of sin and salvation to her personal experience of pain and loss. Religious terminology, beyond specific doctrine, carried Renske through her time of grief, providing both a language for expressing sorrow and a way of managing personal loss.

The De Jongs experienced much personal loss, but throughout their times of grief, Lieuwe and Tjitske's understanding of Reformed doctrine provided stability and comfort. After the death of one of Baaye and Gerrit's children, Lieuwe and Tjitske wrote to them of the hope that they had found in covenantal theology.[65] Reformed covenantal theology posits that God made a covenant with his elect people and their children.[66] Therefore, Lieuwe and Tjitske instructed Baaye and Gerrit to be confident that their child belonged in God's elect, covenant

---

[62] Renske and Albert Hiemstra to Baaye and Gerrit Bakker, New Holland, SD, 7 Sept. 1896, letter 42:135.
[63] Ibid., 19 April 1897, letter 53:153.
[64] Ibid., p. 155.
[65] Lieuwe and Tjitske De Jong to Baaye and Gerrit Bakker, Docers County, SD, 15 June 1902, letter 110:257.
[66] The De Jongs would have understood this covenant as rooted in biblical events, derived from God's covenant with the Old Testament Israelites. See Genesis 12 for the biblical origin of the covenant with God's calling of Abraham.

people and to strive to imitate godly, biblical examples, such as Job, who refused to reject God despite the loss of all his children and earthly possessions. They urged, "Dear children, put your hands on your mouths in this matter and turn to God's word and remember how Job testified and confessed."[67] Lieuwe and Tjitske encouraged their children to hold on to their faith, writing, "Faith does not mean paying lip service, even if that faith as we should profess it is not perfect."[68] For the De Jongs, theology provided comfort; the Bible gave godly examples, and genuine faith in God constructed ultimate meaning for their lives. The De Jong family communicated the depth of their sorrow and loss with religious language, conveying the emotions that secular language could not express. Furthermore, beyond the language itself, their theological beliefs upheld them in difficult times.

The De Jongs' religious convictions informed their entire immigration experience by preserving ties with their former home in the Netherlands, giving importance to church attendance and membership, developing their understanding of education, and providing a response to the hardships of life. In a visible and tangible way, religion had shaped the life of the De Jong family.

Dutch Reformed geography

Just as religion had shaped the De Jongs' daily life, it also influenced their understanding of their new surroundings and the American landscape. The De Jongs' Dutch Calvinist faith connected them to various Dutch Reformed immigrant communities across America. In 1901 Renske's husband Albert considered moving from New Holland to Lynden, Washington, due to its fertile land and its "Christian Reformed congregation."[69] The presence of the CRC gave Albert a connection to what would have been a foreign place. In 1926 Nellie and Nick lived in Ziebach County in western South Dakota, due to the cheap land that surrounded the Native American reservation. Ziebach County, unlike Lynden, Washington, however, had no Reformed church, so Nellie and Nick made plans to start one.

---

[67] Lieuwe and Tjitske De Jong to Baaye and Gerrit Bakker, Docers County, SD, 15 June 1902, letter 110:257.
[68] Ibid.
[69] Renske and Albert Hiemstra to Baaye and Gerrit Bakker, New Holland, SD, 16 Sept. 1902, letter 113:261. This is my own translation of the original "Hervormd Christelijke gemeente." The English translation found in the collection is "Reformed Christian parish."

Nellie described how they held church services in the homes of various families and how she taught the children Sunday school.[70] By 1928 they held church services in the school building with eight or nine families.[71] Nellie and Nick had formed a new Dutch Reformed community, and founding a church played a central role.

Through their travels and personal connections, the De Jongs belonged to a network of Dutch Reformed migrants across America. Nellie accompanied her employer, Mrs. Floete, who lived in Armour, South Dakota, to Iowa, to visit her relatives during the summers of 1896 and 1898.[72] Following their marriage in 1908, Jessie and her new husband John De Haan, accompanied by Nellie, traveled to Sioux Center, Iowa—a Dutch immigrant community—on their way to visit John's family who lived in another area of Dutch American settlement. While in Sioux Center, they stayed with Rev. W. P. van Wijk, a Christian Reformed minister who had previously served their church in New Holland.[73] Members of the wider De Jong family also lived in other Dutch immigrant towns. Jessie describes receiving a letter from her aunt, J. Wassenaar, Lieuwe's sister who lived Fulton, Illinois, a community of Dutch immigrants on the banks of the Mississippi River.[74] Through both church and family connections, the De Jongs created a personal network that encompassed a number of Dutch immigrant communities.

Newspapers, as noted by Hans Krabbendam, connected various Dutch communities beyond familial and personal ties. Krabbendam described newspapers as "the Dutch grapevine," spreading news of various events and travels occurring among other Dutch Americans.[75]

---

[70] Nelly De Jong to Baaye and Gerrit Bakker, Spearfish, SD, 16 Aug. 1925, letter 160:347.

[71] Sy Bakker to Baaye and Gerrit Bakker, Eagle Butte, SD, 26 Feb. 1928, letter 176:389.

[72] Nelly De Jong to Baaye and Gerrit Bakker, New Holland, SD, 9 Oct. 1896, letter 44:137; and Renske and Albert De Jong to Baaye and Gerrit Bakker, New Holland, SD, 1 Aug. 1898, letter 66:179.

[73] Nelly De Jong to Baaye and Gerrit Bakker, Zuni, NM, 17 Oct. 1908, letter 124:283; and John and Jessie De Haan to Baaye and Gerrit Bakker, Platte, SD, 23 Oct. 1908, letter 125:285.

[74] John and Jessie De Haan to Baaye and Gerrit Bakker, Platte, SD, 23 Oct. 1908, letter 125:285.

[75] Hans Krabbendam, *Freedom on the Horizon: Dutch Immigration to America, 1840-1940* (Grand Rapids, MI: Eerdmans, 2009), 266. Suzanne Sinke describes newspaper coverage of social visiting in *Dutch Immigrant Women*, 48-49. Ch. 8 provides an in-depth discussion of the role of both newspapers and letters for the Dutch American community. Conrad Bult's article "Dutch-American Newspapers: Their History and Role," in *The Dutch in America: Immigration, Settlement, and Cultural Change*,

In December of 1927, Baaye and Gerrit's son Sy arrived in New York on board the SS *Volendam*. Sy met his uncles and aunts in South Dakota for the first time, and in a letter to his mother, he described his surprise that the local newspapers noted his arrival. He wrote:

> Things are very different here than in the Netherlands, that was made clear to us recently, because we read in three different papers that we had arrived here, we soon became known here. I also received a letter from a farmer in Corsica [South Dakota] a few days ago! He wanted me to work for him in the winter months, he wanted a Dutch farm hand to feed his cattle.[76]

Newspapers provided information on the wider comings and goings of those within the Dutch network. The arrival of a never-before-seen cousin from the Netherlands (whether a blood relation or not) constituted a newsworthy event. Being part of this network provided Sy with useful connections, receiving job offers from other Dutch Americans less than three weeks after arriving in South Dakota.

The local news section of the *Lynden Tribune* of Lynden, Washington, provides an example of the importance of newspapers and the breadth of the interconnection between Dutch Reformed communities. Lynden, where Albert had considered moving, had (and still has) a CRC and a substantial Dutch population.[77] On November 20, 1919, the newspaper reported that "Dorothy and Bernard De Neui left Saturday for a three-month visit with relatives and friends at Chancellor, South Dakota."[78] A common ethnicity and heritage tied together those within the Dutch American Reformed community. Through years of migration, friends, acquaintances, family members, and simply fellow Dutch Calvinist emigrants, spread from Lynden, Washington, to Chancellor, South Dakota, and, in the De Jongs' case, from New Holland, South Dakota, to Fulton, Illinois.[79]

---

ed. Robert P. Swierenga (New Brunswick, NJ: Rutgers University Press, 1985), gives further detail on the history of Dutch American newspapers. Bult provides extensive coverage of the earlier literature discussing the importance of newspapers for the community.

[76] Sy Bakker to Baaye and Gerrit Bakker, Harrison, SD, 22 Dec. 1927, letter 169:371.
[77] Renske and Albert Hiemstra to Baaye and Gerrit Bakker, New Holland, SD, 16 Sept. 1902, letter 113:261.
[78] *The Lynden Tribune* (Lynden, WA), 20 Nov. 1919. *Chronicling America: Historic American Newspapers*. Library of Congress.
[79] Robert Schoone-Jongen describes the connections fostered by Dutch Americans across these various ethnic enclaves via the pages of the *De Volksvriend*, an Orange City, Iowa, newspaper that included reports from local correspondents

Through the interconnection of these various Dutch Reformed settlements, the community developed a sense of *moral geography*. Defining moral geography, anthropologist Zareena Grewal writes, "Throughout American history, racial and religious minorities . . . have constructed narratives of their . . . marginality, narratives of *countercitizenship* linked to alternative moral geographies that compete with those of the nation."[80] Reformed connections across the United States shaped the De Jongs' understanding of place, transforming relatively insignificant towns, like Fulton, Illinois, and Lynden, Washington, into places with meaning. These connections between Dutch Reformed communities created an alternative geography.

Moral geography or ethnic geography?

Aspects of the De Jongs' faith, such as personal piety, weekly church attendance, a desire for Christian education, and reliance upon biblical language, connected them to a broader Reformed community. But what motivated the De Jongs to so strongly identify with the Dutch Reformed community—Dutch ethnicity or Reformed religion? Alternatively, was the Dutch Reformed community a "moral geography" or an "ethnic geography"? Motivation can never fully be determined, since one cannot untangle the complexity of human emotion. But by seeking to understand the relationship between religion and ethnicity for the De Jong family, we can gain a clearer understanding of the relationship between religion and the migration process.

As described above, when Pete worked in Illinois in 1896, he connected church to the Dutch language and his "own people."[81] Lieuwe also made a connection between religion and ethnicity in the early months of their immigration; he wrote:

> We are here in the far west, I had thought that we would come from the Christian world almost into the pagan world, but God has led us otherwise. I would almost say that if I am not mistaken,

---

in various Dutch communities across the nation. See Robert Schoone-Jongen, "Dateline Orange City, Iowa: De Volksvriend and the Creation of Dutch American Community in the Midwest, 1874–1951," *The Annals of Iowa* 69, no. 3 (2010): 308-31. Suzanne Sinke also discusses the intercommunal connections via newspapers in *Dutch Immigrant Women*, 144-45.

80   Zareena Grewal, *Islam Is a Foreign Country: American Muslims and the Global Crisis of Authority*, Nation of Newcomers: Immigrant History as American History (NY: NY University Press, 2014).

81   Pete De Jong to Baaye and Gerrit Bakker, Capron, II, 2 May 1897, letter 54:157.

many children of God have left the Netherlands to try to find a living in America.⁸²

The De Jongs equated the unknown of the United States and the masses of non-Dutch people with paganism and darkness. In attempting to persuade Baaye and Gerrit to emigrate, Lieuwe wrote,

> The people here serve and fear God, mother [Tjitske] says you [Baaye and Gerrit] had better prepare yourselves for travelling. . . . . We live here on a farm belonging to Fenenga from the island where Jensma is from. Gerrit knows the grown ones, especially his son Gerrit Fenenga."⁸³

Living among Dutch people and fellow Reformed Calvinists in America comforted the De Jongs.

Although closely connected, the Reformed faith was not identical with Dutch ethnicity, and Dutch ethnicity was not the same as being Reformed. Pete's wife Dina became a church member before the birth of their first child. Renske wrote: "[Dina] will be admitted tomorrow as planned. . . . Her parents seem to be quite happy that she is taking that path, they are, said in a Dutch way, modern. . . . Their life is very different, looks good on the outside."⁸⁴ That the De Jongs knew Dina's parents, being nonreligious and not church members, demonstrates that they knew Dutch immigrants unconnected to the Reformed community.

On the other hand, Nellie's work in New Mexico exposed the De Jongs to non-Dutch, but yet Reformed, Christians. In 1906 Nellie served as the first teacher of the Zuni Christian day school, an expansion of the CRC's first school among the Navajo, which started at Rehoboth in 1903.⁸⁵ Renske described how Nellie "works for God's Kingdom" and that she hopes that "things change and . . . that [Nellie] will be a blessing there."⁸⁶ Renske considered Nellie to be working for God and hoped that she could bring Christianity to the Zuni people. Renske's

---

⁸² Lieuwe and Tjitske De Jong to Baaye and Gerrit Bakker, New Holland, SD, 5 June 1894, letter 6:53.
⁸³ Ibid.
⁸⁴ Renske and Albert De Jong to Baaye and Gerrit Bakker, New Holland, SD, 17 Jan. 1903, letter 116:269.
⁸⁵ Scott Hoezee and Christopher H. Meehan, *Flourishing in the Land: A Hundred-Year History of Christian Reformed Missions in North America* (Grand Rapids, MI: Eerdmans, 1996), 31-32.
⁸⁶ Renkse and Albert De Jong to Baaye and Gerrit Bakker, Harrison, SD, 11 Jan. 1909, letter 127:291.

vision of the church stretched beyond the Dutch community. Similarly, in 1911, after Nellie had served in New Mexico for a number of years, Lieuwe wrote:

> But they [the Zuni Mission] have had an unpleasant winter because of the deaths of the Indian children, there was an epidemic of measles amongst them. But how can it be otherwise in this pagan world full of infectious diseases, the children live in the like as animals [sic], sometimes seven a day were buried at the churchyard. Yet not one of them from the Mission has died, hoping that the Lord continues to look after them.[87]

Lieuwe separated the non-Christian children from the Christian children and believed that God protected the Christian children at the mission. Reformed Christianity created a dividing line: Lieuwe saw not only an ethnic dichotomy of Native American and Dutch but also a religious dichotomy of Christian and non-Christian. Just as their Dutch Reformed faith set the De Jongs apart, the Reformed faith of the converted Zuni set them apart from those unreceptive to the mission's message.

The religiously motivated distinctions seen in Lieuwe's letter complicates racial issues within the CRC's missionary outreach to the Zuni and the Navajo.[88] Racial and cultural differences certainly influenced the CRC's missionary efforts. The mission's impact on the Native American community went beyond spiritual conversion and religious teaching. The imparting of Western culture became intertwined with the spiritual goals of the mission, blurring the line between conversion and cultural adaptation. For example, students at the mission school adopted Western clothing, and the mission gave sewing lessons to Navajo women while teaching children Bible lessons.[89]

---

[87] Lieuwe and Tjitske De Jong to Baaye and Gerrit Bakker, Harrison, SD, 4 April 1911, letter 142:313.

[88] The discussion of race, cultural imperialism, and missionary work is much debated, and I do not desire to enter into that conversation here. My discussion of a religious dichotomy is not intended to deny the impact of race in the Zuni and Navajo mission effort; but rather, my goal is to highlight the religious viewpoint of Dutch Americans associated with the mission.

[89] Christian Reformed Church: Board of Foreign Missions, *Navaho and Zuni: Mission Work of the Christian Reformed Church* (Grand Rapids, MI: Grand Rapids Printing Company, 1914), 4, 12-13. Dorothy Dykhuizen, *Go Quickly and Tell* (Grand Rapids, MI: Eerdmans, 1946), 44-45. For more information regarding the Zuni and Rehoboth mission, including a number of primary sources, see the website created by the author: *Blessed Be the Ties that Bind: The Cultural Encounter of Dutch Immigrants and Native Americans*, found at http://bindingtie.omeka.net.

Despite this tendency to combine Western culture and Christianity, Dutch CRC members associated with the mission still maintained religious motivations. Religious desires and racial tension coexisted.

The De Jongs did not close off the Christian Reformed community from others of non-Dutch identity, just as the community did not include every Dutch immigrant. Maybe their personal experience with George rejecting the church opened them up to this possibility, although one cannot be sure how George's separation played a role. Nellie's work at the Navajo mission, however, demonstrated a desire to include Navajos in the CRC subculture. Church membership and religious beliefs, rather than Dutch ethnicity, created the communal boundaries. Pious intentions expanded the moral geography of the CRC community to include Navajos converted through missionary efforts.[90]

Conclusion

Religion formed the center of the De Jongs' life. Their faith held the family together, tied them to their local community, connected them to a broader network of like-minded Dutch immigrants, and motivated Nellie's evangelistic efforts. Religious identity and the community that affirmed it constructed the De Jongs' immigrant experience. The routine of church attendance structured their week, while their moral geography provided a place of belonging and gave shape to their world, giving greater importance to places like Sioux Center, Iowa; Lynden, Washington; and Zuni, New Mexico—communities that meant little to anyone outside of the Reformed faithful.

The De Jong family attests to a competing narrative of religious devotion and ethnicization. Lieuwe and Tjitske De Jong settled on the open prairie of South Dakota, thousands of miles from their home in the Netherlands, only to surround themselves with others of similar ethnic and religious background. Yet, American life created the opportunity

---

[90] Discussing the CRC community in Chicago in the 1960s and 1970s, Mark T. Mulder notes the mobility of the CRC subculture of church and school during "white flight" from the city to the suburbs, allowing the Chicago CRC congregations to avoid changing racial circumstances. In the case of the Navajo and Zuni mission, mobility created the opposite effect. The creation of a Christian Reformed church and school in the desert of New Mexico allowed for racial expansion within the denomination. See Mark T. Mulder, *Shades of White Flight: Evangelical Congregations and Urban Departure* (New Brunswick, NJ: Rutgers University Press, 2014), 31.

for the De Jongs to participate in expanding the CRC community on the basis of common belief rather than ethnic origin. The De Jongs' religious convictions created a paradox in which their Calvinist beliefs fostered ethnic solidarity, while also expanding the boundaries of the religious community to include nonethnic converts, demonstrating that among religiously devoted migrants, faith had the power to both sustain ethnicity and create new communities.

CHAPTER 10

Dutch Immigrants and Nature: Environmental Observations in Letters from Dutch Pioneer Settlers in the United States, 1835–1860

Henk Aay

Human migration is a central dynamic of history. Whether migrants are international refugees, slaves forcibly relocated, those internally displaced, or voluntary immigrants, relocation, to a greater or lesser extent, is invariably a changeover. At the very least, migration entails movement from a country or region where, as inhabitants, people are highly adapted, knowledgeable, and at home to a place where they are strangers, unfamiliar and inexperienced in a new setting. Besides the social, economic, political, technical, and psychological adaptations and adjustments to a new place, this universal changeover experience also has a significant environmental dimension. Migration to rural, and as yet, largely wild, pioneer zones—landscapes where people are more directly engaged with the natural environment by way of farming, forestry, and mining—often poses significant environmental challenges, opportunities, and hardships, and requires new environmental learning and acclimatization.

Beginning with Asian immigrants to a new continent tens of thousands of years ago, continuing with the transatlantic migrations from Europe and Africa from the sixteenth to the eighteenth centuries, to migrations to North America from all corners of the world from the nineteenth century to today, the peopling of North America by those from other environments and cultures has always been accompanied by environmental challenges, adjustments, and adaptations. When the natural home environment, especially as it relates to livelihood, is quite different from the new setting, greater habituation is required than for new arrivals in familiar settings. And still more exacting environmental learning applies to the first ethnic pioneers from abroad who are moving into an as-yet largely unknown area to them.

The first wave of Dutch immigration to North America was to the New Netherland colony (1614-64), settling in what is today western Long Island, Manhattan, northern New Jersey, and the Hudson Valley. By the time England took over New Netherland, from seven- to eight thousand people had settled and served tours of duty in the colony—soldiers and sailors with the West India Company, merchants, traders, farmers, farm laborers, craftsmen, slaves, and those escaping religious persecution.[1] Their descendants further concentrated themselves in the initial settlement zones and spread out farther into Upstate New York.

The second wave of Dutch immigration to the United States began in earnest in 1846. Between 1840 and 1940, more than two hundred thousand Dutch immigrants arrived, settling primarily in the Midwest.[2] During the nineteenth century, the Dutch-immigrant stream was "overwhelmingly a folk migration of rural families seeking cheap land in the United States."[3] Farmers and farm laborers, as well as those employed in the secondary and tertiary sectors supporting the rural economy—artisans, retailers, clergy, and other professionals—made up the bulk of the occupations.[4] Both seventeenth-century New Netherland and nineteenth-century Dutch America in the Midwest and beyond were primary economies: this involved the extraction and collection of natural resources, the cultivation of crops, and the raising of livestock. In these primary industries, relations with the natural environment are fundamental and direct.

---

[1] Jaap Jacobs, "Population and Immigration," ch. 4 in *The Colony of New Netherland, A Dutch Settlement in Seventeenth-Century America* (Ithaca, NY: Cornell University Press, 2009), 32-61.

[2] Hans Krabbendam, *Freedom on the Horizon: Dutch Immigration to America, 1840-1940* (Grand Rapids, MI: Eerdmans, 2009), app. 1, 361-62.

[3] Robert P. Swierenga, "Delayed Transition from Folk to Labor Migration," ch. 2 in *Faith and Family, Dutch Immigration and Settlement in the United States, 1820-1920* (NY: Holmes and Meier, 2000), 35.

[4] Ibid., 57-67.

Primary sources for studying immigrants' environmental observations, knowledge, and behavior

Immigrant and visitor writings, as used in this study, are a principal resource for ethnic environmental history. Private correspondence between immigrants and their families and friends back home maintained bonds and exchanged news and information about loved ones and events from both sides of the ocean.[5] Letters from immigrants may well include environmental observations about the journey over sea and land, as well as descriptions of the environmental conditions, requirements, and successes and failures for life and livelihood at the settlement. Memoirs by immigrants, looking back, that frame, integrate, and interpret personal reminiscences and documents into single accounts, are another primary source. These may also describe the environmental conditions that had to be overcome, adapted to, transformed, or managed at the settlement site.[6] Articles and letters in Dutch American newspapers that include information about environmental conditions and challenges in various parts of the country are another primary source; these have not yet been used to research Dutch American environmental history.[7] Further afield, but relevant for environmental interpretation and fashioning dominant environmental narratives and mythologies, is the body of Dutch American arts and letters—stories, novels, paintings, pageants, and poetry—about emigration, immigrant life, and Dutch American culture, written about and painted by immigrants and their descendants.[8] This

---

[5] Hans Krabbendam reviewed and categorized the studies that have used Dutch immigrant letters and inventoried the published letter collections in his "Avant la Lettre: The Use of Dutch Immigrant Letters in Historical Research," in *The Dutch Adapting in North America: Papers Presented at the Thirteenth Biennial Conference for the Association for the Advancement of Dutch American Studies*, ed. and comp. Richard H. Harms (Grand Rapids, MI: Calvin College, 2001). See also, Krabbendam, "Contact: Letters and Newspapers," ch. 8 in *Freedom on the Horizon.*

[6] A rare example of Dutch American environmental history using memoirs is Jan J. Boersema and Anthonia Boersema-Bremmer, "'The wilderness has been made to blossom': Nineteenth-Century Dutch Immigrants and the Natural World," in *Sharing Pasts: Dutch Americans through Four Centuries*, ed. Henk Aay, Janny Venema, and Dennis Voskuil (Holland, MI: Van Raalte Press, 2017), 25-50. The largest collection of Dutch immigrant memoirs is Henry S. Lucas, *Dutch Immigrant Memoirs and Related Writings*, rev. ed. (Grand Rapids, MI: Eerdmans, 1997).

[7] Conrad Bult, "Dutch-American Newspapers: Their History and Role," in *The Dutch in America; Immigration, Settlement, and Cultural Change*, ed. Robert P. Swierenga (New Brunswick, NJ: Rutgers University Press, 1985), 273-93.

[8] W. Lagerwey, *Neen Nederland, 'k vergeet u niet: Een beeld van het immigrantenleven in Amerika tussen 1846 en 1945 in verhalen, schetsen en gedichten* (Baarn, the NL: Bosch

body of work has also not yet been surveyed for its environmental content and interpretations.

Outside of immigrant and related writings, maps of Dutch American settlements and farming zones in their relationship to the natural environment are another source of relevant primary information for Dutch American environmental history. Settlement locations reveal environmental preferences, opportunities, and skills. Not infrequently, one hears and reads about the proclivity of the Dutch and Dutch Americans for muck soils and soil drainage and for market gardening, greenhouses, and garden centers near cities.[9]

Dutch immigrant letters

As the number of Dutch immigrants increased and mailing costs fell, especially with a postal agreement between the Netherlands and the United States, the number of private letters exchanged between Dutch immigrants and their family and friends back home increased dramatically. Millions of letters were exchanged from the beginning of the second wave of Dutch immigration in 1846 to the post WWII period.[10] Only a very small percentage of these letters have been saved, collected, and archived, and even fewer have been published in collections. The largest archive of Dutch immigrant letters is found in the Dutch Immigrant Papers Collection at Heritage Hall at Calvin College. Nearly all the letters housed there have been transcribed and translated into English. Of the 4,970 letters in this archive, 2,793 are American postings.[11] An assortment of letters from this archive, selected on the basis of the geographic origins of the immigrant writers, their destination and acculturation, and the interest and detail of the letters, was published in Herbert Brink's *Dutch American Voices. Letters from the United States, 1850-1930*.[12] Other letters from the Heritage Hall

---

& Keuning, 1982); Robert P. Swierenga, Jacob E. Nyenhuis, Nella Kennedy, eds., *Dutch-American Arts and Letters in Historical Perspective* (Holland, MI: Van Raalte Press, 2008). That immigration and immigrant stories are not played out as a genre in Dutch American letters is clear from the work of Frisian author Hylke Speerstra: *Cruel Paradise: Life Stories of Dutch Emigrants*, trans. Henry Baron (Grand Rapids, MI: Eerdmans, 2005), and Hylke Speerstra, *The Comfort Bird*, trans. Henry Baron (Oakville, Canada: Mokeham Publishing, 2017).

9   See Swierenga, *Farming the Muck*, ch. 2.
10 Krabbendam, *Avant la Lettre*, 9-11.
11 Dutch Immigrant Papers, 1786-[ongoing], collection no. 78, ACC.
12 Herbert, J. Brinks, ed., *Dutch American Voices: Letters from the United States, 1850-1930* (Ithaca, NY: Cornell University Press, 1995). Earlier, Brinks used excerpts from letters he had collected and housed in Heritage Hall to let immigrants describe

collection and from other college and university archives, as well as from private collections, have also been published in book form, including *Iowa Letters: Dutch Immigrants on the American Frontier* and letters from Wisconsin in *I End with my Pen but not with my Heart: Dutch Immigrant Letters, Memoirs and Travel Journals*.[13] There are also several published collections of letters written by Dutch immigrants to Canada.[14]

Although there are always more letters to collect, transcribe, translate, and publish, these indispensable efforts to bring immigrant letters into public view and make available for analysis, largely carried out during the last fifty years, have prepared the way for the study of these letters from a number of thematic perspectives. Hans Krabbendam has suggested that the study of immigrant letters could usefully be organized into three levels: micro (correspondence from an individual family);[15] meso (letters from a particular region, place, or time period; surveys of particular content, for example, environment, homesickness, faith, politics); and macro (mail costs, transport, and international postal agreements). This study of environmental observations in immigrant letters, therefore, belongs to the meso level of inquiry.

In this essay, I focus on letters written en route to and from the very first pioneer locations settled by Dutch immigrants in the Midwest, beginning in 1846 until 1860, including, but not limited to, the Holland colony in West Michigan; the Wisconsin settlements in Sheboygan, Milwaukee, and Fond du Lac Counties; the Pella colony in Marion County, Iowa; and settlements in Cook County, Illinois. These letters include early environmental observations about areas in America's Midwest from Dutch immigrants to those in the Netherlands

---

in their own words, various settlements, farming, and church life: Herbert J. Brinks, *Write Back Soon: Letters from Immigrants in America* (Grand Rapids, MI: CRC Publications, 1986).

[13] Johan Stellingwerff, *Iowa Letters: Dutch Immigrants on the American Frontier*, ed. Robert P. Swierenga, trans. Walter Lagerwey (Grand Rapids, MI: Eerdmans, 2004). *Iowa Letters* is an English-language edition of J. Stellingwerff's *Amsterdamse emigranten:Onbekende brieven uit de prairie van Iowa 1846-1873* (Amsterdam: Buijten & Schipperheijn, 1975). Several additional collections of letters from Iowa were added to the letters collected by Stellingwerff to produce *Iowa Letters*. Mary Risseeuw, comp., *I end with my pen but not with my heart: Dutch immigrant letters, memoirs and travel journals* (Sheboygan Falls, WI: Sheboygan County Historical Research Center, 2008).

[14] Herman Ganzevoort, ed. and trans., *The Last Illusion: Letters from Dutch Immigrants in the "Land of Opportunity," 1924-1930* (Calgary, Alberta: University of Calgary Press, 1999); Donald Sinnema, ed. and trans., *The First Dutch Settlement in Alberta; Letters from the Pioneer Years, 1903-1914* (Calgary, Alberta: University of Calgary Press, 2005).

[15] For example, Brian W. Beltman, *Dutch Farmer in the Missouri Valley, The Life and Letters of Ulbe Eringa, 1866-1950* (Chicago: University of Illinois Press, 1996).

interested in following in their footsteps. Other pioneer locations and zones, of course, followed from these first areas in subsequent decades (northwestern Iowa, southwestern Minnesota, the Dakotas, northwestern Washington State, to name just a few) but during this earliest period, environmental knowledge was least developed and at a premium. Moreover, unlike the earliest pioneer areas, subsequent migration to new zones was often spearheaded by and certainly included established settlers or their descendants, as well as new immigrants. They had already adapted and, although their environmental knowledge required further adjustment to still other new settings, it was already quite developed. In addition, the settlement of new areas farther west during subsequent decades of the nineteenth century was steered and aided by more widespread and publically available information.

Cover of the pamplet containing J. Pelmulder's letters[16]

[16] Jelle Pelmulder, *Eenvoudige maar zeer Belangrijke Brieven uit Noord-Amerika* (Dockum, Friesland: A. Schaafsma, 1859).

This period was also the time of "bacon letters" (*spek brieven*, stressing how good the immigrant life was), missives that were published (often a number of them together with a title page, introduction, and edits) as pamphlets, sold and circulated in the Netherlands, especially in those regions where immigration fever ran high. Some of these letters were written for publication; the suitability of others for wider distribution was discovered once they reached the Netherlands. These were written by leaders and other immigrants in the United States and made the case for crossing the ocean and for particular destinations in America; they described immigrants' experiences and offered advice. Positive environmental appraisals were an important component of such "bacon" letters, but at the same time, they did not hesitate to explain why other possible settlement areas fell short environmentally.

The distinction between private and public (published) immigrant letters is an important one. Private letters were highly personal, written for family and friends in the Netherlands; by and large, they focused on the here and now: illness, death, birth, family members, crops, prices, land cleared, and except for some pious reflection, there was little generalizing or rumination. Public letters that were published were used for information and promotion. They relayed knowledge and points of view potentially useful to everyone considering immigrating. They were more compelling than third-person accounts because they communicated personal experience and information.

Methodology

I extracted all the private immigrant letters written before 1861 from the Dutch Immigrant Papers Collection in Heritage Hall at Calvin College, and from the three collections of published letters cited above: *Dutch American Voices, Iowa Letters,* and *I end with my pen but not with my heart.* Many letters from these published collections were, of course, also part of the Dutch Immigrant Papers Collection. Together this search yielded 314 letters. In addition, I collected the pre-1861 letters published in pamphlets from a variety of sources and collections: the Dutch Immigrant Papers Collection at Calvin College, the research files and library of the Van Raalte Institute at Hope College, the website of Tresoar, the Frisian History and Literature Center, and Google books. That search yielded thirty-eight public letters published in pamphlets.[17]

---

[17] I am grateful to my colleague, Jan Boersema, for help finding many of these pamphlets.

Archive	Citation		
		No.	Content
1. Worldview/Progress/Development			
2. Weather/Climate			
3. Landscape Description Scenery	on the journey		
	at the settlement		
4. Natural Environment (Soil as Resource)	a. soil		
	b. plants		
	c. animals		
	d. birds		
5. Additional Natural Resources (beside soils)	a. household		
	b. crafts		
	c. farming		
	d. industry		
6. Environmental Practices	a. agriculture		
	b. forestry		
7. Nature's Impact on People			
Quotations			

**Coding sheet for environmental observations
in Dutch immigrant letters**

The environmental observations in each of these letters were identified, classified, and recorded into categories using the coding sheet above, facilitating both quantitative and qualitative appraisals.[18] An environmental observation (or thread) about a given

---

[18] The coding framework went through several iterations as I read through the letters. The results of coding using earlier frameworks were applied to the final version.

topic, practice, or event in a letter could be either a single sentence or several paragraphs. They could be assigned to more than one category. Counts of the coded environmental observations from this body of letters were compiled. Qualitative information was captured in summaries of the environmental observations, as well as quotations from the transcriptions or translated letters. The principal distinction on the check-off list is between what, on the one hand, may be called observations about natural history (such as scenery, landscape, climate, sightings or information about wildlife), and, on the other hand, observations about the natural world (such as resources, amenities and hazards related to and impacting life and livelihood, including references to soil, forest, and weather). Soil, for example, was always perceived as a resource in the letters, never as natural history. The very first category on the check-off list, worldview/progress/development, is clearly not an environmental category but is very relevant for a letter writer's view of earth as modified by human action.

Environmental observations by the numbers

Without checking immigrant writings, one might conjecture that because the Netherlands and the United States are both in the northern midlatitudes, unlike other Dutch immigration destinations such as South Africa or the Dutch East Indies, environmental conditions would be quite similar and therefore observations would be scarcely mentioned. Such sentiment is very clear in a letter from Dirk van Bochove, a carpenter in Brooklyn, New York, to his brother-in-law and sister, H. Tanis and Jannetje Tanis van Bochove, in Ouddorp, Zuid-Holland, the Netherlands. Unlike most Dutch immigrants, van Bochove and his wife Johanna did not push on to the Midwest but lived in Brooklyn for a year and then settled in Hoboken, New Jersey. In a relatively long letter, he described their personal situation (finances, household, English proficiency) and general conditions in the United States (commerce, poverty, government, banking, immigration, the carpentry trade). He finishes with "This ends my American report, and since the New World as far as the realm of nature is concerned has much similarity with Holland, in my view, there is no need to inform you further about this."[19] Many other immigrants, however, who journeyed inland from their ports of debarkation, did comment on the natural

---

[19] Robert P. Swierenga, ed., "A Dutch Carpenter's 'America Letter' From New York in 1849," *New York History* 72, no. 4 (Oct. 1991): 421-38; quotation p. 436.

settings they passed through and then settled into, not only because the settings were different from the Netherlands but also because they left such an impression. This reflects curiosity about their new home, where they had to make a new life. The image below maps the distribution of these Dutch immigrant letters (1835-1860) by state.

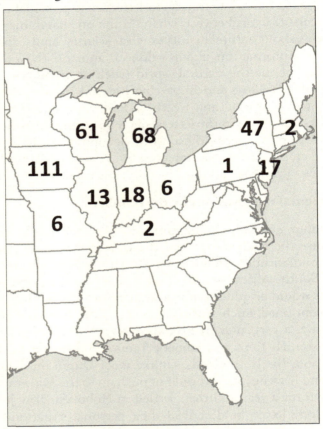

The number of Dutch immigrant letters by state, 1835-60

The number of letters from the state of New York is high, not because it was a primary settlement area during this period but because letters were written either en route or from temporary locations on the way to the Midwest. The higher number of letters from Iowa, Michigan, and Wisconsin reflect the larger number of immigrants who settled in these first pioneer zones.

Dutch Immigrants and Nature 187

The 352 letters contain 451 environmental observations. That statistic alone confirms that this type of information formed one significant strand in immigrant letters; letter writers found the environmental conditions en route and at the settlement as noteworthy and of interest to their relatives and friends. I did not classify the entire content of these letters into categories to establish the ranking of environmental observations compared to other types of commentary about such subjects as church, piety, family, community, finances, and so forth. From reading these letters, I would judge that environmental observations are a minor theme compared to these subjects.

Nearly 45 percent of the private letters include environmental observations—307 in all; 173 letters have no environmental observations. The percentage of environmental observations in public (published) letters is twice (89.5%) that of private letters. There were 144 environmental observations in these public letters and only four letters had none. Published advisory letters for those considering immigrating clearly placed a high premium on positive environmental information and unfavorable counter information about other areas; such reports were seen as encouraging people to immigrate.

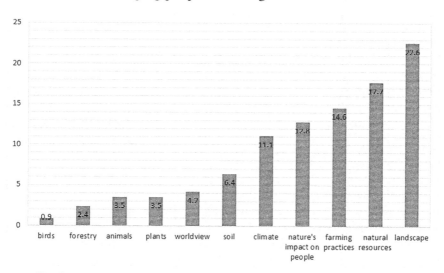

Environmental observations in all surveyed letters, 1835-60

When environmental observations are grouped into categories provided by the coding schema and graphed by percentage of the total observations in ascending order, several patterns become evident. Overall, Dutch immigrant letter writers make fewer remarks about natural history, that is, observations about nature unrelated to human purposes, intentions, projects, uses, and activities. Observations about birds, plants (not crops), and animals on the lower left side are each under 4 percent of the total number. Nevertheless, when one combines those first three categories (7.9%) and adds the highest category—landscape—the visible features of an area of land—then more than 30 percent of the observations are accounted for. It is not surprising that the Dutch immigrant letter writers wanted to tell their family and friends in the Netherlands what they had seen. Many had lived their entire lives in rather small, local, rural areas, centered on market towns. They hardly ever ventured outside their home area. And now, not only had they traveled through the Netherlands to reach a port of embarkation, such as Amsterdam or Rotterdam, and experienced an ocean voyage of a number of weeks, they also had traveled through the eastern part of the United States to reach their destination. They had observed a great deal that was new and different, and it is very understandable that they wanted to share all of this with family and friends. While the journey across sea and land was often harrowing and full of hardships, at the same time, their eyes and minds were filled with new and unfamiliar sights. The natural history observations have less to do with their own lives, goals, and projects and more to do with recording what they had seen and experienced.

The remaining environmental categories—forestry, soil, climate, nature's impact on people, farming practices, and natural resources—mainly on the right side of the graph, tracked higher, together making up 65 percent of the observations. These were very much related to the settlers' livelihoods, their needs and wants, and the ways in which their lives were joined to the natural environment. Drought reduced the crop by 50 percent; trees were felled and branches burned to create fields, and clay was used to fill the gaps between the logs of a home. Again, it is understandable that the bulk of environmental observations in pioneer immigrant letters are related to their reacting and adapting to new natural environments in their lives and enterprises. For most immigrants, success in farming required understanding, accepting, and dealing with new and unfamiliar natural settings and turning their homeland agricultural knowledge and skills to these setttings.

The immigrant letters published at the time of writing had a diverse public readership; the private letters were circulated and read only by family members and friends of the immigrant writer. Not only is the percentage of environmental comments in the public letters twice that of the private ones but the make-up of the environmental categories in each type of letter also shows some notable differences. In the graph below, the composition of the environmental commentary of the private and public letters is shown side by side. The public letters devote a significantly larger percentage of environmental commentary to soil (9.2% vs. 4.6%) and to landscape (35.6% vs. 20.5%).

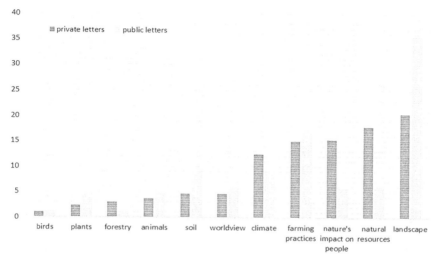

Comparison of public and private immigrant letters by percentage of observations in different environmental categories

This makes sense given the promotional purpose of the public letters and the importance of soil quality to potential immigrant farmers. The environmental commentary of the private letters, on the other hand, gives more weight to nature's impact on people (15.3% vs. 5.8%) and on natural resources (17.9% vs. 5.8%). This is also, I think, understandable. Private correspondence describes the actual operation of particular immigrants' farms; the success and failure of their crops, given weather conditions and soil moisture; the natural resources of wood, water, soil, seed, and weather, necessary for their farm; and the impact of weather on their livelihood and daily lives. The published promotional letters describe beneficial general environmental conditions; they do not recount farm-specific environmental problems and difficulties.

The weight of the categories of the environmental observations may be differentiated for the three states with the greatest number of letters—Iowa, Michigan, and Wisconsin.

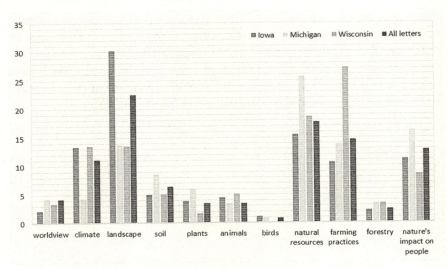

Percentage of environmental observations by category in immigrant letters by state, 1835-60

The settlement zones in Michigan and Wisconsin were covered with mixed deciduous and coniferous forests, whereas Iowa was made up of prairie and mainly deciduous woods in the river valleys. The settlement zone in south central Iowa had a drier and less moderated weather and climate, as well as drier soils than the zone around the Great Lakes. The Netherlands itself earlier had either been largely deforested for farming and pasture land or had consisted of drained wetlands without trees; its maritime West Coast climate, with cooler summers, was considerably more moderate than the more continental climate of the Midwest, with colder, snowier winters and warmer summers. In short, there were plenty of environmental differences to catch the attention of the Dutch pioneer immigrants; these differences may have stood out more in some settlement regions than others.

The comparative table of states, however, does not show many differences in environmental observations by state: soil, plants, animals, birds, natural resources, forestry, and nature's impact on people all have roughly the same percentages. The more general differences between the Midwest and the Netherlands produced a rather convergent categorization of environmental observations. A few differences among the three states stand out: the relatively small number of comments about climate and weather in letters from Michigan compared to Iowa and Wisconsin, the much higher number of observations about landscape from Iowa immigrants, and the greater attention paid to environment as related to farming practices in the letters from Wisconsin. Only the extraordinary focus on the Iowa landscape has a plausible explanation. The rolling prairie was something very different from anything the Dutch immigrants to this state had ever seen; it prompted them to write home about it at twice the rate of those who described the landscapes of the other states.

In their own words: the content of environmental observations in early immigrant letters[20]

The content of these environmental observations and commentary from the letters will be considered and discussed using quotations organized by the broad categories of the coding sheet. The quotations are illustrative, not representative.

Worldview and nature: Seceder environmental theology

Derk and Louise Arnaud, their children, and several relatives sailed for the United States from Hellevoetsluis, south of Rotterdam, on June 4, 1846; their destination was the port of Baltimore, but their passage was marked by a series of storms that blew the ship off course. Their ship anchored in Boston on July 20th, a voyage of more than six weeks. They secured lodgings, and Derk found work as a cabinetmaker, saving money to pay back the loan taken out for their passage and for moving to the Midwest with Van Raalte. During their stay in Boston, the family became acquainted with the city and its immediate surroundings. On September 11, 1846, Louise Arnaud wrote an extensive letter to Rev. Brummelkamp, a leader of the Seceders in Arnhem. Like many letters from Seceders, her letter is replete with religious discourse. The family's hardships, fortunes, and experiences during the crossing and life in Boston are all interpreted through the lens of her Christian faith, prayer, and Bible passages. Louise regards the poverty, public drunkenness, gambling, Sabbath-breaking, and other social ills in the Netherlands as either sinful per se or the result of sin and God's punishment for such wickedness. Puritan-shaped Boston, by contrast, she notes, has more than eighty-two churches, strictly observes the Sabbath, and as a

---

[20] I have checked the available translations in the Dutch Immigrant Papers Collection (Collection 78), ACC, against the original Dutch texts, where possible, and made changes, where appropriate. I am grateful to Nella Kennedy, official translator at the Van Raalte Institute, for help with the translations.

result, suffers from none of these maladies. And then she extends these theological considerations to the natural environment.

> Furthermore, on Sunday, one cannot buy a thing the whole day, and it is very quiet in the otherwise busy city. Many take a walk in the country on Sunday, but no one is able to buy any refreshments. Everywhere rocks can be found, also iron benches, but the most beautiful sight is a cemetery, the quiet place of rest for God's children. My husband walked already early in the morning for an hour and a half in the country; he said it is a delight to see the beautiful rolling landscape, the delicious fruit trees and the lovely cattle. And the fruitful meadows watered with moisture like a fountain springing out of ground. Here one sees that the country greets its Sabbaths with pleasure. Not a week passes but the Lord gives us a mild fruitful rain and soft thunder storms. I have yet to see hail or a downpour which so often ruins the harvest in Holland. All of the fruits here are good, and the curse does not rest upon the land as it is by you. Dear dominee, hasten this way, but tell the congregation that the Lord blesses the land if the people hallow the Sabbaths.[21]

Environmental welfare comes from faithfully following God as outlined in the Scriptures; environmental disruption follows from its opposite. Louise Arnaud's letter of September 11, 1846, as well as another letter written by her from Boston on December 30, 1846, was published in 1847 as part of a nearly one-hundred-page pamphlet, distributed and circulated especially among Seceders in the Netherlands interested in immigrating to America.[22] The pamphlet also included letters from R. Sleijster, a settler in Waupun, Wisconsin; Wyckoff, minister in the old Dutch Reformed Church in America promising help to immigrants; and immigration leader, Van Raalte, about his journey to Detroit and his plans for the settlement colony.

Louise Arnaud's letter was not written for publication, but when Rev. Anthony Brummelkamp, a leader of the Seceders, included it in his pamphlet, it received much attention; the publication went through several printings. While there are more cautious, sober-minded, and

---

[21] Louise Arnaud to A. Brummelkamp, Boston, MA, to Arnhem, Gelderland, the NL, 11 Sept. 1846, published letter and translation, folder 27, box 2, Dutch Immigrant Papers, collection no. 78, ACC.
[22] A. Brummelkamp, *Stemmen uit Noord-Amerika* (Amsterdam: Hoogkamer & Compe., 1847), 26-52.

realistic appraisals of American life in the other letters, Louise Arnaud's perception of a Christian society and a follow-on blessed natural environment in Boston must have helped convince some Seceders to immigrate and replicate this elsewhere.

Weather and climate

Some 11 percent of the environmental observations in these immigrant letters describe weather and climate, usually in contrast to those of the Netherlands and especially about the greater extremes of hot and cold in America. Jan Zahn arrived in Muscatine, Iowa, on the Mississippi River on August 9, 1856, two months after he had left the Netherlands. Between 1856 and 1858, he wrote eight letters to his brothers, sisters, and friends in Zutphen, Gelderland, his hometown.[23] His letters are lively and wide ranging, touching on many family matters, as well as providing diverse and candid observations about life in Muscatine and America. Zahn's descriptions about the severity of Iowa winters against the background of the quite moderate winters in the Netherlands, with infrequent snow and short-lived daytime frost, bring home the lack of awareness of and preparedness for dangerous and disabling frostbite among Dutch immigrants.

> As to the winter here, what shall I write? Imagine the worst and harshest cold, and you still would not know half of what it is like. Oh, oh! The winter season that I am experiencing is something else. For three days it froze so hard here that the Mississippi River was not only covered with ice but hundreds of wagons loaded with wood and other cargo crossed it. The Mississippi is a half hour walking in width at Muscatine and flows through all of America. For several days now the snow has been four feet deep. Now you have to realize that everyone here says this is the beginning, what people in Holland would call a night frost....
>
> Several people here have had frozen ears, hands, nose, etc., and those cannot heal but have to be removed. Last winter Wynand also had a finger removed but this is still nothing; several people have frozen to death.[24]

---

[23] Jan George Zahn to relatives, Muscatine, IA, to Zutphen, Gelderland, the NL, 26 Aug. 1856 to 20 Sept. 1858, eight letters and translation, folder 15, box 76, Dutch Immigrant Papers, collection no. 78, ACC.

[24] Ibid., letter of 17 Dec. 1856.

Landscapes en route

Landscape was the most commonly used category of environmental description with more than 20 percent of the observations. Landscape, of course, is an amalgam of nature and culture—mountains *and* mines, forests *and* farmland, and prairies *and* barns. The transatlantic crossing and land journey to their destination were such once-in-a-lifetime events that early Dutch immigrants were drawn and compelled to write about what they had seen and experienced on their journeys for their relatives and friends back home.

Jelle Pelmulder, a teacher, and his family, travelled from Bornwerd, Friesland, to Pella, Iowa. They arrived in New York City, June 15, 1855, on the ship *South Carolina*, after a crossing of more than six weeks. They then proceeded by train to Philadelphia, Pittsburgh, and Cleveland; by ship over Lake Erie to Detroit; by train to Chicago and Rock Island, Illinois, then the end of the rail line; by river steamboat to Muscatine, Iowa; and, finally, more than a hundred miles to Pella by wagon. They arrived on July 3, 1855. Pelmulder wrote five letters—one to his wife's brother, Jan Klazes Heeringa, during the crossing and four to his pharmacist friend, Jacobus Meinhardi Swartte van Loon, well after the family arrived and settled in Pella. Together, these letters were intended as a single travel account. It is one of the most interesting, insightful, helpful, and well-written travel accounts of Dutch immigration to America available. It was considererd so by Swartte van Loon and others at the time; they arranged the publication of these letters as a pamphlet for sale and distribution to those considering immigration.[25]

In his letters, Pelmulder regularly describes the landscapes his family was passing through on their journey from New York City to Pella, Iowa. He realized that he would not be able to continue his teaching career in America and looked at the land they were crossing as a would-be farmer. As such, he acknowledged his preference for human landscapes governed by the natural world as opposed to urban landscapes; in such geographical settings, Pelmulder felt that the hand of God could clearly be seen.[26] Along the route from New York City to Philadelphia, he wrote:

> Along the railway the ground continually had a reddish tint and was stony. The crops in the field were lean and much land

---

[25] Pelmulder, *Eenvoudige maar zeer Belangrijke Brieven uit Noord-America*.
[26] Ibid., 82.

uncultivated. The cows that we saw walking along the route were thin and small, and I don't remember seeing any that were not red. When we came closer to Philadelphia, the soil became better, and we saw lovely homes and beautiful villages along the route; almost all the houses were painted white. There the land was more cultivated, and cattle gave a better impression. In the distance were extensive forests. I have to tell you, my friend, that the green of the trees never before made more of a pleasing impression on me than in these first weeks in America. Our long sea voyage was a big factor in this; but I do believe that the green of the trees and plants here has a more vivid tint than in the Netherlands.[27]

After leaving Chicago for Rock Island, Illinois, they encountered prairies:

Along the way we encountered endless white prairies, alternating with higher land and occasional wetlands. Many wild roses grew along the route. To me the ground seemed to be less suitable for cultivation than for cattle. After we passed a town named Joliet, there were more hills, and more woods, and here and there, the ground was stony. The further we came, the more woods there were, although always alternating with extensive prairies but not as flat as near Chicago.[28]

Landscapes at the settlement

When seen for the first time, the landscape of the settlement region, either the final or interim destination—planned or unplanned—of the immigrant's journey, does receive attention in immigrant writings. Soon, however, it is no longer the place of a visitor but rather that of a resident, taken for granted, known and unacknowledged, a place for living and for making a living. The perception of the settlement area by its residents has little to do with the aesthetics and curiosity of the traveler and visitor and more to do with the success and contentment (or lack thereof) of the settler's life. In spite of hardships, constant

---

[27] Ibid., 64; Jelle Pelmulder to Jacobus Meinhardi Swartte van Loon, Pella, IA, to Bornwerd, Friesland, the NL, 21 Oct. 1855, transcribed photocopy of letters with partial translation, folder 28, box 15, Dutch Immigrant Papers, collection no. 78, ACC.

[28] Pelmulder, *Eenvoudige maar zeer Belangrijke Brieven uit Noord-America*, 79; my translation.

toil, and loneliness, settlers rationalized and wrote more upbeat letters about their circumstances in their newly adopted places; this was also, in part, to encourage family members and friends to consider joining them in America.

Andries Wormser, a profoundly disillusioned and failed immigrant, wanted none of that. He railed against the publication of what he perceived as deceptive promotional (bacon) letters and booklets promising a paradise in America, written to promote immigration, including the letter of Louise Arnaud.[29] Wormser arrived in Burlington, Iowa, October 29, 1848, with his wife Maria and their four daughters. Two of their daughters died from scarlet fever in the first month. In eleven letters to his brothers, written over six months, Wormser, an urbane office clerk from Amsterdam with military experience, carefully described all that was wrong with America, including unpleasant and very uncomfortable travel, with swindlers at every turn; crude construction and poor workmanship in housing, furniture, and transportation; unending physical farm labor with little to no prospects for economic betterment; and a hurried pace of life, without opportunity for the spirit and the arts.[30] This overall disillusionment understandably extended to his perception of the natural landscape at the settlement site:

> And regarding the enjoyment of nature as we understand it, I dare not predict a great deal of pleasure in this respect. You leave a country where everything is well ordered and beautiful and come here to a wasteland (I do not include the cities). I grant that they can make a deep impression on you initially, but presently it wears off and starts boring you. As you are travelling through the land, you often have beautiful vistas of forest-covered mountains, especially along the [Erie] Canal to Buffalo, but you cannot settle everywhere. In one place, it is too expensive or nothing is available, in other places one is completely isolated and there may not be another individual living for miles around. Where people settle is usually a monotonous woodland. The trees are chopped down, the stumps are not exactly a pretty sight to see, and it will take years to get rid of them. If one has cleared and broken up land, like Budde, there is not a tree in the area. Just imagine a large tract

---

[29] Stellingwerf, *Iowa Letters*, 273-77.
[30] Ibid., ch. 4, "The Disappointment of Andries N. Wormser," 219-325, see also, xvi-xvii, 2-6; Robert P. Swierenga, *Dutch Immigrants in U.S. Ship Passenger Manifests, 1820-1880*, vol. 2, s.v. "Wormser, Andrias Nikolas" (the correct spelling of his name was Andries Nicolaas Wormser).

of farmland that is completely bare and flat, and without even a single little tree; more or less in the center of the land stands a house, and in the distance you see trees all around you.[31]

Unlike most immigrants, Andries Wormser had the means to return to his homeland, and six months after they had immigrated, they were back in the Netherlands.

The natural world: wildlife

The natural environment, of course, includes more than wildlife, but here, as with landscape, I am focused on the kind of perception that belongs to the naturalist—observations about nature unrelated to human use. Soil is included on the coding sheet as part of this category; in the letters, however, soil was invariably regarded as a natural resource. Other components of the natural world, such as water and geology, were coded as part of the landscape category.

Comments about wildlife (undomesticated plants, animals, and birds) add up to almost 8 percent of the environmental observations, a minor theme. Most references to plants are quite generic—woods, grasses, shrubs. Only in the public letters published at the time of writing are trees identified; J. van de Luijster in Holland, Michigan, wrote to his parents and relatives in Hoge Zwaluwe, Noord-Brabant, the Netherlands: "Trees are plentiful and varied; hemlocks, beech, oaks, birch, cedars, and others whose names I do not know."[32] Other named plants invariably are crops. The few identified undomesticated plants are singled out because of their value as food. From Pella, Iowa, Sjoerd Sipma wrote to the residents of his home village of Bornwerd, Friesland, the Netherlands, and all would-be immigrants, in a published pamphlet:

> As far as wild fruits are concerned, there is not much to them: wild apples are good for nothing; wild grapes remain small and are as sour as vinegar; wild plumbs are good and plentiful here; blueberries and hazelnuts, plentiful here, are also quite good."[33]

[31] Stellingwerff, *Iowa Letters*, 292-93.
[32] Jannes van de Luijster to his parents, Holland, MI, to Hoge Zwaluwe, Noord-Brabant, the NL, 15 Dec. 1847, in A. Van Malsen, *Achttal Brieven Mijner Kinderen uit de Kolonie Holland in Amerika* (Zwijndrecht, the NL: J. Boden, 1848), 30. The letters in this pamphlet (but not the endnotes or the postscript) were translated and edited by John Yzenbaard in "'America' Letters from Holland," *Michigan History Magazine* 32, no. 1 (March 1948): 37-65; the quotation is found on p. 62.
[33] Sjoerd Aukes Sipma, Holland, MI, to the residents of Bornwerd, Friesland, the NL, 26 Sept. 1848, in *Belangrijke Berigten uit Pella in de Vereenigde Staten van Noord-Amerika,*

Although a letter writer could readily generalize about plant cover with such labels as "prairies" and "forests," a collective term such as "animals" (mammals, birds, reptiles, and insects) was not helpful. Animals appear as individuals and groups, and observers are obligated to either describe or identify them, if possible. For this reason, there is much more discrete naming of animals than of plants in these immigrant letters. The writers commented on bears, bedbugs, chipmunks, deer, fireflies, foxes, hares, mice, skunks, snakes, squirrels, turtles, and wolves, with wolves and deer receiving multiple mentions. Birds identified in the letters include doves, ducks, geese, hens, partridges, prairie chickens, swans, sand cranes, and turkeys.

Here is one example from Rev. Adriaan Zwemer. In a letter dated August 27, 1859, to his family in Kampen, Overijssel, otherwise given to describing his studies for the ministry in Holland, Michigan, and his experiences serving as pastor and preacher of the Reformed Church in the village of Vriesland, Michigan, Zwemer recounts living next to the church in the woods of Michigan:

> A snake, named "Loopin" here, does not frighten our children, and it is quite common to see hummingbirds (the smallest and most beautiful of birds) flying around the flower garden to get sap from the flowers, Wild cats [bobcats], foxes, raccoons, and other little animals still frequently do damage in the hen houses. When these woods were first settled, the howling of the wolves echoed through the night—now, they are no longer heard. There are still one or two bears in the neighborhood, and they are still seen occasionally. But they seem to understand that the Hollanders have bought these woodlands and that they no longer roam on their own land; they are afraid of people; but the young people wish there were more bears around in order to hunt for them.[34]

In this quotation, based both on Rev. Zwemer's personal observations and what he has heard from area residents, one can recognize the inevitable human-animal interactions that were set into

---

of *Tweede Brief van Sjoerd Aukes Sipma* (Dockum, Friesland: De wed. B. Schaafsma, 1849), 6. A translation of and introduction to this letter are found in Robert P. Swierenga, "A Dutch Immigrant's View of Frontier Iowa," *Annals of Iowa* 38, no. 2 (1965): 81-118.

[34] A. Zwemer to Helenius de Cock, Vriesland, MI, to Kampen, Overijssel, the NL, 22 Aug. 1859. Photocopy with translation, folder 4, box 77, Dutch Immigrant Papers, collection no. 78, ACC.

motion when settlers began to occupy, clear, and convert to agriculture a largely pristine natural area. Larger animals and top predators moved out because of a diminished food supply and a fear of people. Smaller mammals became accustomed to and took advantage of the presence of humans by, among other things, including farm products (and flower gardens) in their food supply. And easy access to game helped to establish hunting, an unknown and illegal pastime for farmers in the Netherlands, among first generation Dutch American young people.

Natural resources

The pioneer settlement zones were untapped, natural-resource frontiers. Survival, livelihood, cultural development, and commerce depended on inorganic materials, living organisms, and the physical geographic setting all supplied by the natural environment, labor, and mid-nineteenth-century technology. Soil, water, woods, grasses, rivers, lakes, and wildlife (plants and animals) separately and together were transformed into personal and common-property resources. Soils became cropland; soil and grass, sod houses; wild animals, game; woods, pastures; wood, timber for buildings, fences, fuel, staves, shingles, and ash; water, a potable resource from springs, rivers, and wells, for people and livestock; water, a transportation resource to reach markets; and undomesticated plants became edible fruits, nuts, herbs, and syrups. All such uses are recorded in these letters.

Because these Dutch immigrant pioneer zones were emerging agricultural economies and drew mainly farmers, farm laborers, and others interested in farming from the Netherlands, environmental observations about soil quality were the most common topic in letters home. One familiar comment was that soils in the settlement areas were especially fertile because no manuring was needed. In an anonymously published book of letters from Pella, Iowa, to people in the Dutch province of Gelderland, the author, most likely Jan Nollen, introduced his readers to the state of Iowa. Toward the end of the book, he describes the Pella settlement and its agricultural hinterland and asks his Dutch readers to imagine setting up a farm.[35] He reviews the labor-intensive tasks of manuring cropland in the Netherlands, an integral component of Dutch agriculture, especially on the sandy soils in the center and east of the country, that is, gathering manure from the stalls, cleaning

---

[35] *De Hollanders in Iowa, Brieven uit Pella van een Gelderschman* (Arnhem, the NL: D. A. Thieme, 1858), 142-76.

stables, gathering straw from fields and adding it to manure, taking manure out to the dung heap, and, finally, carting it out and spreading it over the land.[36] In Iowa such manuring was unnecessary.

> The Creator, however, has blessed the land here with such inexhaustible riches of fertility, that the manure simply presents a burden to the farmer. It is fortunate for him that his horses, cows, and pigs help him with this as much as possible by spreading their manure far and wide in the neighboring woods where they graze.[37]

In much of the higher, sandy central and eastern Netherlands, there was another environmental practice that accompanied the heavy manuring of cropland: cutting sod and gathering soil. Here and elsewhere in Western Europe, beginning already in the Middle Ages, when sandy soils placed severe limits on cropland, farmers practiced what became known as infield/outfield farming. The infields, heavily manured with dung mixed with sods and soil, could be intensively and continuously cultivated with crops. Sods were cut, and sheep were grazed in the outfield. The sods and soil were brought into the barns; the dung was mixed with the sods, and this blend was carted out to the infields.[38]

In a remarkable letter that describes his large family's sixty-two-day transatlantic passage and their overland journey by rail, river boat, and wagon to Pella, Iowa, Teunis van Veenschoten also wrote his family in Lunteren, Gelderland, his home town, about the operation of their newly acquired 150-acre farm, a thirty-five-minute walk from Pella.[39] Like others, Van Veenschoten took pride in the outstanding soil fertility of his farm and region and remarked that their current, very rudimentary,

---

[36] Ibid., 152-53.
[37] Ibid., 153. There is a translation of pages 142-76 of this book in Anonymous, Letters, 1858, 17 items, published letters, translation, Pella, Iowa, to Gelderland, the NL, folder 15, box 2, Dutch Immigrant Papers, collection no. 78, ACC.
[38] An excellent account of the features, origins and development of the infield/outfield farming system in Europe is found in Theo Spek, *Het Drentse Esdorpen-Landschap, Een Historisch-Geografisch Studie*, 2 vols. (Utrecht, the NL: Matrijs, 2004), 726-83.
[39] Additional information about the Van Veenschoten family is found in Robert P. Swierenga, *Dutch Emigrants to the United States, South Africa, South America, and Southeast Asia: An Alphabetical Listing by Household Heads and Independent Persons* (Wilmington, DE: Scholarly Resources, 1983), s.v. "Van Veenschoten, T" 306, and Robert P. Swierenga, *Dutch Households in the U.S. Population Censuses, 1850, 1860, 1870*, 3 vols. (Wilmington, DE: Scholarly Resources, 1987), s.v. "Van Veenschoten, Teunis," 1156.

one-room log house did not matter so much once one took the high quality of the soil on the farm into account.[40] He concluded, "We have an easier and quieter life here than in Gelderland and sleep till the sun rises; no bothering about cutting sods, or collecting soil, or digging ditches."[41] Collecting soil went along with cutting sods destined for the infields in the Netherlands; ditches were commonly dug in stream valleys to drain and improve pastures. All in all, Van Veenschoten found farming in Iowa to be far less labor intensive because of the inherent high fertility of prairie soils compared to the sandy soils of the central and eastern Netherlands. Similar comments were recorded by immigrants in the other pioneer settlement zones; there, too, types and gradations of clays and loams were present, superior to the sand cover of much of the higher Netherlands.[42]

This environmental optimism, however, has to be tempered by the fact that these immigrant farmers were either bringing virgin soil into cultivation or had settled on land only recently converted from its natural ecosystem to agricultural use. Such soils are characteristically nutrient rich and, in forested zones, were made even more fertile from the ash left after burning the woody plants to create fields. After years of continuous cropping, however, even richly endowed soils steadily lose nutrients from the root zone to the crops. Unless soil nutrients are replenished in some way—like manuring—to maintain yields, fertility will diminish. Dutch pioneer farmers rightly assessed that the soils where they settled were of an initial higher quality than in the Netherlands but were mistaken about its durability.

Environmental practices

Other environmental practices were used to manage different natural resources, such as pasture, water, slope, type of crop, and so forth. For Dutch pioneer farmers, however, the environmental practice that left the greatest impression was not related to the daily operations of the farm but to its original creation from the natural environment, a slow, arduous, and one-time process. Letters that describe the journey

---

[40] T. van Veenschoten to relatives, Pella, Iowa, to Lunteren, Gelderland, the NL, 26 Dec. 1855, photocopy with translation, folder 22, box 70, Dutch Immigrant Papers, collection no. 78, ACC.
[41] Ibid., translation, 4.
[42] "Because we do not spread manure here, work goes much quicker than in Holland," G. Heinen to relatives, Sheboygan, WI, to Aalten, the NL, 27 Jan. 1854, folder 13, box 24, Dutch Immigrant Papers, collection no. 78, ACC.

from the East Coast to the pioneer settlement zones, especially by rail, regularly comment on passing through multiple wooded zones with clearings dotted with tree stumps, between which, corn, wheat, and potatoes were grown. Those scenes, as well as the immense forests themselves, must have given those headed for the Midwest some inkling of what was in store for them. At this time, the Netherlands had already effectively been deforested for more than three centuries. Farmers had little to no experience felling and burning trees and clearing other woody growth to create and expand cropland.

Gerard Brandt, with his wife and five children, left Goes, Zeeland, the Netherlands, for Sheboygan, Wisconsin, in the fall of 1848.[43] Their itinerary to the Midwest was followed by many other immigrants: arrival in New York City, steamboat along the Hudson to Albany, canal boat along the Erie Canal to Buffalo, and steamboat on the Great Lakes to Sheboygan. The Brandts homesteaded forty acres of woodland in Oostburg, south of Sheboygan. Dutch emigration records list Gerard Brandt's occupation in Goes as a storekeeper; in Wisconsin, at age fifty-four, Gerard Brandt became a farmer.[44] A year and a half after the family had moved to their farm, Gerard Brandt wrote to his relatives in Goes describing the work involved in converting their woodland into farmland by felling, cutting, debranching, slashing, piling, and burning trees and other woody understory, as well as collecting the leftover ash.

> After that, I chopped down trees with my other two sons all winter. Then the snow lay two and a half feet deep until the fourteenth of April, so that it was difficult work. During that winter, we cut down and burned six acres of trees.... The underground [ground and shrub layer] is cut off level with the ground. That is done first; then this is piled up. Then the small trees are cut down, the thickness of a wagon tongue or a bit thicker, a little above the ground, and then the branches are cut off and thrown on those piles. Next, the large ones are cut down [from] two to two and a half feet above the ground. The branches are often cut up so they can be pulled by two oxen and then they are brought together and ten, twelve, or twenty or more are burned, and when it is all burned up, the ashes are gathered if one wishes to sell them, and a person can get six cents per bushel....

[43] Swierenga, *U.S. Ship Passenger Manifests*, vol. 1, s.v. "Brandt, Gerard," 109.
[44] Swierenga, *Dutch Immigrants to the United States*, s.v. "Brandt, Gerard," 30.

Then when the wood is all burned from the ground, people begin to force split oak logs, usually [from] ten to twelve feet long, and pile them seven or eight feet high and the bottom openings are so narrow that no small pig can get through, and that is necessary because they run around in the woods wherever they please.... The animals roam in the winter as well as in the summer.

In this way we cleared six acres the first winter and on this we had summer wheat and oats and Indian corn.[45]

It is important to realize that these Wisconsin woods, made up of sugar maple, basswood, elm, and oak, were old-growth forests, with mature individuals from seventy to ninety feet tall, a canopy from thirty to forty feet wide, and a trunk from three to four feet wide. It was a physically challenging and hazardous feat to fell such trees for people who lacked the experience of a lumberjack.[46] There are Dutch immigrant writings that report injuries and deaths from falling trees.[47]

In this example, oxen hauled debranched main trunks to the woodpiles for burning; split oak logs were used for fencing to keep livestock out of the cleared field, and wood ash left after the burn could be sold as fertilizer. It is noteworthy that at this location and point in time, the logs could only be burned and not sold as timber for the construction and other industries. Even though Oostburg is situated very close to Lake Michigan, in 1851 there were still no infrastructure or lumber companies to bring timber to urban markets. Such a marketable resource would have made the trees themselves into a crop and would have provided needed capital for such start-up farms.

At a rate of six acres every winter, it would have taken at least another five years to clear all the woods Gerard Brandt and his two sons wished to convert to farmland on their homestead. Moreover, the stumps of the mature trees would have taken up to ten years to decay, making plowing, cultivation, and harvesting more cumbersome and time consuming. In his letter, Brandt moves directly from clearing the woodland to crops without any comment about plowing or cultivating the soil but I think we can assume that, with two oxen available, some

---

[45] Risseeuw, *I end with my pen*, 107.
[46] "Egbert Frederik's Pioneer Memories," in Lucas, *Dutch Immigrant Memoirs*, 68.
[47] Jan Sprik arrived in New York, 11 May 1848, from Brummen, Gelderland, the NL. He went to Vriesland, MI, to farm and died in Sept. 1848 when "a tree fell on him." Brian Jay Nederveld, "The Nederveld Ancestor Tree: Descendants of Jan Sprik," at http://familytreemaker.geneology.com. I am indebted to my colleague, Bill Kennedy, at the Van Raalte Institute for this source.

soil preparation was done before the seed was broadcast. Other letters report crops grown without any soil cultivation for several years after clearing the woodlands.[48]

Nature's impact upon people

The primary relationship to nature in pioneer resource zones (farming, mining, lumbering) is in the direction of people's impact upon nature—the transformation and replacement of natural ecosystems with agroecosystems. When the direction of this fundamental human relationship is reversed, and the impact of the natural world on people is considered, several realities come into play. For one, the natural resources that were harnessed—soil fertility, timber, forest pastures, game, and so on—made human survival and thriving possible. This general state of affairs has already been gauged by environmental observations in the letters classified under the rubric's worldview, landscape, natural resources, and environmental practices on the check-off lists. In this section, nature's impact upon people has a more restricted meaning: nature as impediment and benefit. About 13 percent of the environmental comments fall into this category. Almost all such comments describe the impact of either unusual and extreme or particularly favorable weather and climate on crops and daily life and health; some linked declining mortality and morbidity figures of settlers to progress in clearing the land for farming and, conversely, the increase in diseases to the bad air that emanated from virgin forests and grasslands.[49]

A stock component of private letters from immigrants was letting family and friends know how they, the farm, and the community in general were faring; this typically included standard topics such as their health, yields and prices of crops, livestock and groceries, especially compared to the Netherlands. Not infrequently, the natural world was linked to these circumstances. The negative obstacles that nature had brought their way were, of course, more powerful recollections and

---

[48] En route in St. Louis, MO, Hendrik Barendrecht wrote his immediate family in the Netherlands that they had been advised to go to Michigan for this reason, among others: "We are still advised to go there, because the soil in the woods after the trees have been cut down, yields crops for three years without cultivation. Seeds are just sown over it." Hendrik Barendrecht to family, St. Louis to 's-Gravendeel, Zuid-Holland, the NL, 16 Jan. 1847, folder 1, box 4, Dutch Immigrant Papers, collection no. 78, ACC.

[49] A. N. Wormser to J. A. Wormser, Burlington, Iowa, to Amsterdam, 20 Feb. 1849 (Wormser 30), Stellingwerff, *Iowa Letters*, 293.

stand out. Here are two examples, one from the Holland colony, and one from the Pella colony.

Wouter Jongste immigrated with his brother Cornelis in 1852, from Goederede, Zuid-Holland. In 1859 he was working on a farm in Holland, Michigan, belonging to Paulus den Bleyker, a wealthy immigrant landowner in Kalamazoo. Jongste wrote Den Bleyker no fewer than nine letters in 1859 about, among other things, the state of operations on his farm. In his June 15, 1859, letter, Jongste wrote:

> Again we have had a heavy frost here on the 10th and the 11th of this month. [!] The corn which had sprouted is frozen again, also the winter oats, your wheat is also questionable, the potatoes also suffered much due to the frost. Some in Zeeland have already mowed off five acres of wheat, others seven acres of wheat. So friend, the judgments of God are visible here.[50]

Henriette M. Bousquet-Chabot, married to Pella business leader Abraham Everardus Dudok Bousquet, wrote to Janke Wormser-Van der Ven on September 20, 1849, several months after arriving in Pella from Amsterdam. Her friend Janke was married to Johan Adam Wormser, whose brother Andries also immigrated to Pella. She strongly discouraged Janke from coming to Pella where there were none of the accustomed physical and cultural amenities of Amsterdam. She described the living conditions in Pella:

> It only has to rain for a few hours, and it becomes impossible for women to get outside at all [mud roads], and when you add to that the cold, which everyone describes here as very bad, then I suppose we will not be getting out at all. The wife of a doctor assured me that last winter, she did not get out of the house for five months.[51]

Conclusion

Environmental observations were one distinctive thread of subject material in letters from Dutch immigrants in pioneer settlements during the mid-nineteenth century. Accustomed in the Netherlands

---

[50] W. Jongste to Paulus den Bleyker, Holland, MI, to Kalamazoo, MI, 15 June 1859, folder 10, box 30, Dutch Immigrant Papers, collection no. 78, ACC. Swierenga, *U.S. Ship Passenger Manifests*, vol. 1, s.v. "Jongste, Wouter, 464."
[51] Stellingwerff, *Iowa Letters*, 5-6, 339, quote, 343.

to highly domesticated, small-scale landscapes, with little terrestrial wildlife, Dutch immigrants to the Midwest entered and settled in largely virgin mesic forests and prairies with their wildlife communities. Public letters, published at the time of writing, contained more environmental commentary than private letters—much of it advisory and promotional. In private immigrant letters, unpublished at the time, curiosity about nature as such was secondary to the practical environmental necessities for making a living and a life; they primarily described nature as a resource and reported transforming it into rural landscapes. Many regarded such environmental transformation not only as a necessity but also as a Christian duty. En route from the East Coast to settlement sites, immigrants had the opportunity to convey their impressions about the scale of the continent and the scenery of the environments they passed through; at the settlement site, environmental commentary was related to daily life—practical and prosaic. All these observations gave voice to Dutch immigrants coming to know, to adapt to, and to transform their new natural environments.

CHAPTER 11

A Hunter's Experience: Henry Takken's Memoir and the Demise of the Passenger Pigeon (*Ectopistes migratorius*)

Jan J. Boersema and Nella Kennedy

Introduction

In the 1880s, Holland, Michigan, postmaster Gerrit van Schelven conceived the idea of asking pioneer immigrants to write accounts of their early years of settling. Dozens of people responded to his invitation and sent him their memoirs. The contributions received by Van Schelven have survived and are, together with other items, kept in the Holland Museum Archives and Research Library, in the Van Schelven boxes. In the spring of 2015, while perusing these boxes for the first author's project, "Nineteenth-Century Dutch Settlers and the Wilderness," [1] his attention was caught by a tiny, twelve-page, handwritten memoir entitled "A Hunter's Experience." The tag attached to the memoir reads: "Author unknown. Date unknown."

It was clear that the memoir merited further inspection, and in that endeavor, Nella Kennedy kindly cooperated. We soon figured out

---

[1] See: Jan J. Boersema and Anthonia M. Boersema-Bremmer, "'The Wilderness has been made to blossom': Nineteenth-Century Dutch Immigrants and the Natural World," in *Sharing Pasts: Dutch Americans through Four Centuries*, ed. Henk Aay, Janny Venema and Dennis Voskuil (Holland, MI: Van Raalte Press, 2017), 25-50.

Tag attached to the memoir

that it had been dated after all: "Dec. 28, 1910." It became apparent that the memoir had never been read carefully. But when we started to do so, it turned out to be puzzling in many places. The author's writing is hard to read due to an almost-phonetic spelling and wretched English, but the content of the memoir is fascinating. It describes the hunting practices of the author and his friends shortly after their arrival in West Michigan and provides written proof of Dutch involvement in the tragic demise of American wildlife in the nineteenth century. In this paper we will give a transcription of this document as accurately as possible and explain its significance by putting the content in its historical and geographical context.

The author

Van Schelven's archive is kept in twelve boxes, each with a great variety of documents: memoirs, pictures, letters, translations, clippings, and so forth. In box 9, we found the small, handwritten document: twelve pages of text on paper a little more than four by five inches, with an ornamented cover carrying the name "Foxy." According to the codes on the tag attached to the document, it was either acquired or cataloged in 1937. It was clearly the kind of memoir we were looking for, even more so since it has recollections of the author and his outdoor adventures shortly after his arrival in West Michigan in 1857. The title intrigued us, because hardly any hunter's experiences—certainly from that period—have been written down and preserved in the archives of Dutch immigrants. We were even more curious to know what the document had to say on this topic. The author of the memoir was not

Takken's gravestone at Pilgrim Home Cemetery, Holland, Michigan

named, but he did leave some helpful clues. They showed the date of the writer's arrival (page 1) and mentioned his starting a blacksmith shop in Holland at the corner of Seventh and River (page 3). Combining these data with the existing information from the available records revealed that it could be no other than Hendrik (Henry) Takken (1839-1914).[2]

Hendrik (Henry) was born in Utrecht, the Netherlands, in May 1839, and came to Holland in 1857. In 1866 he may have lived in Grand Haven, where the tax assessment lists him as a repairman of wagons and sleighs, and on page 309 in the *Michigan State Gazetteer Business Directory* of 1875, we find him as a blacksmith in Douglas Township. According to the 1880 census, he still resided in Douglas, but it seems that he lived in Holland as well. He is consistently listed in most records as a wagon maker, owning his own house (mortgaged) at 50 East Seventh Street in Holland. In the late 1850s, he may have been associated with mail carriers who delivered the mail by wagon, for the names of several of these men occur in the memoir.

Henry arrived in the United States in 1852 with his parents, Evert (blacksmith) and Sibylla, and siblings (among whom was his five-years-

---

[2] We are grateful to Earl Wm. Kennedy for helping us discern the most likely author, and for providing information on most of the men mentioned in the memoir. The sources include www.wiewaswie.nl; www.ancestry.com; www.findagrave.com; and "Pillar Church families by head of household," at www.calvin.edu.

Page five of the memoir

older brother Ryk). The family first lived in Buffalo, New York. Henry was married by 1865 to Cornelia de Spelder, and by 1891 had married, as a widower, Anna Bosma. Children by his first wife were Sibylla (Belle), Mary, who died young, Evert (Eddie), and Janie. Henry died at the home of his daughter Sibylla in Fennville in 1914. He was buried at the Pilgrim Home Cemetery.

Diplomatic transcription of the memoir

Punctuation and appropriate capitalization in the document are sparse, so the writer's peculiar phonetic spelling and eccentric capitalization are transcribed as given.[3]

We think such a "diplomatic transcription"[4] captures the authenticity best. Some words have been corrected between square brackets for clarity's sake. The spelling and word order in the document reveal a Dutch background only very occasionally. A question mark

---

[3] In the ongoing process of deciphering the document, Prof. Rolf H. Bremmer, Leiden University, made useful suggestions.
[4] A diplomatic transcription in epigraphic terms is one that records only the characters as they appear on the document, with minimal or no editorial intervention.

between square brackets indicates the meaning and/or transcription is uncertain.

Holland Dec 28 1910

I came to Holland the first time about 1857 to look over the country by the invatation of Janes Konning[5] then Driving the stage from Holland to grand Rapids I was so mutch takken up with the situatiun and mostly what I saw in the shot of game and furs being almost a Naturell Hunter the game part atracted me most
[2]
it was in the spring and at that time in March and it happend at that time ther was high watter and the Muskrats that wer shot and kild that day run into the hundreds 2 men killing over 40 each one was an Indian Iosapt Macksanby[6] be the other was MaCue[7] and ofcoze that was one fratur [factor] that drew me hear [here] and another was I was advised from an Unkell of mine whenever I
[3]
start in buisings [business] to hunt up some New plase that was growing and I would grow up with same now this was before I was Maried wel when that transpired I had not forgoten Unkels advice and the atractions I saw when driven hear [here] and so started to be one of Hollands citizens at that time I started on the corner on River and Sevinth Street with a small Black smith shop
[4]
wher Hidding keeps grozeris [groceries] at that time there was lots of sport fore a Hunter like myself lots of Dees [Deer] boar Muskrat Mink ducks Wild Pigions theas wer so thick at times that you could not see the sky fore ours [hours] now you may think that just a big thing to tell but I think there ar yet a few alive that could coroberate what I say and whill [while] I am at it I want to tell
[5]
I was ones [once] just above grandvill one day when ther was over 50 Hunters shooting theas wild Pigions and yet in all the shooting that was dun you could not keep them from liting [lighting, descending] and fore over 2 ours you could not see the

---

[5] James Koning, a stage coach driver.
[6] Most likely Louis Maksabe (son of Joseph Maksabe, who died in 1849), an Ottawa chief.
[7] Most likely Hiram McCue, b. 1830, lumberman.

skies fore Pigions and ther was thausands of them kild that day I dun nothing fore 2 weeks but shoot Pigions at that time they Nested

[6]

at Pigion Creek and thats what gave it its Names they Nesting their and so it was for a No [number] of years. one year they Nested at Sauth Haven and Pigion River at the same time but they wer yenerly [generally] the thicker when wee had lots of Beach Nuts [beechnuts] and they would fly 60 to 70 Miles each day to feed the farmers and other People yous [used] to goe [go] and get the young ones

[7]

by the wagon Loads before they could fly and at that time they wer as fat as Butter and Heabor Walsh[8] yous [use] to buy them and ship them to Chicago and other placis now nobody nos [knows] wher one is and the United Stats oras [or as] you may say Unkill Sam is ofering [offering] quit [quite] a large som for a few of them

[8]

and when I first started in buisings [business] hear [here] you would Hardly see a doller a munth it was all store order Old man Phanstill yous [used] to keep store at the corner of McBide block[9] ther was at that time thausands open [upon?] thausands of oak stave made and shipt you could get buter and Eggs all you would at 6 cents per oz and the same for and other things in porportiun [proportion] 6 c is coffee

[9]

5 c stiges [?] oz. ther was some Bear also one sunday ther wer three kild just North of the Bridge by Ike Howard and his Brother Henry[10] and MaCue[11] and after that time John Crispell[12] yet living kild a large one just west of the Pine Creek school House and I caught one afte that in a Bear trap but he got aut

[10]

and some otter I recolict [recollect] Old man Hafocatt[13] the Cripell

[8] Heber Walsh, Holland city businessman, druggist, and major shipper to Chicago.
[9] Pieter F. Pfanstiehl, mail carrier and store keeper at the corner of River Avenue and Eighth Street, Holland (McBride block).
[10] Ike and Henry Howard could have been sons of Manly D. Howard, one of the few "Americans" living in Holland from the 1850s on.
[11] Hiram McCue.
[12] Most likely John Crispell, b 1849, married to Elizabeth Ellis.
[13] Most likely Gerrit J. Haverkate, mail carrier and stage driver, first regular driver on the Grand Rapids line.

[Crispell?] caught one in a fuick[14] or hoop Net and I caught one on the Old Howerd dock and C blame [blume?] caught one just abov Scots place and others wer shot and caught in verius [various] ways and they are all you hear and quit [quite] a lot of gray foxes more grays then Reds but they wer both kinds and Black and gray squerils [squirrels] to your Heart's content

[11]

you could get a mes [mess[15]] of them anytime now they are gone I trapt in the River and Marsh I did not mis one spring in over 40 years and I have caught over one hundred in 3 Nites at that time ther youst [used] to be quit[e] lots of Patridge I camenst [commenced] at that time to bring furs in Holland with three Doler that I gave my Wife to take care of and they wer good years.

[12]

at that time ther was quit a lot of Indians camping around Holland and they have about disapeerd [disappeared] and so with the game at that time wher now the fill is wher the Innterurban runs under the PereMarquet[16] I went thruo this with a yall boot[17] that would cary 4 or 5 men with ease now all dry land

Hunting and the Dutch immigrants

As far as we know, Henry Takken and the men who are mentioned by name in his memoir were not professional hunters and fishermen, although they did earn money by it. We may safely assume that some game had been consumed, but for them hunting was primarily recreation, which they obviously practiced with passion, considering the invested time and successes described. One would have to be a trained marksman with thorough field knowledge to shoot forty muskrats in a day. With the exception of Hafocatt [Haverkate]—who dealt with catching otters—the hunters who are mentioned were not immigrants of Dutch origin. A native chief and three non-Dutch Americans appear in the document. Dutch immigrants were not familiar with hunting in their homeland. As in many European countries, hunting rights were reserved for nobility in the Netherlands. Only under the French rule (1810-13) were those rights extended to citizens, provided you were

---

[14] *Fuik* (in the text misspelled as "Fuick") is a Dutch word meaning "hoop net."
[15] A quantity sufficient to make a dish.
[16] Père Marquette was the name of the railroad which ran from Grand Rapids to Holland (and Chicago) between about 1898 and 1924.
[17] A "yall boot" is most likely a "yawl (from Dutch *jol*) boat," a two-master sailing craft similar to a sloop (from Dutch *sloep*).

a land owner (usually farmers). Among townspeople, craftsmen, and agricultural workers, the hunt was unusual, and the possession of a rifle was an exception. From early sources, we know that some Dutch immigrants soon took over the American habit of having a gun at home.[18] With this, it was possible to defend themselves against bears who were trying to steal pigs from styes and/or shoot wolves to collect the premium that was put on their "heads." The killing of young wolves and the collection of a premium is described in the memoirs published by Henry Lucas.[19] We also know from the same sources that early settlers sometimes shot deer for consumption shortly after their arrival, and used rifles to kill wild animals, such as raccoons and squirrels, that caused damage to crops. But in the memoirs we have read, references to, and descriptions of, hunting in that period are virtually absent. The practice of hunting for (profitable) pleasure hardly occurred in the early days among Dutch immigrants to Holland and environs. The story of Henry Takken and the characterization of himself as "being a Naturall Hunter" are exceptional in this respect.

"The Game part"

Takken and his hunting friends were not fussy about their game. They hunted both large and small game and birds. In the short document, no fewer than thirteen different animal names are mentioned.

This hunter's "tableau" is impressive, both qualitatively and quantitatively. Nevertheless, two conspicuous candidates are missing: the wolf and the beaver. Henry Takken arrived in the United States in 1852, and in 1857, he moved to the area around Holland. In the period in which he actively hunted—roughly from 1857 to 1900[20]—the wolf was so scarce in West Michigan (partly due to the hunting premium) that he probably did not meet this animal during his hunting ventures. The beaver population had also fallen sharply since the arrival of Europeans,[21] because their fur was very popular for making hats, but

---

[18] See: Henry S. Lucas ed., *Dutch Immigrant Memoirs and Related Writings* (Grand Rapids, MI: Eerdmans, 1997).

[19] "There was a large bounty on wolves, and one day, one of the Kronemeyer boys came across a nest of young whelps. He called his father, who got his gun and first shot the whelps and then the old wolves when they came. There were seven wolves in all, and each brought $20 or $25." Lucas, *Dutch Immigrant Memoirs*, 1:386.

[20] On page 12 of the document, it reads: "I did not mis one spring in over 40 years."

[21] Gordon G. Whitney, *From Coastal Wilderness to Fruited Plain. A History of Environmental Change in Temperate North America from 1500 to the Present* (Cambridge: Cambridge University Press, 1996), 303.

Name in document	Likely (sub)species	Latin name	Quantity
deer	white-tailed deer	*Odocoileus virginianus*	"lots of"
boar	wild boar	*Sus scrofa*	"lots of"
mink	American mink	*Neovison vison*	"lots of"
muskrat		*Ondatra zibethicus*	"Hundreds"; "2 men killing over 40 each one"
otter	North American river otter	*Lontra canadensis*	Three "caught in a fuick"; "others wer shot"
bear	American black bear	*Ursus americanus*	"three kild"; "kild a large one"; "one got aut"
gray fox	grey fox	*Urocyon cinereoargenteus*	"a lot of"
red fox	red fox	*Vulpes vulpes*	"more grays then Reds"
gray squerils / black squerils	varieties of the eastern grey squirrel	*Sciurus carolinensis*	"over one hundred in 3 Nites" May refer to a different animal; text is unclear
duck	mallard duck	*Anas platyrhynchos*	"lots of"
wild pigion	passenger pigeon	*Ectopistes migratorius*	"thousands kild that day"; "by the wagon Loads"
patridge	grey partridge	*Perdix perdix*	"lots of"

they must still have been present in small but sizable numbers in the terrain covered by Takken. From his accounts, we can see that he was active in the triangle between Grand Rapids, Grand Haven, and South Haven, an area with rivers, marshes, and enough trees, certainly suitable as a biotope for the beaver. It is more likely, therefore, that the beaver is implicitly mentioned in the document when Takken at its end states, "I camenst [commenced] at that time to bring furs in Holland." The "three Doler" mentioned could relate to the sale of one or more beaver pelts. In any case, it was a reasonably credible price for that time.[22]

The memoir further reveals that the huntsmen used a great variety of gear to catch the game. Most of the animals were shot, others

---

[22] It is hard to get reliable information about market prices in Michigan during that period. Some information on prices is given by William Slacum. See: John Forsyth and William A. Slacum, "Slacum's Report on Oregon, 1836-7," *Oregon Historical Society Quarterly* 13, no. 2 (June 1912), 175-224. To quote a passage from page 191: "The price of a beaver skin in the 'Columbia district' is ten shillings, $2, payable in goods at 50 per cent on the invoice cost. Each skin averages one and a half pound and is worth in New York or London $5 per pound; value $7.50."

trapped, caught in a net, or in other "verius ways." The gun appears to be the most prominent device. They might have used a regular shotgun for the passenger pigeons, a so-called 'fowling piece' for ducks, and a bolt-action shotgun for deer and boar. Trapping was also widespread. The Oneida Company in Upstate New York sold its "Newhouse traps" all across the country in different sizes, allowing trappers to catch animals ranging from chipmunks to bears. Takken himself managed to catch a bear in a "Bear trap," but, apparently, to his regret, "he got aut." Interestingly, when the author recollects the catch of otters in a hoop net, he uses the Dutch word *fuik*, although he kind of Americanized it into "fuick."

The memoir's significance

A fascinating document indeed, but what lifts this memoir above a mere curiosity? At first sight, it looks like an authentic but haphazard set of recollections from a hunter. Probably a man with limited formal language education, and, given his sturdy handwriting, accustomed to producing only short notes and accounts, Takken was certainly not accustomed to writing lengthy prose. Why does this document merit publication?

The main reason is that this document puts a "plain" immigrant of Dutch descent in the larger frame of one of the most tragic events in the sad natural history of North America in the late nineteenth century. This event was the eventual extinction of what once was the most abundant bird species on the globe—the passenger pigeon.[23] This piece of history is still fraught with disbelief, shame, and riddles. The passenger pigeon is at the core of Takken's "Hunter's Experience."[24] Almost four pages out of the twelve are devoted to the habits and the "shooting of theas wild Pigions." In this, the author proves himself to be a real outdoorsman and a keen observer. He is surprisingly accurate in his description of the behavior and ecology of the birds, the way they were caught and shot, and ultimately the outcome of all this, at the time he wrote the memoir.

As to the behavior of the birds, Takken noted their apparent tameness. "In all the shooting that was dun you could not keep them

[23] "They numbered from three to five billion and may well have comprised 25-40 percent of North America's birdlife," Joel Greenberg tells us in his well-documented book, *A Feathered River across the Sky. The Passenger Pigeon's Flight to Extinction* (NY: Bloomsbury, 2014), 1.
[24] Michigan, in turn, was at the core of the breeding area of the passenger pigeons.

Pigeon Shoot, an historic illustration from the *Illustrated Sporting and Dramatic News* (July 3, 1875). The passenger pigeons were forming "a feathered river across the sky"—hence the title of Joel Greenberg's book

from liting." Completely befitting their name, the passenger pigeons migrated and tended to do so in large flocks. The birds were gregarious breeders, and once in their breeding area, they would stay close together to roost and to feed on (beech)nuts, acorns, and wheat or corn. These were all behavioral traits that contributed considerably to the ease of shooting them at the same place over a long period of time. That period could really be very long because the birds kept coming. Their migration could last several days, and at times their flocks were immense and their numbers literally innumerable. They would darken the sky, and according to the memoir, "You could not see the skies fore over 2 ours." To the ordinary reader, this may seem grossly exaggerated, but it is not. On the contrary, this phenomenon has been attested to by many naturalists on numerous occasions and pertaining to many places.[25]

---

[25] The famous naturalist, Audubon, wrote about an experience he had had in the autumn of 1813: "The air was literally filled with Pigeons, the light of noon-day was obscured as by an eclipse.... The pigeons were still passing in undiminished numbers and continued to do so for three days in succession." John James Audubon, *Ornithological Biography, or an Account of the Habits of the Birds of the United States of America* (Philadelphia: n.p., 1831), 319-26. More telling citations of J. J. Audubon and others on "Wild Pigeons" darkening the sky for hours can be found on the internet; see http://www.exoticdove.com/P_pigeon/Audubon_Pigeon.html/ and Project Passenger Pigeon: http://passengerpigeon.org/index.html.

Takken also accurately observed the feeding habits of the birds and their subsequent physical condition. In years with an abundant yield of beechnuts, the birds and their young grew fatter. The latter were "as fat as Butter" and an easy prey, since they could be caught before they were able to fly.

It does not come as a surprise that the huge numbers and the "thick" flocks of the pigeon attracted many hunters. "Ther was over 50 Hunters shooting theas wild Pigions," the memoir tells us. With so many birds flying over, it is easy to imagine that the hunters just shot in the air, without the need to aim very accurately. *Pigeon Shoot* (above) gives an artist's impression of how it could have looked. They "kild thausends of them" on a single day and, according to the memoir, Takken himself "dun nothing fore 2 week but shoot Pigions." Sentences like this reveal the scale, magnitude, and one may say, the "madness" of their hunting practices. Although the gun was the greatest killer, a variety of techniques and devices were also used to catch the birds. Sometimes the fat young ones, sitting on sagging tree branches in great numbers, were simply clubbed to death.[26] No wonder such quantities could be transported only "by the wagon loads" to cities like Chicago, Detroit, and New York, where wild pigeons were on the menu until the end of the century. Throughout the nineteenth century, wild pigeons were a welcome and affordable source of animal protein for the average American.[27] Occasionally, concerns about the future of the birds were expressed. In 1857 a bill was even introduced in the Ohio State Legislature seeking protection for the passenger pigeon, yet a select committee of the Senate filed a report stating: "The Passenger Pigeon needs no protection. Wonderfully prolific, having the vast forests of the North as its feeding grounds"; the committee dismissed the suggestion that the species could be destroyed.[28] Due to

---

[26] A. W. Schorger, *The Passenger Pigeon: Its Natural History and Extinction* (Madison: University of Wisconsin Press, 1955); Greenberg, *A Feathered River*, ch. 5: "Means of Destruction."

[27] Robert P. Swierenga pointed out the following passage, taken from George N. Smith's diary from 8 April 1842: "Mr. Martin came, and I went with him to get pigeons; lodged at Superior. I went to the Indians and with them to the pigeons; got each a few live ones, myself a mess of dead ones. Returned." Robert P. Swierenga and William Van Appledorn, eds., *Old Wing Mission: Cultural Interchange as Chronicled by George and Arvilla Smith in their Work with Chief Wakazoo's Ottawa Band on the West Michigan Frontier* (Grand Rapids, MI: Eerdmans, 2008), 118. On the use of (wild) pigeons in the American kitchen, see Caroline F. Sloat, *Pigeons and their Cuisine*: http://www.common-place-archives.org/vol-11/no-03/sloat.

[28] W. T. Hornaday, *Our Vanishing Wild Life. Its Extermination and Preservation* (NY: Charles Scribner's Sons, 1913), 9. See: https://archive.org/stream/ourvanishingwild00horn#page/n7.

their feeding habits, the pigeons were considered a plague and a danger to the grain and corn harvest. As an advertisement in 1857 told it: "Shoot them, or they will prey upon your Wheatfield. They don't make a bad old fashioned pot pie."[29]

At the end of his story about wild pigeons, Takken notes: "Now nobody nos [knows] wher one is and the United Stats oras [or as] you may say Unkill Sam is ofering [offering] quit [quite] a large som for a few of them." This is a really astonishing sentence, keeping in mind that it was written in 1910 and given the fact that the last passenger pigeon was shot in April 1902 near Laurel, Indiana. After that date, there were occasional sightings but no confirmed catches. President Theodore Roosevelt claimed to have seen a bird in Michigan in 1907.[30] It could have been one of the last in the wild and—oh, irony!—protected by a bill introduced in 1897 in the Michigan legislature asking for a ten-year closed season on passenger pigeons. This action was much too late, but Michigan could claim to be the first state to introduce a kind of legal protection.[31] The very last "wild pigeon"—a female named Martha— died in captivity, at roughly twenty-nine years of age. We know that this occurred in 1914—the same year, ironically, that Takken died. Martha passed away at the Cincinnati Zoo on September 1, at one o'clock in the afternoon, and the tragic demise of the once ubiquitous bird was meticulously documented.[32]

How could this tragedy happen? Were the excessive hunting practices to blame for the extinction of the wild pigeon? All the "Takkens" of the nineteenth century undoubtedly ensured that the bird's number fell dramatically; the hunt had had a major influence on the population size. Changes in the habitat of the birds that affected the quantity or availability of food could have had a negative impact

---

[29] *Marshall County Republican* (Plymouth, IN), 10 Sept. 1857, 3.

[30] E. Fuller, *The Passenger Pigeon* (Princeton, NJ: Princeton University Press, 2014), 50-69.

[31] *De Hollander* (17 April 1872) reported that the shooting of pigeons during breeding season was a punishable offense according to the 9th section of the Michigan ordinance of 3 April 1860. The article, copied from the *Grand Rapids Times*, elaborated on its content.

[32] The most recent and best documented account is Joel Greenberg's *A Feathered River* (2014). Wikipedia has an excellent entry on the passenger pigeon: https://en.wikipedia.org/wiki/Passenger_pigeon. As to Martha, her body was shipped in ice by train to the Smithsonian in Washington, DC, subsequently stuffed and put on display in a glass case. See: https://www.npr.org/sections/thetwo-way/2017/11/16/564597936/why-did-the-passenger-pigeon-go-extinct-the-answer-might-lie-in-their-toes?t=1531769014254.

as well. But the question, "Why did they go from billions to *none?*" is far from being answered. Why did tiny populations of this bird not somehow survive in some refugial forest somewhere? Most scientists think it has to do with the genetic makeup of the birds, having become gregarious breeders. The pigeons needed to breed in certain numbers, and if they fell below that threshold, they may have been unable to produce enough offspring to survive.[33] Humans came first and second as causes for their extinction, but the particular reproductive ecology might have been the final blow.

---

[33] This is one of the main reasons why the general idea of recreating the passenger pigeon, as advanced by Ben Novak, has been criticized. See: M. R. O'Conner, *Resurrection Science: Conservation, De-Extinction and the Precarious Future of Wild Things* (NY: St. Martin's Press, 2015).

III. Dutch American Leaders

CHAPTER 12

His Name Was Klijn: Rev. Hendrik Georg Klijn, Reluctant Separatist

Earl Wm. Kennedy

Hendrik Georg Klijn (1793-1883) is best known as the cofounder with Koene van den Bosch of the Christian Reformed Church. In April 1857, these two Dutch-immigrant dominies of the young Classis of Holland, Michigan (along with other dissatisfied members), bade adieu to the old Reformed Protestant Dutch Church[1] in the East. For Van den Bosch, it was a harsh farewell, but for Klijn it was a gentle, brotherly, almost apologetic adieu, one of which he soon repented when he returned to the denomination he had just left. Who was this reluctant, irenic separatist? He has received relatively little attention in the histories of the two American denominations with which he was associated—the Reformed Church in America (RCA) and the Christian Reformed Church (CRC)—probably because he deserted both of them—the one temporarily and the other permanently. He seems to have fallen between the cracks. (But this is to get ahead of the story.)

Hendrik Klijn—also known as H. G. Klijn or Henry George Klyn (anglicized)—stands out in several respects. Like Piet Heyn (the Dutch

---

[1] This was the name of the Reformed Church in America before 1867.

Hendrik Klijn

sea hero in a popular folk song), his name was Klijn (pronounced *klein*), meaning small—his deeds, however, were big (*zijn daden bennen groot*). Klijn surpassed all his immigrant ministerial peers in being the oldest (born in 1793), the longest lived (90 years), the one who preached the most years (about 51), and the one who survived the most wives (3). In addition, he was the initial pastor of three immigrant Reformed Protestant Dutch Church (RPDC) congregations (Graafschap and Grand Rapids, Michigan, and Milwaukee, Wisconsin). A surprising fact is that Klijn was the only pioneer pastor to appear in a volume of *Nederland's Patriciaat* (a kind of *Who's Who* of Dutch families).[2] Finally, he was also unique in having had the worst possible start in life, one so bad, in fact, that he insisted on living his later years under an assumed surname—his mother's (Klijn).

Utrecht: from Lutheran infant to Reformed Seceder minister (1793-1839)

H. G. Klijn was baptized in the Lutheran church in Utrecht in late 1793 as Hendrik Georg Rombach, the youngest of five children; his parents had German roots.[3] When he was not yet six months old,

---

[2] *Nederland's Patriciaat* 32 (1946), 203-14. This series of annual books is better known as *het Blauwe boekje* (the Blue Book); they contain the genealogies of prominent "patrician" (but not noble) families. Two of Klijn's first cousins, as well as two of their sons, were ministers in the Hervormde Kerk (the Dutch public church from which Klijn would secede); two other cousins were medical doctors.

[3] H. G. Klijn's paternal German grandparents settled in Nijmegen, Gelderland, where his father was born in 1749; Klijn's mother, Maria Wilhelmina Klijn (Kleijn or Klijne) (c.1749-1825), was born in Middelburg, Zeeland, but her parents died in The Hague. *Nederland's Patriciaat* 32:203, 213-14; www.wiewaswie.nl; www.zeeuwengezocht.nl.

his father, Christiaan Rombach (originally Johan Georg Christian Rombach), was publicly executed in the most painful way possible—by having his bones systematically broken with a hammer on the rack, the last such execution in Utrecht (May 1794). The senior Rombach had murdered a young Jewish man for some silver coins by slitting his throat with a straight razor. Christiaan, briefly a tobacco merchant in Rotterdam, had fallen on hard times in Utrecht, while his wife worked there as a maid for an aristocratic family.[4]

Little is known about Hendrik's youth, except that his widowed mother took care of him until he was about five years old, when she had to place him in the city orphanage, where he remained until he was thirteen. She saw to it that he was registered there under her maiden name—Klijn, not Rombach.[5] Hendrik grew up to be a wallpaper hanger, marrying Jacoba van de Velde in Utrecht in 1820, when he was twenty-seven. Jacoba, eleven years his senior, was originally from Amsterdam. Together they had two daughters, both of whom would die young.[6] Jacoba also died relatively young, aged forty-nine, in December 1830. Klijn married again only five months later, this time to Cornelia Verbrugh, four years younger than he. She was a farmer's daughter from Maurik, Gelderland, who had worked as a domestic in Utrecht. She would give him a daughter (who died in childhood) and three sons, one stillborn and two who would accompany their parents to the United States in 1849.[7] Klijn earned enough as a wallpaper hanger to be

[4] *Sententie des doods tegen Johan Georg Christiaan Rombach* (Utrecht: Thomas Lieftinck, 1794); G. A. Rombach et al., "Utrechts laatste radbraak," in W. M. J. Bekkers and G. M. F. Snijders, eds. *Recht te Utrecht*, vol. 1 (Utrecht: De Tijdstroom, 1994), 55-68, at http://rozenbergquarterly.com/recht-te-utrecht-utrechts-laatste-radbraak/?print=print. *Nederland's Patriciaat* 32:213, includes this man but is silent about his crime and how he died; it simply gives the standard biographical and family information about him that it does for all the other entries.

[5] Hendrik's two older brothers had also been registered in the orphanage under their mother's maiden name, while the two older sisters remained with their mother in 1794 and eventually conducted a sewing shop with her. The oldest brother became director of public works in Amsterdam, while the middle brother had a less-successful career in the merchant marine and navy. Rombach, "Utrechts laatste radbraak," 61-63.

[6] Jacoba was not employed (but was living at the home of a Mr. Verduin, a prominent Utrecht citizen) at the time of her marriage. Her father (born in East Friesland, Germany), at his death in Rotterdam in 1820, was said to have been living independently. The older Rombach (alias Klijn) daughter, Elisabeth Maria Martha (1822-1836), was named, predictably, Elisabeth, for her mother's mother, but the extra two names may already suggest the parents' biblical piety. The other daughter, named for her father's mother, lived only a few weeks (1826); www.wiewaswie.nl.

[7] The sons were Hendrik Georg (1835-1876) and Johannes Cornelis (1837-1916); the daughter was Cornelia (1839-1842); both sons became printers in the United States;

Klijn's wallpaper store opens, *Utrechtsche Courant*, July 11, 1834

Klijn's business under new management, *Utrechtsche Courant*, January 31, 1840

able to open a store in 1834 in his own house, where he sold wallpaper, carpet, and related items. Klijn employed three men, two of whom were prominent members of the Seceder Reformed church, where he was an elder, and took over his business after his November 1839 entrance into the ministry.[8]

Although the Utrecht newspaper ads and Seceder records (together with the police reports on the Seceders and the orphanage records of the murderer's sons) all give Hendrik's surname as Klijn (or variants thereof) in the 1830s, the city's birth, marriage, and death records of the 1820s and 1830s always name him Rombach. His two sisters (who remained in Utrecht) and his two brothers (who lived

---

www.wiewaswie.nl; www.ancestry.com. For a recent account of Cornelia Verbrugh, see Janet Sjaarda Sheeres, *For Better For Worse: Stories of the Wives of Early Pastors of the Christian Reformed Church* (Grand Rapids, MI: Eerdmans: 2017), 45-65.

[8] These men were A. M. van Beugen and "H. G. Klijn Junior" (in the store's newspaper ads); the latter was incorrectly assumed by C. Smits to be our H. G. Klijn's son, but he was actually Hendrik George Klein [sic] (1816-1895), born in The Hague of an unwed mother, Wilhelmina Henrietta Kleine, possibly a niece of our Klijn's mother. Curiously, an extra dependent, "Henriette Wilhelmina Klein," was living (1813 Utrecht census) in Klijn's mother's household, in addition to her two daughters and her son H. G. Was she the above-mentioned unwed mother (both born ca. 1795)? Also in the same household in 1813 was the infant daughter of the younger (unwed) daughter. *Utrechtsche Courant*, 11 July 1834, 8 May and 14 Sept. 1839, 31 Jan. 1840; C. Smits, *De Afscheiding van 1834*, vol. 4, *Provincie Utrecht* (Dordrecht: J. P. Van den Tol, 1980), 196, 199, 224-26, 254, 464; Rombach, "Utrechts laatste radbraak," 63; www.wiewaswie.nl; www.familysearch.org; Volkstelling 1813 Utrecht inventarissenummer 613, at http://files.archieven.nl.

elsewhere) all retained the name Rombach.[9] It was apparently only Hendrik who wished to shed it, which he managed to do only when he left the city and ultimately the country, remaining "Klijn" for the rest of his days. He became a kind of *anti*-Rombach, presumably seeking to overcome his father's reputation, which dogged him even four decades after his father's death, when a malicious Utrecht teenager called him "Dominie Bloedworst" (Rev. Blood Sausage).[10]

Just why or when Klijn made the transition by the early 1830s from his Lutheran roots to leading a Reformed conventicle (a house-church meeting after Sunday worship for Bible study and prayer), we do not know; he may have been influenced by the Réveil then going on. In any event, in October 1832 (almost two years before Hendrik de Cock's Afscheiding [Secession] from the Reformed public church), Klijn and two other representatives of a Utrecht conventicle petitioned King William I for protection from young hoodlums disturbing their meetings. The Utrecht police reported then that Klijn led "a fanatical group" that regarded all but one Utrecht public church dominie as infected with Arminianism (whose "free-will views were rejected by the Calvinistic Canons [rules] of the Synod of Dort [Dordrecht], 1618-19) and refused to sing the hymns imposed by the public church; his neighbors, moreover, complained about the noise of Psalm singing emanating the whole day from his house church.[11]

When Rev. H. P. Scholte formed a Seceder congregation in Utrecht in December 1835, Klijn (who had just left the local Reformed church with his wife and daughter) became its first elder. In the four years that Klijn served in this office, he was in the thick of the Utrecht Seceders' activities, disputes, and sufferings. He was a delegate to the Seceder national synods of 1836, 1837, and 1840. Klijn stood up to the secular authorities who objected to his Bible "readings" (as exhorter, presumably), was fined for leading an illegal gathering,[12] and even challenged the university-educated Scholte about perceived theological flaws in his Utrecht sermons, for example, external and internal calling. The Klijn-Scholte differences were soon reconciled, after which, Elder Klijn began a year's study for the ministry under Scholte's direction. Klijn was ordained—along with Cornelis van der Meulen (a future

---

[9] www.wiewaswie.nl; Smits, *Utrecht*, 32, 168, 186, 190, 196-97, 201-2, 206-7, 217, 464.
[10] Smits, *Utrecht*, 188, 190.
[11] Ibid., 186-88, 190.
[12] Ibid., 196-97, 201-2, 206-7, 210-12, 223, 254; Klijn's newly born son was the first child to be baptized by Scholte on the day he organized the Utrecht Seceder church in 1835; ibid., 202.

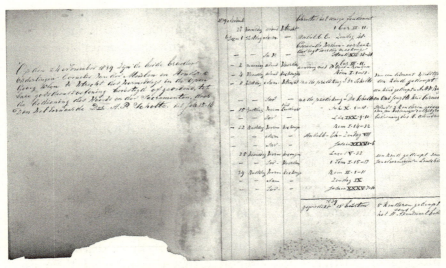

Ordination and first preaching engagements, Nov. – Dec. 1839, Klijn register (*Holland Historical Trust*)

colleague in Michigan)—by Scholte after a long examination. Klijn became a moderate disciple of Scholte but hardly a carbon copy.[13]

Seceder pastor in the Netherlands: Kockengen and Middelburg (1839-49)

The Utrecht consistory only reluctantly released Elder Klijn to become the first pastor of the small Seceder congregation in nearby Kockengen,[14] where he served from the end of 1839 until 1845,[15] when he accepted the call to the larger Seceder church in Middelburg, Zeeland, his deceased mother's hometown. His former fellow student, Van der Meulen, installed him as pastor there.[16] Klijn began his Middelburg ministry by making the controversial but ultimately locally popular decision to don ministerial garb, regarded by some as

---

[13] Ibid., 255-57, 259-60. The examination and ordination by Scholte alone were questioned by some.

[14] Ibid., 255. The Utrecht consistory only agreed to let Klijn go to Kockengen provided that he remain there until his death (and also help the Utrecht church when needed), unless unforeseen circumstances arose, which, obviously, they soon did.

[15] Ibid., 325-27, 330, 332-33. Klijn declined two calls in 1842, one from Noord-Brabant and one from Middelburg; J. Wesseling, *De Afscheiding van 1834 in Zeeland 1834-'69*, vol. 2 (Barneveld: Uitgeverij De Vuurbaak, 1989), 60-61.

[16] Ibid., 66.

a sign of orthodoxy and by others (e.g., his colleagues Scholte, Van der Meulen, and Van Raalte) as "old-fashioned" or "priestly" (i.e., Roman Catholic). But Klijn, already a man of peace, regarded himself as still "united" with his fellow Zeeland pastors (e.g., Van der Meulen), who wore ordinary attire in the pulpit, although the issue was dividing the Reformed Seceders at the synodical level.[17] Furthermore, Klijn, like his mentor Scholte, was flexible regarding the Church Order [government] of the Synod of Dort, which he believed should be adapted to the times, for example, by not insisting on the rotation of elders or on a minister's lifelong service to one congregation.[18]

During his four-year Middelburg tenure, Klijn conducted the usual three services on Sunday (morning, afternoon [catechism], and evening), in addition to serving weeknights in nearby vacant congregations, preaching, administering the sacraments, ordaining elders and deacons, and performing marriages.[19] In August 1848, to his consistory's joy, he declined a call to Dordrecht, but six months later, he received another call, from Graafschap, Michigan, signed by A. C. van Raalte, the West Michigan Dutch Reformed colony's founder. This time Klijn's flock was doomed to disappointment.[20] Some of his ministerial associates had already immigrated to the New World during the preceding couple of years, and several Zeelanders who later became leaders in the Michigan church joined Klijn in the summer of 1849 in crossing the Atlantic.[21] He delivered his farewell sermon to a packed

---

[17] Ibid., 66-67; H. Reenders, "Albertus C. Van Raalte, als leider van Overijsselse Afgescheidenen 1836-1846," in Freek Pereboom et al., *"Van scheurmakers, onruststokers en geheime opruijers..." De Afscheiding in Overijssel* (Kampen: De Ijsselakademie, 1984), 169-75; M. J. Aalders, *De komst van de toga: Een historisch onderzoel naar het verdwijnen van mantel en bef en de komst van de toga op de Nederlandse kansels, 1796-1898* (Delft, Uitgeverij Eburon, 2001), 55-71, especially 58-60.

[18] Wesseling, *Zeeland*, 2:66. Note Klijn's own commitment to serve the Kockengen church until he died! Klijn later told his congregation in Chicago that consistory members should serve until they died or were otherwise impeded; consistory minutes, First Reformed Church, Chicago, 25 Dec. 1863, JAH.

[19] Klijn preached at well over a dozen area churches more than once during his Middelburg pastorate; Wesseling, *Zeeland*, 2:69. At the end of 1848, for instance, he summed up (in the logbook of his engagements) that in the preceding year he had preached 207 times, baptized thirty-one children, administered the Lord's Supper four times, and performed four ordinations and five marriages; furthermore, Klijn's record of biblical texts from which he preached shows that he avoided using the same text twice. H. G. Klijn, "Gepredikte Texten" (1839-83), ms. at JAH.

[20] Wesseling, *Zeeland*, 2:69.

[21] Adriaan Zwemer, the Moerdijk and De Pree brothers, et al., Henry S. Lucas, *Netherlanders in America* (Ann Arbor: University of Michigan Press, 1955), 199.

> Men meldt uit *Zierikzee*:
> „ Ds. *H. G. Klijn*, leeraar bij de Christelijk afgescheidene gemeente te Middelburg, heeft ll. donderdag avond alhier voor eene talrijke schaar eene afscheidsrede gehouden; hoogstwaarschijnlijk vertrekt zijn-eerw. den 19 junij, met ruim honderd zielen, naar Noord-Amerika."

Ordination and first preaching engagements, Nov. – Dec. 1839, Klijn register (*Holland Historical Trust*)

Middelburg church on Sunday, June 17, 1849, on the final words of Christ's Great Commission.[22]

Klijn's call to America was reported in at least a half-dozen Netherlands newspapers.[23] After a five-week crossing to New York, some of it very rough, Klijn made his way to Michigan and was installed by Van Raalte as pastor at Graafschap, near Holland, on Sunday, September 9, 1849.[24]

RPDC pastor before the break: Graafschap, Milwaukee, Grand Rapids (1849-57)

Two problems met Klijn immediately upon his settling in Graafschap. One—soon fairly quickly resolved—was that another Seceder pastor, Koene Sibolts van der Schuur, had just arrived from the Netherlands to serve a breakaway portion of the Graafschap congregation living in "South Holland."[25] The other issue was that Klijn and his wife, being used to city life, disliked the primitive conditions of living in the Graafschap wilderness, so they stayed there only a year and half. In trying to justify to the Classis of Holland his departing Graafschap to serve the congregation in Milwaukee, the irenic Klijn

[22] "Behold, I am with you always, even unto the end of the world," Matthew 28:20. Klijn, "Gepredikte Texten"; Wesseling *Zeeland*, 2:69. The second-hand newspaper account (see image) has Klijn preaching this sermon on a Thursday evening (*Donderdag avond*), but his own record of his engagements states that it occurred in the afternoon (*namiddag*) of Sunday, 17 June.

[23] The call was reported in newspapers in Rotterdam (two), Leiden, Middelburg, Utrecht, and Groningen; "Delpher kranten," at https://www.delpher.nl/nl/kranten/advancedsearch?

[24] "Klijn, Henderik Geert [sic]," in Joh. De Haas, *Gedenkt Uw*, vol. 1 (Haarlem: Uitgeverij Vijlbrief, 1984), 159; Klijn, "Gepredikte Texten."

[25] Classis of Holland Minutes, 31 Oct. 1849, Article 8, in *Classis Holland Minutes 1848-1858* (Grand Rapids: Grand Rapids Printing Company, 1943), 34-35. A Graafschap elder had issued the two separate calls, presumably assuming the legality of the breakaway South Holland "congregation."

claimed that his flock did not love Van der Schuur's South Holland congregation.[26]

In any case, Klijn accepted a call to Milwaukee, becoming its first settled pastor.[27] He remained in Wisconsin until 1854, declining a call in the fall of 1853 to Kalamazoo, Michigan, where he had delivered a sermon urging unity among Christians.[28] Two other evidences of Klijn's "ecumenical" spirit in this period are his well-meaning but naïve and futile proposals in April 1855 that the Classis of Holland seek reconciliation with two congregations that had seceded earlier in the decade and that it keep ties with the Seceded Church in the Netherlands.[29] Klijn's pacific proclivities would quickly be put to the test in his next charge.

Klijn, after more than two months' deliberation, accepted a call from the new, Dutch-language, Second Reformed Church of Grand Rapids, in spring 1854; he had wanted to leave Milwaukee because of the city's supposed evil influence upon his two teenage sons.[30] This move would take him, however, from the proverbial frying pan into the fire, for it was in Grand Rapids that he would encounter Elder Gijsbert Haan.[31]

---

[26] Classis of Holland Minutes, 30 Oct. 1850, Articles 7-8, in *Classis Holland Minutes*, 41. Apparently classis was not convinced by Klijn's argument but let him go anyway. Incidentally, Klijn, usually in good health, was sick and out of the Graafschap pulpit for over two months in late summer and early fall 1850; Klijn, "Gepredikte Texten." De Haas, *Gedenkt Uw Voorgangers*, 1:160.

[27] He also preached occasionally in the small nearby church of Franklin, WI. Klijn, "Gepredikte Texten."

[28] *De Sheboygan Nieuwsbode*, 18 Nov. 1853; Klijn, "Gepredikte Texten," 30 Oct. And 13 Nov. 1853.

[29] Classis of Holland Minutes, 11 April 1855, Articles 8 and 11, in *Classis Holland Minutes*, 171-73. Classis delegated the idealistic Klijn to contact the groups of Jacob Schepers and Roelof H. Smit, as well as the mother church in the Netherlands. Nothing came of these initiatives. Klijn had not been present at the classis meetings when Schepers and Smit had seceded.

[30] Classis of Holland Minutes, 12 April 1854, Article 9, in *Classis Holland Minutes*, 152-53. Earlier, Klijn had bypassed the will of classis about his move to Milwaukee (see note 27 above), but now he sought its advice, which it was reluctant to give. He announced the call (to Grand Rapids) to his Milwaukee flock on 19 February 1854 and his acceptance of the call on 23 April 1854; Klijn, "Gepredikte Texten." The rejection of the earlier call, to Kalamazoo, took him only a couple of weeks; see note 29 above. Interestingly, Klijn's moves to both Milwaukee and Grand Rapids appear to have been motivated by negative factors in his previous charges. He may well, with hindsight, have later wished he had accepted the call to Kalamazoo (where he would later serve) rather than that to Grand Rapids. Was he too controlled by his feelings, as classis suggested? *Classis Holland Minutes*, 30 Oct. 1850, Article 8.

[31] Both men were "interior decorators," Haan being a carpet weaver and Klijn a wallpaper hanger. Otherwise, they seem to have had relatively little in common. For

Gijsbert Haan (1801-1874)

Haan could reasonably claim a more unswerving loyalty to the decisions of the Synod of Dort than Scholte, Van Raalte, or Klijn. Accordingly, at Grand Rapids, Haan led the opposition in 1856 to the election of Geert B. Dalman as elder, whom he claimed was, at best, insufficiently Calvinistic. When, after a great deal of argument in both consistory and classis, Dalman was installed as elder, Haan seceded from the congregation and the RPDC in April 1856, in spite of Klijn's desperate efforts to bring about a peaceful resolution, even calling classis (as its president) to a day of prayer for unity against the schismatic "spirit of the devil."[32] Although depressed by the secession of Haan and his cohorts, Klijn remained at his post as Grand Rapids pastor, declining calls at just this time by churches in Albany and Kalamazoo (to the relief and joy of his consistory and congregation alike).[33]

---

a recent short outline of Haan's career, see Janet Sjaarda Sheeres, ed. and annotator, *Minutes of the Christian Reformed Church* (Grand Rapids: Eerdmans, 2013), 509-10.

[32] Classis of Holland Minutes, 3 April 1856, Article 12, in *Classis Holland Minutes*, 207-8. Of course, to call for prayer against the schismatic "spirit of the devil" did little to appease Haan and his cohorts. Gijsbert Haan, "Voice of One Slandered," typescript, transl. William K. Reinsma (originally G. Haan, *Stem Eens Belasterden* [Grand Rapids: C. Nienhardt, 1871]), 23-25, at ACC.

[33] Klijn, "Gepredikte Texten," 11 and 25 May and 8 June 1856. Consistory minutes, Second Reformed Church, Grand Rapids, 9 May 1856, Article 5; 2 June 1856, Article 4; 23 June 1856, Article 3; at JAH.

Klijn and Haan did not see each other for several months after the latter's secession, but in January 1857, Klijn arranged a meeting with Haan and others to discuss the whole matter of the RPDC. Haan, who knew English and had spent a couple of years getting acquainted with the denomination in the East, was able to persuade Klijn, who knew little English and had not lived in the East, that the bad "rumors" he had heard[34] about the denomination were true, and so Klijn resolved to secede, followed by many of the remaining members of his Grand Rapids flock.

Departure from and return to the RPDC: January to August 1857

Klijn informed his consistory on Monday evening, January 19, 1857, that he was leaving the RPDC. He explained that it was not so much that he believed it was not "the true church," since classis delegates to General Synod, like Van Raalte and Van der Meulen, had testified to its orthodoxy,[35] but rather that the bad rumors about the RPDC, which he could not counter from his own knowledge, had caused some in his flock, presumably the Haan coterie, to have serious doubts about it. Klijn was disinclined to blame anyone, either his beloved fellow ministers who favored the RPDC or others who had testified against it. The gentle, vacillating Klijn was saying, in effect, that he was torn between his old ministerial associates, Van Raalte and Van der Meulen, and his new Grand Rapids Svengali, Elder Haan, but that now God had shown him that the latter's first-hand evidence was correct. Aiming to do the right thing, Klijn had chosen principle over friendship.[36]

The dramatic story of the last-minute attempts of the consistory of Grand Rapids and the "church visitors" of classis (Revs. Van der Meulen and Pieter Jan Oggel) to prevent Klijn's secession; how the

---

[34] Among the many reasons given for the secession of 1857 were the Eastern RPDC's use of hymns, open communion, lax discipline, catechism neglect, involvement in Sunday school and tract societies, and denial that Christ died only for the elect. The sources of the information and "rumors," besides Haan, would have certainly included Rev. John Berdan, a propagandist for the True Reformed Dutch Church, which had left the RPDC in 1822. Classis of Holland Minutes, 8 April 1857, Article 16, in *Classis Holland Minutes*, 242 (reasons given by the Graafschap church for its secession); Robert P. Swierenga and Elton J. Bruins, *Family Quarrels in the Dutch Reformed Churches in the Nineteenth Century* (Grand Rapids: Eerdmans, 1999), 78-87.

[35] The "marks" of the true church are described in the Belgic Confession of Faith, Article 29. Most prominent of the unnamed (in the minutes) delegates to General Synod would have certainly been Van Raalte and Van der Meulen.

[36] Consistory minutes, Second Reformed Church, Grand Rapids, 19, 20, 23-25 Jan. 1857.

elders had tried in vain to bar him from the pulpit on Sunday morning, January 25, 1857; his announcement then to the congregation of his secession and the reasons for it; and the chaotic aftermath appears in vivid detail in the consistory minutes and elsewhere.[37]

Van Raalte was understandably upset about Klijn's defection, commenting in a letter to an RPDC official in the East that he was led "by an [sic] sectarian spirit. Some writings from the so-called True Dutch Church and that separated Elder Haan has [sic] brought him to such a miserable childish conduct."[38]

Meanwhile, more rebellion had erupted in another Dutch congregation in the area, the Noordeloos Reformed Church, led by the recent immigrant, Rev. Koene van den Bosch. Although not an obvious "soul brother" of Klijn, he would nevertheless partner with him in giving birth to what would become the CRC. On March 14, 1857, Van den Bosch penned this curt letter to classis:

> By this I notify you that I can hold no ecclesiastical communion with you, for the reason that I cannot hold all of you who have joined the Dutch Reformed Church to be the true church of Jesus Christ, and consequently I renounce all fellowship with you and declare myself no longer to belong to you. I am the more constrained to do this by the fear of God, on account of the abominable and church-corrupting heresy and sins which are rampant among you. . . .
>
> I hope that your eyes may yet be opened to see your gross sins, to take them to heart, and to be converted therefrom.
>
> (Signed) K. van den Bosch, Minister at Noordeloos

Characteristically, Klijn's letter of separation from the classis, dated April 6, 1857, displayed a very different tone:

> Very Reverend Brethren!
> The God of love unite your reverences in Christ by the power of the Holy Spirit. In connection with the report of my separation from the American denomination, the Reformed Protestant

---

[37] Ibid., 24 and 25 Jan. 1857; Haan "Voice of One Slandered," 27; Egbert Winter, "Historic Sketch. The Second Reformed Church," in "Scrapbook Second Reformed Church 1879-1888," 65. JAH.

[38] Van Raalte to John Garretson, Holland, 16 April 1857, RCA Archives, Board of Domestic Missions, correspondence, folder April- May 1857, box 13; photocopy, Van Raalte Institute; see note 35 above.

Dutch Church, presented to your reverences' assembly by the delegates, I hereby give expression to my cordial thanks for the love and honor enjoyed in the midst of your reverences, together with this sincere desire that your reverences could unite with us on the same standpoint.

Brethren! Ministers of the Gospel, we are together seceded ministers, insofar as your overseers in your midst walked that same path with us in the Netherlands. Yea, we were separated from all Protestant denominations. Brethren, I admonish your reverences in love not, however, to lose this your character. The Church, the Bride of Christ, is a garden enclosed, a spring shut up, and a fountain sealed. The Lord open your eyes, that you may follow your calling, whereby the Church of Christ may walk in one way, to the glorification of his holy name.

I commend myself to a continuance of your fraternal friendship, that no spirit of bitterness may reign in us and among us, for we are brethren, beloved of the Lord, bought by Christ, in order that we should serve him without fear, in holiness and righteousness all the days of our life. The King of Glory dwell in your assembly, that your reverences may observe his will. Now the Lord of Peace himself give you peace at all times and in every way. The Lord be with you all.

Your affectionate brother in Christ,

(Signed) H. G. Klijn, Grand Rapids, Mich.[39]

The marked difference in flavor of these two letters reflects not only the personalities of their authors and their backgrounds in the Netherlands[40] but also the fact that Klijn had had personal ties with these classical brethren in both the Old and the New Worlds, and Van den Bosch had not.

In any event, this odd couple did collaborate briefly in organizing the tiny band of seceders of 1856 and 1857 (the infant CRC) and in writing a letter to the Seceder Reformed Synod in the Netherlands, suggesting that the immigrant separatists were simply an overseas branch of the

---

[39] Classis of Holland Minutes, 8 April 1857, Article 16, in *Holland Classis Minutes*, 240-41, with slight revisions of the translation by the present author.
[40] Van den Bosch had been a rural laborer and Klijn an urban small businessman. Van den Bosch had been trained for the ministry by strict adherents of Dort, while Klijn had been a student of the untraditional maverick Scholte; De Haas, *Gedenkt Uw Voorgangers*, 1:44, 159.

Klijn's record of his 1857 peripatetic seceder ministry

mother church. This idea, however, received no encouragement from the synod.[41]

After about seven months of ministering to the new seceders in Grand Rapids and elsewhere in western Michigan,[42] Klijn's fervor for the separatist cause waned, undermined by a visit from his former fellow student and colleague Rev. Cornelis van der Meulen. Haan would later claim that Van der Meulen had told Klijn that, were he to die, his widow would be left destitute, without the aid of the Reformed Church's Widows' Fund. In any case, Klijn successively informed Van der Meulen and Haan in early August 1857 of his decision to return to the Reformed Church. He also apologized in the pulpit of the Second Reformed Church of Grand Rapids for his secession and wrote emotional letters that same month to the seceders in Grand Rapids and Graafschap, pleading with them to come back to the Reformed fold.[43]

---

[41] The letter's handwriting may be that of Gijsbert Haan. Sheeres, *Minutes of the Christian Reformed Church*, xxii-xxiv, 463-66.

[42] During this period, Klijn preached every Sunday and often during the week. Although the majority of Sundays he was in the pulpit of his own Grand Rapids separatist flock, starting 19 March, he also ministered occasionally in Vriesland, Polkton, Graafschap, Grandville, and Zeeland; in fact, he preached three Sundays in Graafschap and one each in Polkton and Grandville; the remaining visits took place during the week. Klijn, "Gepredikte Texten."

[43] H. G. Klijn to C. Van der Meulen, 5 Aug. 1857, in *De Hollander*, 12 Aug. 1857; Haan, "Voice of One Slandered," 28-29.

Klijn's letter to Grand Rapids offered three main reasons for his return to the RPDC: (1) Jesus' high priestly prayer for the unity of his church (John 17:21), as well as the Apostles' Creed article about the communion of saints; (2) the example of the June 1857 triennial synod of the Christian Seceded Reformed Church in the Netherlands, which had chosen the path of love, narrowly averting a schism; and (3) the letter from the clerk of that synod informing Van den Bosch and Klijn of its unwillingness to recognize the Michigan seceders as a part of the Dutch mother (true) church. Thus, with hope of union with the Christian Seceded Reformed Church excluded, Klijn had to ask himself, "Ought we to stay by ourselves," implying that "we alone are the manifest Church of God?" His conscience, before God, could not endorse such an exclusive standpoint.[44]

Then, three weeks after writing the Haan group in Grand Rapids, Klijn penned a similarly impassioned plea to the Graafschap church, using much the same line of argument, to return to the RPDC as an act of love. He said that the seceders should listen not so much to him ("for I am a changeable human, as you can see") as to Jesus' words that his followers be one (John 17:21), thus abandoning the "way of Afscheiding."[45]

During the period between these two letters, the repentant Klijn invited Van der Meulen and Oggel, the "church visitors" of classis, to see him in Grand Rapids, where he confessed to them that he had sinned against the brethren in classis by not trusting their word as to the Eastern church's orthodoxy—and in believing Haan rather than them—the reason being that he (Klijn) knew little English.[46]

---

[44] (C. Van der Meulen and P. J. Oggel), "Kennisgeving. Aan de Gemeenten tot de Hollandsch gereformeerde Kerk behoorende," in *De Hollander* (26 Aug. 1857).

[45] H. G. Klein [*sic*], "Aan de Gemeente te Graafschap," 27 Aug. 1857, photocopy of the original manuscript, JAH (there is also an English trans. of this letter by Albertus Pieters at the JAH.

[46] Classis of Holland Minutes, 9 Sept. 1857, Article 3, in *Classis Holland Minutes*, 252-53. Klijn's relative ignorance of English is also borne out by his reluctance (refusal) to be a delegate to the General Synod (Classis of Holland Minutes, 5 Sept. 1855, Article 14, and 6 April 1859, Article 11), as well as by his need to read the *Succinct Tract* (see below) in English and the letters in *Dutch* he wrote to Rev. John Garretson (of the RPDC in the East). Three years later, Rev. Adriaan Zwemer wrote Rev. Helenius de Cock in the Netherlands that "the good old man" (Klijn)—his former pastor and "still beloved friend"—"returned [to the RPDC] with unconstrained heartfelt confession of faults, and still at every opportunity he deplores his past mistakes"; moreover, Zwemer noted that the lack of the Michigan immigrants' facility in English contributed to the schism of 1857; Adriaan Zwemer, Vriesland, MI, to Helenius de Cock, 22 August 1859, typescript translation. ACC.

In light of these developments, the classis was guardedly willing, at its regular fall meeting in September, to receive Klijn back, although opinion differed as to what he should do to show he had learned his lesson and would remain true to the RPDC. One suggestion was for the sixty-four-year-old dominie to study a year at New Brunswick Theological Seminary in New Jersey, but classis rejected this as unrealistic and unreasonable. Instead, it was decided that he read—and assent to—the recently published Dutch translation of the *Succinct Tract* that explained and defended the doctrine, discipline, and liturgy of the RPDC. Klijn did this promptly at the same session, after which he was warmly welcomed back into the fellowship.[47]

RPDC pastor after the break: Kalamazoo and Chicago (1857-68)

The next step was for the rehabilitated Klijn to find a congregation in which to serve, since Grand Rapids was no longer available to him.[48] The church at Kalamazoo, vacant for well over a year, contained a good number of Zeelanders, who doubtless knew (of) Klijn; it had already called him virtually unanimously shortly before his secession and now called him again, this time by only a majority vote. In November 1857, Klijn was installed by Oggel as pastor there, where he would remain for nearly five years.[49] By then in his middle sixties, Klijn was still spry enough to preach the standard three sermons on Sunday (as in the Netherlands), as well as occasionally to serve other churches during the week.[50] His wife, however, was ailing, reportedly near death in April 1861

---

[47] The *Succinct Tract* was a pamphlet setting forth the RPDC's orthodoxy in light of attacks by the True Dutch Reformed Church (seceded 1822). *Beknopte Verhandeling over de Geschiedenis Leer en Regering der Hollandsche Gereformeerd Protestantsche Kerk in Noord-Amerika* (NY: Board of Publication of the Reformed Protestant Dutch Church, 1857), a translation of Thomas De Witt, *A Succinct Tract on the History, Doctrines, and Government of the Reformed Protestant Dutch Church in North America* (NY: Board of Managers of the Sabbath School Union, 1848); Classis of Holland Minutes, 9 Sept. 1857, Articles 3 and 7, in *Classis Holland Minutes*, 252-54.

[48] The Grand Rapids church had already been given permission by classis at its April 1857 session to call a man to replace the very recently departed Klijn. Its calls to Oggel and Van der Meulen were declined, and it was not until 1859 that it acquired a new under shepherd. Classis of Holland Minutes, 8 April 1857, Article 15, in *Classis Holland Minutes*, 239; Winter, "Historic Sketch. The Second Reformed Church," 65.

[49] Consistory minutes, First Reformed Church, Kalamazoo, 21 May 1856 and 19 Oct. 1857 (congregational meetings), at JAH. In the three months between his return to the RPDC and his installation at Kalamazoo, he kept busy preaching in Grand Rapids, Zeeland, Graafschap, Grand Haven, Milwaukee, Franklin, Chicago, and (presumably as a candidate) Kalamazoo; Klijn, "Gepredikte Texten."

[50] The fact that Klijn rarely repeated the same biblical text for his preaching may suggest that he did not linger long over sermon preparation, especially given the

(when Klijn was absent from classis meeting for that reason), and died of tuberculosis in February 1862, after over thirty years of marriage.[51]

The still-vital Klijn remarried the following July, once again only about five months after the death of his wife. His choice this time fell on Elisabeth Foute, an unmarried immigrant member of his congregation, a quarter century his junior (born 1819).[52] Many in his flock, including the consistory, appear to have been upset, not by the quick remarriage or the age difference between the pair, but by the fact that they were married in Chicago (by Rev. Seine Bolks) rather than in

---

other demands on his time, e.g., for meetings, pastoral calling, and traveling. He occasionally was spelled by other preachers during his Kalamazoo ministry, e.g.," Mr. P. J. Hoedemaker" occupied Klijn's pulpit six times (June [twice], Sept., and Dec. 1861 and May and June 1862); Klijn, "Gepredikte Texten." Philippus Jacobus Hoedemaker (1839-1910) later made a name for himself in the Netherlands as a theologian, professor, and preacher. When his father, Johannes (later John) Hoedemaker (1811-1876), a book dealer, took as his second wife Christina Pfanstiehl in 1852, Klijn, then visiting in Kalamazoo, performed the ceremony; Klijn, "Gepredikte Texten," 18 June 1852. The second wife died in 1854, and Johannes was married again, this time in Chicago in 1855 to Anna Jacoba (sometimes erroneously named Jacoba Anna) Foute (1820-1901); her older brother would become one of Klijn's elders in Chicago, while her older sister would become Klijn's third wife in 1862. After Anna Jacoba's marriage, she transferred her church membership to Kalamazoo. Surely Klijn had already known the Hoedemaker family well in Utrecht, as their church elder, since Johannes had joined the seceded group there in 1836. The Hoedemakers settled in Kalamazoo in 1851. The Foute siblings, who emigrated in 1849 and 1854, ended up living in both Chicago and Kalamazoo. Smits, *Utrecht*, 32, 261; www.findagrave.com; First Reformed Church, Kalamazoo, membership book, 1852-96, at JAH; Robert P. Swierenga, *Dutch Chicago: A History of the Hollanders in the Windy City* (Grand Rapids: Eerdmans, 2002), 14, 84; www.wiewaswie.nl; www.ancestry.com. See note 53 below.

[51] Classis of Holland Minutes, 17 April 1861 (where he says his wife was very sick), at JAH; Klijn, "Gepredikte Texten," 9 Feb. 1862 (where he notes that he did not preach that Sunday because of his wife's death). The cause of her death is given in http://kalamazoogenealogy.org.

[52] The two "early" remarriages need suggest little more than that Klijn needed a housekeeper (not uncommon in those days). Elisabeth Foute was born in Bennebroek, Noord-Holland, where her father was a housepainter; a native of Württemberg, he died in 1825 when she was only seven; Elisabeth's mother, whose hometown was Bennebroek, died in 1832, leaving several fairly young children. Elisabeth had immigrated in 1854 (with her younger sister and brother), five years after her older brother, Klaas (or Nicholas) Foute. By 1860 Elisabeth was living as part of the well-to-do Kalamazoo household of "John" Hoedemaker, who had married her younger sister five years previous. Because the Hoedemakers then had three young children, ages seven, five, and one (in addition to their student son P. J. Hoedemaker), living with them—and no servant—Elisabeth (for whom no occupation was given in the census) was probably helping care for the children. See note 51 above. www.wiewaswie.nl; www.ancestrycom; Swierenga, *Dutch Chicago*, 14, 84, 88.

their home church in Kalamazoo. Furthermore, the consistory also complained about the nocturnal "outrageous horn and cow bell music" at the parsonage upon the newlyweds' arrival (presumably a shivaree, perhaps unfriendly). Klijn readily apologized for his error of judgment in marrying elsewhere, for which the consistory forgave him. After all, the choice of the wedding venue may well have been influenced by the fact that the bride's family belonged to the Chicago church, where her older brother was also a consistory member.[53]

Klijn's third marriage seems to have lasted less than two years, with Elisabeth Foute dying probably in early February 1864. Oddly, no direct reference to her passing appears anywhere in Klijn's meticulously kept logbook of his ministerial labors, whereas his second wife's death as well as his third marriage are duly noted. No report of Klijn's wife's demise could be found in the usual available (admittedly meager and incomplete) sources, including the consistory minutes of Klijn's churches in the 1860s. The 1870 federal census reports him as a "widower," while the Illinois state enumeration of 1865 lists no female of the right age living with him.[54] The crucial clue appears to lie in the consistory minutes of the First Reformed Church of Chicago, Klijn's next charge after Kalamazoo. The entry for February 10, 1864, states that he opened the meeting in the accustomed way, with prayer and the consistory singing a Psalm verse. This time the song chosen by Klijn was Psalm 89, verse 19, which is about the fragility and shortness of life,

[53] The brother, Klaas Foute, immigrated in 1849 (recorded as "Klaas Voute") and appears in the 1850 census of Holland Township, Ottawa County, MI; like his father, he was a housepainter. Van Raalte baptized his child in February 1853, but Klaas settled in Chicago that October. He was elected deacon in the First Reformed Church there at the end of 1861 and elder at the end of 1862 (shortly after his new brother-in-law, Klijn, had become his pastor), which office he held until his death in 1887; B. de Beij, *De Vertrouwende Verwachting der Gelukzaligheid na dit Leven, Gelegenheids Woord bij de Begrafenis van den Ouderling Klaas Voute* [sic] *en zijne Vrouw* (Chicago: J. and J. G. J. Esnorff, 1887); George Birkhoff Sr., "Historische Schetsen," in *De Hope*, 25 May 1904; www.ancestry.com; Swierenga, *Dutch Chicago*, 14; consistory minutes, First Reformed Church, Chicago, 25 Dec. 1861; 9 and 25 Dec. 1862; Classis of Wisconsin Minutes, 9 Sept. 1863, Article 5, at JAH.

[54] Attestations (letters of transfer of membership) for Klijn and his wife (unnamed) and son (unnamed but presumably his younger son, Hendrik George Jr.) were accepted by the Chicago consistory from the Kalamazoo church; consistory minutes, First Reformed Church, Chicago, 16 June 1863. By the 3 July 1865 Illinois state census enumeration for Chicago, it appears that Klijn had lost a wife and that his son had gained a wife (the latter two are unnamed), so that the elder Klijn has his newly married son and daughter-in-law living with him (both between 20 and 30 years of age). The younger Klijns would be in Pella, IA, by 1870 (federal census). www.ancestry.com.

the threat and unavoidability of death, and the need for God's help, previously given, as he had promised to David, to provide meaning to life and to rescue us from the grave.[55] The meeting's actual business included only two short items, the first of which—and the one important for our purposes—was Klijn's explanation that he had been hindered from acceding to the Milwaukee minister's request to go there "by the illness with which the Lord had visited his [Klijn's] wife."[56] A final hint as to the time Klijn's wife died is that he preached only once on the morning of February 14, 1864 (the Sunday following the consistory meeting); his text was II Timothy 4:7-8, which has been often used as a kind of epitaph: "I have fought a good fight, I have finished my course, I have kept the faith: Henceforth there is laid up for me a crown of righteousness, which the Lord . . . shall give me at that day."[57]

But all this about the death of the elderly dominie's third wife is to get ahead of our story. Klijn's 1862 wedding had occasioned more serious difficulties for him in the Kalamazoo church than merely its location. The consistory was informed then that three years earlier, while still married to his second wife, Klijn had made inappropriate advances (hitherto unreported) to a couple of young women.[58] The offenses were more likely verbal than physical, given the old man's handicap at the time (he was incapacitated with a broken leg) and also the fact that the classis did not subsequently depose or suspend him, for example, for adultery.[59] Klijn readily admitted that the charges were true, whereupon

---

[55] "Gedenk, O Heer! Hoe zwak ik ben, hoe kort van duur: Het leven is een damp; de dood wenkt ieder uur. Zou't menschdom dan vergeefs op aarde zijn geschapen? Wie leeft er, die den slaap des doods niet eens zal slapen? Wie redt zijn ziel van 't graf? Ei! Help ons, als te voren, Gelijk Gij bij uw trouw aan David hebt gezworen!"

[56] Klijn indicates that he was "belet door de ziekte met welke de Heere zijn huisvrouw bezocht heeft." It is not stated in the minutes that the sickness was unto death, although that was not necessarily excluded either. Consistory minutes, First Reformed Church, Chicago, 10 Feb. 1864.

[57] The King James Version is here used to translate the 1637 Dutch *Statenbijbel*. Another minister preached for Klijn that afternoon. Klijn, "Gepredikte Texten," 14 Feb. 1864.

[58] Classis of Holland Minutes, 16 Oct. 1862, Article 18; consistory minutes, First Reformed Church, Kalamazoo, 11, 17, and 21 Aug. 1862.

[59] Van Raalte commented in a letter written from Holland, 24 Aug. 1862, that Klijn had acted "foolish" in marrying at Chicago; he also noted that "an irregularitij [sic] of him [Klijn] form [sic] before three years was brought up against Him: at last taking in consideration his old age, he did ask his dismission, and it is given Him"; Elton J. Bruins and Karen G. Schakel, eds., *Envisioning Hope College: Letters Written by Albertus C. Van Raalte to Philip Phelps Jr., 1857- to 1875* (Grand Rapids: Eerdmans, 2011), 94. Seine Bolks had been deposed from the ministry for adultery in 1851

the consistory, guided by the church visitors Van Raalte and Van der Meulen (Klijn's long-time colleagues), recommended that he resign, which he did in an appropriately humble(d) manner. He was then granted emeritus status by the classis. In the following two decades, Klijn would preach in many places but never again in Kalamazoo.[60]

Klijn's "retirement," however, was of very short duration. He terminated his emeritus standing by the end of the year, returned the little pension money he had received, and became Seine Bolks' successor, in a seamless transition, in pastoring Chicago's First Reformed Church. Klijn began by supply preaching there for half a year (starting December 1862) before he was officially installed by Bolks (June 1863).[61] Klijn served that congregation until late spring 1868. During this time, he continued the practice of occasionally filling other pulpits (both near and far),[62] although, probably as a concession to his advancing years, he now delivered only two sermons per Sunday. The congregation grew markedly, partially due to immigration, so a larger sanctuary had to be built, and Klijn inhabited a new parsonage and launched a Sunday

---

but was soon restored, after repentance. Classis of Holland Minutes, 15 Oct. 1851, Article 7, and 28 April 1852, Articles 8-9, in *Classis Holland Minutes*, 70-78, 87-88; the names of Bolks and of the congregation are omitted in the published minutes.

[60] Klijn last preached in Kalamazoo on Sunday, 10 Aug. 1862. On the following Sunday, 17 Aug., there was *preeklezen* (the reading by an elder of a sermon written by an ordained minister) in the church, followed by morning and afternoon supply preaching on three Sundays in August and September by Revs. Van der Meulen (24 Aug.), Van Raalte (7 Sept.), and Pieters (28 Sept.), with Klijn evidently in attendance; the intervening Sundays would have had *preeklezen*. Klijn himself next preached 16 Nov. 1862, in Grandville, and then regularly for the next month in several places, until he settled in Chicago; Klijn, "Gepredikte Texten." Twice before, the classis had been involved in guiding (or trying to guide) Klijn's pastoral moves, i.e., from Graafschap to Milwaukee and from there to Grand Rapids.

[61] Bolks may have arranged for the "retired" Klijn to supply the pulpit on an interim basis as soon as he (Bolks) left the Chicago congregation, after an unusually short ministry there. He may have intended to benefit not only the flock he was leaving but also his senior colleague Klijn. It should be recalled that Bolks had officiated at Klijn's controversial wedding and also that Bolks, like Klijn, had been forced out of the ministry because of sexual misconduct (see note 60), and, finally, that Klijn's new wife's brother was already a member of the Chicago consistory. With Bolks presiding over a congregational meeting, Klijn was elected pastor of the Chicago church in March 1863 by a nearly unanimous vote of its male communicant members; he received 29 of 31 votes cast. Consistory minutes, First Reformed Church, Chicago, 4 and 26 Nov. 1862; 9 March 1863; Klijn, "Gepredikte Texten."

[62] For instance, he presided over the organization of the Reformed congregation in Fulton in Western Illinois, which he presumably reached by train. He preached in this infant, pastorless church three Sundays in 1865 and 1866. Klijn, "Gepredikte Texten," 10 Sept. 1865, 17 June, and 27-28 Oct. 1866.

school,⁶³ as well as a parochial day school.⁶⁴ In addition, collections were received for sick soldiers during the Civil War,⁶⁵ with consistory endorsing Klijn's proposal in 1863 to hold a prayer meeting for the nation every two weeks.⁶⁶ His generally irenic temperament displayed itself again by the conciliatory way in which he responded to a man in the congregation who was upset about something the dominie had supposedly said to him.⁶⁷ In 1867, however, toward the end of Klijn's tenure, some members seceded, partly because they were dissatisfied with their aged pastor's ministry, to form what would become the First Christian Reformed Church of Chicago. In a sense, history was repeating itself, with Klijn firmly opposing schism, as he had initially done in Grand Rapids in 1856, but this time his loyalty to the RPDC never wavered.⁶⁸

---

63 Consistory minutes, First Reformed Church, Chicago, 17 and 31 March 1863; 13 June 1865.
64 Ibid., 3, 23-24 Jan., 7 Feb., 2, 16, 30 May, 22 Aug. 1865; 10 April and 15 Oct. 1866. Klijn had earlier presided over the opening of a parochial school in Grand Rapids on 3 Dec. 1855; H. G. Klijn to John Garretson, Grand Rapids, 25 Feb. 1856, RCA Archives, Board of Domestic Missions, correspondence, box 12, folder Jan.-April 1856, photocopy, VRI. Garretson and his wife had just visited Klijn and his wife and sons, evidently in Grand Rapids. Did the sons act as translators? Klijn wrote several "business" letters in Dutch to Garretson and one to Rev. Isaac N. Wyckoff between 1853 and 1856; apparently, they all needed to be translated into English in New York, presumably at the time.
65 Consistory minutes, First Reformed Church, Chicago, 28 July 1863, 12 Jan. 1864, and 21 March 1865.
66 Ibid., 30 June 1863. Klijn's "Gepredikte Texten" suggests, however, that he both previously and subsequently conducted prayer meetings not only for the nation but especially for foreign missions.
67 Klijn tried (unsuccessfully) to deflect the accusation by conceding that the member may have *thought* he heard Klijn say what he in fact did not say (which was substantiated by an eye witness's testimony to the consistory); the accuser remained adamant and was eventually disciplined. Consistory minutes, First Reformed Church, Chicago, 6 Sept. 1864; 21 March, 4 April, 16 May, 27 June, and 27 July 1865. Consistory also rebuked some women who were gossiping about Klijn; the nature of the gossip was not mentioned; consistory minutes, 8 March 1864.
68 A fine, detailed account of Klijn's Chicago pastorate appears in Swierenga, *Dutch Chicago*, 100-108; see also Birkhoff, "Historische Schetsen." Because the consistory minutes of the First Reformed Church of Chicago are missing for a number of years beginning Jan. 1867, the principal (virtually primary, albeit hostile) source for the 1867 CRC secession is B. de Beij and A. Zwemer, *Stemmen uit de Hollandsch-Gereformeerde Kerk in de Vereenigde Staten van Amerika* (Groningen: G J. Reits, 1871), 154-56. Strangely, the secession is not mentioned in the minutes of the Classis of Wisconsin or in those of the General Synod (the latter being of course largely dependent on the former). Nevertheless, something of the outflow of members from Klijn's church can be gathered from the congregational statistics for the year 1867-68, appearing in the June 1868 General Synod minutes: 24 communicant

Emeritus pastorates: Grand Haven, Milwaukee, Chicago, Pella (1868-1878)

After Chicago, Klijn, now in his seventy-fifth year, received emeritus status once again. Although he continued to preach in various places (for which he may have received some slight compensation) until his long life's end, he became largely financially dependent upon the largesse of the Chicago congregation, the Classis of Wisconsin, and the RCA General Synod (the disabled ministers' funds of the latter two were not, however, always reliable); his requests for this support (either $300 or $400 per year, probably about half of his preretirement salary) appear regularly in the classical minutes.[69] Given the poverty of Klijn's earliest years, he may be forgiven were he to have been a bit anxious about his income in his final years; one brief, initial threat to his peace of mind in that regard seems to have been the 1867 secession from the Chicago church, which temporarily reduced its ability to contribute to his retirement support.[70] Nevertheless, the probate of Klijn's last will and testament, composed a year before his death, in April 1883, when he was eighty-nine years old, suggests that he had managed his meager estate prudently; he even left a legacy of forty dollars for the Board of Foreign Missions of the RCA.[71]

---

members were dismissed (although 47 were received by letter and 12 by confession of faith), in contrast with only three dismissed the previous year (1866-67); *The Acts and Proceedings of the . . . General Synod of the Reformed Protestant Dutch Church, . . . June 1867* (NY: Board of Publication of the RPDC), 233; *Acts and Proceedings, June 1868*, 457. The secession may have been partly due to dissonance between a new wave of immigrants from the province of Groningen who did not fit in well with earlier immigrants from the province of Zuid-Holland; Swierenga, *Dutch Chicago*, 105, 107-8; De Beij and Zwemer, *Stemmen*, 155. The congregation appears to have grown considerably in its first year under Klijn's energetic successor, Rev. Bernardus de Beij; *Acts and Proceedings, June 1869*, 620.

[69] Classis of Wisconsin Minutes, 22 April 1868, Article 6. The minutes are missing from 1869 to Sept. 1877. Klijn's requests for support (approved by classis) appear annually in the minutes from April 1878 to April 1883.

[70] In June 1869, the Classis of Wisconsin memorialized the General Synod about setting up "a fund to sustain the Emeriti Ministers of our Church. . . . The occasion of this request was the case of a Pastor who, having been declared emeritus, and promised an annuity, was deprived of his expected support by a division of the congregation." The classis was informed that there already existed a "Fund for Disabled Ministers," to which the classis should apply for an appropriation. *Acts and Proceedings* (1869), 658. Almost certainly, the church mentioned here is Chicago (with its CRC exodus in 1868), and the minister is Klijn (retired 1868). This seems to be the only reference (albeit oblique) to the Chicago CRC secession in the minutes of either the classis or the General Synod.

[71] In addition to the $40 given to the RCA, his estate was sufficient to pay for his burial and gravestone in a Keokuk cemetery and to pay off a $90 debt of his surviving son;

Financial considerations aside, Klijn kept preaching throughout the fifteen years of his second retirement. From June 1868 to September 1869, he regularly filled the pulpit of the Grand Haven, Michigan, Reformed congregation, following which, he supply preached at his former church in Milwaukee from January to September 1870.[72] Between May 1871 and May 1878, Klijn held forth periodically in Pella at its three Dutch-language Reformed churches (as well as in some neighboring communities), except for several weeks in 1874 and 1876 when he supplied Reformed pulpits in Chicago and vicinity. His changes in locality may have been dictated partly by housing provided by his offspring. Klijn's older son, who resided in or near Pella, where his father preached regularly until December 1875, died in early Feb. 1876. Klijn's younger son made his home in Chicago during the 1870s, until moving to Grand Rapids by 1877. Klijn preached in Chicago from the end of February to late July 1876, after which he returned to Pella.[73]

---

he also left $154 and $19 to his two daughters-in-law. His Dutch books sold for $46—probably not a very large library. Henry George Klyn, Iowa, Wills and Probate Records, 1758-1997, Lee County, Will Records, South Keokuk, vols. 1-2, 1868-1902, at www.ancestry.com; *The Fifty-Second Annual Report of the Board of Foreign Missions of the Reformed Church in America for the Year ending April 30th, 1884* (NY: printed for the board, 1884), 107.

[72] The 1870 federal census for Milwaukee reported him as a widower living in the household of Emme Janssen and his wife. Janssen, a long-time pillar of the First Reformed Church of Milwaukee, was one of its first elders when it was organized in 1849. He was also several times a delegate from the Milwaukee church to the higher RPDC/RCA assemblies. Klijn filled the Milwaukee pulpit in the interim in 1870 between the pastorates of Revs. John van der Meulen and Adriaan Zwemer. It was here, 11 Sept. 1870, that he delivered the last sermon he ever gave based on the Heidelberg Catechism. Klijn, "Gepredikte Texten"; www.ancestry.com (1870 census); membership records, FRC, Milwaukee, 1856-1939, ms. At JAH; *First Reformed Church Seventy-Fifth Anniversary Souvenir*, 12; Classis of Wisconsin Minutes, 22 April 1868, 19-20 Sept. 1877; *Minutes of the Particular Synod of Chicago, 1867, 1868, 1869, 1870, 1872, 1874, and 1875* (Chicago: various publishers, 1867-70, 1872, 1874), 36, 54, 71, 90, 138, 190, 215.

[73] The older son, Henry George Klyn Jr. (1835-1876), a printer, became a member by letter of transfer from Chicago in March 1864, of Hope (Reformed) Church, Holland, MI (English language), and was dismissed from there in 1873, although he was evidently living much of this time elsewhere with his wife, an Amsterdam native (like his father's first wife), whom he had married in Lee County, Iowa, in 1867, and with whom he was living in Pella in the 1870 census; he died 6 Feb. 1876 intestate in nearby Jasper county, Iowa. The son's wife, Wilhelmina ("Mina") Catharina van We[e]rden (1837-1918), the daughter of a "confectioner" born in Utrecht (the dominie's hometown), had come with her parents and siblings to the United States in 1854, settling in Keokuk, the county seat of Lee County, Iowa. The younger son, John C. (earlier Johannes Cornelis) Klyn (1837-1916), was once a member of Van Raalte's (Dutch-language) church in Holland, MI, where he was living as a recently wed man, according to the census of 1860; he was later a 2nd lieutenant in the

Klijn's preaching engagements gradually became fewer, and he traveled less. An unnamed illness suddenly struck him January 16, 1877, and for that entire year, he made no entries in his logbook of texts, dates, or places of various "talks" (*toespraken*) he gave. But then, as he says, the Lord granted his request (citing the prayer of Jabez, I Chronicles 4:10b), so that he was able to return to fairly frequent preaching in Pella's Fourth Reformed Church by February 1878.

Final years: ministry in Keokuk (1878-1883)

Klijn's final move was from Pella in central Iowa to Keokuk in the southeast corner of the state, in June 1878. Klijn had never preached there before but would henceforth preach nowhere else until his death five-and-a-half years later. He lived in Keokuk with the widow of his older son, Henry George Klyn Jr., and their only child, Kate, who was about seven years old upon his arrival.[74] The obvious attraction of Keokuk for him was a caregiving family (his daughter-in-law had roots and family there), although he may also have hoped to revive a ministry to the remnants of a short-lived RCA congregation disbanded

---

infantry from Iowa (Pella?), 1862-63, in the Civil War and an off-and-on printer (typesetter); he may well have lived with his wife and growing family in Chicago from the days of his father's pastorate there. The young couple was probably (anonymously) in the elder Klijn's household there in the 1865 Illinois state census; he (with his family) also appears in Chicago in the 1870 census (as a postal clerk) and in the 1872, 1873, and 1876 Chicago city directories; his father was boarding with him in 1876, when he was a constable; he was listed in the Grand Rapids city directory for 1877, appearing there subsequently for the rest of his life. John C. Klyn was married to a niece of pioneer Sheboygan *Nieuwsbode* publisher Jacob Quintus; this fits with his frequent employment as a printer. www.ancestry.com (federal and Illinois state censuses; Chicago and Grand Rapids city directories; Civil War draft registration; marriage records; cemetery records; Iowa Wills and Probate Records, 1758-1997, Jasper County Administrator's Bonds); www.wiewaswie.nl; www.findagrave.com; Bevolkings registers, 1851-53, 1853-63, Stadsarchief Amsterdam. Klijn, "Gepredikte Texten," shows that he preached in outlying congregations near Pella, e.g., Otley, Bethel, Sand Ridge, and Elk Creek; he also preached at the High Prairie (Roseland) church near Chicago in the short time he was in that area. His record of sermons delivered at the Fourth Reformed Church of Pella provides a rare bit of information about that elusive, ephemeral congregation.

[74] Had Klijn been boarding with the widow of his son in or near Pella from the middle of 1876 until she moved back to her hometown of Keokuk in 1878? For particulars on the daughter-in-law, see preceding note. Mina remained in Keokuk with Kate (who as a young adult became a school teacher and a Presbyterian) until almost the end of her life, when they moved to Minnesota when Kate married. Mina died soon after this and was buried in her hometown beside the old dominie; www.findagrave.com.

**Klijn's record of his preaching from bed,
starting October 7, 1883**

thirteen years earlier.[75] The old dominie delivered sermons (or at least homilies on biblical texts) in his new home on most Sunday afternoons for the rest of his life. His Keokuk "congregation," numbering about a dozen people, bought him an "easy chair" in 1880, so he could sit while delivering his messages.[76] Klijn remained on the rolls of the Classis of Wisconsin until his death and, ever loyal to the RCA, a gift of $21, collected in his house, was sent in his name to its Board of Foreign Missions in the final year of his life.[77]

The entries in Klijn's preaching register continued in his quivering hand until December 1882, the start of his ninetieth year; the following

---

[75] Klijn's daughter-in-law's family, the Van We[e]rdens, was well established in Keokuk; her elderly parents lived there into the 1890s; www.ancestry.com. The young Rev. Jacob Baay had served the newborn RPDC in Keokuk from 1860 to 1865, when it dissolved, and he became a Presbyterian. Russell L. Gasero, *Historical Directory of the Reformed Church in America 1628-2000* (Grand Rapids: Eerdmans, 2001), 12, 569.

[76] *De Volksvriend*, 10 June 1880.

[77] This was in addition to the previously mentioned legacy of $40 for the foreign missions board. *Annual Report of the Board of Foreign Missions for the Year ending April 30th, 1884*, 107. See note 72 above.

month, the records began to be written by someone else (perhaps his daughter-in-law). Then, after preaching almost every Sunday afternoon in 1883, the register for September 20 reports that he did not preach because he had become sick. The next entries, for four Sundays in October and the first three Sundays in November report that he *uit bet gepredikt* (preached from bed).

Klijn's last sermon text was Psalm 71:6, 7, and 9.

> By thee have I been holden up from the womb: thou art he that took me out of out of my mother's bowels: my praise shall be continually of thee. I am as a wonder unto many: but thou art my strong refuge. . . . Cast me not off in the time of old age; forsake me not when my strength faileth.[78]

There are worse ways to go. Klijn had turned ninety just the day before this and died only a week and a half later, eleven days after his birthday.

Rev. Egbert Winter, pastor of the First Reformed Church of Pella (1866-84), where Klijn had sometimes substituted in the pulpit in the 1870s, conducted the funeral, with many area Dutch people attending, in the United Presbyterian Church of Keokuk. This was a Psalm-singing, English-language congregation (founded 1853),[79] of which Klijn's daughter-in-law and granddaughter may well have been members. It may also have been the church that Klijn himself, before he became an invalid, attended on Sunday mornings (his English had presumably improved, at least enough to communicate with his granddaughter Kate).[80] In any case, he was laid to rest in the Oakland Cemetery in Keokuk, and Mina, his faithful daughter-in-law, was buried beside him thirty-five years later.[81]

Assessment of Rev. H. G. Klijn

In a substantial obituary written at the time for *De Hope*, the Dutch-language RCA weekly for Midwestern immigrants, Winter reported that Klijn "was indefatigable until the end, still at work in the proclamation

---

[78] King James Version; Klijn, "Gepredikte Texten."
[79] S. W. Moorhead and Nelson C. Roberts, *History of Lee County, Iowa*, vol. 1 (Chicago: S. J. Clarke Publishing, 1914), 324, at https://archive.org/details/storyofleecounty01robe.
[80] H. G. Klyn Jr. and his wife were doubtless bilingual, having been young enough when immigrating to learn English very well. He had even, as a young adult, joined the English-language Hope Church in Holland, MI; see note 74 above.
[81] www.findagrave.com. No gravestone exists for them there.

of the grace of God. When he could not stand anymore, he did so seated, and when he could not sit in his chair anymore, he did so from his bed."[82] Winter gave a short overview of Klijn's spiritual pilgrimage, beginning with his conversion during the spiritual awakening in the Netherlands, presumably in the 1820s, and continuing through his study for the ministry under Scholte. Nothing was said of Klijn's role in the 1857 CRC secession, although Winter did note that the man had his shortcomings, like the best of God's servants. In this connection, he told of his having heard that Klijn had at one time been influenced by the *lijdelijke richting* ("passive party" among the seceders) that "enervates the gospel." Winter is here referring to the tendency in some pietist Reformed circles to emphasize divine sovereignty to the exclusion of human activity, so that sinners, including children of the covenant, can only wait passively for the Holy Spirit to give them regeneration, faith, good works, assurance of election, and so forth. This involved a heavily introspective piety, that mainstream Reformed Seceders, like Van Raalte and Winter, believed to be a kind of perverted mysticism, undercutting the free offer of the gospel and human responsibility.[83] Winter's obituary, however, goes on to say that he had detected nothing of this in Klijn's gospel preaching in the 1870s, in Pella, where the old dominie had proclaimed the good news of God's grace, pure and simple.

There have been a few more recent assessments of H. G. Klijn. In the early twentieth century, the historically minded stated clerk of the RCA Classis of Holland, described him as "a man of limited education, pious, mystical, emotional, often led by his feelings rather than his judgment."[84] But, more positively, an historically minded carpenter and

---

[82] E. Winter, "In Memoriam," *De Hope* (11 Dec. 1883), 6 (transl. Nella Kennedy), in H. G. Klijn file at the VRI.

[83] K. Dijk, "Lijdelijkheid," in F. W. Grosheide and G. P. van Itterzon, eds., *Christelijke Encyclopedie*, 2nd ed. (Kampen, NL: J. H. Kok N. V., 1959), 4:450-51. A member of Klijn's flock in Grand Rapids had complained that his pastor overemphasized divine election; consistory minutes, Second Reformed Church, Grand Rapids, 26 Jan. 1856, Article 2, manuscript at JAH. Earlier, the Classis of Holland (with Van Raalte as clerk) had asserted that Klijn had based his decision to go from Graafschap to Milwaukee upon his feelings rather than upon the Word of God; Classis of Holland Minutes, 30 Oct. 1850, Article 8, in *Classis Holland Minutes*, 41; this may or may not be a reference to his *lijdelijkheid*. Klijn may have been introduced to experiential piety during the 1820s, when the *Réveil* was spreading in the Netherlands. That he was not a consistent "extremist" in his pietism is suggested by the fact that he advertised the writings of Wilhelmus à Brakel, a popular, moderate experientialist, in the *De Nieuwsbode* of Sheboygan, WI, e.g., 20 Dec. 1853 and 3 Jan. and 14 Feb. 1854.

[84] Gerhard De Jonge, manuscript commenting on the ministers of First Reformed Church, Grand Haven; in the Gerhard De Jonge file, JAH.

former member of the church in Chicago who had settled there just after Klijn left, described him (presumably based on the testimony of others) as being a man of "fine culture," having "courteous manners worthy of a minister of the gospel" and a "very mellifluous voice."[85] An examination of Klijn's carefully handwritten business letters—in Dutch—to RPDC officials in the East in the mid-1850s shows that he had mastered good penmanship and that he had strived to make a good impression, using acceptable but rather stilted, old-fashioned (even for then), pious language.[86]

Possibly the best overall, albeit succinct, recent characterization of H. G. Klijn comes from an RCA minister raised in the CRC, working only with the English-language sources in print a quarter century ago. He concludes that Klijn was an "accidental separatist," "caught in the middle," having a "malleable will, ... guileless diplomatic engagements," and an "earnestly irenic heart."[87]

Although Klijn's "irenic heart" appears intermittently throughout his long career; it may be that his early Reformed pietism contributed to his brief un-irenic involvement in the birth of the CRC; this is because this mysticism would have been uncongenial to the "evangelicalism" of the Americanized RPDC, as represented by Egbert Winter, a graduate of the denomination's seminary in New Brunswick, New Jersey.[88] Possibly,

---

[85] Klijn was "een man van fijne beschaving, had hoffelijke manieren waardig een Evangelie dienaar. Zijn stem was zeer welluiden." Birkhoff, "Historische Schetsen." Gerrit (very quickly George) Birkhoff (1827-1910), who immigrated with his family in 1869, reportedly erected the first building in Chicago after the 1871 fire. www.ancestry.com; www.findagrave.com.

[86] Klijn also made a few, relatively common, spelling (but not grammatical) errors. See note 65 above.

[87] Ron Rienstra, "Caught in the Middle: A Character Study of an Accidental Secessionist," in *Historical Highlights* 41 (June 1994), 8. Rienstra's lengthier version: "1) Klein [sic] was, at best, refreshingly guileless, at worst, he was hopelessly naïve with regard to the political issues which are too frequently a part of church government; 2) Klein was a somewhat unpredictable figure. Though not always indecisive, he was susceptible to rapid changes of opinion, and his pliable will was perhaps too often swayed by the strong personalities around him; and 3) nevertheless, Klein was a kind, open, honest man, well-respected by his colleagues, and at least an innocent and irenic figure caught in the middle of a largely political and personal struggle." Ibid., 3. One might question the use of the word "political," but overall this seems to be a fair description of the man.

[88] Could Klijn's theological training under Scholte have planted a seed that ultimately undermined his early inclination to Reformed pietism? Of course, Van der Meulen (another Scholte protégé) and Van Raalte—with whom Klijn had formed bonds of collegiality if not friendship over the years—were more open than the CRC to the American "evangelicalism" of much of the eastern RPDC.

too, the subjectivism of the "passive" way may have played a role in Klijn's vacillating, erratic behavior in 1857. However this may be, it is evident that he was ill-cast as the cofounder of the CRC and is undeserving of a place in its pantheon of progenitors. Rather, Gijsbert Haan is far more qualified for that honor, as the virtual Svengali of the "malleable" Rev. Hendrik Georg Klijn, who, when left to himself, purposed to be a kind of anti-Rombach, desperately desiring to do the right thing: loving the brotherhood, seeking the unity of the church of Jesus Christ, and persevering to the end. Klijn's death went understandably and deservedly unnoticed in the pages of the weekly *De Wachter* of the CRC, the denomination he had cofounded but abandoned in its infancy, while that weekly gave his partner in 1857, Rev. Koene van den Bosch, an understandably and deservedly large, front-page obituary in 1897. After all, *he* had stayed the course.[89]

---

[89] *De Wachter* (24 Nov. 1897), 1. This extensive obituary by Van den Bosch's Grand Haven pastor was preceded by a short notice the previous week announcing the death and promising further coverage. The Holland, MI, weekly *De Grondwet*, 4 Dec. 1883, stated, without comment, that the "the old Dominie H. G. Klijn" had died in Keokuk early in the morning of the preceding Thursday.

CHAPTER 13

The Michigan Years (1888-1893) of Geerhardus Vos

George Harinck

In general, the small, American, nonestablished theological schools founded in the nineteenth century had in their first years a teaching staff of ministers who taught part time at the school and ministered part time in their congregations. And almost all of these teachers had no academic credentials beyond their ministerial studies (formal or informal). In nineteenth-century Dutch American communities, this is the case with both Calvin Theological Seminary (founded 1876) in Grand Rapids and Western Theological Seminary (founded 1884) in Holland. There was, however, one exception to this rule. A decade after the Theological School of the Christian Reformed Church—Calvin seminary's name in the nineteenth century—started, it hired a professor of theology who had studied at the best seminaries and universities in the United States and Europe, had defended and published a dissertation and more, who had never ministered in a congregation, and was wanted as a professor by several academic institutions. His name was Geerhardus Vos (1862-1949).[1]

---

[1] Vos earned a PhD degree in Arabic studies from the University of Strassburg, Germany (now Strasbourg, France), in 1888.

In this article, I will focus on three questions: Why did this bright academic take a job at a theological school with only two other professors and a student body of about twenty? What was his role and influence in the five years he taught in Grand Rapids, and why did he leave?

Ending up in Michigan

The Dutchman Geerhardus Vos knew very well the school in Grand Rapids that hired him in 1886. When he emigrated in 1881 with his parents from the Netherlands to Grand Rapids, where his father became the minister of Spring Street CRC, he was nineteen years old and had just finished his secondary education at the Amsterdam municipal *gymnasium*.

The option to enroll at a Dutch academic institution had evaporated. Instead he became a student at the small CRC Theological School in Williams Street, Grand Rapids. This school had started in 1876 with seven students and one docent, Rev. G. E. Boer, and was located on the first floor of the Christian primary school on Williams Street.[2]

The curriculum of the school was a copy of the curriculum of its sister institution, the Theological School of Kampen: four years of literary education and two years of theology.[3] Boer taught twenty-one hours in five days and two more for the "Circle"—an informal meeting with students, a pattern that Boer knew from his student days at Kampen Theological School.[4]

Because Boer had to combine this teaching load with pastoring his congregation, students also had to educate each other.[5] New students varied in their level of educational training, some had nothing but primary education. Vos, with his classical training, was a rare exception. Boer's teachings were satisfactory, though his students were rather critical at times,[6] and they had the impression he did not prepare the dogmatics class well.[7] They deplored the fact that Boer taught in Dutch:

---

[2] J[acob] Noordewier, "De oorsprong van onze Theologische School," in *Semi-Centennial Volume. Theological School and Calvin College 1876-1926* (Grand Rapids, MI: Published for the Semi-Centennial Committee [by Tradesman Co.], 1926), 13-14.

[3] George Harinck and Wim Berkelaar, *Domineesfabriek. Geschiedenis van de Theologische Universiteit Kampen* (Amsterdam: Prometheus, 2018), 66.

[4] Harinck and Berkelaar, *Domineesfabriek*, 50.

[5] Notulen curatoren, 16 March 1880, Art. 6, ACC. All translations of the Notulen have been done by Heritage Hall at Calvin College.

[6] Notulen curatoren, 15 April 1880, art. 3, 4.

[7] Ibid., 16 March 1880, art. 11.

the younger generation preferred learning in English. One student asked in 1880 for a leave for one year to practice his English among English-speaking Americans. The curatorium did not allow this.[8]

Such was the school Vos entered in September 1881. He skipped the literary education, except for the Hebrew class.[9] He immediately started the theological course, which he finished in June 1883.[10] He excelled as a student and even had adequate spare time. Vos studied without a scholarship from the church but soon earned his own income. From April 1882 until the summer of 1883, he worked as an assistant to Boer, first for $300 and then soon for $600 a year.[11]

The four members of the curatorium wanted to hire Vos as a docent, but Synod decided in May 1883 that, at twenty-one years of age, he was too young for this position, and on top of this, the curators preferred a docent from the Netherlands. Synod therefore appointed him temporarily as an assistant again, until the docent would come.[12] In June, Vos declined this temporary job. Synod called the aged professor Anthony Brummelkamp from Kampen, but when the curatorium had not received an answer from him by August, at the start of the academic year, Vos was offered the job of assistant docent for a full year, with the restriction that he would withdraw when Brummelkamp accepted.

Vos had to decide immediately, but he had already resolved to enroll at Princeton Theological Seminary and was in contact with professors there. He was dealing with Princeton registrar William H. Roberts about exemption from the first year, for he already had a diploma in theology from the Grand Rapids school:

> It would suit me best to enter the middle class. As the catalogue does not give evidence on this point, I must trouble you once more and ask:
>
> 1. Will I be admitted to the middle class?
> 2. Is it possible by studying successively or simultaneously all the branches to take a full course in two years?

---

[8] Ibid., 22 June 1880, art. 8.
[9] Ibid., 28 June 1881, art. 4.
[10] Ibid., 26-28 June 1883, art. 7. He had to preach on Ephesians 1:4. This text led him to a moderate suprlapsarianism, see G. Vos to B. B. Warfield, 7 July 1891, James T. Dennison, ed., *The Letters of Geerhardus Vos* (Phillipsburg. NJ: P&R Publishing, 2005), 162.
[11] Noordewier, "De oorsprong van onze Theologische School," 14.
[12] Notulen curatoren, 7 Feb. 1883, art. 8; *Handelingen van de synodale vergadering der Hollandsche Christelijke Gereformeerde Kerk, gehouden te Grand Rapids, Michigan den 23 mei e.v.d. 1883* (Holland, MI: n.p., 1883), art. 20.

3. To what kind of diploma or certificate will I be entitled when entering the middle class and leaving the senior after a study of two years?[13]

Vos's mind was thus already focused on Princeton, and he would start his studies there on September 20, in the middle class. Only an unconditional offer from the CRC might have stopped him from leaving Grand Rapids. Since the curatorium now preferred Brummelkamp, Vos declined the call.[14] He left for Princeton, and then Brummelkamp declined the call of the CRC as well. Rev. G. K. Hemkes was appointed assistant,[15] and subsequently, in 1884, Hemkes—not Vos—was appointed as the second docent.[16] On August 28, 1884, Hemkes gave an inaugural address in Dutch on the practice of preparatory disciplines.[17] At that time, there were two docents and about twenty students.

So when Vos on June 17, 1886, was appointed by Synod as its third docent at the Theological School,[18] he already had a history with this institution, and the CRC had not forgotten him. He also knew that the school and his future role there were on the mind of his father, one of the school's curators from 1882 until 1891 and again from 1892. Though Vos had left Grand Rapids in 1883 and studied in Berlin, Germany, since the fall of 1885, on a Princeton fellowship, he clearly recognized the themes addressed in his letter of appointment as issues from his student days:

> [The] Holland Christian Reformed Church in America is becoming more and more convinced that in the interest of the future offspring and the preservation of our church, preaching in the English tongue has become a pressing need. More than one Classis has requested that . . . our students at our theological school receive more instruction than currently in the English tongue so that the future ministers, as a result, also can preach in that language.[19]

---

[13] Vos to William H. Roberts, 17 Aug. 1883, Dennison, *Letters*, 115-16.
[14] Notulen curatoren, 7 Aug. 1883, art. 4, 7.
[15] Noordewier, "De oorsprong van onze Theologische School," 14.
[16] *Handeling synode 1884*, arts. 53 and 62. Hemkes got 48 votes. Geerhardus Vos had also been nominated and got 18 votes. The Kampen professor D. K. Wielenga had been the third nominee. Vos's father asked the Synod not to call his son but Wielenga, in case Hemkes would decline.
[17] Notulen curatoren, 29 Aug. 1884, art. 1.
[18] *Handelingen synode 1886*, art. 94. Vos got 42 votes, J. Y. De Baun 26.
[19] Letter of call, addendum to notulen curatoren, 24 Aug. 1886. The letter was composed in the meeting of 22 June 1886. Since Sept. 1884, student O. Stuit had

Synod therefore decided "that a third docent be called to the theological school of our church, whom we feel is able to serve in this capacity or, preferably, who can fully serve in this capacity." His task would be to:

> 1. Teach the English language to the students. 2. Teach in English, exclusively, the literary subjects assigned to you after deliberation with the other docents and the Curatorium. 3. To preach on Sundays in English at least once in Grand Rapids, or now and then elsewhere when it is so desired, as much your strength allows and without [causing] interference with the teaching.

The curators knew that Vos was in the midst of his PhD studies, but they hoped he would accept "and come here [as] quickly as possible in order to be here at the start of the new school year, or at least not long thereafter."

The letter from Synod was received by Vos in July 1886, at an inconvenient time. In May he had been approached by the Vrije Universiteit (Free University) of Amsterdam to succeed F. W. J. Dilloo, professor in Semitic languages who also taught Old Testament, but who had resigned in December 1885 and returned to Germany.[20] Vos was reluctant to negotiate with the Vrije Universiteit, because he planned to return to the United States after finishing his dissertation. Vrije Universiteit persisted, and Vos met several of its professors and curators in Amsterdam. He felt attracted to this new university, so to accept the call to Grand Rapids, after having come halfway through the process with Amsterdam, became comparatively less appealing.[21] He had made a favorable impression in Amsterdam, and in September 1886, Vos was invited to the Vrije Universiteit.

Vos told the Amsterdam curators that he would not decide without having consulted his parents. His parents cabled him to

---

given English lessons to his fellow students, but in Feb. 1885, he had been dismissed from the school because of an "intimate relationship" with his girlfriend. Notulen curatoren, 29 Aug. 1884, art. 3; Notulen curatoren, 18 Feb. 1885, art. 2. In the academic year 1887-88, English was taught by Rev. De Baun. Notulen curatoren, 3 Aug. 1887, art. 19.

[20] Maarten J. Aalders, "F. W. J. Dilloo en zijn mislukte integratie," in Maarten J. Aalders, *Gereformeerden onder elkaar. Elf opstellen en een preek* (Barneveld: Vuurbaak, 2015), 71-92.

[21] Professor F. L. Rutgers to president-curator J. W. Felix, 28 Aug. 1886. *Archief-curatoren*, Vrije Universiteit Amsterdam. Vos had several questions about the letter of call from Grand Rapids, Notulen curatoren, 24 Aug. 1886, arts. 13, 14.

decline and come to the theological school in Grand Rapids. This was a disappointment, because over the summer, his sympathy for the Vrije Universiteit had grown, and in July, Herman Bavinck, professor at Kampen Theological School, had spent a week with him in Berlin, visiting tourist locations and attending classes at Berlin university.[22] The Dutch context felt like home. His parents did not join him in his shifting sympathy, and he felt obliged to obey them and accept Grand Rapids' call, declining "with much sorrow" the call from the Vrije Universiteit.[23]

Vos was disappointed about this outcome and did not look forward to joining the theological school; a year later, he regretted his decline of the call from Amsterdam ("I still sometimes doubt if I may or even should return").[24] His task teaching English especially distracted him. It was not English and English ideas he favored, but Dutch and Dutch ideas, especially those developed by Kuyper and Bavinck.

The curatorium in Grand Rapids had agreed that Vos would stay in Europe until the summer of 1887, but when, due to heath problems, he was unable to finish his dissertation in that academic year, it accepted another year's postponement.[25] Early in 1888, Vos received his doctorate, and in the middle of May, after having visited Bavinck in Kampen, he took the boat to New York, never to return to Europe.

Vos's standing and influence

On June 12, 1888, Vos presented himself to the curatorium in Grand Rapids, and in the following weeks, he acted as examiner at the theological school. At his request, he was discharged from the duty of preaching.[26] In a public meeting in his father's Christian Reformed church on Spring Street in Grand Rapids on September 4, Vos was installed by curator Rev. Lammert J. Hulst. That evening, he gave "a very thorough"[27] inaugural address in the same church, in Dutch, on the "Prospect of Theology in America," for a large and mixed audience. In this address, he analyzed the pragmatic, fragmentary, and ahistorical character of American culture as detrimental to Reformed theology.

---

[22] Dagboek, 23-30 July 1886. *H. Bavinck Papers*. Historisch Documentatiecentrum voor het Nederlands Protestantisme, Vrije Universiteit Amsterdam (HDC).

[23] Vos to A. Kuyper, 7 Oct. 1886, Dennison, *Letters*, 121.

[24] Vos to H. Bavinck, 16 June 1887, Dennison, *Letters*, 121. The chair at the Vrije Universiteit was still vacant.

[25] Notulen curatoren, 3 Aug. 1887, art. 16.

[26] He seldom preached, but he did so in the late Van Raalte's Pillar Church in Holland, see *De Grondwet*, 19 Feb. 1889; *De Wachter*, 26 June 1889, also mentions an occasion.

[27] *De Wachter*, 12 Sept. 1888.

In a letter to Bavinck, Vos had already expressed his worries about the growing influence of the American language (that is, English) and culture on the theological school.[28] He also acknowledged the upside of this culture, with the freedom of religion as its major asset. In Kuyperian language, he praised the "sphere sovereignty" of the church, a freedom rooted in Calvinism. Reformed theology in America, therefore, should strive

> to hold high its character as ideal science over against all practical, realistic striving; continuously reflect on its principium and maintain it without weakening over against all lack of principle reflection; and protest unflaggingly against all lack of historical sense by means of a calm taking up and continuing the historical line of our forefathers.[29]

Vos stressed the need to develop the Reformed theological tradition, especially by learning from Scottish Presbyterians and staying in close contact with developments in the Reformed tradition in the Netherlands of the last fifty years in order to preserve "the true Dutch exemplar": "No matter how far we may be ahead of the old fatherland materially, we cannot do without it in spiritual and theological concerns."[30] He did not lay out a theological program but ended on the positive note that "out of a high awareness of our glorious heritage and our beautiful calling, we may find both courage and strength for the building of an American Reformed theology!"[31]

There were Kuyperian overtones in his lecture, for example, when he pointed to the importance of Calvinism, the distinction between archetypal and ectypal theology,[32] the close relation between knowing and believing, and his aim to overcome the isolation of theology among the sciences.[33] In the light of his take on theology as laid out in his

---

[28] Vos to Bavinck, 16 June 1887, Dennison, *Letters*, 125.
[29] "The Prospects of American Theology. Address by Prof. G. Vos, PhD on the acceptance of his position as professor of theology at the Theological School in Grand Rapids, Mich. on 29 August 1888." Copied by J. B. Hoekstra, Pella, IA (7 May 1889), 49. ACC.
[30] Vos, "Prospects," 70.
[31] Ibid, 71.
[32] In archetypal and ectypal theology, Kuyper distinguishes between God's self-knowledge and our knowledge of God.
[33] "Science" and "scientific," in Kuyper, and in this article, in relation to theology, are translations of the Dutch *wetenschap* and *wetenschappelijk*, referring to theology's place among the scholarly disciplines, and are of course not intended to suggest that it is a natural or a social science.

inaugural address, Vos was very positive about Kuyper: "He has done more than anybody else for the revival of the old orthodoxy and the old orthodox theology in Holland," he wrote to Princeton professor Benjamin B. Warfield in 1889, "and unites in a wonderful manner the practical gifts of the leader of a religious movement, with a well-trained systematic mind."[34]

Given Kuyper's critical view of American culture, however, Vos did not expect him to find a broad readership in the United States, but in Presbyterian circles, his work might be appreciated. It could help to strengthen orthodoxy in these circles, but also among the Dutch immigrant circles of his own CRC and the RCA, where his orthodox colleague, Nicolaus Steffens of Western Theological Seminary, was not understood in his opposition to American influence.

Vos wrote Kuyper: "It seems to me that isolation is the only thing that can protect us against washing away with the current."[35] Vos therefore in 1889 promoted the translation of Kuyper's *Encyclopaedie der Heilige Godgeleerdheid* (Encyclopedia of Sacred Theology). He wrote Warfield: "It would be the first modern attempt to write on the Encyclopedia of Theology from a reformed-Calvinistic point of view."[36] Vos encouraged Kuyper and also Bavinck to publish in English. Instead of working in Amsterdam next to Kuyper, he became his and Bavinck's translator and intermediary in introducing neo-Calvinism in America.

The theological school started the 1888 academic year with three docents and about twenty-five students. It was still located on the second floor of the Christian school on Williams Street and had six rooms; it was the former house of the schoolmaster. Three of the rooms

---

[34] Vos to B. B. Warfield, 22 Oct. 1889. *B. B. Warfield Papers*. Special Collections Luce Library, Princeton Theological Seminary. Dennison, *Letters*, 129, misses a whole paragraph in this letter: "So far as I know" has to be followed by this insertion: "it would be the first modern attempt to write on the Encyclopedia of Theology from a reformed-Calvinistic point of view. I have no doubt but the writer [Kuyper] is eminently qualified to do the work thoroughly. He has done more than anybody else for the revival of the old orthodoxism and the old orthodox theology in Holland and unites in a wonderful manner the practical gifts of the leader of a religious movement, with a well-trained systematic mind.

Now the question appears to have risen with both him and his publisher on whether it would not be preferable to publish the book in English. The Holland language is very little read outside of the small country in which it is spoken, while to an English book not only the new, but also a large part of the Old World lies open, English being read everywhere."

[35] Vos to Kuyper, 12 July 1890, Dennison, *Letters*, 142.

[36] Vos to Warfield, 22 Oct. 1889.

were classrooms, and one was the lecture room: "They are not de luxe . . . [but] they are all high, fresh, and have a good ventilation."[37] With three docents—since 1891 called "professors"[38]—the building was relatively small, and the prospect was a further increase in students. Aside from that, its location was far from ideal, close to a marshaling yard for trains with seventeen tracks, a lot of steam and maneuverings, and a Christian school with 100 children on the ground floor.[39] On top of that, this school planned to switch to teaching in English and would need more room in the near future.

In 1890 there was a debate in the press about relocating the school to either Zeeland or Holland. Vos did not participate in this public debate. The students were in favor of Grand Rapids, and Synod—representing about one hundred CRC congregations—decided in June by an overwhelming majority that the school would stay in the city.[40] At the same time, Synod discussed a new building. Hemkes did not think a new building was needed, and Vos preferred a better library over a better building. Synod decided for a new building.[41] Early in 1891, a lot on the corner of Madison and Fifth Avenue was purchased by the trustees, and a new school building was dedicated there in September 1892.

Vos made a big impact in the five years he taught at the school. Respected for his learning, he got the curriculum adapted to improve academic standards. After his first academic year at the school, upon his request, an examination in English grammar was added by the curatorium to the literary exam, and an exam on metaphysics was replaced by one on the history of philosophy. As to theological studies, metaphysics was included in natural theology, and a separate course on the history of religions was added.[42] All these disciplines were taught by Vos. Every week he taught eight subjects: three hours dogmatics, two hours exegesis, two hours history of philosophy, eight hours Latin and Greek, two hours English, two hours Hebrew, two hours isagogics and homiletics, and one hour history of dogma.[43]

Through Vos's influence, the school "particularly broadened, enlivened, and deepened the courses of instruction."[44] His best known

---

[37] *De Wachter*, 23 April 1890; see also 28 May 1890.
[38] Notulen curatoren, 23 June 1891, art. 7.
[39] Hemkes in *De Wachter*, 17 Sept. 1890.
[40] *Handelingen synode 1890*, art. 31, 33.
[41] Ibid., art. 29; *De Wachter*, 17 Sept. 1890.
[42] Notulen curatoren, 21 June 1889, art. 32, 33.
[43] Ibid., 26 July 1893, art. 6.
[44] G. D. de Jong, "The History of the Development of the Theological School," in *Semi-Centennial Volume*, 29.

student was Henry Beets,[45] who arrived at the school from Orange City at the end of Vos's first year and graduated a year after Vos left. Early in 1893, Beets wrote an RCA minister about Vos:

> We have a splendid professor in Dr. Vos. He is a Calvinist of the most pronounced type and a supra-lapsarian at that. And of course we, as his pupils, his disciples, are becoming his enthusiastic followers in supra-lapsarianism also. I am very much pleased with Dr. [Vos]. I wish you could form his acquaintance. He is a young man of thirty and as kind and obliging and humble as I never saw a man before. And what a treasure of knowledge he may call his own![46]

Student John van der Mey graduated in 1893 and studied at the school during Vos's years. He wrote Kuyper in 1896 that most ministers in the CRC sympathized with his neo-Calvinism. The reasons for this were twofold in Van der Mey's opinion. In the first place, the teaching of Boer and Hemkes was poor and unattractive. When their students became ministers, they realized they did not know enough and started studying again, this time by reading Kuyper. Secondly, "those who were taught by dr. Vos went over to your side, thanks to the solid education enjoyed under Vos. Vos led us to Kuyper."[47]

Indeed, Vos's influence in the CRC was the strongest through his students. He did not mix in public debates, partly because he was a reserved person.[48] Boer and Hemkes wrote on a regular basis in the CRC weekly *De Wachter*, Vos hardly ever.[49] The two other professors lectured and spoke at annual meetings of CRC-related organizations; Vos never did. Professor Steffens of Western Theological Seminary liked him and attended his inaugural address but did not subsequently see him or hear from him.[50] Steffens' colleague, professor Henry Dosker,

---

[45] Beets was later the longtime stated clerk of the CRC, editor of the CRC weekly, *The Banner*, and first major historian of the denomination.

[46] Henry Beets to Rev. Dirk Scholten, 6 Feb. 1893, *H. Beets Papers*, ACC.

[47] J. van der Mey to Kuyper, 18 Feb.1896, *Kuyper Papers*.

[48] Richard B. Gaffin Jr., ed., *Redemptive History and Biblical Interpretation. The Shorter Writings of Geerhardus Vos* (Phillipsburg: P&R Publishing, 1980), xiii.

[49] The first time was in *De Wachter*, 30 April 1890 and 28 May 1890, in a discussion with Rev. J. Riemersma on church polity. In the issue of 7 May 1890, Vos reported on an anti-secret societies conference in Chicago he attended. *De Wachter, Christelijk weekblad*, weekly of the CRC, issued since 1868.

[50] N. M. Steffens to Kuyper, 1 Dec. 1888: "I see or hear nothing of Dr. Vos. Last August he visited me, and in September I saw him in Grand Rapids on the occasion of his installation. Since that time, I have lost sight of him." Translation of the original

complained that he had had contact with Vos and called him "dry" and a "bookworm."[51] But it is clear that Vos had changed the character of the school and had had a formative influence on his students by his vast knowledge and character and especially by introducing them to Kuyper.[52]

Less clear is the influence of the CRC community on Vos. He had already been worried about the American influence on this community before he returned to Grand Rapids, and these worries were aggravated in the years he taught at the school. He started already without many expectations: "I am going to America with the feeling that my place is not there."[53] Though he appreciated the loyalty of the CRC members to the Reformed tradition, he was struck by the narrow mindedness of many. Steffens had the impression that Vos got along well with the ecclesiastical point of view of the CRC,[54] but Vos confessed to Bavinck that he had distanced himself from the strict opinions on the church he had had in his student days.[55]

In 1891 Vos succeeded in getting Article 4 of the rules for the theological school amended, which modified the exclusiveness of the institution:

> The Curatorium will not allow any docents to serve the school other than those who are members of the Dutch Christian Reformed Church or the Christian Reformed Church in the Netherlands, unless the Synod stipulates otherwise.[56]

This "unless" made it possible to follow Vos's advice and call Professor Steffens in 1892, after Vos had declined Princeton's first call. He left the CRC's theological school disappointed; maybe he had overrated its possibilities for theological development. Polemics on the covenant and supralapsarianism taught him that the CRC was satisfied

---

letter in Dutch in George Harinck, *"We live presently under a waning moon." Nicolaus Martin Steffens as leader of the Reformed Church in America in the West in years of transition (1878-1895)* (Holland, MI: Van Raalte Press, 2013), 144.

[51] H. E. Dosker to Bavinck, 25 Feb. 1893, in George Harinck en Wouter Kroese, *"Men wil toch niet gaarne een masker dragen." Brieven van Henry Dosker aan Herman Bavinck, 1873-1921* (Amsterdam: HDC, 2018), 115, transl. by author.

[52] Vos to Kuyper, 1 Feb. 1890, Dennison, *Letters*, 135.

[53] Vos to Bavinck, 16 June 1887, ibid.

[54] Steffens to Kuyper, 1 Dec. 1888. *Kuyper Papers*.

[55] Vos to Bavinck, 3 July 1893, Dennison, *Letters*, 176: "I do not like an excessive *churchism*, although I myself did that before."

[56] Notulen curatoren, 3 Sept. 1891, art. 17.

with what the seventeenth-century Synod of Dordrecht had to offer and was not interested in theological development.

Polemics and departure to Princeton

But new ideas flowed in. In the 1880s, the CRC became familiar with the names and ideas of Bavinck and Kuyper through *De Wachter*. When Vos arrived in 1888, the editorship of this weekly shifted from Hulst to docent Boer, who extended *De Wachter*. That fall Boer published six meditations of Kuyper in *De Wachter* and an article by Bavinck on the church, and their books were advertised. This seemed to support Vos. But Steffens doubted in 1888 if Vos was in the right place at the theological school: "True learning is not valued in our Dutch American circles," he wrote Kuyper. "The people are not sufficiently informed to value it."[57]

Boer's editorial policy for *De Wachter* was freedom of expression but no polemics. In a community that was developing, with hundreds of new immigrants per week, its members growing in means, and with poorly educated ministers and one highly educated professor, an open publication forum was a risk. Still, debates developed. Vos admitted that he himself had provoked them.[58] In July 1891, he wrote Warfield:

> I happen to be a supralapsarian in the matter of predestination, though in a very moderate sense, and not so much on logical grounds as for exegetic reasons (Rom. IX, Ephes. I, III). In some way the idea has been started that the doctrine of an eternal covenant and supralapsarianism are inseparable. I have never been able to discover an *objective* nexus causalis between the two. There may be some affinity however between the subjective tendencies that underlie both views.[59]

The CRC was dominantly infralapsarian, and supralapsarianism was new to them. Vos's views clearly had the marks of Kuyper: supralapsarian, consistently theocentric, with a stress more on the

---

[57] Steffens to Kuyper, 1 Dec. 1888, Harinck, *"We live presently under a waning moon,"* 144.
[58] Vos to Kuyper, 21 Feb. 1891, Dennison, *Letters*, 149.
[59] Vos to Warfield, 7 July 1891, ibid., 162. Dennison transcribes Ephesians I, III (chs. 1 and 3) incorrectly as Ephesians 1:3.
[60] James D. Bratt, "De erfenis van Kuyper in Noord-Amerika," in C. Augustijn, e.a. (ed.), *Abraham Kuyper. Zijn volksdeel, zijn invloed* (Delft: Meinema, 1987), 208.

objectivity of regeneration than on the subjectivity of conversion, and a scientific theology, developed from its principle of God's sovereignty.[60] Both Boer and Hemkes were infralapsarians.[61]

After Vos's first year at the school, curator Hulst requested him to stay within the boundaries of Reformed doctrine. This exchange was not in public, but Hulst was not the kind of man to keep silent on doctrinal issues. He was a fierce debater, for example, in 1889, on subjects like baptism, Sunday school, and the church. In the summer of that year, a critical article in *De Heraut* on Kuyper's view of election was republished in *De Wachter*.[62] Issues like election, covenant, and predestination often triggered debates.

In December 1889, Boer started a series on the covenant of grace and on the difference between predestination and covenant. The readership showed interest in these topics.[63] In June 1890, Hulst started to comment on Kuyper's view of presumptive regeneration, which he considered untenable.[64] That same month, a series started on the issue: what is Calvinism? *De Wachter* was not in favor of polemics, already considering the debates detrimental to the growth of the readership. Boer therefore extended its range of contributors in order to diversify opinions: "May this contribute to avoiding fruitless controversy."[65]

It did not help. In September 1890, Vos became rector of the theological school, and eleven new students enrolled. It turned out to be his heaviest year in Grand Rapids. In previous years, he had been busy preparing his lectures,[66] but now ecclesial issues occupied his mind. In November 1890, *Holland City News* reported "another tempest in the ecclesiastical teapot": Boer and Hemkes were said to have accused Vos of heresy. Both colleagues issued a statement in *De Wachter* stating

---

[61] Henry Beets, *De Chr. Geref. Kerk in N. A.: zestig jaren van strijd en zegen* (Grand Rapids, MI: Grand Rapids Printing Company, 1918), 294, 301. Supralaparianism and infralapsarianism, debated at the Synod of Dort, have to do with the logical order of God's eternal decrees in regard to salvation and damnation, i.e., whether God chose to elect and reprobate humans before or after his decree to permit the fall (*lapsus*, Latin).

[62] *De Wachter*, 10 July 1889. *De Heraut* was a weekly, edited by Abraham Kuyper, and was approximately the equivalent in the Netherlands of the CRC's *De Wachter*.

[63] *De Wachter*, 2 April 1890.

[64] Ibid., 11 June 1890. Kuyper promoted the long controversial doctrine of the presumptive (or presupposed) regeneration of the children of the covenant, whose believing parents could bring them for baptism with the presumption that they were regenerate and sanctified in Christ, at least until the opposite should be apparent as they grew up, by their faith and life.

[65] *De Wachter*, 18 June 1890.

[66] Vos to Kuyper, 12 July 1890.

that this was untrue and that no one in Grand Rapids knew anything of this.⁶⁷ Vos did not confirm the statement of his colleagues and kept his mouth shut about the issue. Some weeks later, Steffens commented to Kuyper: "Dr. Vos has a more conservative environment than I; but he is not understood in his circles because he deals with well-meaning but uneducated and narrow-minded people."⁶⁸

This rumor was only the beginning. In January 1891, Hulst started a series in *De Wachter* on infra and supra, soon followed by Rev. D. J. Vander Werp; they defended the infra position. Or better: they rejected the supra position as a philosophical scheme. Steffens informed Kuyper about Vos's position:

> Presently he is being harassed from all sides in "De Wachter" because of his supralapsarian view. It is true, Rev. Hulst has no quarrel with him but with you, but "the initiated" understand that he is the one. It is too bad that that young man wastes his powers in those circles ... he is a conscientious scholar who works with great exactness. One can say nothing against his principles. I love him.⁶⁹

In March, Boer joined the discussion with an article on the topic. The debates, however, became harsh. The editorial committee therefore in March restricted the publication of new contributions to the subject and tried to limit the discussion.⁷⁰ Others asked in *De Wachter* for a more respectful attitude of the contributors toward each other and for a more relaxed approach: "What I *do* understand is that the whole supra-infra system is *not* understood by the readers, and I believe with certainty ... that the outcome will not be worth the effort, ... to the contrary will always do harm, for both systems, infra and supra, when consequently, in the end run aground."⁷¹ In June, Hulst was forced by the editor to stop writing on this issue,⁷² but he decided to continue his argument in a brochure that was published at the end of 1891.⁷³

---

67 *De Wachter*, 3 Dec. 1890. The statement was dated 26 Nov. 1890.
68 Steffens to Kuyper, 25 Jan. 1891, Harinck, *"We live presently under a waning moon,"* 151.
69 Ibid.
70 *De Wachter*, 11 March 1891.
71 F. Kniphuizen in *De Wachter*, 25 March 1891.
72 *De Wachter*, 3 June 1891.
73 L. J. Hulst, *Supra en infra. Een woord van verdediging en toelichting der confessioneel gereformeerde leer en practijk, omtrent de praedestinatie en het genadeverbond* (Grand Rapids, MI: D. J. Doornink, 1891); also published in the NL (Nijkerk: Callenbach, 1892).

Vos was not a "leader in public affairs," as Steffens put it,[74] but he did follow the debates intensely. He wrote to Kuyper that the theological issue was not supralapsarianism; from a confessional point of view this was just the weakest spot. The real target was Kuyper's view on baptism and covenant, taking election into account. This issue triggered Vos. He believed Kuyper was right in connecting baptism and covenant with election, but he just did not know how. Vos did not enter the debate, mainly because in his opinion it was so dominated by ignorance about the Reformed tradition, that anything was possible.[75]

Vos decided to research the issue from not a systematic but an historical viewpoint: "It occurred to me that it would be a useful thing to describe the historical development of the covenant idea in Reformed theology and to show how intimately it has been connected from the outset with the practical side of the dogma of predestination."[76] He asked Kuyper and Warfield for information on supralapsarianism and on the covenant.[77] His rectoral address on September 2, 1891, on *De verbondsleer in de gereformeerde theologie* (the doctrine of the covenant in Reformed theology) was the result of his studies.[78]

In the historiography on the subject, this lecture is praised, but there is hardly any appreciation from American contemporaries, since the lecture was published in Dutch only.[79] In *De Heraut*, Kuyper calls it the best publication on the subject in recent years and a welcome token of the fact that the struggler for a scientific Reformed theology was not waged in the Netherlands only.[80] *De Wachter* quoted this, and then Boer added, in a rare public compliment for Vos, that the lecture was "through and through Calvinistic."[81]

---

[74] Steffens to Kuyper, 25 Jan. 1891, Harinck, *"We live presently under a waning moon,"* 151.
[75] Vos to Kuyper, 16 July 1891, Dennison, *Letters*, 165-66. Dennison dates this letter 30 July.
[76] Vos to Warfield, 7 July 1891, Dennison, *Letters*, 162.
[77] W. Geesink wrote a memorandum on supralapsarianism for Vos, see: Vos to Kuyper, 16 July 1891; Vos to Warfield, 29 Aug/ 1891, Dennison, *Letters*, 165-66.
[78] G. Vos, *De verbondsleer in de gereformeerde theologie. Rede gehouden bij het overdragen van het rectoraat aan de Theol. School te Grand Rapids, Mich. den 2den sept.* (Grand Rapids, MI: Democrat, 1891).
[79] Vos had the intention to publish a condensed English version for *The Presbyterian and Reformed Review*, but this never happened; see Vos to Warfield, 28 Sept. 1891, in Dennison, *Letters*, 169. The first English translation was published in 1971: *The Covenant in Reformed Theology* (Philadelphia: K. M. Campbell, 1971).
[80] Quoted in *De Grondwet*, 23 Feb. 1892 and *De Wachter*, 2 March 1892, from *De Heraut*, 7 Feb. 1892.
[81] *De Wachter*, 2 March 1892.

The day after the lecture, the criticism of Vos by Hulst reached its climax, when he submitted a letter of protest to the Curatorium:

> The Undersigned:
> Considering that he, also as curator, is bound by the standards of the Reformed churches and thus is obliged to be watchful with the other brothers that the current instruction at our Theological School always is given in complete agreement with our creeds; Considering that now already for the past two years it has become apparent from the examinations that the instruction at our school, entrusted to our care, particularly in dogmatics, has moved beyond the boundaries of our standards, and that for that reason already objectionable matters have come to light; Considering, that he, for two years already, at the assembly of the Curatorium has proposed to request Dr. G. Vos, particularly in his instruction of dogmatics, stay within the boundaries of the standards of our church without having received support in the Curatorium; Considering that the Curatorium also is unwilling to place this question before the forthcoming Synod, so that it may decide whether or not the Curatorium then is bound by the standards; Considering all of that he is compelled consequently to protest against the introduction of supralapsarianism and everything connected with it at our Theological School, and therefore protests against the position of the Curatorium, which is unwilling to do anything against this.
>
> The Curatorium is asked to include this protest in its minutes, so that the undersigned has the opportunity to appeal these matters at Synod.
>
> Grand Rapids
> 3 September 1891, L. J. Hulst, curator.[82]

The polemics and Vos's contribution to it confirmed Vos's decision not to stay in Grand Rapids forever. He had received several offers before to work at a Presbyterian school, but had always turned them down, for his calling was to teach at the theological school of his church. But in 1891, he decided not to stay much longer. Theologically, he would prefer a return to the Netherlands, but socially, he was tied to the United States: "There is a certain charm in the American life from

---

[82] Notulen curatoren, 3 Sept. 1891, art. 19.

which it is hard to withdraw," he wrote Bavinck, who had asked him to consider a position at Kampen Theological School.[83]

On January 14, 1892, Princeton Theological Seminary's Old Testament professor Charles A. Aiken died unexpectedly, and within a few weeks, rumors went around that Vos might succeed him.[84] And indeed, at the end of February 1892, Vos received a call from Princeton. It was the talk of the day in CRC circles. *De Volksvriend* stressed the honor bestowed on Vos, being so young, and congratulated him.[85] *De Wachter* stressed the honor being called by Princeton, and also the sacrifice Vos would make if he stayed in Grand Rapids:

> Here he often has . . . to fulfill the role of schoolmaster and language teacher and teach the first principles to the young men; there he works with students who come from a college. Here there are many subjects; there it is one large subject, and how important, how attractive: Biblical Theology.[86]

Vos's students—and colleagues—were attached to him and asked him to stay. On March 15, he informed the curatorium he had declined Princeton's call. He now taught twenty-nine hours a week and saw the theological school making progress.[87] The call came too early for Vos. If he would have gone, he wrote to Warfield:

> The better part of our people would lose courage, our seminary would receive a blow that might prove fatal. I cannot but consider it of great importance to preserve our Dutch people for old calvinistic faith. . . . Though shrinking from too many unpleasant features of this work, I do not feel at liberty before God to abandon it.[88]

But such a call could happen again. Princeton had to fill several vacancies, and the fear among faculty was that the seminary might go down, and as a result "the cause of orthodox theology and evangelical religion will receive a heavy blow."[89] Princeton professor William H.

---

[83] Vos to Bavinck, 30 June 1891, Dennison, *Letters*, 159.
[84] See *De Grondwet*, 16 Feb. 1892.
[85] *De Volksvriend*, 3 March 1892.
[86] *De Wachter*, 2 March 1892.
[87] Ibid., 23 March 1892.
[88] Vos to Warfield, 18 March 1892, Dennison, *Letters*, 170.
[89] W. H. Green to Vos, 19 March 1892. Copy from Richard B. Gaffin.

Green, therefore, urged Vos to reconsider his decision: "Is a man at liberty to decline a public duty in a time of general peril however willing he may be to remain in obscurity and whatever local value may attach to his less conspicuous labour?"[90] Princeton Theological Seminary stressed Vos's quality by granting him an honorary doctor of divinity degree within months after he declined the call.

The curatorium was alarmed by this attention for its professor and did all it could to keep Vos.[91] Boer was urged to reduce his work for *De Wachter*, particularly to decrease Vos's workload,[92] and Synod proposed to call a fourth professor. Vos suggested that this docent could teach dogmatics instead of him.[93] Vos preferred to concentrate on exegetics, the discipline he liked best.[94] The result was that Synod, in June 1892, gave in, in reaction to Vos's decision to stay. Steffens of the RCA seminary in Holland, Michigan, was called as fourth docent, but Vos was urgently requested to remain as docent in dogmatics. This plea was supported by a similar request of the students.[95] Steffens turned down the call, and so, after him, did D. K. Wielenga from Kampen,[96] who visited Grand Rapids in the summer of 1892, together with Bavinck.

Vos and Bavinck were friends, and Bavinck spent many hours in Vos's study room.[97] Wielenga stayed with Hulst.[98] Undoubtedly, Vos and Bavinck discussed their similar situations, working as well-educated academics at small ecclesiastical seminaries.[99] A fourth docent was not found when the new academic year started, so Vos gave in and kept on teaching dogmatics. The new year started in the new building, with more than fifty students, the school having already produced thirty-

---

[90] Green to Vos, 18 March 1892. Copy from Gaffin.
[91] Notulen curatoren, 11 March 1892, arts. 2, 3.
[92] When Synod decided to call a fourth professor, Boer continued as editor of *De Wachter. Handelingen synode 1892*, art. 59.
[93] Notulen curatoren, 15 June 1892, arts. 4, 5.
[94] De Jong, "History of the Theological School," 30; Henry Zwaanstra, "Louis Berkhof," in David F. Wells, *Reformed Theology in America. A History of its Modern Development* (Grand Rapids, MI: Eerdmans, 1985), 169: "Vos's first love was biblical theology, not dogmatics."
[95] Notulen curatoren, 30 June 1892, art. 42.
[96] *De Wachter*, 23 Nov. 1892. Wielenga's letter of decline was published on the front page of *De Wachter*, 30 Nov. 1892.
[97] V. Hepp, *De Reformatie*, 2 May 1924 (review of G. Vos, *Grace and Glory, Sermons Preached in the Chapel of Princeton Theological Seminary*).
[98] *De Wachter*, 3 Aug. 1892.
[99] See: George Harinck, "Herman Bavinck and Geerhardus Vos," *Calvin Theological Journal* 45, no. 1 (2010), 18-31.

four ministerial candidates.[100] It was a time of good prospects, and Boer, looking back, wrote that the CRC could not have imagined at the start of the school in 1876, "that it would really have in 1888 a doctor graduated at a university (not just a doctor honoris causa)."[101]

But for how long could the theological school keep Vos? Some asked why the CRC maintained a theological school if it could not get a fourth docent, while others complained about the rising costs for the new building.[102] New irritation about Kuyper came to the fore when he downplayed the issue of membership of Reformed people in Masonic lodges, an important reason for the recent spurt in growth of the CRC. Further annoyance was caused when Dutch theologians like Kuyper, Bavinck, and prof. M. Noordtzij spoke out on the futility of the differences between the RCA and the CRC.[103]

In April 1893, a new call came from Princeton, and this time Vos was ready to go: "The young people who study are so poorly educated that despite the diligence of instructors, the results that they accomplish are so small that you have to lose heart."[104] The curatorium was willing to make his work as agreeable as possible,[105] but Vos said there was nothing that needed to be changed to accommodate him.[106] When Vos informed the school on April 17 that he had accepted the call, the CRC gave in, though some bemoaned his decision.[107] *De Wachter* of May 31, 1893, published a farewell poem for Vos by J. C. van der Ven.[108]

The theological school and what Vos had done for this institution was the talk of the town: "We suffered a big loss now Dr. Vos is leaving us. This is the main cause of our solicitude. We suffer damage, and the doctor makes a bold step. But this the doctor himself has to account for."[109] Later Vos's colleagues formulated some criticism of his departure from both the school and the CRC. In Princeton he joined the Presbyterian church. Especially in the RCA, some saw Vos's moves as a blow to the CRC.[110]

---

[100] *De Wachter*, 21 Sept. 1892.
[101] Ibid., 7 Sept. 1892.
[102] Ibid., 7 Dec. 1892.
[103] Boer and Hulst wrote almost weekly in *De Wachter* against Kuyper and others from the end of Nov. 1892 until June 1893.
[104] Vos to Bavinck, 3 July 1893, Dennison, *Letters*, 175.
[105] De Jong, "History of the Theological School," 32.
[106] Notulen curatoren, 11 April 1893, art. 6.
[107] *De Wachter*, 12 July 1893.
[108] In ibid., 28 June 1893.
[109] Ibid., 2 Aug. 1893.
[110] *De Grondwet*, 26 Sept. 1893, criticized the RCA weekly *De Hope* for its journalism and defended Vos's decision to join the Presbyterian church.

Could anything have stopped him from going to Princeton? This time, personal relations may well have played a role in his decision. In May 1893, Vos became engaged to Catherine Frances Smith (1865-1937), assistant at Grand Rapids public library. She was a Congregationalist and not acquainted with the Dutch American immigrant community. They married September 7, 1894, without announcing this in the Dutch American press, as was commonly done.

Wielenga was called again by the theological school, but in June 1893, he declined once more. So when Vos left, the school was in great difficulty, having two vacancies and no students around.[111] In July it was decided that five ministers, including Vos's father for dogmatics and Hulst for exegesis, would act as assistant docents and take Vos's eight classes.[112]

Vos's legacy

The exams of June 1893 convinced Vos once more that leaving was the right choice. Boer and Hemkes did not offer solid teaching. The curatorium was grateful for what he had done, but there was no public farewell. In the 1920s, Vos's departure was still seen as one of the most severe losses to the theological school.[113] Vos believed the school should be reorganized radically in order to survive. In his opinion, the two docents did not do much solid work, and yet it was impossible to find two or three better ones.[114] Some in the CRC feared that, with Vos's departure, the end of the school was at hand.[115]

---

[111] Vos's father made inquiries in the Netherlands "with and regarding docent Wielenga, and the ministers, Bos, Elzinga, Biesterveld, Ten Hoor, Noordewier." Notulen curatoren, 4, 5 April 1894, art. 15.

[112] Notulen curatoren, 26 July 1893, art. 6: "The division of the classes taught by Dr. Vos is discussed at this time. With unanimous approval it is stipulated that the class time will be allotted as follows:
3 [hrs.] Dogmatics – J. H. Vos
Exegesis – L. J. Hulst
Intro. To Dogmatics and history of Philosophy – K. Kuiper
Latin and Greek, 3rd and 4th class – G. D. De Jong
English – Berkhof
Hebrew – Hemkes. In exchange for the last-named subject three hours, will be deducted from his honor's teaching schedule
Isagogics and Homiletics – K. Kuiper
History of Dogma – Hulst."

[113] Beets, *The Christian Reformed Church in North America* (Grand Rapids: Eastern Avenue Book Store, 1923), 95; Beets, *De Chr. Geref. Kerk in N. A.*, 294; Hepp, *De Reformatie*, 2 May 1924.

[114] Vos to Bavinck, 3 July 1893, Dennison, *Letters*, 175.

[115] Noordewier, "De oorsprong van onze Theologische School," 19.

Vos's legacy is the memory of a brilliant scholar shining at the start of what is today Calvin College and Calvin Theological Seminary. The school had begun as a barely viable institution, dependent on the goodwill of some ministers, and theologically poor, but in the historiography, Vos's presence is viewed as giving glory to these humble beginnings. This interpretation is summarized in James D. Bratt's description of Vos as "West Michigan's donation to the Princeton Seminary faculty."[116]

Vos's legacies to the theological school are his extensive lectures on dogmatics, introduction to dogmatics, history of philosophy, New Testament Greek, and idolatry,[117] as well as his well-received address on the covenant. But his decades at Princeton largely overshadow his Michigan years, which is only partly deserved when we take into account the context in which he had to operate. It was quite a feat that he had worked systematically, undisturbed by the rumors and polemics around him, not distracted by the teaching load he had assumed and the mixed quality of his students. His friend, Nicolaus Steffens, on the contrary, always got himself involved in the debates of the time, so his theological legacy, therefore, is negligible. Vos stuck to his theological studies and, even in the challenging conditions of the Christian Reformed community around 1890, was able to produce solid and valuable theological work that can still be appreciated.[118]

---

[116] James D. Bratt, "The Dutch schools," in Wells, *Reformed Theology in America*, 142.

[117] Noordewier, "De oorsprong van onze Theologische School," 18; cf. Zwaanstra, "Louis Berkhof," in: Wells, *Reformed Theology in America*, 155: "Vos did, however, leave his reputation and unpublished lectures in dogmatics behind."

[118] Vos's dogmatics has been translated and published recently in a 5-vol., hardcover set (1359 pages): Geerhardus Vos, *Reformed Dogmatics*, transl. and ed., Richard B. Gaffin Jr. (Bellingham, WA: Lexham Press, 2014-16).

CHAPTER 14

John Henry Vanderpoel—Who?

Nella Kennedy

Introduction

The number of visitors entering the Art Institute of Chicago (AIC) was especially large on May 4, 1911. They had not gathered to view art. Rather, they had come to pay homage to a beloved and recently deceased AIC teacher, whose casket had been placed in its Fullerton Hall, where the funeral was to be conducted.[1] The throng included the instructor's fellow artists and more than five hundred of his students.[2] It was an amazing tribute to the Netherlands-born John Henry Vanderpoel, whose life and accomplishments are virtually unknown to the Dutch American scholarly community of today,

---

[1] The morning funeral was conducted by Rev. Philip F. Matzinger, a Princeton Theological Seminary graduate and pastor of the Campbell Park Presbyterian Church, who had studied at the AIC and could well have been a student of Vanderpoel. The *Chicago Daily Tribune* of 3 May 1911 headlined the article about the artist's death, "Pupils Mourn Dead Artist: Demise of J. H. Vanderpoel Causes Gloom at Art Institute."

[2] Newton Bateman and Paul Selby, eds., *Biographical and Memorial Edition of the Historical Encyclopedia of Illinois* 1 (Chicago: Munsell Publishing Co., 1915), 717-20.

275

although he was once renowned as "one of the foremost teachers of academic drawing that this country has produced," whose talents had gained him "universal recognition."[3] It was even said at the time of his death that "the Chicago field of art had never been called upon to face a greater loss."[4] On June 8, 1911, a month after Vanderpoel's death, the trustees of the AIC passed a unanimous resolution to record "their sorrow for this loss." Furthermore, they declared that Vanderpoel, in his more-than-thirty years there, had done "more than any other person to [contribute to] the high reputation of our school. In his specialty of academic drawing, he was unsurpassed, and his personal qualities endeared him in a remarkable degree to pupils and associates."[5]

Reminders of his contribution to the world of art in Chicago are visible even today. One can still travel on the long Vanderpoel Street in Beverly—a suburb of Chicago—which intersects the even-longer Ninety-Fifth Street. Vanderpoel Elementary School and Vanderpoel Art Gallery are nearby. His accomplishments in the field of art, however, reach well beyond Chicago. Vanderpoel's manual on drawing (more about that later) is still available worldwide and continues to be reprinted, most recently in 2017. Incongruously, his father, who had been acclaimed as "possibly the best-known Dutchman in Chicago"[6] is all but forgotten, while his son's artistic legacy continues to this day,[7] albeit not among Dutch Americans.

It is my intent in this article, therefore, to induct John Henry Vanderpoel into the as-yet imaginary "Dutch American Hall of Fame." I myself was unaware of Vanderpoel's existence but learned about him from Michael and Astrid Griffin, who shared with me a spiral-bound volume about the Rijsoord art colony, founded in the Netherlands by Vanderpoel.[8] The art colony began informally in 1887, with his invitation to fellow expatriate artists—like himself, studying in Paris—to join him in painting and drawing the people and rural environs

---

[3] Ibid., 719.
[4] Ibid., 719-20.
[5] *Bulletin of the Art Institute of Chicago* 5, no. 2 (Oct. 1911), 18.
[6] *Onze Toekomst*, 6 Aug. 1909, in Robert P. Swierenga, *Dutch Chicago* (Holland, MI: Van Raalte Press; Grand Rapids: Eerdmans, 2002), 687.
[7] Chicago mayor Richard M. Daley proclaimed 11 April 1992, as "John H. Vanderpoel Day," in recognition of his contribution and commitment to the beauty of art. Jimmie Lee Buehler, *Beverly Review*, 28 Oct. 1992.
[8] There were many such colonies in the Netherlands from the last two decades of the nineteenth century until the Second World War. They were especially popular with American artists. See, for example, Annette Stott, ed., *Dutch Utopia: American Artists in Holland, 1880-1914* (Savannah, GA: Telfair Books), 2009.

of his ancestral village of Rijsoord in the province of South Holland, where many of his relatives still lived. Since the information about the artist was sketchy in the booklet shared by the Griffins, I was stimulated to learn more about this Dutch American. Why was he so acclaimed? Was it his teaching, his skills as a draftsman, or his painting oeuvre? A combination of all three? And to what extent did his life in the United States confirm his Dutch roots?

Dutch roots

John Henry Vanderpoel, beginning life as Johannes van der Poel, was born in Haarlemmermeer, province of North Holland, November 1857.[9] His father, Jan van der Poel, and mother, Maria Van Nes, both born and raised in Rijsoord, had moved the year before to the newly reclaimed Haarlemmermeer (Haarlem Lake), where farmland had been opened for purchase in 1853. Although the majority of the land was in the hands of a few wealthy landowners, the entrepreneurial Jan apparently saw opportunity there.[10] He opened a hotel and a second-hand store (*uitdragerij*) at the intersection of two roads in 1856 and organized the first grain exchange there in 1863,[11] subsequently named De Beurs (the exchange).[12]

Van der Poel also functioned as a broker of grains and rapeseed, cattle, shorn wool, houses, and land. On Wednesdays, tenant farmers came to his exchange with samples of their produce to sell and to settle their accounts.[13] For a time, Jan owned a livery stable for transients, and he was even a bookseller.

---

[9] Johannes, the future artist, had an older brother, Jan (1851-1898), both of whom, together with their father (also Jan), appear as "John" (the standard English translation of Johannes and Jan) in the 1870 and 1880 federal censuses for Chicago. By 1880 the artist had added "H." (for Henry) as his middle initial, while the older brother would later be simply John Vanderpoel Jr. Incidentally, the surname was misspelled in the 1870 census record as "Vanderboel." See: www.wiewaswie.nl; www.ancestry.com; US federal census 1870 and 1880.

[10] Economic necessity may have been the main motive. Jan had worked his ancestral farm in Rijsoord with two of his brothers; the income would have been meager to support his growing family.

[11] www.gemalen.nl. *De Nederlandse Gemalen Stichting*, updated 18 Jan. 2002.

[12] De Beurs is now on the municipal monument list. Cultuurhistorisch Haarlemmermeer, *Meer-Historie*, June 2011. The new polder contained many public houses, and alcohol abuse was common.

[13] References to Jan Van der Poel's business appeared in a number of local papers, for example, in the *Opregte Haarlemsche Courant*, of 3 Nov. 1863, in which he advertised by "private contract, a farm house, with stable for twenty cows, with 19, 25 or 30 hectares meadowland (top clay soil)," and an ad in the *Weekblad van Haarlemmermeer*, 15 July 1863, that invited grain dealers to come to Wednesday sales.

Hoofddorp, Bondshotel "de Beurs," Haarlemmermeer, late nineteenth century (*courtesy Haarlemmermeermuseum Cruquius*)

What made Jan decide to emigrate to the United States in 1868? Several neighboring families had already left the new polder for America in 1867, so he was not the first to undertake such a venture. Moreover, many others from the Haarlemmermeer evidently shared his intention to leave. The mortality rate for children was twice that of other parts of the Netherlands, and many of the polder people had died in the "cholera year" of 1866. Being tenant farmers, with perhaps few prospects to own land themselves, made it easier to leave. Furthermore, in the early years of the Haarlemmermeer settlements, farmers suffered from poor harvests and low commodity prices. This must have affected Van der Poel's business, since he had accrued debts he could not pay.[14] To make matters worse, Jan, father of ten, had lost his wife on May 17, 1867. His world was collapsing. The *Weekblad van Haarlemmermeer* of June 2, 1868, reported:

> The innkeeper at *De Beurs* . . . J. van der Poel, left for America without giving any notice of this to his friends or creditors. . . . On Tuesday morning, one could see strangers and family members hastily emptying the furniture from the house, and soon people

---

[14] *Meer-historie*, June 2011.

were acquainted with the fact that J. van der Poel had already left two days ago."[15]

The Van der Poel family, including the ten-and-a-half-year-old Johannes, embarked from Bremen, Germany, on the SS *New York*, a passenger cargo vessel of the Norddeutscher Lloyd Bremen steamship company. That they were quartered in steerage is an indication of the family's shortage of funds. After arrival in New York on June 25, 1868, Jan van der Poel had to borrow money to travel to Chicago.[16] Is there official evidence of a hasty flight to escape creditors? The Dutch emigration records list father Jan as an innkeeper, "less well to do." Perhaps (predictably—or euphemistically) the official reason recorded for the forty-year-old's departure was "the desire for adventure."[17] The US ship record lists his occupation as laborer, consistent with the 1870 Chicago census information that "John Vanderboel" was employed in a planing mill.[18] For the resourceful John, however, factory work would be of short duration.[19]

Becoming Vanderpoels

Amazingly, Jan van der Poel, having become John Vanderpoel in Chicago, was soon able to build a career as a public servant in that city, rising quickly from postmaster of the suburban Blue Island post office to a clerical position in the Cook County tax office (1880 census),

---

[15] Jan van der Poel wrote an undated letter to his mother and siblings from Bremen, the day before the ship's departure at the beginning of June 1868, thanking them for the letters they had sent and for their personal farewells. He asserted that, although he could not "excuse" his drastic step, he did not feel obligated to repent, for he had done his duty and followed his conscience. The letter expressed his pain at this departure multiple times, but also mentioned that he had left everything in God's care. Institutional Archives of the AIC (IAAIC), Vanderpoel letters.

[16] Jimmie Lee Buehler and Joel Dryer, "John Henry Vanderpoel (1857-1911)" in the *Illinois Historical Art Project*. http://www.illinoisart.org/john-henry-vanderpoel. The date of passage is verified by Robert P. Swierenga, compiler, *Dutch Immigrants in U.S. Ship Passenger Manifests, 1820-1880* (Wilmington, Delaware: Scholarly Resources, 1983), 982; https://1909ventilo.me/2012/06/28/mar-31-1858-norddeutscher-lloyd-bremen-launched-the-ss-new-york-a-passenger-cargo-vessel.

[17] Robert Swierenga, compiler, *Dutch Emigrants to the United States, South Africa, South America, and Southeast Asia, 1835-1880* (Wilmington, DE: Scholarly Resources, 1983), 277.

[18] In a letter on 25 Feb. 1871, John wrote his family that they were doing well, with increased living comfort, and that three of the family were employed in "honest manual labor," without having to incur debts; "Oh! Indeed, never again." IAAIC, Vanderpoel letters.

[19] His well-written letters exhibit education and intelligence.

ultimately becoming the chief clerk in the folio department of the county recorder's office, where he was still employed at his sudden demise at age eighty-two.[20]

The Americanization process was swift. John Sr. became active in politics soon after his arrival in Chicago, soon proud to call local and state politicians his friends.[21] His name appeared in the *Journal of the Senate* a few times, for example, with an article in 1903 on the safety of the postal savings bank.[22] John's sons also found employment; the 1880 Chicago federal census indicates that three of them were machinists, and one was an apprentice druggist, while son John H., at age twenty-one, was listed as an oil painter.[23] In fact, "John H." had already made his appearance as an "artist" in the Chicago city directory for 1877, published when he was but seventeen years old, living (as he did for the next few years) with his "clerk" father John and "machinist" brother John.[24]

Dutch Newsboy, drawing with highlights, c. 1874.[25]

---

[20] Swierenga, *Dutch Chicago*, 687. The death certificate, 29 July 1909, lists the cause of death as "heat stroke," with a contributing cause being "acute meningitis." www.ancestry.com.

[21] *Onze Toekomst*, 6 Aug. 1909.

[22] *Public Policy: A Journal of the Correct Understanding of Public Policy: Questions and the Development of Good Citizenship* (2 May 1903), 8:280. Another article appeared in the *Journal of the Senate*, 8 Oct. 1900.

[23] www.ancestry.com (1880 federal census).

[24] www.ancestry.com (*U.S. City Directories, 1822-1995*). Two employed older brothers of John H. were also reported as living in the same household in the 1877 and 1878 city directories.

[25] The drawing was created when Vanderpoel was only 17. Information from Irene Testa, Vanderpoel Art Gallery, Beverly (Chicago).

Postcard of the Art Institute of Chicago (n.d.)

Training, junior teacher, and travel

John Henry had begun art classes as a youth in high school, perhaps already then guided by Hermann Hanstein, supervisor of drawing in the Chicago schools.[26] No doubt Vanderpoel also attended the Chicago Athenaeum, where Hanstein taught free-hand, mechanical, and architectural drawing in the evenings and on Saturday mornings. From 300 to 350 students were taught there and produced such excellent work that their results were displayed at art fairs in major cities.[27]

The article on John H. Vanderpoel in the *Bulletin of the Art Institute of Chicago* of 1911[28] mentions that he had received instruction—on a Uranus H. Crosby scholarship—at the Chicago Academy of Design.

This poorly run institution, which began in 1866 and was led by artists, was taken over by civic and business leaders and renamed the Chicago Academy of Fine Arts in 1879. Three years later, in 1882, it became the School of the Art Institute of Chicago (SAIC).[29]

After Vanderpoel's death in 1911, an article in the *Bulletin of the Art Institute of Chicago* included a lengthy description of his life, indicating that he was a "distinguished student" at the Art Institute before becoming a junior teacher.[30] Puzzling, however, is an entry in the *United States Art Directory* of 1882, which lists Vanderpoel already

---

[26] *Bulletin of the Art Institute of Chicago* (July 1911), 5:1, 3.
[27] Alfred Theodore Andreas, *History of Chicago from the Earliest Period to the Present Time*, 3 vols. (Chicago: A. T. Andreas Company Publishers, 1886), 3:424.
[28] *Bulletin of the AIC* 5, no. 1 (July 1911), 3.
[29] The Department of Drawing and Painting at the School of the Art Institute of Chicago.
[30] *Bulletin of the AIC* 5, no. 1 (July 1911), 3.

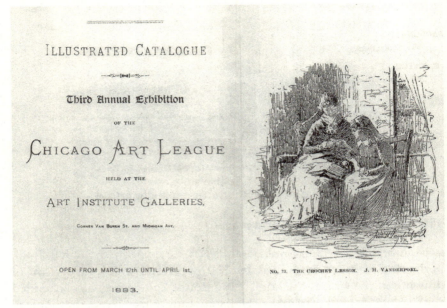

The Crochet Lesson (Catalogue of the Third Annual Exhibition of the Chicago Art League, 1883)

as an instructor in "still-life painting, pen, ink and pencil drawing, and etching."[31] The *Bulletin*'s tribute certainly must refer to his having been a student at the SAIC's precursors, not at the SAIC itself. That he was an instructor in 1883 is, however, incontrovertible. The catalogue of the first annual exhibition of the Art Institute on January 13, 1883, lists him as an instructor of "still life in oil colors."[32]

His appointment as an instructor at the SAIC terminated his internship/job as a "general handy-boy" in the studio of C. V. Schwerdt, a German portraitist in Chicago. When he began to work for this painter is not known, but by 1882, Vanderpoel had been succeeded by another aspiring artist, Joseph Birren.[33]

[31] S. R. Koehler, comp., *The United States Art Directory and Yearbook: A Guide for Artists, Art students, Travellers, Etc.* (NY: Cassell, Petter, Galpin & Co., 1882), 1:28.

[32] Lawrence Earle and Henry F. Spread are listed among the handful of instructors in the catalogue and are also mentioned in the 1911 *Bulletin* as having been Vanderpoel's instructors at the SAIC.

[33] The following year, 1883, Birren became an early pupil of Vanderpoel at the newly organized classes at the SAIC, and in the late 1880s, also went to study at the Académie Julian. A. T. Andreas, *The History of Chicago: From the Earliest Period to the Present Time*, vol. 3, *From the Fire of 1871 until 1885* (Chicago: The A. T. Andreas Co., 1886), 421.

While teaching, Vanderpoel also found time to produce art. The *Illustrated Catalogue of the Third Annual Exhibition of the Chicago Art League*, held at the Art Institute in March and April 1883, exhibited four Vanderpoel works. It provided a reproduction of one of them named *The Crochet Lesson*, an "original sketch."[34] It is likely the first verifiable piece by Vanderpoel of which we have an image.

Vanderpoel was so highly thought of that the Art Institute granted him a "traveling" scholarship to go abroad in 1885. Others had corroborated this appreciation of Vanderpoel's talents, for the third volume of the history of Chicago, issued in 1885, mentions him as a "rising artist in the city," with a "specialty in figure painting and portraits."[35] His passport application states that he had planned to travel in England, France, Germany, Holland, and other European countries.[36] It was in Paris, however, where he was to spend the majority of his time during these two years. Vanderpoel would not study at the prestigious art academy, the École nationale supérieure des Beaux-Arts, presumably because he would have had to pass an extremely rigorous French-language examination. Most Americans, therefore, opted for one of the many art academies open to foreigners, and Vanderpoel chose the esteemed Académie Julian. Twice a week,[37] students received instruction there from notable artists such as Gustave Boulanger, William-Adolphe Bouguereau, and Jules Joseph LeFebvre.[38] These older artists had been

---

[34] *Catalogue of the Third Annual Exhibition of the Chicago Art League* (1883), 28. This drawing was one of several of his submissions for this exhibit. It may have been his first public exhibition at the AIC. Many such exhibitions of his work would follow in subsequent years.

[35] Andreas, *History of Chicago*, 421.

[36] Application dated 24 Aug. 1885. He states in the application that his father John Vanderpoel had become a US citizen when he was still a minor. Furthermore, John H. Vanderpoel is described in this document (in the time before passports had photographs) as being (only) 4'11'', with a medium forehead, dark-brown eyes, rather prominent nose, medium mouth, rather long and square chin, light brown hair, light complexion, and a rather narrow and long face; www.ancestry.com (US Passport Applications 1795-1925). The specific locations where Vanderpoel painted or drew—indicating where drawings or paintings were made in a brochure of the memorial exhibition in 1912—show the extent of his travels within the United States and abroad in his lifetime. "Memorial Collection of Works by John H. Vanderpoel," AIC, 1912.

[37] Alexandra Gaba-van Dongen, *Dromen van Rijsoord: Wilhelmina Douglas Hawley, 1860-1958* (Bussum: Thoth, 2005), 29. Women, however, received instruction only once a week, but they paid almost twice the tuition fees.

[38] Lefebvre, the most popular teacher among the American students in Paris, had possibly the greatest influence on Vanderpoel. The former taught the necessity of absolute precision when the students drew from life. Vanderpoel liked to tell his

Académie Julian students c. 1885, J. H. Vanderpoel, *front right*

trained at the aforementioned Beaux Arts academy in the classicist and idealist style, which had dominated French instruction since the late eighteenth century. They produced canvases that were highly finished, often allegorical and predominantly of women. They eschewed impressionism, and the emerging postimpressionism, symbolism, and pointillism, to name a few of the then avant-garde movements.

The Académie Julian itself did not insist on traditional classicism, thus permitting modernism to be expressed by students. Childe Hassam, the American impressionist, was at the academy with Vanderpoel and so was Robert Henri (founder of the Ash Can School, although he was still producing impressionist canvases at that time).

There were plenty of new ways of artistic expression in Paris in the early 1880s. The Societé des Artistes Indépendants held its second and third exhibitions during the years Vanderpoel was in Paris, but it is not known whether he viewed the exhibitions. Given the authority of the majority of Académie teachers, and the general antimodernist views at

---

students of an occurrence in one of his classes at the academy. One of his teachers had ridiculed him for drawing a model's foot with six toes, but the anatomical abnormality was in fact true and had been observed only by the latter. Thomas C. Buechele and Nicholas C. Lowe, *The School of the Art Institute of Chicago*, Campus History Series (Chicago: Arcadia Publications, 2017), 27.

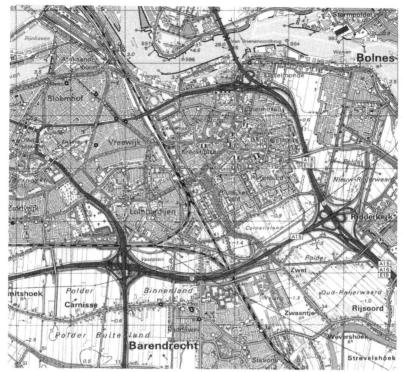
Rijsoord, province of South Holland

the AIC, he was not likely to have had great fondness for the works of Cézanne, Seurat, Gauguin, and others exhibited there.[39]

Since the art academies in Paris closed over the summer, students were able during those months to study elsewhere in Europe. Early in the summer of 1886, John Henry traveled to Germany and Italy, returning to the Netherlands for the remainder of the summer. The weekly Holland, Michigan, newspaper *De Grondwet* found this significant enough to report that the "*American* artist Joh. van der Poel Jr." was planning to reside in Rijsoord until September.[40] It should be recalled that his parents were born and raised there, and many of his near relatives still worked and resided there. While there, John Henry

---

[39] Sue Ann Prince, ed., *Old Guard and the Avant-Garde: Modernism in Chicago, 1910-1940* (Chicago: University of Chicago Press, 1990), 196. Gaba-van Dongen, *Dromen van Rijsoord*, 30.

[40] *De Grondwet*, 13 July 1886. "Rijsoord, 15 June. The American artist Joh. van der Poel Jr. will reside here until the beginning of September this year"; translation and emphasis mine.

stayed at the ancestral farm, Burghoeve, on the Pruimendijk, where some of his older siblings had been born.

Rijsoord was a small village then, surrounded by an arm of the Waal River, whose water was used to process flax,[41] cultivated abundantly there.[42] It is not surprising, therefore, that Vanderpoel saw this rural setting as a haven for artists. Although not far from the much bigger town of Dordrecht, Rijsoord was still pretty much untouched by city culture. Getting there was easy, for artists could reach Rijsoord via a good road from The Hague, and the spacious Hotel Warendorp could accommodate them. In the summer of 1887, Vanderpoel took a number of Académie Julian students with him to travel in the Netherlands, finally settling with them in Rijsoord in July. It was a picturesque place for the Americans, who painted *klompen*-shod farm folk engaged in the processing of flax, and women, in their highly distinctive headdress and ear irons, washing laundry from landings in the river. A student recalled in 1893 that "the simple-minded folk had never seen an artist to that time."[43]

The success of this venture led ultimately to a kind of loosely structured art colony that flourished until the First World War.[44] The students did not all come from Académie Julian; several came from other art schools in the United States.[45] Vanderpoel returned to Chicago in the fall of 1887 but not before he and other American artists in Rijsoord had treated school children to a Fourth of July celebration. Rijsoord residents made twenty-five carriages available (decorated with Dutch and American flags) so that the children and the Americans could ride in a procession through the village.[46] Vanderpoel returned to Rijsoord in 1888,[47] 1889, and intermittently after that.[48]

---

[41] The Van Nes family had been flax growers for generations; Maria Van Nes was John Henry's mother.
[42] The flax was made into linen and rope.
[43] https://rijsoord.dordtenazoeker.nl. Vanderpoel's sisters, Cornelia and Mathilda (the latter also an artist), spent the summer of 1887 in Rijsoord as well, staying with family. A good example of a typical American response to "quaint" Holland is "A Holland art village," by Elizabeth Leypold Good, *Catholic World* (Rijsoord) 70, no. 418 (1900), 514-26.
[44] See Gaba-van Dongen, *Dromen van Rijsoord*, and Annette Stott, *Dutch Utopia*.
[45] For example, the Pratt Institute in Brooklyn, the Art Students' League in New York City, and the California School of Design in San Francisco.
[46] *Nieuwsblad gewijd aan de belangen van De Hoeksche Waard, IJsselmonde, Kralingen & Vlaardingen* 10, no. 991 (6 July 1887).
[47] *Nieuwsblad* (25 July 1888), 11, reported that Vanderpoel had arrived with a couple of women. There were about twelve American gentlemen and ladies spending the summer months painting the beautiful area *en plein air*. It was, however, a wet and

Since the Académie Julian did permit women to study there[49] (the Beaux Arts academy did not admit women), many American women flocked to Rijsoord, where they ultimately outnumbered the men. The men stayed in Hotel Warendorp, while the women lodged in the newly constructed (1889) and spacious dwelling of one of Vanderpoel's cousins, Volksje (van Nes) Noorlander.[50] The large attic provided plenty of room to paint and to display "the catch of the day."

Teaching at the School of the Art Institute of Chicago

Once back in Chicago, Vanderpoel resumed his teaching at the School of the Art Institute of Chicago (SAIC). Students at the SAIC received rigorous instruction and could graduate after three years. One of Vanderpoel's students, Minerva Teichert, recalled that the morning would begin with having to draw plaster copies of antique statuary and then move to drawing from life models.[51] Vanderpoel and seven instructors taught this class, attesting to the view of the SAIC that drawing was a basic and foundational tool for beginning students.[52] They were not allowed to do any work in color unless they showed they could draw well, which generally took from seven to eight months to learn.[53]

Some of the courses were taught by Vanderpoel and only one other (generally notable) instructor, including the nude-life class, the advanced head-and-draped-model class, and the head-and-costumed-life class, but Vanderpoel was especially cherished for a course that only he taught on the scientific and artistic construction of the features of the head and the entire human figure.

Vanderpoel illustrated his lectures by creating large drawings while speaking. Students were impressed by the surety and confidence of his

---

cold summer, which destroyed the crops in Rijsoord. The students organized a song and dance event in Hotel Warendorp to raise money for the poor there.

[48] *The Bulletin of the Art Institute of Chicago* 2, no. 1 (July 1908), indicates that Vanderpoel had returned after a year in Europe. He had received a year's paid leave of absence beginning in Oct. 1907 to work abroad.

[49] Women did study in separate rooms, where they were permitted to draw or paint nude male models.

[50] Anna H. Stanley, one of John Henry's students, had laid the first stone.

[51] Marian Eastwood Wardle, "Minerva Teichert's Murals: The Motivation for her Large-Scale Productions," MA Thesis (Provo, UT: Brigham Young University, Sept. 1988), 31.

[52] *Bulletin of The Art Institute of Chicago school of drawing, painting, sculpture, designing, architecture, circular of instruction for 1902-03, with catalogue of students 1901-02* (Chicago: Lake Front, Opposite Adams Street, 1902), 22.

[53] Ibid.

Torsos

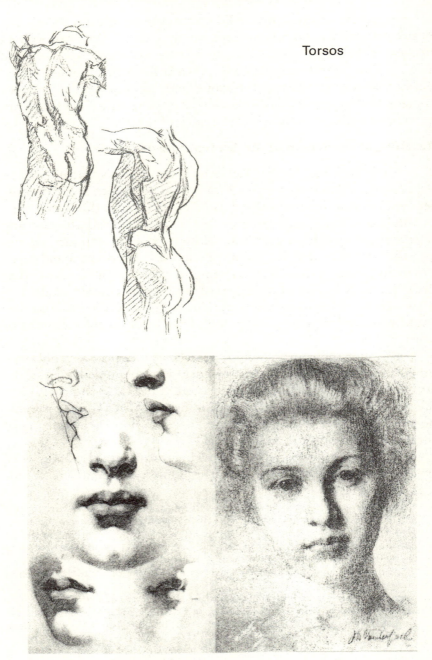

Faces, from Vanderpoel's *The Human Figure*

draftsmanship, which demonstrated "a wonderful analysis of form."[54] A former pupil described Vanderpoel as a "quiet, gracious personality," with "carefully chosen words,"[55] showing his "intent profile" while studying a model. Another mentioned his "slender, marvelously skilled hands."[56] Since this course was offered during the day, as well as at night, Vanderpoel was able to teach numerous students over the years.[57] Many of these considered him to be the "best teacher living of the drawing of the human figure" and even "the greatest draftsman on earth" who had "made the Art Institute great" and was "the nation's leading authority on rendering the human figure."[58] Georgia O'Keeffe, a student at the Art Institute in 1905-6, although not liking the emphasis on realism, wrote in her autobiography that Vanderpoel was "one of the few true teachers she had ever known."[59]

His colleagues respected him as well. One former student of Vanderpoel—and from 1900 to 1911, a colleague—was effusive in his praise. Grateful graduates, he wrote, did not include only painters but also "illustrators, designers, mural decorators, and workers in the minor arts."[60] That the AIC mounted an exhibition of his sketches and his oil and watercolor paintings a year after his death in February 1912 is further testimony to the artist's lasting influence, which established the AIC as "a school of severe [sic] drawing."[61]

[54] Ibid., 21. The Dutch newspaper, *Nieuwsblad*, in various articles in the last decades of the nineteenth century, often remarked about his entertaining an audience by *sneltekenen*, i.e., making quick sketches on a large piece of paper. The *Rotterdamsch Nieuwsblad* of 1 Sept. 1888 also describes this gift: http://rijsoord.dordtenazoeker.nl.
[55] He was also known for criticizing students in class who favored modern artistic trends. Prince, *Old Guard*, 196.
[56] Thomas Wood Stevens, *The Inland Printer: The Leading Trade Journal of the World in the Printing and Allied Industries* 47, no. 5 (Aug. 1911), 690.
[57] Records show that these lectures began to fill more of his teaching load, thus reducing his normally scheduled courses; IAAIC, Vanderpoel papers. He gave public lectures as well. The *AIC Bulletin* 3, no. 3, of Jan. 1910, lists a forthcoming lecture by Vanderpoel entitled "An Artist's Jaunt in Italy," which he would illustrate with sketches, 42.
[58] *AIC Bulletin* (1911), 4. Wardle, "Minerva Teichert's Murals," 10, 17n14. Eleanor Jewett, in *Chicago Daily Tribune*, 30 Sept. 1928. Sue Ann Prince, *Old Guard*, 196.
[59] http://www.okeeffemuseum.org. She attended the SAIC for only one year (1905-6), due to a bad case of typhoid fever. In her autobiography, she tells that she looked forward to the Vanderpoel lectures, and the instruction of the "very kind, generous little man" was treasured by her. He ranked her drawings first and gave her "several honorable mentions." *Mount Greenwood Express*, Midlothian, IL (29 Dec. 1983), n.p.
[60] Stevens, *The Inland Printer*, 690.
[61] *A Memorial Collection of Works by John H. Vanderpoel Exhibited from February 1 to February 28, 1912*, in the Art Institute of Chicago.

Jury selecting paintings, Columbian World's Exposition, Chicago, 1893. Vanderpoel in center

Vanderpoel and the traditionalism of the School of the Art Institute of Chicago

That Vanderpoel was on a jury selecting American oil paintings for the Columbian Exposition of 1893 shows his importance in Chicago's art world. The long-term president of the AIC, Charles L. Hutchinson, lent his very own Vanderpoel painting to the exhibit, additional proof of the artist's reputation.[62] Although this jury (and similar bodies) allowed some of the art to reflect modern notions,[63] that was not the norm. On the whole, the exposition's famous "White City," with its traditional architecture and sculpture,[64] conformed to the classical con-

---

[62] Another was the "Portrait of a Lady" owned by his in-laws, the J. B. Humphreys, in Gallery 9, number 660. *World's Columbian Exposition Official Publication ... Department of Fine Arts* (Chicago: W. B. Conkey Publishers to the Exposition, 1893), 28. A total of five paintings by Vanderpoel were exhibited at the exposition.

[63] On display were works of art by American Impressionists, such as Frederick Childe Hassam (not a Monet or Renoir in sight in the French Pavilion), and the Dutch Hague School artists Mauve, Willem Maris, Neuhuys, Blommers, etc. There were a great many paintings from past centuries as well.

[64] A good example of this was the huge sculpture by Frederick William MacMonnies of Columbia arriving in her ship, the focal point in the Court of Honor.

structs of the nineteenth-century French style and harmonized with the conservative positions held by the AIC. This outlook endured in the Chicago art world for decades.[65]

It is ironic that, in terms of architecture, new ground had been broken a decade earlier with the use of steel-frame construction and large plate-glass windows. The contemporary architect, Louis Sullivan, whose design for a building at the exposition departed from the rest, opined that the Columbian Exposition had set Chicago back many years.[66] Sullivan's verdict, however, was verified in 1913, two years after Vanderpoel's death. School of the AIC students protested the avant garde art on loan from the International Exhibition of Modern Art in New York (better known as the Armory Show). Sullivan's loyalty to the Beaux-Arts tradition and hence his antimodernist views (also shared by many on the faculty) had undoubtedly influenced the artistic views of his students.[67]

Student evaluations

Vanderpoel's popularity with students, however, was not primarily based on his conservative views. Rather, it was his superb draftsmanship and effective teaching methods that made him so attractive. He had a cheerful, gentle, and lovable disposition, despite his having to cope with major physical handicaps and a small stature. He had been severely crippled by a gymnasium accident at the age of fourteen, with many months of recovery to follow. Furthermore, from 1892 on, he had vision in only one eye.[68] A student, recalling Vanderpoel

---

[65] Prince, *Old Guard*, 196-97. The tide had already begun to turn in France in the late nineteenth century, and painting and sculpture in the traditional academic style was derisively termed *l'art pompier* (fireman art) by modernists.

[66] The AIC's conservative position is made quite clear in an article about an exhibition of German contemporary artists (such as Kandinsky, Feininger, Nolde, to name a few) on their premises, in the *Bulletin of the AIC* 2, no. 4 (April 1909), remarking that the "German point of view [read Expressionism] [is] so different from American, but also from Parisian art [read Fauvism, Cubism, etc.]."

[67] The steps of the AIC became the stage of a mock trial of Matisse's paintings, with a ceremonial burning of copies of his work. The heading in the *Chicago Daily Tribune* of 17 April 1913, "Cubists Depart; Students Joyful," voices the student sentiments which Vanderpoel himself had frequently expressed. Prince, *Old Guard*, 193-94, 196-97. The *Chicago Daily Tribune* wrote (tongue in cheek) that "no infection of new ideas has been reported. Long live the past!" (18 April 1913), 8. It, however, was not the students' and faculty's first exposure to avant-garde art, for the work of the artist Arthur Davies, the principal organizer of the Armory Show in New York, had been exhibited at the AIC in 1911.

[68] *Bulletin of the Art Institute of Chicago* 5, no. 1 (July 1911), 3. *American Art Annual: American Federation of Arts* 9 (NY: MacMillan Company, 1911), 318-19. *Biographical*

some years after having been instructed by him, told her granddaughter, "We almost worshiped that little hunch-backed man who we felt, was so big and so high up there that he walked with God. Don't we wish America could again produce a giant like that?"[69]

During the years he taught at the AIC, Vanderpoel spent many summers teaching in various places, such as St. Joseph, Michigan; Oregon, Illinois (the Eagle's Nest art colony); and frequently Delavan, Wisconsin. In Delavan he cotaught with the Englishman Charles Boutwood, who had also been taught by Bouguereau.[70] The schedule in Delavan was probably identical to that in the other art colonies in which he instructed. In the morning, students painted a local inhabitant outdoors, in an action pose of some sort, and in the afternoon, they took trips to the countryside to paint. One student reflected on her fear after she had shown Vanderpoel her first sketch, for he could be exacting, but instead she found him very kind and helpful.[71]

The Human Figure

Vanderpoel's excellence in teaching and his outstanding draftsmanship led many of his students to encourage him to publish a book to make available to a wider public what he had taught for so many years at the AIC. The illustrated manual, *The Human Figure*, was published in Chicago by the Inland Printer Co. in 1907,[72] with a second edition just one year later. This book has been reprinted multiple times and, although the front cover has undergone changes over the years, the content has remained the same. One edition shows an addition to

---

and Memorial Edition, 717-20. This biography lists Vanderpoel as having received instructions at "Turner Hall." Since there was no Turner Hall in Chicago, could this have been one of the many buildings in Chicago functioning then as a *turnverein* (hence called "Turner Hall"), where males could exercise and occasionally take courses? He could well have injured himself there in a wrestling match that caused his physical handicaps.

69 Wardle, "Minerva Teichert's Murals," 10n14. The irony of Vanderpoel's insistence on depicting the human body in its most beautiful and perfect form could not have escaped him or his students. Prince, *Old Guard*, 193.

70 John H. Vanderpoel oversaw the summer sketching classes, which began in 1892 under the auspices of the SAIC. He described the idyllic setting in poetic detail in a Delavan newspaper in 1899. http://www.gazettextra.com/20150118/delavan. Margaret Plevak, "Delavan countryside was their canvas," *Gazette*, 18 Feb. 2017.

71 Louise Riedel, "Student Life at Delavan," in *Brush and Pencil* (June 1898), 115-19.

72 The Inland Printer Co. began as an international journal for the letterpress and lithography industries in 1883. Besides being a printing plant, the company also published practical manuals.

John Henry Vanderpoel, *The Human Figure*, 1907

the title on the front cover: "*Over 300 Drawings and Marginal Sketches, an Inspiration for the Art Student . . . The largest selling book on the subject of figure drawing ever published.*"[73] It continues by praising:

> the great classic for its clear, detailed presentation of thousands of fundamental features of the human figure. . . . The plentiful illustrations provide anatomical detail and direct the viewer to subtle points of shading, curvature, proportions, foreshortening,

Muralist

Vanderpoel's drawing expertise made him a sought-after muralist. There had not been much patronage for murals on public buildings in the United States in comparison to Europe to date, but the 1893 Exposition, with its construction and decoration of huge (albeit temporary) buildings, changed that. Consequently, Vanderpoel, often with another artist, executed murals in various places. These were often

---

[73] John Henry Vanderpoel, *The Human Figure: Life Drawing for Artists* (NY: George B. Bridgman, n.d.). *The Bulletin of the Art Institute of Chicago* (Oct. 1907), 15, gushed that the manual had long been expected. The last reprint was issued in 2017.

painted first in oil on canvas and then transferred to walls or ceilings. Unfortunately, none of his murals has survived, but the design for a series of thirty-foot-high murals in the banquet hall of the Alexandria Hotel in Los Angeles in 1906 have survived. The series, entitled *The Vintage Festival*,[74] was later included in Vanderpoel's *The Human Figure*.

Position at the People's University

A year before his death, Vanderpoel moved to St. Louis, at the invitation of Edward Gardner Lewis, founder of the People's University in University City, a suburb of St. Louis. Vanderpoel had accepted the headship of the Drawing and Painting Department of the Art Academy at the university,[75] while apparently continuing certain obligations at the AIC. This was a capstone in Vanderpoel's career, for Lewis had selected an "incredibly talented staff."[76] While at the university, Vanderpoel had to cancel a lecture at the AIC[77] for health reasons, but it was subsequently reported in the institute's *Bulletin* that his health had recovered. His weak heart, however, did give out a few months later, his death occurring at the home of his friend, John A. Campbell, in University City, May 3, 1911.

Commemorating John Henry Vanderpoel

The AIC's public mourning of the deceased long-time teacher at its Fulton Hall was just the beginning of many tangible commemorations of Vanderpoel's life and influence. In 1912 the AIC bought four of Vanderpoel's drawings to include in their permanent collection.[78]

---

[74] Also, the catalogue of the 1910 AIC exhibition showed studies for the mural ceiling decoration of the theater at De Paul University, Chicago. The ceiling is no longer extant. The exhibition also included forty-seven pencil and charcoal sheets included in his manual of 1907.

[75] Shortly before the St. Louis job began, the Royal Academy in London had come to the United States to inquire if Vanderpoel would be interested in taking the position of head drawing master. William L. Klug, *Catalogue of the Annual Exhibition of the John Henry Vanderpoel Art Association*, 1928.

[76] Sidney Morse, *The Siege of University City, the Dreyfus Case of America* (University City, MO: University City Pub. Co., 1912), 44. Vanderpoel's death came just a few years before the collapse of Edward Gardner Lewis's financial enterprises.

[77] The SAIC had granted Vanderpoel a year's leave of absence, with the proviso that he "continue his lectures here upon the Head in Figure, in three series, during the year." *Bulletin of the AIC* 4, no. 3 (Jan. 1911); and ibid. 4, no. 4 (April 1911), 64.

[78] *Bulletin of the AIC* 5, no. 4 (April 1912), 50. The IAAIC presently lists only one Vanderpoel graphite drawing in its collection, *Log Cabin in Woods*, of 1881 (The Leonora Hall Gurley Memorial Collection, no. 1922.1873).

John H. Vanderpoel teaching students at the People's University Art Academy, 1910-11 (*courtesy University City Public Library*)

In 1913 the Art Students' League of the Institute established a John H. Vanderpoel Scholarship.[79] That same year, the Chicago board of education named a new public elementary school in the suburb of Beverly, on South Prospect Avenue, the John H. Vanderpoel School, "in honor of our lamented teacher and artist." The building still exists, and the school continues to bear his name.[80] That same year, one of John Henry's sisters, Marie Leenheer, alerted John A. Campbell about the sale of her brother's paintings by an art club, and he and his wife raised sufficient funds ($650) to buy a painting to be hung in the school. This work, *The Buttermakers*, made at the summer art colony in Delavan, was donated to the school in 1914.[81]

Campbell's efforts to memorialize his friend did not stop there. In 1915 the John H. Vanderpoel Art Association was founded.[82] Its purpose was to solicit works of art from Vanderpoel's former students, colleagues, and friends for placement in the school. The response was so gratifying that ultimately the school had no more room to display

---

[79] *Bulletin of the AIC* 7, no. 1 (July 1913), 12.
[80] It has been renamed the John H. Vanderpoel Magnet School, and the John H. Vanderpoel Humanities Academy is attached to it.
[81] See this painting above on the lower left of the Vanderpoel paintings in the Vanderpoel Art Gallery.
[82] The over-five-hundred members supporting the venture all lived in the immediate locality of the school. Pamphlet of the John H. Vanderpoel Art Association, 1922, in Ryerson and Burnham Libraries, AIC. Eleanor Jewett, "Vanderpoel Gallery Unique in Art World: Memorial to Loved Institute Teacher Made by His Pupil," *Chicago Daily Tribune* (30 Sept. 1928), 8.

them all. With association funding, a three-thousand-square-foot, skylit gallery was constructed at the south end of the Ridge Park Field House on South Longwood Drive. In 1939 it was estimated that 700 works by 350 artists (all with a connection to Vanderpoel) had been collected. Although fire, theft, weather, and negligence have reduced that number over the years, it is still a splendid collection.[83]

Vanderpoel paintings in the Vanderpoel Art Gallery.[84]

Accolades by Vanderpoel's students and colleagues were profuse after his death, primarily in praise for him having been a most effective and influential teacher, whose "singularly vital personality" was expressed "most fully in his instruction." "Many thousands of us," a former student wrote, "remember how he explained away our difficulties with charcoal."[85] Vanderpoel had given his students a foundation of draftsmanship to further their subsequent artistic careers, especially in drawing the human figure.[86]

---

[83] John Henry Vanderpoel was a long-time resident of Beverly, a new Chicago suburb, where he bought a house. For a thorough history about the weal and woe of the John H. Henry Vanderpoel Art Gallery, see https://www.chicagoreader.com/Chicago/separation-anxiety/Content?oil=912396. See also, Marielle Shaw, "The Art of Inspiration: VanderPoel Art Collection in Beverly A 'Hidden Treasure,'" in *Arts & Entertainment*, 29 June 2014; Howard Ludwig, "Priceless Vanderpoel Art Collection Tucked Within Beverly's Ridge Park," *Arts & Entertainment*, 29 May 2014.

[84] The fourth painting on the top is an oil portrait of J. H. Vanderpoel, painted by a student. He is flanked on the left by a painting of a woman's profile, painted by sister Mathilda.

[85] Stevens, *The Inland Printer*, 690.

[86] Stevens also mentions in his glowing tribute that a recent "important Eastern exhibition" included five contributors trained by Vanderpoel, and that that number would undoubtedly be higher in "Western exhibitions"; ibid.

Vanderpoel paintings in the Vanderpoel Art Gallery

Continued fame or obscurity?

But how can Vanderpoel be evaluated as an artist? His sketches in *The Human Figure* show his superb mastery of drawing, his surety of line and anatomy, shading and light. But he also painted using the media of oils, pastels, and water colors. The AIC, in the introduction to the retrospective of Vanderpoel's art in 1912, speaks with regret about his limited oeuvre—a natural consequence of his teaching schedule. Yet it lauded what he had accomplished in his characteristic "tonal quality and refinement of color."[87] His works—oils, pastels, and water colors— were so pleasing and accomplished that they gained him prizes at expositions.[88] Vanderpoel's paintings have always sold well—both then

---

[87] *Bulletin of the AIC* 5, no. 4 (April 1912), 50.
[88] For example, he won a bronze medal at the Louisiana Purchase Exposition in St. Louis in 1904 for the oil called *Little Miss Moffett*; ibid.

The Empty Cradle, 1894, watercolor

The Perplexing Problem, n.d., oil

and now.[89] A recent advertisement of his *Portrait of a Lady* of 1891 had a ticket price of $26,000.[90]

Nonetheless, books and articles on the many Americans who went on to depict the picturesque Netherlands refer to him at best as founder of the Rijsoord art colony and teacher at the AIC, without further comment. At the same time, however, these sources elaborate on the lives and art of other Rijsoord painters.[91] Perhaps this lack of recognition of Vanderpoel is because many of his students produced paintings that were superior to his. Or it may be due to his limited oeuvre. Possibly his resistance to participate in and learn from the revolutionary changes that were taking place in the art world during his lifetime impeded his attaining further, and perhaps deeper, artistic accomplishments.

Dutch American connections

Did the Dutch American community in Vanderpoel's day recognize his skills? And how does his life and art reflect his birth in the Netherlands and his upbringing there until he was not yet eleven? What was his contact with the Dutch American community? John Henry and his father, and perhaps some of the in-laws of his siblings, were active in the Holland Society (Nederlandsche Vereeniging) of Chicago. The members of this organization had to prove Dutch ancestry as well as American citizenship, and in spite of commemorating Dutch historical events and honoring the Dutch royal family at various events, the members were clearly patriotic Americans.[92] The twofold requirement for membership had led some people to consider the society elitist. It had not, however, deterred the artist Vanderpoel in 1902, who, as a

---

[89] The Arche's Club bought *Threading the Needle* for $1,000 in 1892, and the following year, tycoon C. T. Yeskes bought *Twilight Reverie* for $200. Both paintings were purchased at exhibitions of the Chicago Society of Artists. Buehler, *Beverly Review*, 1992.

[90] http://www.markmurray.com/john-h-vanderpoel-paintings-for-sale. I am thankful to Donald Luidens for calling this to my attention.

[91] Hans Kraan, *Dromen van Holland: buitenlandse kunstenaars schilderen Holland, 1800-1914* (Zwolle: Waanders Uitgevers, 2002), 225. Annette Stott, *Holland Mania: The Unknown Dutch Period in American Art & Culture* (Woodstock, NY: Overlook Press, 1998), 68-74; Annette Stott, ed., *Dutch Utopia: American Artists in Holland, 1880-1914* (Savannah, GA: Telfair Books, 2009), xix, 112, 208.

[92] Swierenga, *Dutch Chicago*, 529. The letter that John Vanderpoel Sr. wrote to his family on 25 Feb. 1871, is full of praise about the United States, this "great land and people, where the lowest worker can be a citizen, a voter, and can himself be elected, and where there is freedom of religion and free education."

member of the Holland Society, was present at a mass rally of the society in support of the South African Boers. The report lists J. H. Vanderpoel as one of the sixty-six *active* members.[93]

John Sr. was active in the Holland Society first and certainly was a member early on. In a letter to his family in the Netherlands in 1877, he alerted them about a visit from a Dutch American friend traveling in the Netherlands. The friend was there, probably among other things, to buy Dutch books for "our town library" in the "beloved mother tongue," to be paid for by the Holland Society.[94]

That John Henry had attained some fame as an artist among Dutch Americans is made clear in Rev. Peter Moerdyke's "Chicago Letters."[95] The artist, Moerdyke writes, was present at a dinner of the Holland Society in 1898, together with two of his sisters and their husbands.[96] The setting of the banquet room resembled a Dutch village. Moerdyke wrote about the yearly gathering in April to commemorate the defeat of the Spanish Duke of Alva in Den Briel in 1572.[97] It was there that "Mr. J. H. Vander Poel," "teacher of art in our Art Institute" was asked to draw four colored "admirable sketches," of which, three illustrated some events of the Dutch Eighty-Years' War with Spain (1568-1648).[98] Moerdyke explained that Vanderpoel was an "ardent Hollander" but spoke Dutch "brokenly." The "Letter" also intimated that Vanderpoel had shown his drawing skills earlier at a meeting(s).[99]

[93] His father is listed as an honorary member that year and the year following. John Sr. is one of eight members, including Abraham Kuyper and Professor Bergen of Hope College.

[94] John Vanderpoel Sr., letter, 17 Aug. 1877. He added that he hoped that the family would also contribute books as gifts to the society, for "the use of all Dutch folk here." The letter also mentions that he had participated in establishing a library in Chicago (there were then several "outposts" with small collections) and had personally contributed Dutch books to the collection.

[95] Peter Moerdyke, born in the Netherlands in 1845, died in Toronto in 1923. He was pastor of Trinity Reformed Church in Chicago from 1892 to 1907. His "Chicago Letters" were published regularly in the Reformed Church in America's denominational paper the *Christian Intelligencer*.

[96] The third annual banquet was held that year in honor of William of Orange and was a grand affair. Women were given portraits of Princess Wilhelmina (crowned later that year as queen), and the men received a pipe and miniature "jugs of old Holland gin." "The Holland Society of Chicago" in *Paint, Oil and Drug Review* 25, no. 2 (5 Jan. 1898), 17. A detailed report on the festivities also appeared in the Flemish monthly *Neerlandia* 2 (Jan. 1898).

[97] Swierenga, *Dutch Chicago*, 529.

[98] Ibid. The fourth depicted a "real Dutch Madonna and child"—perhaps in Dutch costume?

[99] De Nederlandsche Vereeniging (Holland Society) met at Trinity Reformed Church in Chicago (Moerdyke was its pastor then). *Christian Intelligencer* (16 April 1902), 253.

Knowledge about Vanderpoel as an artist was not restricted to Dutch Chicago or American Chicago. He had also become known in the Netherlands, at least in the area around Rijsoord. A regional paper in the Netherlands reported in 1890 about the fame of "Johannes Van der Poel" in Chicago, printing an excerpt from an article in the Dutch-language Chicago weekly *De Nederlander* about "our Dutch painter."[100] The writer praises Vanderpoel's career as teacher and artist and is fairly specific about his style:

> His painting of this year, *Give us this day our daily bread*, is also a domestic subject [of] a humble family in poor surroundings, ready to eat the midday meal, over which they pray a blessing.... One is drawn by the same religious feeling of the *Angelus* (by Jean-Francois Millet). The painter had to say something here that was worth saying.[101]

Vanderpoel's frequent return to Rijsoord also speaks to a continued connection to his native land, which provided him with many Dutch-themed sketches and paintings. Thus, catalogues of his exhibitions list, in addition to works without Dutch subject matter include: *Meal Time, Holland; The Home Coming on the Dijk; Canal Boat, Holland* (pencil sketches); *In Holland, Dutch Milk Maid* (watercolor); *Dutch Interior; Old Dutch Woman at Tea*; and *Wash Day, Holland* (oils).

Vanderpoel's brothers and sisters married Dutch-immigrant spouses, some of whom had connections in or near Rijsoord. His youngest sister Mathilda (Machteldje) was also a graduate of the AIC and taught there for many years. She never married.[102] John Henry married Jessie Elizabeth Humphreys, of non-Dutch descent and ten years his junior, who with their two children, frequently traveled with him to the Netherlands. Although most Dutch immigrants maintained contact with others from the Netherlands through membership in an RCA or

---

[100] https//rijsoord.dordtenazoeker.nl. *Nieuwsblad* 13 (9 July 1890), does not give the date of issue of *De Nederlander* from which the citation came. Although it was in print for several decades, no issues of this Chicago Dutch-language weekly are extant. The article had several inaccuracies about Vanderpoel's life. The *Nieuwsblad* reported frequently about Vanderpoel and the artists in Rijsoord.

[101] Ibid. Translation mine. The 1912 AIC commemorative Vanderpoel catalogue lists a pencil sketch with this title.

[102] Mathilda Vanderpoel and Jean Sherwood organized the Holland House Association in 1908 with the purpose of providing a place in Boulder, CO, where "tired working women" from Chicago could vacation. Funded by many, the organization lasted for forty years.

CRC, this was not the case with John Vanderpoel Sr. After settling in Chicago, he took his children to the Methodist Episcopal church on Halsted Street, where the hymnbooks had English and Dutch texts.[103] Connections with other Dutch Americans (outside his family) seem, therefore, to have come through membership in the Holland Society. The ideals expressed there were not only to remember the Old Country but also to prize being an American.

His father's association with non-Dutch Illinois and Chicago politicians;[104] his choice to join the Methodist church, a mainstream American denomination, rather than a Dutch Reformed church; his public life in city government; and his desire to have his children involved in the arts and sciences,[105] resulted no doubt in the rapid Americanization of himself and his family. John Henry's marriage to an American-born woman and his associations with the Chicago art world—not well populated with Dutch Americans[106]—may have limited his connections with the Dutch American world. The high esteem felt by his "American" students, colleagues, clients, and others in the Chicago art world, both before and after his death, indicates how well the Dutch immigrant Johannes van der Poel had morphed into the American artist and teacher John Henry Vanderpoel.

---

[103] Buehler, "John Henry Vanderpoel (1857-1911)." The Halsted Street Methodist Episcopal Church, organized in 1867, had its first bilingual (Dutch/English) pastor in 1882. The Methodist church was a thoroughly middle-American denomination, often Main Street, with an emphasis on revivalism, and rooted in the anti-Calvinist theology of John Wesley. *Northwestern Christian Advocate* 51, no. 32 (23 Aug. 1903), 2, at https://books.google.com/books; English-speaking Calvinistic churches, e.g., Presbyterian, were readily available in Chicago, but the (senior) Vanderpoels, for whatever reason, chose to not identify with any of them. The artist, nevertheless, was buried in a service led by a Presbyterian minister, albeit one of his students; see note 1.

[104] "The Passing of Mr. John Vanderpoel," *Onze Toekomst*, 6 Aug. 1909. He was proud of calling Chicago and Illinois politicians his friends.

[105] John Vanderpoel Sr., letter, 17 August 1877. His penmanship is very good; the letters show erudition and are at times almost poetic.

[106] Rachel Cranston of St. Peters, MO, descendant of John Henry's brother Arie, mentioned in a telephone conversation with the author in 2017 that her great-aunt Lizzie (sibling of the artist) had destroyed the Vanderpoel drawings of unclad models, finding them objectionable. It is conceivable that some more orthodox Dutch (and other) Americans may have disapproved of the display of the bodies of nudes in his manual.

CHAPTER 15

A Mini Biography of Dutch American Astronomer G. P. Kuiper

Huug van den Dool

Introduction

In the summer of 2015, NASA spacecraft *New Horizons*, launched in 2006, made a flyby of Pluto. This was feel-good news in the United States for days on end, as ever-more detailed pictures of the popular dwarf planet were sent back to earth. The mission was truly a huge success. Pluto had been discovered only in 1930 and for a long time was considered the ninth planet of our solar system. Not satisfying all criteria of being a planet, Pluto was demoted in 2006 to the newly defined status of "dwarf planet." The national news in 2015 also mentioned the Kuiper Belt, which makes our Dutch American heart rate go up a bit: Who was Kuiper? What was his life about? Why is there a cosmic belt named after him? And what exactly is the Kuiper Belt?

A case of recent history

G. P. Kuiper (1905-1973) was a noted Dutch American astronomer who came to the United States in 1933. His career in the middle of the twentieth century is described by more sources than can be digested for this short essay, and he is quite a presence on the internet—including Wikipedia.[1] Some of the more pertinent information we relied on came from a scientific "obituary," written by one of Kuiper's few students in the United States, Dale P. Cruikshank,[2] and a curious and admiring piece of local history from Harenkarspel, the birthplace of Kuiper, written around the time (c. 2000) that a statue was unveiled to honor their famous son.[3]

Early life and education

Gerrit Pieter Kuiper, or GPK,[4] was born December 7, 1905, in West Friesland (a section of the province of Noord-Holland), in the small village of Tuitjenhorn, in the municipality of Harenkarspel. His parents were Gerrit Kuiper (a tailor) and Antje de Vries, who were very poor. He was the oldest of four children; he had a sister, Augusta Alida Margaretha (1909), who would become a teacher, and two brothers, Pieter Nicolaas (1914) and Nicolaas Cornelis (1918), who would both become engineers. The parents were Nederlands Hervormd (Netherlands Reformed, the Dutch public church), according to town records, but are also listed on the "humanitarism" website,[5] usually indicative of an environment of humanism, pacifism, vegetarianism, opposition to smoking and drinking, fairly socially progressive, and politically left leaning (or some combination thereof). This movement was particularly strong and idealistic between 1900 and 1940. Its ideals included a good education for children, and Gerrit and Antje laudably succeeded in that pursuit, despite poverty and the distance to education beyond the mandatory local elementary school. By "distance" I mean not only the literal distance in kilometers to the nearest suitable secondary school but also the distance enforced by a class-conscious society that made it hard for the poor to succeed.

Speaking a dialect was, until very recently, a serious handicap in the Netherlands in general, where snobbish speakers of Algemeen Beschaafd Nederlands (ABN, standard Dutch) would make fun of those

---

[1] https://en.wikipedia.org/wiki/Gerard_Kuiper.
[2] Dale P. Cruikshank, *Gerard Peter Kuiper 1905-1973: A Biographical Memoir* (Washington DC: National Academy of Sciences, 1993), at http://www.nasonline.org/publications/biographical-memoirs/memoir-pdfs/kuiper-gerard.pdf.
[3] "Professor Doctor Gerard P. Kuiper," *Zicht op Haringcarspel* (publication of the "Historische Vereniging Harenkarspel), 10, no. 19 (1 May 2001), 6-10.
[4] GPK also stands for Gerard Peter Kuiper, the name he adopted in the US.
[5] http://www.humanitarisme.nl/personen/index.php?m=family&id=I79565.

who did not or could not speak standard Dutch, and a strong dialect was spoken in West Friesland, something GPK would be reminded of regularly. Appreciation for dialects and local languages would not emerge until about 1970. This discrimination was especially felt in the educational system. Pupils in elementary school were sometimes lucky enough to have a teacher from the same area who would share their language form; otherwise, teachers tried to stamp out any dialect. In the elitist university environment, the ABN-speaking, well-to-do students would pick on their fellow students from a modest background who spoke with an accent.

GPK was an excellent pupil in elementary school and skipped a grade.[6] His teacher, Meester (Master) Blad, convinced young GPK's parents that he should go on to secondary education. In those days, the highest achievement for the lower strata of society in the Netherlands was to become an elementary school teacher.[7] In line with that self-limiting expectation, GPK was sent, at age eleven or twelve, to a secondary school in Haarlem, likely called the Kweekschool (teacher training school), far away from home, thus requiring him to board at a young age. GPK was again found to be quite smart, and he skipped another grade., GPK had meanwhile decided he wanted to be an astronomer, but he found himself in the wrong school for that pursuit. His interest in astronomy dated back to his young childhood—at least to the day that his father and grandfather had given him a small telescope, and Meester Blad helped him make night-sky observations from the neighbor's roof. So, in addition to his final exam at the teacher's school, he volunteered to take some additional, difficult, secondary-school examinations in the area of the exact sciences in order to be admitted to a university. This could easily have cost him an extra one or two years. But because of his intelligence and determination, this turnabout caused him surprisingly little delay. He was enrolled at the University of Leiden in 1924.

Higher education and emerging interests

G. P. Kuiper may not have realized how lucky, in a sense, he was. Both the physics and astronomy programs (two sciences that are closely related) at Leiden University were nearly the very best in the world in the 1920s. The physics program had benefitted immensely from the singular talents of Nobel Prize winners Hendrik Antoon Lorentz

---

[6] "Professor Doctor Gerard P. Kuiper," *Zicht op Haringcarspel*, 6-10.
[7] This is my interpretation. The parents of the author were in this category.

(1853-1928) and Heike Kamerlingh Onnes (1853-1926). Astronomy as a science in the Netherlands had been catapulted into prominence by the extraordinary renown of Jacobus Cornelis Kapteyn (1851-1922), professor at the University of Groningen. Nearly all astronomers of some fame were the highly intellectual children or grandchildren of Kapteyn. GPK began his university education in this environment of high expectations and standards and was awarded his bachelor's degree in 1927.

Successful as this may sound, GPK encountered an atmosphere of discrimination at Leiden.[8] I can imagine that young Kuiper, very self-assured by nature and too smart for any school he had attended so far, was put in his place by other students because of his lower-class background and dialect. Not to be discouraged by such distractions, however, GPK immediately started a PhD program with Danish astronomer Ejnar Hertzsprung (1873-1967), professor at Leiden and son-in-law of Kapteyn. Like almost all astronomy students, Kuiper was enlisted to observe a solar eclipse, for which an expedition traveled to Indonesia in 1928. As a little extracurricular activity, he stayed in that country, then a Dutch colony, for eight months. Apparently, he learned Malay in that period.

GPK would ultimately focus on the dynamics of solar systems (not just our own solar system). His work with Hertzsprung that resulted in a PhD in 1933, was on so-called binary stars in a simple type of solar system. Binary stars involve the confluence of two stars—one of which may not even be visible—that orbit around a common center of gravity. By appearance, they can be interpreted as a sun and a single huge planet. At that time, it was not known whether a sun with order-ten planets (that is, a sun with about ten planets), as is the case in our solar system, was exceptional or common. Speculation at that time was that only a very small percentage of stars (or suns) in the universe had multiple planets. Kuiper would later give ever-increasing probabilities of stars being surrounded by multiple planets. The discovery of Pluto in 1930—the first new planet discovered in our own solar system in almost a century—caused great excitement, and student GPK must have shared in that excitement.[9]

[8] Cruikshank, "*Gerard Peter Kuiper*, 260.
[9] Never mind that Pluto is no longer considered a planet; the excitement in 1930 was real.

An invasion of astronomers

During the first half of the twentieth century, Leiden and other Dutch universities cranked out numerous well-educated and ambitious students, as well as first-rate astronomers, but there were very few jobs in the Netherlands at that time. By sheer luck, there was a country somewhere else in the world with the exactly opposite problem. Despite hard times brought on by the Great Depression, the United States did make money available for building several big telescopes, so there was a huge demand for capable astronomers to come from the other side of the ocean. Thus began another unique chapter of Dutch American history. To put it in the words of historian Klaas van Berkel: "The Netherlands was growing astronomers for export,"[10] as if they were a crop and the principal customer the United States. A partial list of US immigrants who were all well-known Dutch astronomers, includes:

	Arrival
Willem Luyten	1921
Peter van de Kamp	1923
Dirk Brouwer	1927
Bart Bok	1929
Jan Schilt	1933
Gerard Kuiper	1933[11]

All of them would have a large impact on astronomy in the United States, and in fact worldwide. All would be internationally known, but Kuiper embraced the US scene perhaps more than some of the others. Bok moved on to Australia after some years in the United States, and van de Kamp returned to the Netherlands after retiring. In addition to these well-known people before WWII, the export of astronomers would go on for decades, and Dutch astronomers would dominate the international scene until 1980 or so. Around 1935, Kuiper considered moving on to Indonesia (Dutch East Indies at the time) after two years in the United States, but circumstances prevented that. One of these "circumstances" was his marriage to Sarah Fuller, whose family had donated the land

---

[10] Klaas van Berkel, "Growing Astronomers for Export: Dutch Astronomers in the United States before World War II," in *The legacy of J. C. Kapteyn: Studies on Kapteyn and the Development of Modern Astronomy*, ed. Piet C. van der Kruit and Klaas van Berkel (Dordrecht, NL: Kluwer Academic Publishers, 2000), 151.

[11] Van Berkel, "Growing Astronomers for Export," 171-74.

for the Harvard Oak Ridge Observatory. If this marriage was a tactical move on GPK's part (we do not know), it was superb. Astronomy is one of these appealing human enterprises greatly helped by wealthy benefactors. Moreover, his wife-to-be seemed to understand his lengthy absences required to make nighttime observations.

Our solar system

Solar systems take a long time to form, and we see but a snapshot late in the process. How can we interpret what we see? Our solar system has eight or nine planets orbiting the sun. The four small planets nearest to the sun are Mercury, Venus, Earth, and Mars. Going farther outward, we encounter four large planets: Jupiter, Saturn, Uranus, and Neptune. These eight planets are revolving around the sun on nearly the same plane (the ecliptic)—like on a gramophone record—with the outer planets revolving much more slowly around the sun. An empirical finding made several centuries ago suggests the distance of the planets from the sun is not random but follows the Titius–Bode Law.[12] Based on that law, one can surmise that there may or should have been another planet between Mars and Jupiter. Instead of a planet, however, we find an asteroid "belt," with bigger and smaller pieces of material spread out along and around the entire orbit. From this belt, many of our asteroids originate. Asteroids hit the earth about one thousand times a year on average.

GPK made an hypothesis in the early 1950s: beyond Neptune, there ought to be another planet, or in its place, a broad belt full of debris that did not coalesce into a planet. His speculation was based primarily on his knowledge of the origin of comets. His theoretical debris path came to be known as the Kuiper Belt. Prior to 1990, however, nothing at all had been observed in the Kuiper Belt, except Pluto. In the outer reaches of our solar system, where the sun's attraction is small and its reflected light weak, old-style observation was at a huge disadvantage. Since the launch of the Hubble Space Telescope in 1990, it has been possible to observe the heavens without interference from our own atmosphere, and many objects in the Kuiper Belt have now been seen. Pluto (one-seventh the mass of our moon) is now understood to be just one of many pieces of debris of roughly that mass and size. The idea of a ninth or tenth planet going around the sun (one full revolution in

---

[12] A calculation that suggests the distance of planets from the sun and from each other.

many hundreds of years) has not been given up, yet nothing has been observed to the satisfaction of astronomers.

Interlude

We have already answered our introductory questions: Who was Kuiper? What was his life about? Why is there a cosmic belt named after him? And what exactly is the Kuiper Belt?

For the reader who wants to know more about his phenomenal career, I have organized some highlights in tables 1 and 2 below, but this is an incomplete list. I shy away from even an abbreviated biography; Kuiper's career was vast, and writing a biography should be left to an astronomer or planetary scientist (I am a meteorologist).

Instead, I want to end with a discussion about Kuiper and language. This is a very important topic for understanding the experience of any immigrant and especially for the AADAS audience intent on comprehending the immigrant experience.

Kuiper and language

For every immigrant—and their children to some extent—there is the question of adaptation. Language is one big aspect of adaptation. There is no question that Kuiper embraced the United States and its language without reservation. Around 1935 he changed his name from Gerrit Pieter to Gerard Peter; perhaps he or his wife-to-be thought that would be easier in the United States. He probably reveled in a society that was less class conscious than the Dutch, and although Americans would notice his accent, it would not be held against him; accents were to be expected in a country full of immigrants. Immigrants also face the reciprocal question as to how they maintain (knowingly or unknowingly) their first language. One can imagine Kuiper spoke very little Dutch in the United States, especially after he married an American woman. Some immigrants almost lose their original language, and Kuiper appears to be one of them.

Cornelis ("Kees") de Jager (b. 1921) wrote a column about a visit by Kuiper to Utrecht in 1946 while de Jager was a student (soon a famous Dutch astronomer). To the astonishment of his audience, Kuiper refused to speak Dutch in his personal discussions with students because, he claimed, he "had forgotten" the language.[13] Critics

---

[13] Cornelis de Jager, "Gerrit Pieter Kuiper," *Zenit* (monthly magazine of the Netherlands Weather and Astronomy Organization; Dutch acronym KNVWS) (June 2012), 8.

sarcastically commented that he had never known Dutch in the first place, reminding each other of his upbringing in West Friesland, with its strong dialect (even its own language). More sympathetic analysts recognized that Kuiper had experienced discrimination at Leiden because of his lower-class background and saw that as his reason to refuse to use Dutch.

This kind of story is somewhat at odds with other claims about Kuiper's talent for language. According to his daughter, he had learned Malay during his short visit to Indonesia in his student years. Because he knew German, he was selected to be part of the American group of military personnel and scientists who tracked down German scientists in the last weeks of World War II, before the Russians scooped them up. Kuiper's German was an asset for this so-called Alsos Mission. If he had acquired German, he certainly should have remembered Dutch, even if they spoke it a little differently at Tuitjenhorn.

Much later, this oddity in Kuiper's mind became apparent in a situation in full public view. In the 1960s, Kuiper was going to give a seminar at Utrecht University. At that time Marcel Minnaert (1893-1970) was the leading astronomer there. Minnaert was not only a stellar scientist,[14] but he was also a language purist in the extreme. He had fled his native Belgium at the end of WWI because he had been convicted for pro- ("Dutch"-speaking) Flanders activities during the German occupation of Belgium in WWI. This was treasonous in the eyes of the Francophone Walloons. Minnaert carried on his defense of proper Dutch as a refugee in the Netherlands where he was very, very pure about his own (Dutch) language, fighting against words imported from other languages (Germanisms, Anglicisms) and inventing Dutch equivalents for any new words and notions.

So after a rousing introduction of Kuiper at the University of Utrecht, Minnaert added it would be a great pleasure for their famous Dutch son to give a seminar in his own language—meaning Dutch. Uncharacteristically, Kuiper momentarily lost his composure, but he carried on, giving his seminar in English, leaving Minnaert flabbergasted. English, yes, but with a strong West Frisian accent, according to De Jager, who was in the audience.[15] One cannot forget everything.

We should not blame Kuiper—focused on research as he was—for not knowing, seemingly, all the sensitivities surrounding language in

---

[14] Minnaert wrote the classic, *Light and Color in the Outdoors* (NY: Springer-Verlag, 1993).
[15] De Jager, "Gerrit Pieter Kuiper," *Zenit* (June 2012), 8.

Belgium. But he, however, was not entirely oblivious. In an article by Janet Sheeres, we learn of a curious incident in 1942-43, during World War II, when the Dutch royal family was in exile in London. Bernard Fridsma (1905-2005),[16] a language professor of Frisian descent living in Grand Rapids, Michigan, petitioned Queen Wilhelmina for the independence of Friesland from the Netherlands. Interest in Frisian independence was surprisingly strong among Frisians who, in fact, had left Fryslan and immigrated to the United States. In order to bolster his case, Fridsma tried to enlist the support of well-known Dutch Americans (not all of them Frisian). That Kuiper was one of them shows he was already well known in 1942 and still connected to other emigrants from the Netherlands. Kuiper refused to sign the petition on the ground that the Nazis would misuse this issue to strengthen their grip on occupied Netherlands by applying the "divide and conquer" principle. (We might add—on behalf of Minnaert—just as the Germans had done famously with Flanders vs. Wallonia in Belgium in World War I.)

Concluding remarks

Gerard Peter Kuiper and the United States of America were made for each other. He, a singularly gifted and focused person wanting to apply himself to planetary science (not a popular field of study c. 1930) within astronomy, and the United States, spending huge resources on manned missions to the moon and unmanned missions to other planets. Backed by millions of dollars, Kuiper made very good use of the opportunities afforded, even of the Cold War aspects of his work, including the space race with the Russians. According to Carl Sagan,[17] a student of Kuiper, Kuiper even had a secret project with the US military to detonate an atomic device on the moon.

To the end, G. P. Kuiper remained an enigmatic personality:

- He was extremely hard working, expecting nothing less from others; very self-assured; highly driven; producing very original work.
- He worked the US system from the inside, more than many of his contemporary Dutch immigrant scholars, such as Edward William Bok, Peter Van de Kamp, and Willem

---

[16] Janet Sjaarda Sheeres, "Bernard J. Fridsma: A Frisian Ambassador in the United States," *Origins* 24, no. 2 (2006), 35.

[17] Carl Sagan's television programs on astronomy in the 1980s made him a national celebrity in the US.

> Jacob Luyten. He was anything but a helpless immigrant; he became as American as anybody.
> - Kuiper was a great scientist and researcher and a very ambitious manager. He directed others and took advantage of opportunities.
> - He never doubted the importance of his work and ambition.
> - He was gifted with unusually sharp eyesight (a feature of many astronomers).
> - He avoided teaching as much as possible, since it took time away from his research.

Kuiper died of a heart attack in Mexico City on December 24, 1973, while on a trip with his wife and a colleague. He and his wife had two children, Paul and Sylvia, born in 1941 and 1947, respectively.

Acknowledgments

The request to present a biography about G. P. Kuiper came originally from Gerlof Homan, who came across that name in his research on Adrian Barnouw. Gerlof made several contributions to the PowerPoint presented at the 2017 AADAS conference. I dedicate this paper to Gerlof, who died a few months later, in November 2017. I also acknowledge input from David R. Rodenhuis, who critically read this manuscript. I am not attempting to acknowledge all the numerous sources about GPK one can find on the internet.

Table 1

From Gerrit Pieter Kuiper's biodata

- 1905: born in Tuitjenhorn to *humanitarian* parents, Gerrit and Antje de Vries
- Had a sister (Augusta A. M. 1909-2005) and two brothers (Pieter Nicolaas 1914-2007) and Nicolaas Cornelis (1918-)
- Grandfather and father (both tailors) gave him a small telescope
- Sent to secondary school in Haarlem to become an elementary school teacher
- 1924-33: student at Leiden: BSc (1927), PhD Leiden on Binary Stars / Prof. Hertzsprung (1933)
- 1929: eight months in Sumatra (including a solar eclipse)
- 1933: to the US, postdoc at Lick Observatory (CA); changed name to Gerard Peter but was called GeePeeKay; 1937 US citizenship
- 1935: to Harvard College Observatory
- 1936: marriage to American Sarah Fuller (whose parents donated land for the observatory); 2 children: Paul b. 1941 and Sylvia b. 1947
- 1936: moved to Yerkes Observatory and University of Chicago
- 1937: associate professor Chicago; 1943 full professor Chicago
- 1943-45: WWII leave of absence
- 1947 - : stints as director of both Yerkes and McDonalds (Texas) Observatories
- 1960: left Chicago for University of Arizona
- 1973: died on a visit to Mexico City

Table 2

Some highlights of Kuiper's work and service to the nation

- 1943-45: worked on RADAR at Harvard (war effort)
- 1945: part of Alsos Mission in 1945 to find German scientists before the Russians did (Max Planck)
- Discoveries: several moons of Uranus and Neptune (dogged and painstaking work)
- Discoveries: chemical composition of several planets' atmospheres, e.g., the greenhouse of Mars
- Discovery: Titan (Jupiter moon) has an atmosphere
- Pioneered "seeing" in the infrared, over and beyond the visible light
- Astronomical observations from high flying planes. (Kuiper Airborne Observatory)
- Edited several atlases of the moon, sun, and several planets
- Hypothesis 1951: A belt of icy debris beyond Neptune, now called Kuiper Belt
- Advised US and NASA about landing spots on the moon
- Wrote several books, one about the atmosphere (meteorology!) of the planets
- Origin of the solar system had his interest, questions about a second moon around Earth, Titius Bode law
- Founding director of Lunar and Planetary Observatory in Tucson, AZ

Name Index

A

Aiken, Charles A., 269
Akker, Harry, 133
Akker (van Akkeren), Sjabbe, 134
Albregts, Jan, 113
Albright family, 113
Ameele, Susan Tack Brill, 118
Arens, John, 46
Arens, William, 46
Arnaud, Derk, 191
Arnaud, Louise, 191-93, 196

B

Bakelaar, Adriaan, 114
Bakelaar, Jan, 114
Bakker, Baaye, 154, 157, 160, 162, 164-68, 171, 173
Bakker, Gerrit, 154, 162, 165-68, 171, 173
Bakker, Sy, 165, 171
Balkema, Joseph, 21
Balkema, Peter, 21
Balkema, Rudophus, 27
Barber, Bryant, 60
Barendrecht, Hendrik, 204
Barnouw, Adrian, 312
Bavinck, Herman, 258-60, 263-64, 269-71
Beets, Henry, 262
Berends, John, 50
Birren, Joseph, 282
Blad, *Meester* (Master), 305
Blaukamp, John, 46
Blaukamp, Ralph, 46
Blauwkamp, Albert, 44, 46, *47*
Blauwkamp (née Bosgraaf), Sadie, 46
Blauwkamp, Terry, 46-47
Blommert, Willemina, 112
Bodnar, John, 144
Boer, G. E., 254, 262, 264-67, 270-72
Bohannan, J. H., 94

Bok, Bart, 307
Bok, Edward William, 311
Bolhuis, Gerrit, 44
Bolks, Seine, 239, 242
Bom, Peter, 114
Bont, John, 50
Bos, C. J., 32
Bosgraaf, Ben, 46
Bosgraaf, Jack, 46
Bosgraaf, Jerry, 46-47
Bosgraaf, Ralph, 46-47
Bosgraaf, Ted, 46
Bosgraaf, Tom (Tiete), 44, 46
Bosma, Anna, 210
Bosma, Donald, 40
Bosma, Richard, 40
Bouguereau, William-Adolphe, 283
Boulanger, Gustave, 283
Bousquet-Chabot, Henriette M., 205
Bouwens, Pieter, 114
Brandt, Almon, 51
Brandt, Gerard, 202-3
Bratt, James D., 273
Bridge (Brugge), Jenny, 118
Bril, Jacob, 114
Brink, Herbert, 180
Brink, John R., 51
Brouwer, Dirk, 307
Brower, Chester, 46
Brower, Harvey, 46
Brower, Willard, 46
Bruijnooge, Jozias, xvi, 115-16
Brummelkamp, Anthony, 191-92, 255-56
Bruzijn/Brusijn, Jan, 113
Buerman (Buurman), Jacobus A., 117-18
Buist, Andrew, 50
Buist, Dale, 49
Buist, Robert, 49
Butijn/Butin, Elizabeth, 114
Butin, J., 112
Buurma, Anco, 55
Buurma, Frans (Frank), 54-56
Buurma, Gerry, 55
Buurma, Hank, 55
Buurma, Jack, 56
Buurma, John, 55
Buurman, Johannes, 115
Buurman, Levinus, 115
Bytwerk, Albert, 44

C

Caillieux, Pieter, 114
Callieux, Elizabeth, 114
Campbell, John A., 294-95
Cappon, Jan, 113
Cappon, Jannis, 113
Cepilina, Ed, 36
Chester, Herbert, 85
Clicquennoi, Adriana, 114
Clicquennoi, Marinus, xvi, 114-15
Cowley, Betty, 79
Cranston, Rachel, 302
Crispell, John, 212-13
Cruikshank, Dale P., 304

D

Daane family, 32, 113
Daane, Peter, 77
Dalenberg, Arnold, 67, 74
Daley, Richard M., 276
Dalman, Geert B., 232
Damhoff, John, 134
Damhoff, John J. (son of John), 133-34
Danbom, David, 140
Day, William Henry, 17, 62
de Bruijne family, 114
de Bruijne, Sara, 114
De Bruin, Cornelius, 21
De Bruin, Marinus, 21
De Bruyn, Donald, 50
De Bruyn family, 28
De Bruyn, Robert, Jr., 50
De Bruyn, Robert, Sr., 50
De Die, Jan, 114
De Feyter, John, 27
De Good, Earl, 46

Name Index 317

De Graff, Ted, 67, 74
De Graff, Walter, 67, 74
De Haan, Jessie, 161, 165, 170
De Haan, John, 165, 170
de Jager, Cornelis ("Kees"), 309-10
De Jong, Baaye. *See* Bakker, Baaye
De Jong, Dina, 173
De Jong family, 154-76
De Jong, George, 154, 164-66
De Jong, Jessie, 154
De Jong, Lieuwe, xvii, 154, 156, 158-59, 161-62, 166, 169-70, 173-75
De Jong, Nellie, 154, 157, 159-60, 162, 164-65, 169-70, 173, 175
De Jong, Nick, 154, 161, 169-70
De Jong, Pete, 154, 159-60, 172-73
De Jong, Rika, 164-65
DeJong, Selina Peake, 74
De Jong, Teake, 154
De Jong, Tjitske Lijkeles Memerda, 153-54, 156, 159, 162, 166, 167-69, 173, 175
De Kruif (De Kruijft), John, 113
De Kruyf, John, 112
De Lelys (de Lelijs), D., 113
De Master, John E., 77
den Bleyker, Paulus, 205
De Neui, Bernard, 171
De Neui, Dorothy, 171
Den Hartogh, Suzanne E. Wisse, 118
den Hollander, Maarten, 114
De Ruijscher family, 114
De Ryke family, 32
de Spelder, Cornelia, 210
Deursma, J., 32
De Visser, Johannes, 114, 116
de Vlas, Ulbe, 157
De Vos, Julius E., 62
de Vries, Antje, 304
De Weerd, Norman, 46
De Witt, Fred, 46
De Young, Arend, *25*
De Young, Hank, 35

Didama, Simon, 112
Diekema, Gerrit, 142
Dilloo, F. W. J., 257
Dosker, Henry, 262
Douma, Michael, 140
du Bois, Isaac, 114
Dudok Bousquet, Abraham Everardus, 205
Duerwarder family, 32
Dusold, Fred, 76
Dusseljee, Kenneth, 27
Dyke, Bernard, 46
Dyke, Jacob, 44
Dykema, Albert, 46
Dykema, Clarence, 46
Dykema, Dick, 46

E

Earle, Lawrence, 282
Eaton, J. M., 134
Eding, Alvin, 28
Eding, Dale, 28-29
Eding family, 35
Eding, Henry, 28
Eding, Jeff, 29
Eding, Mike, 29
Eding, Ron, 28-29
Eernisse, Abraham, 114
Eernisse family, Jacob Pieter, 113
Eernisse family, Jacobus, 113
Eernisse, Magdalena, 119
Elias, Magdalena, 118-19
Ellis, Elizabeth, 212
Emelander, John, 46
Emelander, Stanley, 46
Englebert, Rudolph, 112
Enterprise, Albert Lea, 16
Ettema, Alvin, 51
Ettema, Bernard, 51
Ettema, Heine, 51
Ettema, William, 51

F

Faas, Ed, 77
Faas family, 114

Faas, J. B., 77
Faas, Leendert, 114
Faro, Isaac, 118
Fellows, W. C., 133
Fenenga, Gerrit, 173
Ferber, Edna, 74
Fisher, Bernard, 40
Fisher, Casey, 36, 40
Fisher, Joe, 40
Floete, Mrs., 170
Foute, Elisabeth, 239-40
Foute, Klaas, 240n53
Frank, James, 29
Fridsma, Bernard, 311
Fuller, Sarah, 307, 313

G

Gelder, Andrew, 44
Gelder, Gerrit, 43
Geldersma family, 32
Gemmen, Henry, 46
Gernaat, John, 27
Gernaat, John, Jr., 24, 27n18
Gernaat, John, Sr., 27
Gilsy (Gillis), Carry, 118
Gjerde, Jon, 141, 155
Glewen family, 82
Gouwens, William, 67, 74
Grasman, Case, 46
Grasman, Simon C., 46, 50
Grasman, Stanley, 46
Green, William H., 269-70
Grewal, Zareena, 172
Griffin, Astrid, 276-77
Griffin, Michael, 276-77
Groenewoud, Arthur, 52

H

Haaksma, Elmer, 47
Haan, Gijsbert, 231-34, 237, 251
Hafocatt ("Old man"), 212
Hahn, Arvin, 69
Hamburg, Wally, 46
Hancock, George, 29
Hanson, Marilyn Wassink, 80

Harms, Richard H., 156
Harris, Harry, 52
Hart, Mart, 47
Hassam, Frederick Childe, 290
Haverkate, Gerrit J., 212-13
Heeringa, Jan Klazes, 194
Heimstra, Hieltje, 158, 160
Heimstra, Renske, 154, 157-60, 164, 166, 168-69, 173
Hekkema, Albert, 40
Hemkes, G. K., 256, 262, 265, 272
Henri, Robert, 284
Hertzsprung, Ejnar, 306, 313
Heyn, Piet, 223
Hiemstra, Albert, 154, 157-58, 169, 171
Hijnolf/Hinolf (Hinold), Jacob, 113
Hoedemaker, P. J., 239n50
Hoeksema, Fred, 51-52
Hoeksema, John, 52
Hoeksema, Warner, 51
Hoeksema, William, 52
Hoekstra, Wybren, 27
Hoeltzel, Bob, 123
Holstege, Gerrit, 50
Holstege, Harvey, 50
Holstege, Henry J., 50
Holstege, Jay, 50
Holstege, Leonard, 50
Holthof, Albert, 44
Holthouse, Ken, 58
Holthuis, Alice, 57
Holthuis, Dena, 57
Holthuis, Grace, 57
Holthuis, Harm, 57
Holthuis, Jacob, 57
Holthuis, Jan, 57
Holthuis, John, 57
Holthuis, Jordon, 57
Holthuis, Ken, 57
Holthuis, Kevin, 57
Holthuis, Kirk, 57
Holthuis, Mark, 57
Holthuis, Rudy, 57

Name Index 319

Holthuis, Stanton, 57
Holthuis, Steve, 57
Holthuis, Wayne, 57
Homan, Gerlof, 312
Houtman, Adolph, 27
Houtman, Jerry, 27
Howard, Henry, 212
Howard, Ike, 212
Howard, Joseph K., 85
Howard, Manly D., 212
Huenink, Ben, 76
Huenink family, 76
Huenink, J. B., 76
Huenink, John, 76
Huibregtse, Sam, 77
Huizenga, John, 28
Huizenga, Peter, 50
Hulst, J. B., 149
Hulst, Lammert J., 258, 264-66, 268, 270, 272
Humphreys, Jessie Elizabeth, 301
Hutchinson, Charles L., 290

J

Jaarsma, Louis, 134
Jacob, Pieter, 114
Jager, Jake, 52
Jager, Lewis, 52
Janssen, Emme, 245n72
Jensma, 173
Jobse, Arnold, 113
Johnson, Henry, 54
Johnson, Lyndon B., 34
Jongste, Cornelis, 205
Jongste, Wouter, 205
Joosse family, 114

K

Kain, Mary E., 134
Kapteyn, Jacobus Cornelis, 306
Kapteyn, Melvin, 50
Kearns, J. B., 134
Kelder, John, 50
Kelder, Peter, 50
Kelder, Thomas, 50

Kelder, William, 50
Keppel, Ruth, 143
Kieft, Fred, 32
Kieft, Jan (John), 29, 32
Kieft, Martin, 29-30, 34
Kieft, Martin (Ted), Jr., 30-31, 35
Kieft, Larry, 29, 31-32, 35
Kieft, Paul, 32
Kieft, Peter, 30
Kieft, Tom, 32
Kiekover, Gerrit, 46, 50
Klijn, Hendrik Georg, xx, xxi, 223-51, *224*, 227
Klijn (Klyn), Hendrik George Jr., 240n54, 245n73, 246
Klijn, Maria Wilhelmina, 224n3
Klooster, Clarence, 27
Klooster, Melvin, 27
Klop family, Arie, 32
Klug, Herbert, 36, 40
Kollen, Gerrit J., 142
Koning (Konning), James (Janes), 211
Kooiman, Abe, 32
Koole, Arie, 87, *89*, 90-91
Koole brothers, 86-91
Koole, Leendert (Leonard), 87, *89*, 91, 94, 96
Kooy family, 105
Kooy, Peter, 98, 101-5
Kooy, Ralph, 105
Krabbendam, Hans, 140, 157, 170, 179, 181
Kraker, Howard, 49
Kramer, Vernon, 50
Krikke, Chester, 46
Krikke, Stuart, 46
Kroes, Rob, 140
Kroll family, 49
Kroll, Harriet, 49
Krool, Dena, 49
Kuiper, Augusta Alida Margaretha, 304, 313
Kuiper, Gerrit, 304

Kuiper, Gerrit Pieter, 303-14
Kuiper, Nicolaas Cornelis, 304, 313
Kuiper, Paul, 312-13
Kuiper, Pieter Nicolaas, 304, 313
Kuiper, Sylvia, 312-13
Kuyper, Abraham, 163-64, 258, 260-67, 271, 300

L

Laarman, Andrew, 51
Laarman, Cora, 51
Laarman, Peter, 51
Langeraad, Katherina Plattenberg, 118
Leenheer, Marie, 295
Le Febre, Fred, 49
LeFebvre, Jules Joseph, 283
Lewis, Edward Gardner, 294
Lorentz, Hendrik Antoon, 305
Lousma, Sidney, 52
Louters family, Peter, 60
Louwerse, Pieternella, 113
Lubbers, Gerald, 50
Lubbers, John, 50
Lucas, Henry, 110, 214
Luitwieler, Hubertus, 113
Luyten, Willem Jacob, 307, 311-12

M

Machiele, Andrew, 46
MacKay, Angus, 86-87
Macksanby, Iosapt, 211
MacMonnies, Frederick William, 290
Maksabe, Joseph, 211
Maksabe, Louis, 211
Marsh, Alvin W., 119
Martinie, Gordon, 46
Mason, Alice, 106
Mast, Clarence, 50
Matthews, August, 104, 106-7
Matzinger, Philip F., 275
Mayow (Mahieu), Susan, 118
McCue, Hiram, 211-12
McIntosh, W. H., 109
McMillan, P. D., 60
Meints, Art, 27

Meyers, Harriet, 56
Miedema, Gerald, 47
Miedema, Ron, 47
Miedema, Ted, 47
Millet, Jean-Francois, 301
Minnaert, Marcel, 310-11
Miskotten, Edward, 29
Moerdyke, Peter, 300
Moorman, William, 35
Morris, Jonathan F., 116
Mulder, John, 32
Mulder, Mark T., 175
Munneke, John (Jan), 134
Myrick, Hobart D., 93

N

Nanninga, Henry, Sr., 24
Nevenzel, John, 28
Noble, Charles S., 86, 94-96, 99-101, 104-8
Nollen, Jan, 199
Noordtzij, M., 271
Noorlander, Volksje (van Nes), 287
Nyenhuis, Jacob E., 50
Nykamp, Art, 46

O

Oggel, Pieter Jan, 233, 237-38
O'Keeffe, Georgia, 289
Onnes, Heike Kamerlingh, 306
Ostergren, Robert, 145

P

Paarlberg, James, 74
Paarlberg (née Waagmeester), Antje, 74
Palmbos family, 44
Palmer, Asael, 90, 94, 99
Palmer, Harry E., 51
Pals, Howard, 67, 74
Payne, George H., 60
Peeters, F. F., 62
Pelmulder, Jelle, 194-95
Penning, Henry, 27
Peper, Abraham, Jr., 112
Peper, Maatje, 113

Name Index

Peper, Abraham, Sr., 111-13, 121, 123
Peterson family, 32
Pfanstiehl, Christina, 239n50
Pfanstiehl, Pieter F., 212
Phanstill ("Old man"), 212
Planck, Max, 314
Platschaert, Johannes, 115
Pleijte family, 114
Pleijte (Plyte), Isaac, 114
Poel, Adrian, 32
Posthumus, Claus, 27
Posthumus, George, 27
Posthumus, Henry, 61
Prange, Herbert, 81
Prange, Sharon, 81
Puijenbroek, Jacob, 114

R

Reed, W. H., 93
Regnerus, J., 28
Risseeuw, David, 83
Roberts, William H., 255
Robinson, B., 134
Rodenhuis, David R., 312
Roelofs, Harold, 50
Roeters, William, 46
Rombach, Christiaan, 225
Rombach, Elisabeth Maria Martha, 225n6
Rombach, Hendrik Georg. *See* Klijn, Hendrik Georg
Roosevelt, Theodore, 219
Roossien, Harm, 30, 32, 35
Roossien, Henry, 30, *33*
Roossien, Lou, 50
Roossien, Peter, 30, *33*
Roth, Marty, 32, 37
Roth, Nate, 32
Ryskamp, Henry, *25*
Ryskamp, Lester, *25*

S

Sagan, Carl, 311
Sall, Albert, 49
Sall, George, 50
Sall, Russell, 49
Salmon family, 35
Saunders, Charles, 86
Schilt, Jan, 307
Schippers, Henry, 24
Scholte, Hendrik Pieter, 227
Schoone-Jongen, Robert, 145
Schoone-Jongen, Terence G., 140
Schreuder, Martin, 27
Schreur, Andrew, 46, 48
Schreur, Arie, 44
Schreur, Bruce, 46-47, *49*
Schreur, Ellie, *49*
Schreur, Eric, 47, 49
Schreur, Gerrit, 43-44, 47, *48*
Schreur, Gerrit (grandchild), *49*
Schreur, Grace, *49*
Schreur, Heather, *49*
Schreur, Herman, 46-48
Schreur, Mitchell, 47, *49*
Schreur, Richard (Rick), 46, 48
Schreur, Sheryl, *49*
Schut, Albert, Jr., *45*
Schut, Albert, Sr., *45*
Schut, George, *45*
Schut, Harold, 46
Schut, Lambert, *45*
Schuur, Henry, 27
Schuur, Mike, 27
Schwerdt, C. V., 282
Scott, Nelson, 36
Sinke, Suzanne, xvii, 167
Slager, Jacob W., 27
Slager, Jon, 27
Sleijster, R., 192
Smallegan, John, 50
Smith, Catherine Frances, 272
Smit, Henry, 46
Smith, Harry, 133
Smith (Smit), Thomas Pieters, 125
Smit, John, 44, 46
Snor, Ann, 63
Snor, Cornelia, 63
Snor, John, 62

Snor, John (Jan Jacob), 63
Souter, George H., 28
Spanish Duke of Alva, 300
Spoelman, Cornelius, 44, *45*
Spread, Henry F., 282
Sprik, Jan, 203
Stanley, Anna H., 287
Steenwyk, Clarence, 50
Steenwyk, Ray, 50
Steenwyk, William, 44
Steffens, Nicolaus, 260, 262-64, 266-67, 270, 273
Sterenberg, Fred, 133
Stoutenburg, Willem, 113
Stryker, John, 51
Stuyvesant, Peter, 112
Sullivan, Louis, 291
Swartte van Loon, Jacobus Meinhardi, 194
Sytsma, John, 62

T

Tack, Margaret Wisse, 118
Takken, Evert (Eddie), 209-10
Takken, Hendrik (Henry), 209-10, 213-19
Takken, Janie, 210
Takken, Mary, 210
Takken, Ryk, 210
Takken, Sibylla (Belle), 209-10
Talsma, Clarence, 50
Talsma, Gene, 47
Talsma, William, 47
Tamminga, John, 50
Taylor, George, 20-21
Teichert, Minerva, 287
Te Ronde family, 80
Tesselaar, Vincent, 62
Teune, John, 46
Timmerman, Casey, 41
Ton, Jon, 53
Ton, Richard, 53
Tuff, Lorenzo P., 88
Turner, John, 95, 100

Tysman family, 32

U

Unkill (Uncle) Sam, 212, 219

V

Van Arkel family, 32
van Berkel, Klaas, 307
van Bochove, Dirk, 185
van Bochove, H. Tanis, 185
van Bochove, Jannetje Tanis, 185
van Bochove, Johanna, 185
van de Kamp, Peter, 307, 311
Van Dellen, Al (Alje), 134
van de Luijster, Jannes, 197
Vandenberg, Marinus, 51
Vanden Berg, Reinder, *25*
van den Bosch, Koene, 223, 234, 235n40, 251
Vander Driest, Jan, 113
Vander Driest, Pieter, 113
Vander Kolk, Gerrit, *22*
van der Meulen, Cornelis, 114, 227-28, 233, 236-37, 242
van der Meulen, John, 245n72
VanderMey, Albert, 62
van der Mey, John, 262
Vander Ploeg, Arthur, 51
Vander Ploeg family, 51
Vanderpoel, Arie, 302
Vanderpoel, Cornelia, 286
Van der Poel family, 279
van der Poel (Vanderpoel), Jan (John), Sr., 275-77, 279
Vanderpoel (van der Poel), John (Johannes) Henry, Jr., xxiii, 279-302
Vanderpoel, Lizzie, 302
Vanderpoel, Mathilda (Machteldje), 286, 301
van der Schuur, Koene Sibolts, 230
van der Ven, J. C., 271
Vander Werp, D. J., 266
van de Velde, Jacoba, 225
Van Dyken, Charlie, 50

Van Eck, Marinus, 40
Van Hinte, Jacob, 110, 122
Van Laar, Jack, 56
van Löben (Löven) Sels, Pieter Justus, 61, 62n67
Van Nes family, 286
Van Nes, Maria, 277, 286
Van Raalte, Albertus C., 110, 114-15, 121, 163, 191-92, 229-30, 233-34, 241n59, 242, 249
van Schelven, Gerrit, 207-8
Van Singel, Peter, 41
Van Timmeren, Cal, 49
Van Timmeren, John, 49
Van Tuyl, John G., 52
Lone (née Van Tuyl), Bertha, 52
van Veenschoten, Teunis, 200, 201
van Weerden, Wilhelmina ("Mina") Catharina, 245n73, 248
van Wijk, W. P., 170
Veldhoff, Paul, 29
Ver Berkmoes family, 32
Verbrugh, Cornelia, 225
Ver Hage, Ernest, 46
Ver Hage, Martin, 44, 46
Ver Hage, Terry, 46
Verhulst, Henry, 77
Ver Sluis, Arthur, 27
Ver Sluis, Lewis, 21, 27
Visser, Casey, 50
Vlieg, Henry, 51
Vlieg, John, 51
Vlieg, Ralph, 52
Vogel, Cornelius, 134
Vos, Geerhardus, xxi, xxii, xxiii, 253-73
Voss, Henry, 61
Vredeveld, Lucas, 50
Vredeveld, Ted, 50

W

Wagenmaker, Alvin, 40-41
Wagenmaker, Gordon, 41
Wagenmaker, Jacob, 36, 40-41

Walsh, Heber (Heabor), 212
Walters, Dennis, 49
Walvoord, Carl, 70
Warfield, Benjamin B., 260, 264, 267, 269
Warnshuis, J. W., 116
Wassenaar, J., 170
Wassink family, 80
Weesies, Claude, 40
Weesies, Edward, 40
Weesies, Elizabeth, 40
Weesies, Harry, 40
Weesies, John, 40
Welling, Jake, 32
Welling, John, 32
Wenke, Chris, 27
Westrate, Marinus, 50
Westrate, Matthew, 50
Wielenga, D. K., 270, 272
Wiers, Ben, 59
Wiers, Corwin, 58, 59
Wiers, Ed, 59
Wiers, Edd, 58, 59
Wiers, Eddy, 58
Wiers, Edwin, 59
Wiers, Frank, 58
Wiers, Garrett, 58
Wiers, Henry, 58
Wiers, Jerry, 59
Wiers, Jim, 59
Wiers, John, 59
Wiers, Norman, 58
Wiers, Tom, 59
Wilhelmina (queen), 62, 300, 311
Wilhuis, William, 113
Willbrandt, Bruce, 41
Willeboordse, Aplonia, 113
William III (king), 62
Williamson (Willemsen), George, 86, 96-101, 104-8
Winter, Egbert, 248-50
Withage, Chris, 91
Withage, Neil, 91, 94
Wobick, Otto, 95, 100

Woordes, Henry, 77
Workma, John, 50
Workman, Bill, *38*, 39
Workman, David, 39
Workman, Jim, *38*
Workman, John, *38*
Workman, Simon, Jr., *38*
Workman family, Simon, 35, 36
Workman (Werkman), Simon, Sr., 35-38
Workman, Tom, *38*
Wormser, Andries, 196-97, 205
Wormser, Johan Adam, 205
Wormser, Maria, 196
Wormser-Van der Ven, Janke, 205
Wyckoff, Isaac N., 192

Y

Yonker, Peter, 50
Yonkers, Albert, 43
Yonkers, Lambert, 43
Yonkman, Frank, 51

Z

Zachariase, Pieternella, 113
Zahn, Jan George, 193
Zwemer, Adriaan, 198, 245n72

Van Raalte Press Publications from 2007 to 2019 in Chronological Order

Van Raalte Press

Swierenga, Robert P., Jacob E. Nyenhuis, and Nella Kennedy, eds. *Dutch American Arts and Letters in Historical Perspective*. Association for the Advancement of Dutch American Studies, 2007 (2008)

Nyenhuis, Jacob E., Suzanne M. Sinke, and Robert P. Swierenga, eds. *Across Borders: Dutch Migration to North America and Australia*. Association for the Advancement of Dutch American Studies, 2009 (2010)

Van Den Broeke, Leon. *"Pope of the Classis"? The Leadership of Albertus C. Van Raalte in Dutch and American Classes* (2011)

Ester, Peter. *Faith, Family, and Fortune: Reformed Upbringing and Calvinist Values of Highly Successful Dutch American Entrepreneurs* (2012)

Kennedy, Nella, Mary Risseeuw, and Robert P. Swierenga, eds. *Diverse Destinies: Dutch Kolonies in Wisconsin and the East*. Association for the Advancement of Dutch American Studies, 2011 (2012)

Harinck, George. *"We live presently under a waning moon": Nicolaus Martin Steffens as leader of the Reformed Church in America in the West in years of transition (1878-1895)* (2013)

Cox, John D. *The City in its Heart: The First 100 Years of Maple Avenue Ministries, Holland, Michigan, 1913-2013*. Historical Series of the Reformed Church in America Congregational History Series, no. 1 (2014)

Swierenga, Robert P., Nella Kennedy, and Lisa Zylstra, eds. *Dutch Americans and War: United States and Abroad*. Association for the Advancement of Dutch American Studies, 2013 (2014)

Hemenway, Stephen I. *Hope Beyond Borders: The Life and Letters of Paul Fried* (2014)

Swierenga, Robert P. *Faithful Witness: A Sesquicentennial History of Central Avenue Christian Reformed Church, Holland, Michigan, 1865-2015*. Historical Series of the Reformed Church in America Congregational History Series, no. 3 (2015)

———, and Jacob E. Nyenhuis, eds. *Historic Dutch Sites in the Holland/Zeeland Area: An Illustrated Tour Guide* (2015)

———. *Park Township Centennial History, 1915-2015* (2015)

Luidens, Donald A. *Seeds of Hope, Seeds of Hate: A Love Story* (2016)

Schafer, Robert. Sheet music for "I Will Lift Up Mine Eyes." Sesquicentennial Anthem (2017)

Aay, Henk, Janny Venema, and Dennis Voskuil, eds. *Sharing Pasts: Dutch Americans Through Four Centuries*. Association for the Advancement of Dutch American Studies, 2015 (2017)

Luidens, Donald A., and JoHannah M. Smith, eds. *Jack: A Compassionate Compendium. A Tribute to Dr. Jacob E. Nyenhuis, Scholar, Servant, Leader*. Historical Series of the Reformed Church in America, no. 93 (2018)

Schaaf, Kenneth A. *In Peril on the Sea: The Forgotten Story of the* William & Mary *Shipwreck*. Historical Series of the Reformed Church in America, no. 92 (2018)

Kennedy, Earl Wm. *A Commentary on the Minutes of the Classis of Holland, 1848 – 1876: A Detailed Record of Persons and Issues, Civil and Religious, in the Dutch Colony of Holland, Michigan*. 3 vols. Historical Series of the Reformed Church in America, no. 94 (2018)

Nyenhuis, Jacob E. et alii. *Hope College at 150: Anchored in Faith, Educating for Leadership and Service in a Global Society*. 2 vols. Historical Series of the Reformed Church in America, no. 95 (2019)

Kennedy, Earl Wm., Donald A. Luidens, and David Zwart, eds. *Dutch Muck—and Much More: Dutch Americans in Farming, Religion, Art, and Astronomy*. Association for the Advancement of Dutch American Studies, 2017 (2019)

Van Raalte Press in Cooperation with Wm. B. Eerdmans Publishing Co.

Ester, Peter, Nella Kennedy, and Earl Wm. Kennedy, eds. *The American Diary of Jacob Van Hinte*. Historical Series of the Reformed Church in America, no. 69 (2010)

Bruins, Elton J., and Karen G. Schake, eds. *Envisioning Hope College: Letters Written by Albertus C. Van Raalte to Philip Phelps Jr., 1857-1875*. Historical Series of the Reformed Church in America, no. 71 (2011)

Nyenhuis, Jacob E. and George Harinck, eds. *The Enduring Legacy of Albertus C. Van Raalte as Leader and Liaison*. Historical Series of the Reformed Church in America, no. 81 (2014)

Swierenga, Robert P. *Holland, Michigan: From Dutch Colony to Dynamic City*, 3 vols. Historical Series of the Reformed Church in America, no. 80 (2014)

Heideman, Eugene P. *Hendrik P. Scholte: His Legacy in the Netherlands and in America*. Historical Series of the Reformed Church in America, no. 84 (2015)

Van Raalte Press Forthcoming

Verhave, Jan Peter. *A Constant State of Emergency: Paul de Kruif, Microbe Hunter and Health Activist*. Historical Series of the Reformed Church in America, no. 92 (2019)

Baer, Marc and Allison Utting. *Making Music: Hope College's Music Department, A History* (2019)

Swierenga, Robert P. *Train, Equip, Inspire: A History of Timothy Christian Schools of Chicago* (2019)

Made in the USA
Monee, IL
05 October 2020

43968651R00204